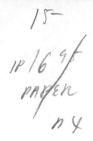

Dr. America

Dr. America

☆ ☆ ☆

THE LIVES OF
THOMAS A. DOOLEY,
1927–1961

James T. Fisher

University of Massachusetts Press
Amherst

A volume in the series

CULTURE, POLITICS, AND THE COLD WAR

Edited by Christian G. Appy

Copyright © 1997 by
The University of Massachusetts Press
All rights reserved
Printed in the United States of America
LC 96-48652
ISBN 1-55849-067-1
Designed by Jack Harrison
Set in Berkeley Medium by Keystone Typesetting, Inc.
Printed and bound by Thomson-Shore, Inc.

Library of Congress Cataloging-in-Publication Data
Fisher, James T., 1956–
Dr. America : the lives of Thomas A. Dooley, 1927–1961 /
James T. Fisher.
p.   cm. — (Culture, politics, and the Cold War)
Includes bibliograhical references and index.
ISBN 1-55849-067-1 (alk. paper)
1. Dooley, Thomas A. (Thomas Anthony), 1927–1961.
2. Missionaries, Medical—Asia, Southeastern—Biography.
3. Missions, Medical—Asia, Southeastern—Biography.
4. Asia, Southeastern—History—1945–
5. United States—Civilization—1945–
6. Cold War.   I. Title.   II. Series.
R722.32.D66F57   1997
610'.92—dc21
[B]   96-48652
CIP

British Library Cataloguing in Publication data are available.

All photographs are from Saint Louis University Archives, except where noted.

To Kristina

CONTENTS

Illustrations follow pages 114 and 210.

ACKNOWLEDGMENTS

This book project was christened in the great nor'easter of December 10, 1992, when my rented home in Brant Beach, New Jersey, welcomed in a bit of the Atlantic Ocean through a portal created when a picnic table sailed through the living room window. Nearly all of my Tom Dooley research materials survived even as the ocean swept beneath the floors over three days and nights of high tides. As darkness fell over the fourth day my mother and father arrived, having waited through the afternoon for the waters to recede from the causeway with the same patient spirit and good cheer that endured over the years I was writing this book. Five minutes after their arrival my friend Mike Young appeared in his '64 Newport: I thank him as well for friendship and inspiration spanning several decades.

The semester at the Jersey Shore was made possible by a Morse Fellowship from Yale University, where my research was also generously supported by the Griswold Fund and the Program on Non-Profit Organizations. I am also grateful to the American Council of Learned Societies, which provided me with a grant-in-aid at an early stage in the project, and to the Danforth Foundation for funding a position at Saint Louis University that has been a real blessing to me, not least because of the support offered by my two departmental chairpersons, Bill Shea of Theological Studies and Don Critchlow of History.

I began the research at the Western Historical Manuscript Collection, University of Missouri—St. Louis, where I was welcomed back on return visits by Anne Kenney and Pat Adams, then later by Ann Morris and Kenn Thomas. At the Saint Louis University Archives, John Waide and Randy McGuire are not only gentlemen and scholars but the finest ambassadors the university could ever wish to find. Laura O'Keefe of the Manuscripts and Archives Section of the New York Public Library was enormously helpful in locating materials; she also generously shared her own remarkable insights concerning the mystery of Dr. Tom Dooley. I am also grateful to Sr. Rosalie McQuaide, of the Catholic Relief Services archives, and to archivists and librarians at Boston University, the Center for the Study of the Vietnam Conflict at Texas Tech University, the Hoover Institution on War, Revolution and Peace, Indiana University–Purdue University Indianapolis, the University of Massachusetts, Amherst, Michigan State University, the National Archives and Records Administration, the University of Notre Dame, and to the outstanding staff at Pius XII Memorial Library, Saint Louis University. I also wish to thank Jeff Burns, a historian and archivist: though I have yet to visit his shop, he has been a true inspiration and a source of great encouragement.

I received invaluable assistance from nearly two hundred individuals who agreed to be interviewed for this book or who otherwise provided leads and suggestions. My deepest gratitude extends to each and every one of them. Professor Joel Halpern of the University of Massachusetts, Amherst, one of the first American scholars to work in Laos, was uniquely helpful and encouraging. My friends Patrick Allitt and Glenn Wallach read portions of the manuscript; despite my initial trepidation I am lucky they agreed to offer their insights. The Reverend Paul Myhre and Steven Taylor offered expert research assistance, and Tina Klein and Jonathan Nashel were an extremely sympathetic audience as fellow cultural historians seeking to understand what Americans were doing in Southeast Asia in the 1950s. I wish to add a special thanks to everyone who worked with me in American Studies 191.

Clark Dougan of the University of Massachusetts Press recalled for me in vivid detail a presentation he made in the eighth grade concerning the jungle doctor of Laos. He subsequently provided steady encouragement over the course of this project, and arranged for the manuscript to be read by Maurice Isserman—not only an expert on the political culture of the cold war but the author of a forthcoming biography of Tom Dooley's classmate Michael Harrington—and Chris Appy, who offered the most searching and incisive commentary I have ever received.

The strange yet compelling life of Dr. Tom Dooley was rich in issues sufficient to engage scholars from a host of disciplines, a few of whose territories I have crossed into without any illusions as to the limitations of my endeavor. I do hope that if others choose to pursue some of those issues, this book will serve as a useful guide. In my own field, the history of American Catholicism, the late Timothy J. Sarbaugh represented everything a scholar and teacher could ever strive to become. Tim was a wonderful person who is missed terribly; his example and his inspiration will never be forgotten.

NOTE TO READERS

I have not corrected the unorthodox spelling and grammar found in Dr. Tom Dooley's letters, with the exception of obvious typographical errors. I realize that in deciding which errors to correct I am susceptible to errors of my own, but I do not wish to highlight Dooley's eccentricities any more than I hope to convey something of his unique mode of self-expression.

Dr. America

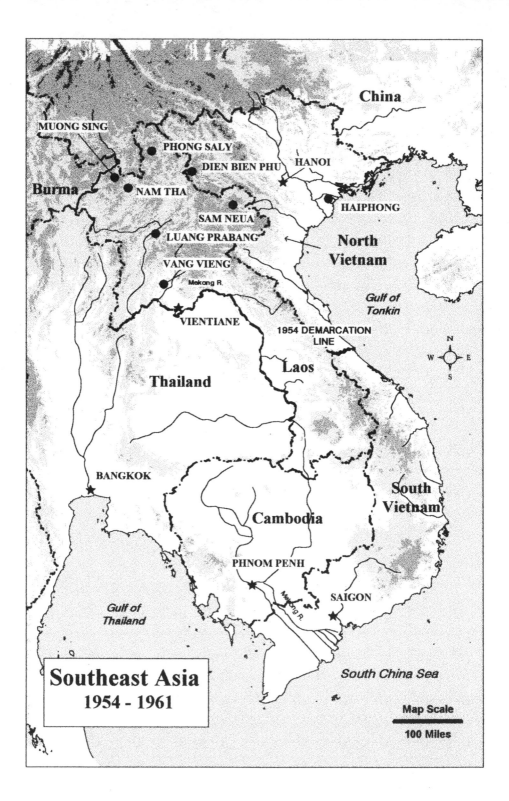

Southeast Asia
1954 - 1961

The Man in the Song

This time tomorrow
Reckon where I'll be
In some lonesome valley
Hanging on a white oak tree

Hang down your head, Tom Dooley
Hang down your head and cry
Hang down your head, Tom Dooley
Poor boy, you're bound to die

Prince Souphan of Laos arrived at Lambert Field on November 30, 1959, to a proper St. Louis reception led by the deputy mayor and the head of the board of aldermen. The young prince was in town to attend a dinner sponsored by the Junior Chamber of Commerce honoring a thirty-two-year-old native St. Louisan who—seven years after being nearly expelled from a local medical school—was returning home as a hero, celebrated the world over for providing medicine and inspiration to Vietnamese refugees and Lao villagers. The prince told reporters assembled at the airport that Dr. Tom Dooley, better known to his grateful Lao admirers as *Thanh Mo America* ("Dr. America"), had made such a profound impact in Southeast Asia that communist radio broadcasts frantically denounced him as an American spy and regularly demanded his expulsion from Laos.[1]

The Jaycees had backed Dr. Dooley's work since 1956, when he had first traveled to Laos to build a clinic financed in part by royalties from *Deliver Us from Evil*, a best-selling chronicle of his central role in the U.S. Navy's autumn 1954 campaign to transplant Catholic North Vietnamese refugees to a newly created state in the South. Crawford King, a St. Louis Jaycee who ran his family's burial monument business, had volunteered to supervise the entertainment of the visiting dignitary during his brief stay in the Gateway to

1

the West. The prince told King that he wanted to see some American dancing girls.[2]

On the evening of December 2, at a testimonial dinner at the Sheraton-
Jefferson Hotel, the Jaycees presented Tom Dooley with a check for over
$18,000. He excitedly told the crowd of fifteen hundred that the twin-
engine Piper Apache aircraft to be purchased with their gift "will enable me
to get our new hospital started in Ban Houei Sai [Laos] and to give a lot more
of my time to new MEDICO projects in South Vietnam, Cambodia, and
other places." MEDICO (Medical International Cooperation) was an expanding program cofounded by Dooley in 1958, devoted to providing non-
governmental, nonsectarian medical aid to people who, in the words of a
former Dooley aide, "ain't got it so good," particularly those living in "developing nations" threatened by communism.

The *St. Louis Post-Dispatch* reported that "the slim, wiry young doctor"
also received on that first evening in December a citation from the Reverend
Paul Reinert, S.J., president of Saint Louis University, in recognition of "his
personal devotion to the poor and suffering in a stricken land." Dooley was
deeply touched by the honor, but he could not have been surprised to learn
that Father Reinert—a steady and often courageous presence at the university through four decades—had just quelled a near insurrection fomented by
his medical school faculty. While Dooley was by far the most celebrated
alumnus of the school, especially outside of the medical profession, many of
his former professors continued to dismiss him as a West End playboy who
had taken five years to graduate 109th in a class of 116 (Dooley was surely
the only member of the class whose ranking could be found in a CIA
document). Tom had at least fulfilled the terms of a perhaps apocryphal
bargain enshrined in campus folklore—that in return for his diploma in
1953, he had promised the faculty never to practice medicine within the
United States.[3]

After the banquet Prince Souphan and his Lao entourage were escorted
to the conveniently titled Royal Suite of the elegant Sheraton-Jefferson.
Though it was well after midnight, Dooley then turned to Crawford King
and Bob Copenhaver, a publicist on loan from the Mutual of Omaha life
insurance company, complaining that he was tired of the endless trail of
fundraising and speech making; he wanted to "sneak away, and have a beer,
and put my feet up." Suddenly he insisted that they all go out to the Chase
Club in the city's West End, just down Lindell Boulevard from the Petit
Pigalle (where he had occasionally played cocktail-hour piano during medical school) and other favorite haunts. Dooley wanted to meet the members
of the Chase Club's enormously popular featured act, the Kingston Trio,

young folksingers who would be certain to perform the song that had made them stars: "Tom Dooley."[4]

This death-row ballad—with which the jungle doctor of Laos would be associated indissolubly—was already by 1959 an almost "century-old Blue Ridge Mountains folk tune, originally titled 'Tom Dula.'" The song was inspired by the trial and execution of a twenty-two-year-old veteran of Company K, Forty-second Regiment, North Carolina Infantry, who was convicted in October 1866 of murdering Laura Foster, "a poor girl, 21 years of age at the time of her death." The prosecution in the case convinced a jury that "a criminal intimacy had existed" between Dula and the deceased, as well as "between the prisoner and Ann Melton, a married woman" and the third party to the "fatal triangle." Ann Melton was apparently the last of the trio to contract syphilis; amid the ensuing acrimony Dula allegedly murdered Laura Foster. Melton was similarly charged, but, despite self-incriminating remarks she had made about her part in the killing, she was acquitted when, on the eve of his hanging in 1868, Dula declared himself solely responsible for the deed.[5]

At the conclusion of John Foster West's *Lift Up Your Head, Tom Dooley,* an exhaustive, luridly detailed account of the case (Ann Melton, we learn, possessed "almost all the faults one woman could have"; in addition to being "temperamental, demanding, and aggressive," this uneducated rural lady "was also lazy, with no interest in household duties"), the author declared in a somber anticlimax that "however cruel and demoralized Tom Dula might have been, however distasteful his lifestyle, whether or not he actually murdered Laura Foster or conspired in her murder," he should never have been charged in the first place. Among other procedural errors attending his arrest and confinement, explained West, the state failed to produce a murder victim during the first six weeks of Dula's incarceration.[6]

The origins of the ballad of Tom Dula are shrouded in a fog at least as thick as that beclouding the circumstances of its inspiration. Though the trial and execution were covered by the *New York Herald,* it is far from certain that Dula "made himself up a ballad" en route to the hanging ground "and sang it in his sour baritone, playing the tune over on his fiddle between every verse," as was claimed by the renowned folk musicologists John A. and Alan Lomax. There is general agreement, however, that the tune "lived on among the people of the Great Smokies as a ballad epitaph of a bitter returned veteran of the Civil War." According to folk musicologist Robert Cantwell, the song "entered tradition in Tennessee and North Carolina, where in 1938 an ingenuous young mountaineer from Pick Britches Valley, North Carolina, Frank Proffitt, sang it for a folksinger-collector named

Frank Warner." Warner in turn provided Alan Lomax with a version of the song for inclusion in his influential anthology, *Folk Song USA*. In 1957 the Kingston Trio—who had progressed from entertaining fraternity and beer hall audiences in northern California to a lengthy gig at the Purple Onion nightclub in San Francisco—heard a singer audition for the club with a rendition of a tune now entitled "Tom Dooley." While the Lomaxes reported that "since *Dooley* sings much more easily than *Dula,* that's the way the song has come to us from that flavorsome North Carolina singer, Frank Warner," John Foster West insisted that the name was always pronounced "Dooley" in "the old ballad."[7]

The trio decided to record the song for its first album with Capitol Records; in July 1958 disc jockeys Bill Terry and Paul Colburn of KLUB radio in Salt Lake City found themselves spinning the platter incessantly and quickly touted it to friends in other markets. Capitol responded by releasing "Tom Dooley" as a single: it hit the *Billboard* Top Ten Singles chart in October and remained there for four months, eventually selling more than three million copies. By the time the group arrived in St. Louis at the end of November 1959, a new recording, "Here We Go Again," was poised to become "one of four Kingston Trio albums in Billboard's Top Ten for the week of December 7, 1959," an accomplishment "surpassed only by the Beatles in 1964."[8]

Following their last set at the Chase Club in the early morning hours of December 3, the members of the trio were introduced to the "real" Tom Dooley, who quickly enticed them in his unique fashion to haul their equipment to the Sheraton-Jefferson and favor Prince Souphan with a jam session. A star in his own right, Dooley was also about to hit some impressive charts. When the Gallup Poll's annual Christmastime ranking of the "most admired" men in the world was released several weeks later, Dooley's name occupied seventh place, just below such towering figures as Winston Churchill, Pope John XXIII, and Dooley's official idol and fellow jungle doctor, Albert Schweitzer. But Tom did not need to await the results of a popularity contest to arouse a celebration. He had just completed a grueling, two-month-long fundraising junket that swept through thirty-seven cities, even as he recuperated from radical surgery for the removal of a malignant melanoma on his chest. Bob Shane, who along with Dave Guard and Nick Reynolds comprised the Kingston Trio, noticed the young physician's difficulty in shaking hands and assumed it was caused by the loss of musculature in Dooley's right side. A bottle of Whyte & MacKay scotch was quickly produced; as dawn broke vigorous handshakes were exchanged all around.[9]

It had been quite a night. The trio performed from their eclectic repertoire of calypso, folk songs, and cowboy music, shifting gears at three in the morning to croon a rendition of "Scarlet Ribbons" over the telephone to Dooley's pregnant sister-in-law in Detroit. Dr. Tom taught the band the lyrics to his mission's new theme song, "I Was a Cooley for Dooley," an uplifting version of the trio's smash hit, while the prince—clad in pajamas and bedroom slippers—kept time on an overturned wastebasket. During two days and nights in St. Louis, not only had the youthful scion obtained the G-string of an authentic burlesque queen (the headliner at downtown's Grand Burlesque was "Kalura, the Puerto Rican Bombshell," supported by "Johnny D'Arco, the Singing Buffoon") and later ceremonially presented it to Dooley, but he had sat in with one of the most popular singing groups in the Free World. Dooley told Copenhaver to remind him "to drop a hint to the prince that he ought to do something for the Kingston Trio. He might send them an elephant or something."[10]

The easy banter and instantaneous camaraderie between Dooley and the members of the trio, young American celebrities all, seemed so natural that no one present in the Royal Suite that evening was likely to have imagined he was witnessing a special moment, the kind that proves the world does truly change over time. Sainthood and show business had commingled in a wholly new fashion. On that swinging night in the heartland, Tom Dooley, who had begun his ascent as a Catholic folk hero, confirmed his "crossover" status as a transcendent American youth-culture icon. The Kingston Trio, for their part, represented a new musical and cultural hybrid: folksong-crooning pop idols who had liberated the genre from its confinement in left-wing and "purist" enclaves. Drawn together by the unlikely intercession of a song, the piano-playing jungle doctor and the self-styled, deceptively so-phisticated young musicians were forged at that moment into a kind of celebrity juggernaut capable of gleefully subverting the conventions of med-ical, musical, and spiritual "authenticity." In the freshness of their com-plementarity, they even hinted at new versions of American identity yet to emerge.

The meeting had even been eerily prefigured in March 1959, when the members of the Kingston Trio narrowly escaped injury after their six-passenger Beechcraft crash-landed in an Indiana field. They had been en route to a concert engagement at Tom Dooley's undergraduate alma mater, the University of Notre Dame. Just weeks after Buddy Holly, Ritchie Valens, and J. P. Richardson (the Big Bopper) had died in an Iowa cornfield, the Kingston Trio not only survived a crash but immediately made their way to the Notre Dame fieldhouse for the scheduled concert. As Dave Guard re-called: "Here we'd gone from nearly being killed to getting the greatest audience reception we'd ever experienced. We talked out onstage and the cheering was just deafening. We announced to the crowd that the only reason we were alive was because we were playing Notre Dame on a Friday." At the university Reverend Theodore M. Hesburgh, C.S.C., a visionary leader as well as Dooley's friend and admirer, was in the midst of creating a modern yet fully Catholic institution fit to tackle a rapidly changing world. Yet not even the "new" Notre Dame would have welcomed the appearance of a typical 1950s folk group such as the Weavers, tainted as they were by association with leftist causes. In contrast, the modishly apolitical Kingston Trio, though unchurched, fully embodied both the breezy "collegiate good time ethic" and the lighthearted idealism percolating on a wide variety of campuses in the twilight of the Eisenhower era.[11]

The synchronicity of the Kingston Trio's hit song and Dooley's rise to stardom occurred less than one year before the election of John F. Kennedy, America's first Roman Catholic president. Tom Dooley bequeathed his most ardent constituency to the young politician he knew and admired. In many ways Dooley served as a bridge between the grim Catholic cultural politics of the McCarthy era and the tremulous euphoria witnessed by the end of the 1950s. If Philip Rieff was correct in arguing that "as cultures change, so do the modal types of personality that are their bearers," Dooley was without peer in leading his subcultural community into the blinding glare of late modernity.[12] The personal and historical forces that helped compose the mystery of Dr. Tom Dooley—including the dark romance of his secret life as a "compromised" homosexual, beholden to elements of the U.S. intelligence community—ranged far beyond the conventional limits of his religious background and identity; in fact, Dooley came to view himself as the prophet of a postdenominational American spirituality. Yet all the roles of his life led ultimately to a common stage, where both his public and his intimate identities as a Catholic exacted their tribute.

Tom Dooley had grown up within the upper reaches of an extraordinarily insular St. Louis Catholic community (a columnist and product of that world noted that "newcomers to our city are surprised to find everyone is related").[13] Secular popular culture was eschewed by Dooley's parents as well as by the Jesuits who instructed him at Saint Louis University High School. At Notre Dame in the mid-1940s he was urged to enlist in the titanic and possibly final clash between Christian civilization and godless communism; he would be "discovered" in Vietnam in 1954 while presenting impassioned lectures to sailors confused by the crucifixes found in the rafts of refugees from the North. Dooley's first book, *Deliver Us from Evil* (1956), perfectly captured the militant parochialism of his inheritance. By the time he dramatically resigned from the U.S. Navy in 1956 to return to Southeast Asia as a crusader armed only with love, faith, and pharmaceuticals (which he had administered in Vietnam almost as a surrogate Eucharist), Dooley had indelibly personified a Catholic patriotism that even the wariest of old-stock Americans could scarcely resist.

Yet if in 1956 it would have been absurd to liken Dooley's crosscultural appeal to that of irreverent young pop stars, by the end of 1959 critics of rock and roll who continually exalted him as a wholesome alternative to Elvis Presley had at least found the right church, if the wrong pew. Dooley himself enjoyed teaching "Shake, Rattle, and Roll" to children in Lao villages. The Kingston Trio, for their part, claimed roots far west of Elvis's American heartland, in Hawaii—Tom Dooley's favorite halfway house—where in 1947 Bob Shane and Dave Guard had met as students at Honolulu's Punahou School. Five years later they left the island for schools in California—Guard to Stanford, and Shane to Menlo College, where he quickly befriended Nick Reynolds, the son of a naval officer. Together they made for a likable, fun-loving unit who tapped and then reshaped a new spirit redolent of collegiate life, the golden West, and velvety smooth pop music. Their name was designed to suggest Ivy League cockiness as well as the calypso rhythms made popular by Harry Belafonte, yet for all their casual charm the trio grappled with a lingering orthodoxy as demanding in its own way as the dogma of Dooley's Roman Catholic Church. Folk music purists—the kind who later jeered the amplified Bob Dylan from the stage of the Newport Folk Festival—disdained the trio's eclectic repertoire and teen-pleasing showiness, only further alienating them from the older generation of folk groups such as the Weavers; "Shane, Reynolds and Guard," wrote one observer, "*never* considered themselves folksingers, going more for the spirit of the genre than for the authenticity of it."[14]

While many of Dr. Tom Dooley's critics denied that he was a legitimate jungle doctor, he surely captured "the spirit of the genre" with a rare fervor. His affinity for the Kingston Trio oriented a new future he was charting for young Americans in the late 1950s, especially young Catholics. Their culture had been defined for a decade by its ferocious anticommunism: one of their fallen idols, Sen. Joe McCarthy, still evoked in many American liberals and pundits images of autocratic prelates with Romish designs on the republic of virtue. Tom Dooley won his fame saving the Catholics of North Vietnam from rapacious communists, but by 1956 he found himself working as a civilian among Lao villagers who practiced none of the religions he had ever heard of in St. Louis. During his speech at the Jaycees dinner three years later, Dooley turned to a prominent St. Louis Jesuit and less than half-jokingly remarked: "keep away from His Royal Highness, Prince Souphan, who is seated beside you tonight, because he is a good Buddhist, and he probably wants to remain that way."[15]

In urging his audience toward an appreciation of a world wider than parish boundaries, Dooley also provided a bridge from the darker impulses of secular youth culture (which had provoked near hysterical anxieties over violent comic books and surly actors portraying juvenile delinquents) toward a mystique of service to others that many observers found deeply compelling. The Kingston Trio members were kindred spirits in gently guiding their young listeners away from strictly escapist musical fare. As the "authentic" folk singer Will Holt explained, "The Kingston boys sing good folk music and manage to do it in a way that's readily acceptable to teenagers, as well as other age groups. They are 'sincere' without being 'serious' . . . the Kingston boys are also comforting to teenagers in another way: Those who buy Kingston records can assure themselves they are listening to a 'better kind of music' than rock 'n' roll. The trio forms a bridge on which teenagers can safely escape from subteen music."[16]

Dooley's interest in young people reflected his mystical desire for a post-sectarian future. His example broke down some of the walls that trapped Catholics in an outdated posture of resistance to global citizenship, just as the Kingston Trio turned the music of left-wing connoisseurs into everybody's music and liberated folk from its ongoing preoccupation with McCarthyism. Like Dooley, they were dismissed by elitists as middle-brow opportunists, yet they managed to forge, as he had, a protean audience that transcended the stagnant cultural politics of the era.

The neat symmetry of their respective vocations was confirmed by the phenomenon of "Tom Dooley." When the song was initially recorded, the trio had scant awareness of the jungle doctor of Laos and certainly had no intention of publicizing his cause through their music. At the same time, Dooley's most ardent Catholic disciples, discerning a sinister plot, "despised the song because of the association of names." The author of a Tom Dooley children's biography explained: "The Communists decided on a terrible way to 'get even' with Dr. Tom. They would use a song and make him look foolish." But Dooley himself "insisted that it was good fun as well as good music, and he was sure that the song's popularity also made people think of him, and therefore in some way benefited MEDICO."[17]

The jam session at the Sheraton-Jefferson drew together figures on the leading edge of a sea change neither they nor their constituents could fully divine. In an issue devoted to "the explosive generation," *Look* magazine called the trio "Pied Pipers to the New Generation," while Dooley was often photographed romping with adoring Lao children or, on his visits to the United States, regaling hordes of collegiate acolytes. The boyish celebrities shared bonds of idealism and a dashing, slightly rakish superstardom: at Stanford Dave Guard "had earned a reputation as a sort of stubble-bearded prebeatnik," while Dooley occasionally jarred admirers with his offhand, "bohemian" pronouncements.[18]

Less discernible were the roles Dooley and the Kingston Trio played as intuitive if premature postmodernists. Their distinctive identities were constructed around a dizzying array of influences, rearranged at will to suit performative circumstances. The trio's music was played on pop, rhythm and blues, and country music radio stations ("Tom Dooley" earned them a Country and Western Grammy award for 1958; a "Folk" category was not established until a year later). The "Kingston Trio sound" was indebted to the "slack-key" Hawaiian guitar of Gabby Pahinui (Dave Guard called it "a hula beat with an oceanic feel") as well as to Burl Ives, Frank Sinatra (who considered Bob Shane's vocal turn on "Scotch and Soda" one of the truest performances ever captured on vinyl), the show tunes of Lerner and Loewe, and "Polynesian tribal musicians whose names have been lost to time." Bob Shane always insisted that versatility took precedence over concerns for musicianship or folk purity: "I would tell people that you should use an instrument for whatever it is that you *want* to use it for, and don't be embarrassed by it."[19]

Tom Dooley unabashedly trumpeted his mastery of modern advertising and public relations techniques, utilized for the greater glory of his mission. As he brashly replied to his critics: "If you're gonna be a humanitarian today you've gotta run it like a business. You've gotta have Madison Avenue, press relations, TV, radio." Yet after MEDICO was cut loose in 1959 by its original sponsor, the International Rescue Committee, Dooley's savvy handlers were replaced by woefully inexperienced aides, and the program depended entirely on his brilliant choreography of the roles demanded by his public: Catholic anticommunist, rakish Irishman, gentle healer, nature mystic, manic taskmaster, master propagandist.[20]

Dooley's self-presentation was especially dramatic in light of the traditional wariness with which many American Catholics viewed secular vehicles of mass communications. Critics of all stripes rarely missed an opportunity to contrast him with his putative mentor, Albert Schweitzer, who though no stranger to the art of public relations, presented a much more conventional image as a stately Christian physician-savior. The array of forces Dooley harnessed in the late 1950s traced a jaunty swath across a landscape in which the sacred and the secular, the image and the reality were dislodged from their customary spheres and grafted into the composite likeness of this "Madison Avenue Schweitzer."

Tom Dooley was always entranced by show business. As his tastes in music evolved—from the classics and opera favored by members of St. Louis society, to a brief collegiate stint as a chorus boy in the supper club act of the noted chanteuse Hildegarde, to the folk-pop sounds of the Kingston Trio—he drew closer to the heart of America, extending the immigrant journey of his grandfather's generation toward more elusive horizons. He cultivated a large and loyal following in Hawaii, at the midpoint between his homes in Laos and the American mainland. Students at Honolulu's exclusive Puna-hou School, along with Catholic schoolchildren, raised thousands of dollars for MEDICO. Photographs of Dooley at a 1960 cocktail party in Honolulu depict him in a mode of unusual relaxation; sporting a Hawaiian shirt and natty Italian boots, he looked as though he were preparing to audition for the Kingston Trio. It was on this visit that he saw the members of the group for the final time. On July 17, 1960, the group saluted him from the stage of the Waikiki Shell by performing "their song."[21]

The trio performed several benefit concerts for Dooley's work during 1960. That fall, as he suffered a recurrence of cancer, the group's original lineup collapsed amid disputes over financial and musical strategies. The trio also became embroiled in a futile legal battle over the arrangement rights to "Tom Dooley" that ominously foreshadowed the unseemly struggle soon to be fought by claimants to the "real" Tom Dooley's legacy. In 1961 twenty-one-year-old John Stewart replaced Dave Guard; a year later the group dedicated their album *New Frontier* to the volunteers of the Peace Corps, a program launched by President John F. Kennedy in part to keep Dooley's spirit alive.[22]

John Stewart was invited to join the Kingston Trio just a few months after Tom Dooley's death. A graduate of a Catholic high school in Pomona, California, he shared with Dooley a background that seemed to set him somewhat apart from the remaining original members of the group. Stewart's account of his initial attraction to the trio movingly captures the nature of their appeal; had Dooley been given to introspection he might have recognized yearnings of his own in Stewart's reflections:

> Bobby [Shane] and Nick [Reynolds] were very *organic* musicians; there was nothing cerebral about their musicianship. It was totally *natural,* and that was a great part of the magic of the Trio; it was that *thing,* that natural energy, that made them connect with millions of people. . . . They were totally themselves. They enjoyed singing music and playing music; but it was not so much an obsession and an escape for them, as it was with me, because they had nothing to escape *from.* They were very comfortable with themselves and with the world.[23]

Tom Dooley worked feverishly throughout his life to present himself as a "natural." This desire had fateful consequences, for he met fellow Americans in Southeast Asia all too willing to aid in the careful sculpting of a public image for him, so long as it furthered aims of which Dooley had little knowledge and less understanding. In his frenzied quest for authority to define America for the people of Vietnam and Laos, Dooley reveled in his access to individuals "on the natch," as Nick Reynolds characterized the seemingly effortless poise of his bandmate Bob Shane. The Kingston Trio, Walt Disney films, and the Sears catalog provided the all-American mythology Dooley then served up to his patients in his role as high priest of international brotherhood. He loved reporting to his American audience that his Lao "kids" only learned to pronounce his name after hearing "Tom Dooley" played on a battery-operated record player.[24]

Although they spent but a few hours together, Dooley and the Kingston Trio remain joined in popular historical memory. Mention of the jungle doctor's name to many Americans born between 1920 and 1950 inevitably provokes the query, "Wasn't there a Kingston Trio song about him?" The manner in which the song came to be "about" the jungle doctor of Laos orients us toward some of the mysterious cultural undercurrents Dooley traversed in the late 1950s, as he grew from an undisciplined Irish American rake into a celebrity-saint. Though he was to jungle doctors what the Kingston Trio was to folk music, Dooley's practice in the show business of medicine was intimately connected to the very real and dangerous game of cold war intrigue being played on a world stage.

To many Americans of a certain age and religious upbringing—who *know* Tom Dooley from the Kingston Trio—the jungle doctor will forever evoke memories of a youthful romance with the mystique of self-sacrifice, embodied in the image of a charismatic man dying young. Many have testified that on hearing Dooley speak, they were overcome with a desire to spirit themselves to Laos and join his crusade. He usually resisted their entreaties; at times it almost seemed like Tom Dooley wished to experience in solitude the opening act of his nation's consuming romance with Southeast Asia.

☆ 1 ☆

What Tommy Knew

Between late December 1955 and the first week of 1956, Dr. Thomas A. Dooley III signed publishing agreements with *Reader's Digest* and the prestigious New York firm of Farrar, Straus and Cudahy. To support the massive publicity campaign for his first book, *Deliver Us from Evil*, Dooley supplied "biographical" materials to his sponsors. His invention as a public figure was launched in these sketchy documents that, among other fictions, reported that he "completed his undergraduate work at the Sorbonne in Paris." For the remainder of his life Dooley revised and rewrote his life story with brazen disregard for consistency, as though his experience was meaningful only as it could be invoked to serve the demands of the moment. Given license to continually reinvent himself, he simply intensified patterns that had marked his earlier years. Between 1946 and 1958, for instance—in completing a series of passport applications—Dooley alternately listed his father's birthplace as Hannibal, Joplin, Springfield, or St. Louis, Missouri (Thomas A. Dooley Jr. was born in Moberly, Missouri, in 1885).[1]

Dooley's imaginative renderings of his own life proved contagious to others, particularly those who wrote of his youth. One of his hagiographers erroneously reported that he was a high school track and swimming star who "soloed with famous orchestras." Those who sought to debunk Dooley's legend were no less prone to lapses in factuality: a journalist writing in the

Los Angeles Times Magazine in 1991 claimed that Dooley's father "was a railroad foundryman, a hard drinker who hoped that his namesake would become a prizefighter." Thomas A. Dooley Jr.'s status as a wealthy, refined, second-generation executive and pillar of the St. Louis Catholic establishment actually ranks among the less contested facts of the Dooley saga.[2]

Between Dooley hagiography, timeless and eternal (a cover story in the *Liguorian,* a Catholic magazine, from June 1991 is virtually identical to devotional works written during his lifetime), and the resentful exposés that emerged in the wake of the Vietnam War, one might hope to discover the "historical" Tom Dooley. But the precelebrity, presainthood version is only faintly accessible to us, due in part to the influence Dooley's public image inevitably exerted on the memory of his friends and acquaintances. In light of Tom Dooley's adult reputation as a manic extrovert, even the surviving artifacts of his childhood feature a rather impersonal tone, as though he had already learned to present versions of himself to others (and even to his scrapbooks) while deferring the emergence of a "stable" identity.

In the absence of the core personality that custom demands we first locate in a subject's childhood, the Dooley legend spawned dark rumors about "a missing diary" that could provide insights unobtainable through traditional methods of invasion. As there is no such diary and the belief in its existence only enriches the quality of his elusive genius, we are left in an encounter with this uniquely vulnerable individual who so often resembled a lost boy.

Thirty years before Dr. Tom Dooley met the Kingston Trio at a nightclub in the Chase Hotel, a testimonial dinner was held in an adjoining banquet hall at the Chase honoring his grandfather, Thomas A. Dooley Sr., for fifty years of service to the American Car and Foundry (ACF) Company of St. Louis. The seven-course meal served on that February night in 1929 included medallions of halibut with egg sauce; breast of chicken, nonpareil; artichoke bottoms, florentine; and harlequin ice cream with cardinal sauce. The three hundred distinguished guests were entertained by the Maxwell Goldman Orchestra, the St. Louis Quartette, "Our Own Jack Ryan, Storyteller," and a production of ACF Motion Pictures, "In the Service of Transportation." The *St. Louis Post-Dispatch* reported that the seventy-three-year-old Mr. Dooley "appears unusually active for his years. He is a resolute walker and each morning, rain or shine, tramps from his home at 6314 Waterman Avenue to Art Hill [located across spacious Forest Park]. An automobile takes him the rest of the way to the plant. It's a rare occurrence for him to miss a day at work."[3]

Thomas A. Dooley, district manager of American Car and Foundry Company, was a self-made captain of industry whose labors subsidized the carefree youth of his grandson. A large, robust man, he had earned the plaudits bestowed on him at that testimonial dinner through a lifetime of earnest toil. Because the onset of the Great Depression was but months away, the banquet represented one of the final tributes to that buoyant spirit of American enterprise which originated—according to historian T. J. Jackson Lears—half a century earlier, at a time when "the stout midriff was a sign of mature success in life. Affluent Americans devoured heavy meals at huge banquets. They accepted the congratulations of afterdinner orators. The speaker announced the marriage of material and spiritual progress. His audience nodded approval. There was no limit to American abundance. There was no impediment to the partnership of Protestantism and science." Although it was an "age of confidence," as Lears argues, the self-satisfaction of the late nineteenth-century industrial elites barely obscured the gnawing dread of "overcivilization" that affluence had wrought. By 1929 business leaders had long grappled with a much more tangible concern: the very immigrants whose labors generated industrial fortunes also threatened Protestant cultural authority with their unfamiliar languages and religions. As the historian of St. Louis's business elite wrote, "In a population consisting of a variety of linguistic and religious groups, a largely native American, Protestant business community could hardly hope to provide a universally accepted cultural leadership." It would not be for lack of effort that they would know only limited success.[4]

The stewards of wealth in St. Louis had more practical experience with cultural diversity than did their counterparts in most American cities. Since the town's founders and many of its earliest prominent families were French Catholic, there was no Protestant creation narrative akin to those of Boston or Philadelphia. There had even been a small group of prefamine Irish Catholic immigrants who achieved wealth and some status. John Mullanphy arrived in St. Louis in 1804 and "virtually cornered the cotton market following the War of 1812"; he soon became St. Louis's first millionaire. Richard C. Kerens, a transportation director for the Union Army, established a tradition of Irish success in the railroad industry as a prominent investor in the Iron Mountain, the St. Louis, and the Arkansas and Texas railroads. Thousands of impoverished Irish immigrants arrived in St. Louis in the 1840s; most settled in the notorious "Kerry Patch" on the city's near North Side. Nativist violence and gang warfare rendered the famine-era Irish unsavory in the eyes of the Protestant establishment: as late as 1878 a city guidebook claimed the "chief amusements" of Kerry Patchers "consist of punching each other's eyes." Still it was not so unusual for a postfamine Irish migrant to St. Louis like Thomas A. Dooley to rise steadily through the ranks—from carpenter to foreman to manager—as it would have been in an eastern concern.[5]

Like so many other Irishmen, Dooley had vigorously pursued railroad work in a career that took him from Glendale, Ohio, to Moberly, Missouri (an early hub of the Wabash and Pacific railways), and finally to St. Louis, where he found employment as a carpenter with the Missouri Car and Foundry Company. He married Annie Hogan, an Irish Canadian woman who gave birth to Thomas A. Dooley Jr. in 1885. Missouri Car and Foundry operated a small shop that produced eight to ten wooden cars daily prior to merging with several other car companies to form the American Car and Foundry Company. By the early years of the century, with Dooley at the helm as district manager, ACF's St. Louis plant employed three thousand workers and produced 2,250 boxcars per month. In his greatest personal triumph, Dooley designed and supervised the production of the first all-steel railcars in time for use by the United States military during World War I, for which the firm reaped over $100 million in government contracts. In a 1919 letter to W. K. Bixby, one of the founding partners of ACF, Dooley described the platinum, gold, and enamel Tiffany watch presented to him in gratitude by the corporation: "The engraving on the face is as follows: 'Nothing easy, but nothing impossible.'"[6]

Thomas A. Dooley Sr. combined an adherence to the work ethic embedded in that maxim with a devotion to corporate authority. "One of my axioms all through my life has been loyalty," he exulted in the 1919 letter to W. K. Bixby. Bixby was one of the true giants of St. Louis commerce and society: a director of the dazzling 1904 World's Fair and a collector of great art and rare books who retired before the age of fifty to his magnificent home on Portland Place, one of St. Louis's fabled "private streets." Bixby embodied an interlocking directorate of the St. Louis industrial elite dubbed "The Big Cinch" by muckraking journalist William M. Reedy in the late 1890s. "Less than twenty men run it," he wrote. "They dare do anything. They control the banks, the trust companies, the street railroads, the gas works, the telephone franchises and the newspapers."[7]

Bixby was a director of both St. Louis Union Trust and Boatmen's Bank; when the Wabash Railroad fell on hard times in 1905 a federal judge appointed Bixby receiver even though he headed a company that made railroad cars. He was a major benefactor of the Missouri Historical Society, Washington University, the St. Louis Public Library, the Bibliophile Society, and the First Congregational Church of St. Louis, as well as being "one of the most important backers" of Charles Lindbergh's flight from New York to Paris in 1927. Letters from Thomas A. Dooley Sr. to Bixby featured a masterly blend of camaraderie and deference, confirming his role as steadfast lieutenant in the corporate chain of command: "The photograph of you hanging in my office, with the inscription: 'T. A. D. With very best wishes of his old friend, W. K. Bixby,' is such a matter of pride, that all visitors visiting my office, and there are many of them from all over the United States, especially since we are working on the Government cars, that it gives me great pleasure to see them reading the inscription under the photo and to have them know that Mr. W. K. Bixby is Tom Dooley's old friend."[8]

Mr. Dooley carefully avoided overreaching himself: though he had moved his family from an immigrant neighborhood in South St. Louis to a fashionable West End address, he evaded the wrath directed at some of his new neighbors by the likes of society columnist "Virginia Dare," who sneered: "The West End is full of folk who cannot achieve the Imperial Club and will not if they strive till judgment day." Along with the far wealthier Busch family, whose vocation as brewers was viewed with disdain by the cream of St. Louis society, the Dooleys were not members of the Saint Louis Country Club, nor were they invited to join the Bogey Club, founded by, among others, W. K. Bixby (on land adjacent to the estate Thomas A. Dooley Jr. would purchase in 1940). The elder Dooley was content with an offer of membership from the perfectly respectable Glen Echo Club. His grandson, Thomas A. Dooley III, would grow up close to the sources of St. Louis privilege and employ his social graces to great effect later in life, but he also betrayed the resentment of one who experienced a vague yet persistent sense of exclusion from the inner circles where he knew he belonged. A brilliant stage Irishman, Dooley would flamboyantly transgress the same bounds of decorum his grandfather reverentially observed.[9]

Thomas A. Dooley Sr. died in 1934, leaving a sizable fortune to his namesake (and sole surviving son) and to his grandsons in trust. Thomas A. Dooley Jr. attended Culver Military Academy in Indiana and the Jesuit Saint Louis University before going to work as an assistant manager at American Car and Foundry in 1911. On the last day of 1925, shortly after his fortieth birthday, he married a thirty-year-old widow, Agnes Wise Manzelman. From a distinguished family with deep roots in Pennsylvania, she was a Daughter of the American Revolution whose grandfather, Capt. William W. Wise, had died for the Union cause in the battle of Murfreesboro. When Agnes was thirteen her family moved to St. Louis and there, in 1917, she married Earle Henry Manzelman in an Episcopalian ceremony. Manzelman was a flight instructor in the "Cracker Box" Air Force who was soon posted to Hickam Field in the Territory of Hawaii. The couple's first child, a girl named Betty Jane, died for lack of proper medical care at the age of six months. Mrs. Dooley soon became pregnant again and returned to St. Louis to await the birth of her second child. On October 14, 1922, Earle died in a training accident; his son, Earle Henry Manzelman Jr., was born the following February.[10]

Agnes Manzelman became a Roman Catholic in order to marry the devout Mr. Dooley; her parents were so impressed by her newfound faith they joined the Church as well. The couple's first child, Thomas Anthony Dooley III, was born at St. Ann's Hospital on January 17, 1927, weighing in at a hefty twelve pounds. The Dooleys lived on Pershing Avenue in the West End of St. Louis, not far from the imposing residence of Thomas A. Dooley Sr. Shortly after the death of the elder Dooley in 1934, the family (which by then included Tom Dooley's two younger brothers, Malcolm and Edward, and Earle, whom Mr. Dooley had adopted) moved to his home at 6314 Waterman. In 1940 they completed their westward journey through the prestigious suburbs of St. Louis by settling into an estate at Fair Oaks in Ladue, situated amid pastoral elegance in St. Louis County.

Thomas A. Dooley Jr. suffered the dilemma common to sons of self-made men, particularly those who pursue the same line of work as their fathers. Though determined to cement the family legacy in the annals of St. Louis industry, he was not as dynamic as his father and fell into a career at American Car and Foundry, where he ultimately assumed his father's old position as general manager; for years the two men lunched together each day in the firm's executive dining room. Beholden to inherited wealth, he failed to command the authority of his own father but insisted on maintaining the outward trappings of genteel manners. The Dooley boys were required to dress in jacket and tie for dinner, served promptly at 6:30. The family employed a cook, a maid, and a chauffeur-houseman named Norvell Simpson who tended to their dinner table in a starched white jacket.[11]

Mr. Dooley was caught in a snare of history, lodged between the imposing image of his own father, the quintessential industrialist, proud exemplar of what the historian Warren Susman called the "culture of 'character,'" and his flamboyant, extroverted elder son, who became a virtuoso performer and Catholic pioneer of an age exalting the power of "personality." By the early 1940s the Dooleys found it increasingly difficult to maintain upper-class appearances, however: family finances were possibly mismanaged; Mr. and Mrs. Dooley drank heavily from behind their shuttered windows; visitors to the darkened home grew rare. Years later in *Redbook* Mrs. Dooley presented a composite view of the family's various homes which characteristically centered their emotional life around her talented if unpredictable son: "We lived in a large, pleasant house which stood on an acre of ground with many splendid trees, and except for the winds of Tom's volatile temperament, ours was a calm and orderly household."[12]

Before moving to exclusive Ladue in 1940 (St. Louis historian Ernest Kirschten called it the "swankiest of the dormitory satellites") the Dooleys lived in the Parkview section of the West End, near Washington University. Parkview was among the most attractive of St. Louis's famed "private places" (the section of Parkview in which the Dooleys resided was located in University City, a community adjoining the western border of the city). The neighborhood was an enclave of affluent professionals including a fair share of Irish Americans, with physicians and attorneys predominating over industrialists like Thomas A. Dooley Jr. In St. Louis—as in most northern and midwestern cities—Catholics were known by the parish to which they belonged. Tommy Dooley attended St. Roch's parochial school until 1936, when he was enrolled in the fourth grade at the more prestigious Barat Hall, a private school operated by the Religious of the Sacred Heart at City House, a convent located behind the "new Cathedral," as St. Louisans still refer to the Romanesque edifice on Lindell Boulevard that was actually completed before World War I.[13]

The boys of St. Roch's admired Dooley's older half-brother, Earle, for his athletic prowess, but Tommy remained aloof from their ballgames and forays through the neighborhood. A speech problem heightened his isolation from the boys of Parkview; he preferred instead to play at "curing" sickly dolls with a girl from the neighborhood. At Barat Hall, located several miles east of Parkview, the schoolday lasted from 8:30 until 5:30. In accordance with the civilizing mission of the Sacred Heart nuns, Tommy Dooley studied French and received instruction in the fine arts. By one account he was sent to Barat Hall because "Mr. Dooley was having labor troubles at his car and foundry plant, and kidnap threats had been made. The boys were driven by the family chauffeur to school, where a watchman was in attendance throughout the day."[14]

Since Thomas A. Dooley Sr. had made provisions in his will for the education of his grandsons, Barat Hall may have reflected the family's more comfortable circumstances as much as fear for the children's safety. But the alleged threats evoke a pattern of discourse connected with the Dooley family—perpetuated later by Tom's admirers—in which hints of dark chaos always threaten that image of a buoyantly devout clan they worked so hard to promote. Tommy Dooley's nonconformity emerged as well in his early years at Barat Hall: "Sometimes," conceded a hagiographer, "he received less than perfect conduct marks with comments like: 'he talks too much.' "[15]

The Dooleys summered at Lawsonia, a former estate on Green Lake in Wisconsin. Tom's brother Malcolm recalled: "In those quiet summers just before World War Two, the Dooley boys had their world with vanilla icing on it." Home movies from 1936 and 1937 provide the first recorded evidence of Tom Dooley's performing self: while his parents and brothers respond bashfully to the camera, Tommy always occupies the center of the frame, blowing kisses in grand gestures to the sky, dangling a big fish from the dock, or beaming from atop a fine-looking horse. He appears as remote from members of his family as he is intimate with the camera. Dooley also spent several summers at a camp operated by Benedictine monks at Holy Cross Abbey in Canon City, Colorado, a popular destination among the St. Louis Catholic elite. The camp's former director recalled that Mrs. Dooley often personally accompanied her sons to Colorado in a limousine driven by the family's chauffeur; she was impressed by the range of activities available to the boys for what seemed to her such low cost. Her sons learned some Native American folklore and horsemanship while encamped at the monks' lodge, overlooking their base camp from an elevation of 8,000 feet in the Rocky Mountains.[16]

In 1940 Tom Dooley entered Saint Louis University High School, the oldest school west of the Mississippi. Founded in 1818 as Saint Louis Academy by Bishop William du Bourg, it was transferred to the custody of the Jesuits in 1827. With an enrollment of 650 students, the "U High" played a central role in training the Catholic elite of St. Louis. For decades St. Louisans have routinely determined the social position of strangers by inquiring, "Where did you go to high school?" Contemporaries of Dooley who attended one of the numerous St. Louis schools that were conducted by other religious orders, or by the archdiocese, often recalled several decades later the special sense of privilege associated with students at Saint Louis University High. In 1941 the official archdiocesan newspaper proclaimed of the school's mission: "It is the humble endeavor of an all-Jesuit faculty, assisted by five highly qualified laymen, to produce real Catholic men who will take their place as future leaders in St. Louis." Yet while some observers and Dooley's classmates recalled him as being quiet and pleasant, and others remembered a cocky showoff, all agreed that he remained aloof from the conventional groupings that comprised the student body. Tom Dooley was unathletic and uninterested in politics or intellectual issues, and while he performed well enough in some of his classes, he failed to make a lasting impression on either his teachers or his peers.[17]

Dooley focused his energies instead on the highly elaborate milieu of St. Louis Catholic society, becoming the male equivalent of a debutante. Between 1920 and 1940, American Catholic leaders had dramatically intensified their efforts to organize the laity through the creation of a wide range of institutions which, while often mirroring secular organizations, featured clerical supervision. A renewed conviction of the Church's mission in serving the Mystical Body of Christ energized the corporatist ideology promoted by a variety of zealots and reformers, from the social theorist Msgr. John A. Ryan (dubbed "the Right Reverend New Dealer" for his affinity with Democratic legislative efforts in the 1930s) to the immensely popular "radio priest," Father Charles Coughlin.[18]

Coughlin's increasingly divisive message won him his share of adherents in Depression-era St. Louis, but the local Catholic scene featured a relatively self-confident outlook, especially compared with that found in the major dioceses to the north and east. Tom Dooley blithely traveled in the same social circles as such prominent debutantes as Ann Farrar Desloges, a member of a highly prominent French Catholic family; in 1946 she was crowned "Queen of the Veiled Prophet" at the climax of a vaguely "pagan" annual event that marked the high point of the social calendar for prosperous St. Louisans of many persuasions.[19]

A prominent St. Louis Jesuit and Dooley family friend, Daniel Lord, was national director of a devotional fraternity for young people, the Sodality of the Blessed Virgin. By the time Tom Dooley joined in the early 1940s, the Sodality had enrolled over two million members nationwide. Lord "revitalized the Sodality both through the force of his own personality and by linking the organization to the newly emergent concept of Catholic Action." Pope Pius XI (1922–39) encouraged lay involvement in promoting the Church's "corporatist interests." But in heavily Catholic cities like St. Louis (as early as 1842 Charles Dickens could write, following his visit there, that "the Roman Catholic religion . . . prevails extensively"), the Church's organizing principle extended well beyond conventional devotional activities. Daniel Lord helped found the Gallery of Living Catholic Authors, which annually chose the Best Ten books by authors "in communion with the Universal Catholic Church." He also launched the Catholic Theater Conference in 1937, and with his encouragement parish dramatic clubs flourished in St. Louis in the 1930s and 1940s.[20]

While Tom Dooley dutifully participated in devotional groups like the Sodality of the Blessed Virgin, he could also derive rich yet fully legitimate pleasures from the dances of the Fleur de Lis Catholic Cotillion, which held monthly formals under Church auspices in order for young people to acquire social graces and meet a variety of appropriate members of the opposite sex. They were directed to proper non-Catholic sources of recreation as well: Dooley joined the Civic Music League and frequented symphonic and operatic performances at Kiel Auditorium. After demonstrating a precocious aptitude for music, he was sent at a young age to the Leo Miller Studio for instruction in piano but, according to his mother, "Mr. Miller told us he lacked just some special thing, perhaps a bit of Latin blood or perhaps a bit of Jewish blood, that would keep him ever from becoming a pianist of any magnitude."[21]

Yet even as he cultivated his secular interests, Tom Dooley was continually reminded of the claims of the spirit. Father Daniel Lord wrote to Tom in February 1944 to apologize in advance for missing his upcoming piano recital: "I shall be in retreat at the time," he explained. Spiritual retreats were gaining prominence among affluent, devout Catholic youths in the late 1930s; the boys from Saint Louis University High made theirs at the Jesuits' White House, a secluded facility located along the banks of the Mississippi River. Dooley's notes meticulously preserved the tone of a retreat he experienced in 1943. "Every little thing must die," the retreat master had intoned. "Death is ever with us. The way we live is the way we die."[22]

The Jesuits expected their charges to integrate the spiritual insights nurtured on retreat into each facet of their lives. In what he called "a preposterous coincidence," the renowned democratic socialist visionary Michael Harrington was Dooley's classmate at Saint Louis University High: Tom "arranged my first date and we and the young ladies went to the movies in his family's chauffeur-driven limousine." In his autobiographical *Fragments of the Century* (1973), Harrington explained that at Saint Louis University High School, "something of the spirit of being shock troops of Christ on the perimeters of the Faith still persisted." As a budding intellectual Harrington was more impressed than Dooley by the *Ratio Studiorum* ("the traditional Jesuit theory of education formulated in 1559"), with its emphasis on Latin, Greek, and classical literature. Yet according to Harrington, the Jesuit principle came alive as well when a young scholastic spent an entire class period "discussing a popular song, 'Wrong, would it be wrong to kiss, seeing we feel like this?' It was, he argued, a typical example of the rampant relativism and hedonism of the culture." The Jesuit system, for Harrington, represented "the philosophical analogue of the daily experience of a closed, Catholic world." A nonintellectual like Tom Dooley had greater difficulty than Harrington in recognizing the boundaries of that world, but his old classmate knowingly argued that "each of us was motivated . . . by the Jesuit inspiration of our adolescence that insisted so strenuously that a man must live his philosophy."[23]

As a "pious apostate" from Catholicism, Michael Harrington could depict the "ghetto Catholicism" of his upbringing with a cool detachment Tom Dooley never affected. Harrington enjoyed an only slightly less privileged boyhood than Dooley's. "And yet," he wrote, "even that happy, secure and relatively unresentful world was a ghetto . . . we did not know British imperialists, Yankee bosses, or Protestant princes first hand, yet they haunted our every waking moment. Above all, our ghettoization had been institutionalized by a Roman Catholic Church which had been engaged in a defensive struggle against the modern world for four hundred years or more."[24]

Catholic leaders in St. Louis thus reinforced their authority among young elites by offering a separate experience, spiritual as well as social, and by promoting an appreciation of secular high culture when they could not provide a surrogate of their own. Tom Dooley was shielded from the popular culture of the many rural Southern whites who had migrated to St. Louis, and remained a stranger to the extensive African American milieu of the city. Dooley surely missed the opportunity to hear his contemporary Miles Davis, son of a dentist from East St. Louis, apprenticing with trumpeter Clark Terry and other local musicians at places like the Riviera Club. (The Riviera, located at Delmar and Taylor, just a few crucial blocks north of Dooley's grammar school, occupies a large space in jazz folklore because it was there Miles Davis first heard bebop pioneers Charlie Parker and Dizzy Gillespie; Davis left for New York in 1944 and later condemned St. Louis as "racist to the bone.") Less than a mile to the northeast of the Riviera, Charles Edward Anderson Berry was born at 2520 Goode Avenue in October 1926, just three months prior to the arrival of Thomas A. Dooley III. Chuck Berry would invest *his* knowledge of all the musical cultures of St. Louis—from white country to pop to rhythm and blues—into the new music he helped invent, rock and roll.[25]

Tommy Dooley's musical innovations were less ambitious, but he still managed to earn his reputation as a nonconformist while serving as the organist at the elegant Annunziata Church in Ladue: during Mass he enriched the sacred music with licks drawn from such pop tunes as "Largo" and "Sleepy Lagoon." Dooley was also notorious, in his role as an altar boy, for whacking his friends under the chin with a paten designed to prevent the consecrated Eucharist from falling to the ground during the offering of Communion. Annunziata was a new parish reflecting the migration of Catholics toward the wealthy suburbs of St. Louis County, although there was still but one other Catholic family in Fair Oaks when the Dooleys moved to that "private place" in 1940. A member of that other family, Maryanne Sell, was Tom's age and quickly befriended him; she kept a diary that poignantly captured the sense of youthful gaiety shattered by events suddenly intruding on their teenage idyll.[26]

On the gray afternoon of December 7, 1941, Tom and Maryanne traipsed through the woods behind her house to feed the ducks at the Bogey Golf Club, before returning to hear the news that permanently altered the course of their lives. Soon Dooley's older brother Earle, a graduate (like his adoptive father) of Culver Military Academy, departed from Georgetown's School of Foreign Service to enlist in the army. Yet on the surface, life proceeded with a minimum of disruption for the young Catholic socialites; war rationing and shortages interfered only slightly with their affairs. In 1943 the patronesses of the Cotillion decided that, in light of "existing conditions, particularly with regard to the new shoe regulations . . . while they prefer dinner coats or formal dress, dark suits with matching trousers and black or brown shoes will be acceptable."[27]

Maryanne and Tom continued to skate on Bogey's pond, attend the concerts of the Civic Music League (where Dooley specialized in cadging backstage autographs of touring musical dignitaries), and party in the basement "rathskellers" at the homes of their many friends. Tommy Dooley was quite a romantic. The night that he "played beautifully" on a radio broadcast, he brought Maryanne "a dark red rose that had won a blue ribbon in the flower show." On April 25, 1943, the sixteen-year-olds had lunch at the Statler Hotel, attended a touring production of *Macbeth* with Judith Anderson and Maurice Evans, took in an evening movie, and joined three carloads of friends at Crossroads, a drive-in restaurant in suburban Clayton favored by night people and adolescents with automobiles. Maryanne was a student at Villa Duchesne, an exclusive high school for Catholic girls run by the same Sacred Heart nuns who operated Barat Hall. Once, while she was on retreat on the school grounds, Tommy telephoned the convent for no apparent reason, causing her much fear and embarrassment. Not long afterward, Dooley suddenly grew emotionally distant, and Maryanne discerned a puzzling, inexplicable change in his temperament during his last year in high school that resulted in the end of their friendship.[28]

Dooley had always been the center of attention at parties and routinely walked into the homes of his friends "like he owned the joint," but now he often acted surly and distant. To many of his acquaintances he represented an odd mixture of extrovert and loner, capable of swaggering into a party to immediately commandeer the piano (once he even played from the back of a pickup truck moving down Grand Avenue) and just as suddenly disappear. At his senior prom, held at the exclusive Missouri Athletic Club, Dooley convinced some male friends to ditch their dates and join him for a dip in the club's pool. Despite such antics Tommy Dooley was generally viewed as an affable, if unpredictable, fellow who chose to reserve a large private space between himself and his friends, especially where any discussion of the Dooley family was concerned.[29]

He began spending time with a girl suffering from degenerative rheumatoid arthritis; they would bake cookies while spraying flour all over themselves and around the kitchen. Some of his friends believed this relationship provided an early glimpse of a compassionate spirit that belied the frivolity of most of his youthful activities; many acquaintances later recalled a "serious side" beyond his frantic showmanship. In 1943 Dooley began the extensive traveling that dominated the remainder of his life. He toured Mexico in July, then spent several weeks that summer with his family at the elegant Monmouth Hotel along the "Irish Riviera" in Spring Lake, New Jersey (a girl he met there said that for the Irish Americans, vacationing at Spring Lake "was like you had died and gone to heaven"). From there it was on to New York for the symphony and Broadway shows, lunches at the Oasis Room of the Waldorf Astoria (he would bivouac exclusively at the Waldorf during visits to New York in the years to come), and Masses at St. Patrick's Cathedral.[30]

Travel may be broadening, but Dooley's cultural baggage was highly portable. Along the road he consorted almost exclusively with fellow well-to-do Irish Catholics who shared most of the assumptions of his St. Louis friends—"swell fish" like Bill Burke, the young tennis pro at the Monmouth Hotel. A girl he dated at Spring Lake sent him the prayer to St. Jude that he might pass his college entrance examinations. Another girl wrote to confirm her spiritual legitimacy lest Dooley resist her charms: "I promise that I will not bicker with you, But, BUT, I would like you to know that I am a very good Catholic and with a grandmother by the name of Fitzsimmons, Irish . . . I want to set you on the right track."[31]

In November 1943 the Catholic Foreign Mission Society of America responded to his inquiry by inviting Tom Dooley to visit their St. Louis office regarding "the important matter of your vocation." Dooley also contacted the army's Aviation Cadet Training program and took the qualifying test for the navy's wartime college program. His brother Earle was fighting in Europe, and Tom Dooley—who graduated from high school just as he turned seventeen in January 1944—felt he too should serve, but his parents insisted that he begin college instead. Making a choice among schools was not difficult. Tom had received adequate high school grades; the University of Notre Dame not only was the most prestigious Catholic college in America, but also offered extensive opportunities to combine military training and service with the pursuit of a higher education. Dooley was accepted for admission and enrolled for the 1944 winter semester. "I am very pleased to hear that you are going to Notre Dame," wrote a Brooklyn Irish girl he had met at the Jersey shore. "That is my favorite college and Boy! what a team they have."[32]

Tom Dooley was not a fan of collegiate football, but he became Notre Dame's most celebrated product despite spending only five erratic semesters and one summer in South Bend. He left without his degree in 1948 after being admitted to the medical school of Saint Louis University; premedical students of that era were often admitted after three years and Dooley's wealth of St. Louis connections may have compensated for an indifferent undergraduate record. He later forged a public relationship with Notre Dame that provided an archetypal model for all of his mythmaking; he came to symbolize the Notre Dame mystique even as he reshaped it in his own image, while remaining personally aloof from the communal ethos that suffused the institution. The paradox of Dooley's character is rehearsed as well in the memories of his classmates, who recall a cocky, loquacious boy who was at the same time a "bitter," "rebellious" loner.[33]

The war years dramatically affected the college experience everywhere, but at few institutions were the changes more evident than at Notre Dame, which housed the largest navy officer training program "of any Catholic school, and one of the largest in the country." In 1943 nine hundred officer candidates in the navy's V-12 program joined the twelve hundred men enrolled in the midshipmen's school established at Notre Dame the previous year; by the time Tom Dooley matriculated only seven hundred civilian students remained on campus. After deciding that he wanted to become a physician, Tom obtained his parents' grudging permission to enlist as a U.S. Navy medical corpsman with only two semesters of college work completed. He was in training at the Great Lakes Naval Station when word arrived that his half-brother Earle had been killed in Germany on November 18, 1944, at the battle of Hurtgen Forest. Earle had written an impassioned if illogical letter to his family to be read in the event of his death; he charged them to "see to it that any attempt to begin this slaughter anew is crushed *at once,* by force of arms if necessary!"[34]

After being trained as a pharmacist's mate at Great Lakes, Tom Dooley began his medical career tending to the broken bodies of servicemen returned from combat to the naval hospital at St. Albans, in Queens, New York, and later the Marine Hospital at San Diego. Since he "received patients in battle dress" at San Diego, presumably combat casualties, he could later claim to have served in "the Pacific theater of war." Shortly before the war ended Dooley was transferred to the U.S. Marines Medical Corps, but following additional training at Quantico, Virginia, he was shipped to Puerto Rico as part of a detail responsible for detonating surplus ammunition.[35]

Returning to Notre Dame in 1946 Dooley, like many veterans, sported a distinctly worldly air along with his U.S. Navy pea coat and combat boots; he enjoyed boasting about the many circumcision procedures he had performed as a pharmacist's mate. Notre Dame's legendary disciplinary code rivaled that of the service in its austere rigor and added a dose of muscular Catholicism for good measure: students were required to attend at least three weekly Masses in the chapels housed in each residence hall (Notre Dame's few non-Catholic students conducted check-ins for their fellows). Complaining about the system, then revering it in maturity, was a Notre Dame art form that Dooley celebrated in his legendary 1960 deathbed letter to the University's president, the Reverend Theodore Hesburgh, C.S.C.: "Do the students ever appreciate what they have, while they have it? I know I never did. Spent most of my time being angry at the clergy at school: 10 P.M. bed check, absurd for a 19-year old veteran, etc. etc. etc."[36]

Before Tom Dooley's time at Notre Dame, to "skive" meant "to absent oneself from a hall, without permission, after hours, at night, for private reasons . . . skivers caught were compelled immediately to pack their trunks and forever go." An accomplished skiver, Dooley enjoyed a rare knack for ignoring rules without paying consequences, a source of much of his rakish mystique. Resident Notre Dame students were not allowed to keep cars on campus, yet several classmates recall the Cadillac convertible in which Dooley once tooled up alongside Cavanaugh Hall, accompanied by the attractive young female whose wealthy father owned the vehicle. Dooley never failed to attract a crowd when the time was right; classmates remembered him as a wisecracking, 1940s-style "character" who told bawdy jokes: "I was driving with my girlfriend and she said 'please use two hands,'" began one such effort. "I'm sorry," said Tom, "I need one to drive with." On another occasion a hallmate stopped by his room to accompany Dooley to Sunday Mass only to be informed by Tom that, in the absence of a confessor on duty, he could not take Communion because on the previous evening he had visited a South Bend tavern and wound up examining firsthand a bluebird tattoo imprinted on the breast of a woman he had met there.[37]

Notre Dame students were not permitted to leave the campus overnight without letters of permission from their parents, yet Dooley frequently spent weekends with his sophisticated friends along the midwestern horse show and fox hunt circuit. He also spent a great deal of time at neighboring Saint Mary's College, a women's school where he played the piano and became a favorite of the college's poet-president, Sister M. Madeleva Wolff. He even made an appearance during 1944 in the chorus line at the fabled Empire Room of Chicago's Palmer House Hotel, where impresario Merriel Abbott booked the nation's most glamorous entertainers. The enormously popular chanteuse Hildegarde was rehearsing one afternoon for a performance when she saw a young man wheeling a piano across the stage of the Empire Room, histrionically wiping feigned perspiration from his brow. She introduced herself to the young collegian and on learning he was a Notre Dame student invited him to accompany her to the 2:00 A.M. "swinger's Mass" at St. Mary's Church in Chicago.[38]

Dooley was able to appear in Hildegarde's chorus line because, while still in his teens, he had become a highly spirited participant in the homosexual subcultures of the American armed forces, the Catholic Church, the hunt circuit, and various urban centers including New York and Chicago. Hildegarde was herself a devout Catholic with a large gay following: her campy nightclub act was rife with allusions to "Kinsey's whimseys" (after 1948) and other euphemisms for homosexuals in currency among entertainers of the period. Allan Bérubé, the chronicler of gay life in World War II, noted that "although nightclub entertainment was never publicly identified as gay, such performers as Hildegarde and Tallulah Bankhead attracted a devoted gay following, sometimes dropping veiled hints or singing lyrics with double meanings directed at their admirers."[39]

From the time that Dooley's homosexuality was first discussed publicly in 1989, it has been widely assumed that he must have suffered terribly for his sexuality. This view is not wholly unfounded, but it is equally true that from his adolescence onward, Tom Dooley made little effort to conceal his sexuality. He made frequent passes at male acquaintances; according to his classmate Michael Harrington, Tom had a sexual relationship with a young cleric that was anything but secretive, at least so far as Harrington was concerned. A gay friend who served with Dooley as a marine corpsman recalled that far from being confused or tormented by his sexuality, Tom confidently exploited his appeal to gay officers in order to receive choice assignments.[40]

In fact Dooley's precocious talent for trumping military authority and protocol—often a function of his gay connections—may have caused him later to overestimate dangerously his own prowess. In *Promises to Keep,* Agnes Dooley proudly described Tom's coup in arranging for an impromptu visit by Hildegarde to the U.S. Navy Hospital at St. Alban's, where he was stationed in 1945: "Hildegarde had arrived on schedule, all right, but she refused to budge unless Corpsman Dooley personally escorted her through the hospital. Followed by all the Navy brass—'It was the first time in my life I preceded anyone of rank,' Tom wrote—Hildegarde took Tom's arm, went into Tom's ward, entertained Tom's patients, and then toured the entire hospital."[41]

Long before his sexuality became an issue, Dooley was known for his compulsive if often charming nonconformity. The Notre Dame dean responsible for premedical students recalled "there were times when he was a student here that I could have wrung his neck with pleasure; certainly he had a brashness that must have irked the braid of the high brass in the Navy." Yet when he was not acting out his flamboyant public roles Dooley appeared genuinely touched by the pervasive spirituality of Notre Dame. He regularly served Mass for an Irish priest, Father Lawrence Broughal, a philosophy teacher and a popular confessor who spoke often of the responsibility of Catholics to apply the Church's teachings to public affairs. Notre Dame banned social fraternities in favor of a more inclusive vision of brotherhood. Dooley later recalled the urgency of religion professor Father Paul Doherty's pronouncements on the "oneness of mankind" when he asserted: "My years in Asia have proved to me that the brotherhood of man exists as certainly as does the fatherhood of God." Dooley was among the few Anglo members of Notre Dame's Inter-American club, dedicated to promoting hemispheric cooperation (José Napoleon Duarte, the future president of El Salvador, was also a member of the club; he and his brother had decided to attend Notre Dame after viewing the film *Knute Rockne, All American,* starring Pat O'Brien and Ronald Reagan).[42]

Dooley's public religiosity was often dismissed by his later critics as mere showmanship: his December 1960 letter to Reverend Hesburgh featured a tone suitable for the framing it later received. Yet while the letter demonstrated a mastery of the often sentimental piety of Notre Dame, it also hinted at Dooley's struggle with the limits of the genre, a central issue in his writing as in his life. His was the spiritual journey of a complex individual who persisted in the effort to reconcile wildly conflicting impulses, for the sake of his audience as well as for himself. He wrote to Hesburgh that despite his illness, "nothing human or earthly can touch me. A milder storm of peace gathers in my heart. What seems unpossessable, I can possess. What seems unfathomable, I fathom. What is unutterable, I can utter. Because I can pray. I can communicate. How do people endure anything on earth if they cannot have God?"[43]

Dooley understood that he owed something to the millions of American Catholics who partook of the mystical dimension of Notre Dame. Shortly after his death an engraved copy of his letter to Hesburgh was placed in the Grotto of Our Lady, a lovely replica of the shrine at Lourdes and the focal point of personal spirituality at Notre Dame, as well as an immensely popular attraction for campus visitors. In 1986 a statue depicting Dooley with adoring Lao children was placed nearby; his is the dominant human presence at the Grotto. In 1960 Tom traveled to the original Lourdes shrine, despite his own reservations about the shrine's healing powers or his own worthiness to receive them. The derivative language of his message to Hesburgh barely conceals a similar desire for the sentiments to acquire an authentic life of their own, as if in vindication of their author:

> But just now, and just so many times, how I long for the Grotto. Away from the Grotto, Dooley just prays. But at the Grotto, especially now when there must be snow everywhere and the lake is ice glass. . . . If I could go to the Grotto now, then I think I could sing inside. I could be full of faith and poetry and loveliness and know more beauty, tenderness and compassion. This is soggy sentimentalism, I know. . . . So, Father Hesburgh, Notre Dame is . . . always in my heart. That Grotto is the rock to which my life is anchored.[44]

Of Notre Dame the novelist Richard Sullivan wrote simply, "The story is a mystery story . . . this place, this present, living fact of Notre Dame, is unfathomable." Remembered by one classmate above all for his haunted laughter, Dooley glimpsed at Notre Dame the source of some of that mystery; gifted with a peculiar genius, he went on to extend his presence in the Mystical Body to an audience who—without surrendering their fealty to the Fighting Irish—yearned for the bolder spiritual adventures embraced by the jungle doctor of Laos.[45]

In June 1948 Tom Dooley sailed for Paris aboard the SS *Marine Marlin* as a reward from his parents for gaining admission to medical school. He wrote almost daily to his family, a habit that greatly facilitated the composition of his first book. These letters are the earliest extant samples of Dooley's writing and reveal—aside from his jealousy of the "Princeton men" heading for a regatta in England (an early indication of the status worries that helped fuel his ambition)—the dutiful son he would remain through many hundreds of missives addressed from Southeast Asia to his mother. Yet puzzling hints of disorder occasionally disrupted the charmed tone of this abundantly blessed young man. Tom had planned to travel with a Notre Dame friend, but "then something came up which was not very nice" and he wound up living alone in a Paris pension but frequently hosting "numerous other fellows" he had met along the way.[46]

Through his old girlfriend Maryanne Sell, whose father was in the foreign service, Dooley was introduced to a distinguished Parisian family. Agnes Dooley's account of this meeting offers a representative sampling of Dooley mythology, with a focus on his spontaneity and effortless grace:

> The Haizet family . . . invited him to tea at their elegant apartment "right on the Seine near the Tour Eiffel." While Tom was there, some Chopin scores were delivered to Madame Haizet. "She asked me," wrote Tom, "whether I could play what she had and, by sheer accident, I could. Nor could I have had a better setting for Chopin. I just let myself go and played Chopin for nearly an hour. They are leaving Paris and going to their summer villa in Brittany. I have been invited to spend a few days there in August."[47]

Dooley desultorily attended a few lectures at the Sorbonne, but mostly he traveled; in his highly convincing guise as suave young American socialite, he cased American Express offices for well-heeled fellow countrywomen. He cadged elegant dates to the racetrack at Longchamps and the opera from a woman who, he confided to a St. Louis traveling companion, had to be worth at least $6 million. The friend noticed a trait Dooley later refined to perfection: an astounding ability to travel in first-class splendor on virtually no money. Nearing the end of the European holiday, he wrote from Brussels:

"My heart is a little heavy in leaving Sorbonne days, Paris nights, Geneva fetes, Lucerne music festivals, Matterhorn heights, Brittany hospitality and all, but I shall be so glad, so very glad to see that Lady of Liberty and all she stands for." Within a decade Tom Dooley would be celebrated as one of the world's greatest and most self-sacrificing humanitarians, but for now he anxiously upgraded his return passage on a luxury liner to avoid the "many D.P.'s" (displaced persons) fleeing those parts of Europe not on the itinerary of indomitable young Americans.[48]

If Notre Dame planted the seed of Christian service in Tom Dooley's soul, his disastrous, humiliating years at Saint Louis University School of Medicine provided the incentive that drove him to seek worldly acclaim as a physician-savior. The precise reason why Dooley was forced to repeat his final year—a well-tended secret at the medical school—spawned an array of theories that meshed neatly with the broader outlines of Dooley folklore. Mrs. Dooley blamed a vindictive faculty member, a theme that would recur whenever Tom clashed with authority figures. Others cited Dooley's frequent appearances in the society pages of the *St. Louis Post-Dispatch* and his habit of turning up late for class still clad in riding attire. Variants on this theme place Dooley at either the Kentucky Derby during final exams in 1952 or perched atop the celebrated jumper "Miss Budweiser" in a horse show at Madison Square Garden. Even his mother admitted that he "thought nothing of cutting an exam for more engaging activities like a fox hunt." Tom was also alleged to have spent more time lining up wealthy female St. Louisans as future patients for his practice as a "society obstetrician" than in fulfilling his clinical duties. He was reported to have telephoned a professor on the eve of a final examination asking that he be excused. Once he had talked his way out of taking the test, Dooley reportedly exulted: "It's a good thing, since I'm calling from Paris."[49]

Just as he had at Notre Dame, Dooley became in medical school a highly conspicuous figure and an object of fascination, envy, and disdain while remaining totally remote from the daily life of the institution. A 1950 clipping from the society page of an Indianapolis newspaper provides a hint of the life Dooley pursued with much greater vigor than he lent his medical studies: "Last Saturday night at Woodstock Jeanne Robinson and Tom Dooley of St. Louis, Dave Moxley's week-end house guest, were having a wonderful time waltzing away amid the hearts and flowers setting of the Valentine's dance. They thought the floor surprisingly deserted, only two other couples were enjoying with them the Viennese waltzes. Then they found out why! They were participating in a waltz contest!"[50]

David Moxley was a member of the Yale class of 1943 who as an army officer in World War II socialized with the horsemen of the Philadelphia Troop, a famed corps of gentlemen officers whose organization dated to the Revolutionary era. Moxley, who had met Tom Dooley on the midwestern hunt circuit, found him to be an aggressively charming young man whom he was pleased to introduce to distinguished friends at the Trader's Point Club in Indianapolis. He recalled that Dooley "was not of the Methodist persuasion" when it came to accepting a cocktail; his companions never feared a dull moment or lull in the conversation so long as the young St. Louis horseman was in the room. Dooley was one of the few riders to whom Moxley would gladly loan a horse and "give a leg up"; it was Tom's "surgeon's hands," he recalled, that separated him from the common herd of riders.[51]

Dooley commuted to medical school in his yellow convertible from the comparatively modest West End home where the family had moved during the war. His father had supervised the production of more than fifteen thousand army tanks at American Car and Foundry, but neighbors believed that reversals in Mr. Dooley's personal finances plagued the family. In November 1948, while his wife was "knitting argyll socks" and his sons Tom and Eddie Mike were visiting their brother Malcolm at Notre Dame, Mr. Dooley was stricken by a fatal heart attack outside Our Lady of Lourdes Church on Forsyth Boulevard in University City. Thomas A. Dooley Sr.'s death had been front-page news in St. Louis, but although his son had succeeded him as district manager of ACF, Dooley Jr. was relegated to a modest notice on the obituary page, the photograph revealing a rather haunted-looking sixty-three-year-old man. Several years earlier he had written to his eldest surviving son on ACF letterhead as Tom prepared to leave for Notre Dame; no adjustment for the rigid proprieties of the era can ameliorate the pained distance evident between these men or the father's faltering efforts to establish a bond between them, in signing the letter "always your pal."[52]

Although Tom Dooley and his father had never been close, the latter's death removed a source of authority that moderated the more frenetic aspects of Tom's nature. Agnes Dooley later claimed that despite his father's death, her son "went right on with his kind of double life—the one face buoyant, gay, garrulous and the other high-minded, compassionate and reflective." Yet few others in St. Louis observed the latter attributes, recalling instead the day Tom put his new horse on the elevator at St. Mary's Hospital to impress a patient on his internship rounds, or the time he impulsively dragged a friend into Archbishop Glennon's residence for an unannounced visit (years later, Francis Cardinal Spellman of New York told Dooley that he had heard of the incident from Glennon himself). He established a tremendous rapport with younger patients and routinely skipped classes and missed tests to take children to the circus or for rides in his convertible, often stopping for ice cream at Frank Monaco's drugstore on the South Side. Tom was especially fond of young "delinquents." "They looked like thugs," his mother recalled, "but they were Tom's friends." Dooley often brought these youths to the family home, and "after they left," according to his brother Malcolm, "mom would count the silverware."[53]

The faculty at the medical school were enraged by Dooley's irresponsibility, but his family's prominence (an otherwise modest Jesuit at the university surprised one of Dooley's friends by boasting that he socialized with Tom's parents) placed them in an awkward position. Although Saint Louis University and the city had come a long way since nativists trashed the fledgling medical school in 1849 (the sight of parts of a cadaver on the grounds inflamed Know-Nothing hysteria over Catholic "abuses, cruelties, and profanations perpetrated in hospitals"), Dooley's antics threatened to rekindle the disrepute Catholic educators had struggled so hard to overcome. In fact many Catholic universities had adopted a disciplinary model akin to that at Notre Dame precisely to bolster the image of their schools as rigorous, highly respectable institutions. The year before Dooley entered the medical school its longtime dean, Alphonse M. Schwitalla, S.J., resigned due to failing health. Schwitalla had been a leading proponent of rigorous standards for Catholic higher education but he lacked medical training; his departure signaled an opportunity for a "medical man" to elevate the school's reputation.[54]

Melvin A. Casberg, a peripatetic medical educator and a Protestant with a great interest in missionary work, was appointed dean in 1949, only to clash immediately with the school's Jesuit regent, Edward T. Foote. Casberg was highly sympathetic with Tom Dooley's impulsive worldliness and his resistance to authority; he became a key patron who bailed Dooley out of more than one self-created predicament. But Casberg was forced out of his position in 1952 by the rather dour Father Foote, who, with the encouragement of several prominent faculty members, promptly declared open season on Dooley and other miscreants among the student body. One of Dooley's few friends at the medical school was a young Hawaiian of Chinese descent (Tom was also close to the only female student in his class) who ultimately failed to graduate and who later insisted that Father Foote did indeed have a personal vendetta against Dooley; even if this is true, however, Tom had supplied more than ample grounds for his own expulsion. Dooley was repeatedly warned to reform his ways, but feeling immune from threats of expulsion or disgrace, he persisted in his carousings and received the shock of his life when the administration finally called his bluff, shortly before the class of 1952 graduated. Informed that he must repeat his entire senior year, a chastened Dooley told a Notre Dame friend that he would sell his convertible as well as Jim Hawkins, his horse.[55]

The convertible may have been relinquished but the horsemanship was too precious for Dooley to give up for long. His new social headquarters in St. Louis was the Bridlespur Hunt Club, founded by August A. Busch Jr. in the mid-1920s after he was apparently blackballed by the Saint Louis Country Club. Dooley regularly cooled his heels at the club while evading the scrutiny of his adversaries at the medical school, who were generally content to travel by foot, public conveyance, or automobile. Reporting on Bridlespur's first annual horse show in 1928, the *St. Louis Post-Dispatch* had noted that "the competitors were the club's charter members, and the spectators ranged from those noted in the Social Register to those lucky to be found in the telephone book." According to Stephen Birmingham, chronicler of America's would-be aristocracy, "some sports purists claim that fox hunting is not properly a sport at all . . . it is, they argue, merely an equine fashion show at which the hunters display their custom-made pink coats, their skin-fitting white breeches, and their three-thousand dollar boots; a pastime for social climbers."[56]

Tom Dooley was so proud of his pink jacket that he sometimes wore it to class at the medical school. Although his "innocent arrogance" later proved no match for the East Coast patricians and intelligence operatives who tended the aura that flickered around him, Bridlespur rewarded a bravado that confirmed Dooley as not just another wisecracking urban Irishman on the make. Even if after more than a half-century the Dooleys are still retrospectively denied a place within what an acquaintance called "the cream of St. Louis society," Tom certainly acted the part and could scarcely have imagined the price he would later pay for lacking a genuine mastery of the world's harsher workings.[57]

☆ 2 ☆

The Storyteller on Ice
in Haiphong

On May 12, 1955, Premier Ngo Dinh Diem of South Vietnam awarded Lt. (jg) Thomas A. Dooley III, United States Navy, "the highest honor that his country can give to a foreigner, pinning on him the medal of an Officier de l'Ordre National de Viet Nam." In one of the photographs taken to commemorate the occasion, the lanky young medical officer looks with respectful solemnity on the much shorter, dapper chief of state, clad as usual in a white double-breasted suit. In the background, framed by the two principals, stand Capt. Walter Winn, United States Navy, and a Father Khue, an ascetic-looking Vietnamese Catholic priest. The photograph orients our gaze back and forth from Diem to Dooley, mediated by representatives of two agencies whose interests would converge just long enough to anoint Dr. Tom Dooley the symbol of U.S.-Vietnamese friendship.[1]

This event, occurring nearly a decade prior to the "Americanization" of the Vietnam War, is never mentioned in histories of the conflict. Dooley's name is missing from the indexes of virtually all of the scores of well-known studies of the war, as if the hopes he represented were buried under an avalanche of bloodletting and national catastrophe. Yet no American played a larger role in announcing the arrival of South Vietnam as a new ally whose fate was decisively bound to that of the United States. Dooley's enormously popular 1956 account of his work in Vietnam, *Deliver Us from Evil,* quite literally located Vietnam on the new world map for millions of Americans.[2]

Dooley stumbled into history as a result of his medical school debacle, which was a topic of bemused conversation in St. Louis, especially within those circles where he had hoped to flourish as a society doctor. The medical faculty had decided it was not enough that he repeat his senior year; he was deemed too immature to begin a residency and was ordered to extend his internship an additional six months, an offer Tom declined. He decided to rejoin the military, where he had enjoyed the travel if not the discipline during his tenure as a navy corpsman. In the summer of 1950 he fulfilled a medical school requirement by serving in an army ROTC program at Letterman General Hospital in San Francisco. On August 25 of that year the U.S. Navy hospital ship *Benevolence* sank in thick fog just west of the Golden Gate bridge after colliding with a freighter. According to his brother Malcolm, "Tom was at the hospital but off duty at the time of the tragedy and immediately joined in the rescue effort. People in California still talk of the young man who went out into the fog-shrouded bay in a small boat and time after time dove into the water to pull out survivors. Tom himself was hospitalized after this exploit and was later commended by the Army for his selfless display of courage." While no evidence of Dooley's heroism is to be found in San Francisco newspaper accounts of the accident, or from U.S. Army sources, he may indeed have aided in the rescue. The episode entered the Dooley canon in the numerous versions he shared with acquaintances: in the future his good works were usually performed with a media escort on hand.[3]

A return to the service promised Tom Dooley a life of travel and freedom from the scornful glare of the civilian medical establishment. A prominent St. Louis physician who was a family friend and Dr. Melvin A. Casberg—who had been Dooley's intercessor at Saint Louis University Medical School—pleaded with U.S. Navy Surgeon General Lamont Pugh to overlook Dooley's woeful record ("when my slate was so soiled," as Tom put it) and admit him to the Navy Medical Corps. In April 1953 he was appointed lieutenant (jg) and assigned to an internship at Camp Pendleton, California, in preparation for duty at the U.S. Naval Hospital in Yokosuka, Japan. On July 14, 1954, he received "Temporary Additional Duty" orders to report from Yokosuka to the USS *Montague* "in connection with medical matters."[4]

The *Montague* was dispatched to the Philippines for amphibious exercises and practice landings in preparation for the naval operation that inaugurated United States military involvement in the Vietnamese revolution. Following the defeat of the French by the Viet Minh at Dien Bien Phu in April 1954, an unsigned "Final Declaration" was issued at Geneva on July 21, ending the First Indochina War:

> The Geneva Accords of 1954 provided for a cease-fire, and for the temporary partition of Vietnam at the 17th parallel, followed by nation-wide elections in 1956 to determine the future of the country. Neither part of the country was to join any military alliance, and no new military equipment or personnel were to be brought into either area from outside, nor were there to be any foreign military bases. An International Control Commission, composed of representatives from Canada, Poland, and India, was to supervise the truce.[5]

Article 14 of the Geneva Accords required the governments of North and South Vietnam to permit and assist all individuals who wished to transfer from one zone to the other until May 1955, when the Viet Minh would assume full control of the North and the borders would be closed. In the meantime the French were conducting fitful negotiations with Emperor Bao Dai over the creation of a new, presumably pro-Western government in South Vietnam. The United States refused to be a party to the Geneva treaty since the agreement recognized the legitimacy of a communist government in the North, but President Eisenhower and Secretary of State John Foster Dulles decided that a naval presence would facilitate the transfer of refugees to the South and demonstrate American resolve against the spread of communism in Southeast Asia. The French were also committed to supervising a refugee operation, but in late July, "doubting that the French could handle the task alone," Ngo Dinh Diem "advised the United States Ambassador, Donald Heath, in Saigon that South Vietnam would need help in transporting Catholics and other anti-Communists from the North to the free zone of Vietnam."[6]

Tom Dooley's letters to his mother throughout Operation Passage to Freedom—from late summer 1954 through the spring of 1955—were redolent of the last innocence known by Americans in Vietnam. It turned out that Dooley was but a factotum in a massive exercise conducted by American intelligence operatives in country; what he did not know about this larger campaign would eventually fill a book. Since he was as anxious to maintain steady communication with his mother as he was intent on protecting her from his personal life, the letters provided a fairly credible account of his duties (compared with the highly stylized version presented in *Deliver Us from Evil*) and offer perhaps the best surviving firsthand account of the opening chapter in America's long, slow descent into the Vietnam quagmire. As raw materials, the letters paralleled Dooley's gradual evolution into a polished propagandist. His experiences in Vietnam in 1954–55 were far less important than a fortuitous sequence of events that rendered him increasingly useful to Premier Diem's American handlers.

By the time the *Montague* arrived in Subic Bay, the Philippines, Dooley had already antagonized several officers and established his informal authority over the enlisted men through his spirited lectures on the causes and prevention of venereal diseases: "They are appreciative of this knowledge, and really desire to have it." Well aware of his lack of intellectual or scientific credentials, Dooley quickly won over the sailors on the deck of the *Montague* by approaching them as people hungry for knowledge, susceptible to simple formulas, and wary of haughty "experts." On August 15, the Feast of the Assumption (like many Catholics of the 1950s Dooley often dated his correspondence according to the Church's holy calendar), Dooley wrote from the harbor of Tourane (later Da Nang), just south of Hue, in the land he continued to call "Indo China." He described the logistics of the evacuation just beginning, noting that "they are going to be poor refugee, Vietnamese who are trying to escape from the Communists to whom they have been sold by the French."[7]

With Dooley aboard as medical officer, the *Montague* journeyed between the supply depot at Tourane and Baie d'Along, a small harbor thirty miles south of Haiphong where refugees were picked up and transported to Saigon for debarkment. By August 26 Dooley had already contacted the *St. Louis Post-Dispatch* with a "run down of this trip . . . I believe all will be interested in it." On liberty in Saigon, he noted the similarities of that colonial city to Paris, but although Tom's advanced tourist's knowledge of the French language aided his rapid ascent in the refugee operation, disillusionment with French personnel in Vietnam became a constant theme in the letters: "Like the French, complacency is the keynote. Three blocks from the docks (which is like the river is to St. Louis) I was sitting in sidewalk cafes listening to new French music, watching people scurrying, and with no obvious cognizance of the horrible load of mutilated refugees that we had just debarked."[8]

The refugees were transported in French vessels from Haiphong to Baie d'Along where Dooley, acting as interpreter, was waiting to supervise their transfer onto the landing craft "called a LSM which is about 100 yds long, with a large well deck, and the mouth of it opens up."

> My job is to interpret all the commands that the captain gives to the captain of the French ship as she pulls along side. You can just shout from one bridge to the other, or with a megaphone. I do the yelling . . . just as the connecting gangway is putt down I go over to the LSM and have the control people taken off first. These are the priests, nuns, the Vietnamese officers who handle the

mobs . . . Then they start up. Milling thousands in total. Miserable, filthy lame, blind, crippled and war wounded come aboard. I am sure you have seen the newsreels. Eighty percent are very old men and women, and the others are infants, all swollen with malnutrition and starvation, and literally dozens without limbs. They have a few paltry bags on sticks, called yokes, with two bags on each end. This is the only things they have left in the way of possessions.[9]

Dooley was far from the trails of the Bridlespur Hunt Club; although he thoughtfully continued using country club geography in his letters as a basis for comparison with the landscape of Vietnam, he was beginning to undergo a profound conversion in his view of the world and his potential role therein. "You can see they keep me busy," he wrote, "but I couldn't be more content. I am getting to see and learn a great deal about this whole thing." He so impressed the navy that on September 1, 1954, Rear Admiral Lorenzo S. Sabin "offered" Dooley a special assignment working with a small team of physicians and corpsmen on medical intelligence in Haiphong and in Laos (which Dooley continually misspelled as "Loas"), "high in the Himalyas." When Dooley asked why, since Hanoi "goes red in six weeks," the navy would be concerned with epidemiology in Vietnam, the admiral reportedly replied: "America never knows where she may have to fight next. Malaria almost stopped World War II. Hemorrhagic fever almost stopped the Korean War. This time we want to be ahead of the game."[10]

In early August, Capt. Julius Amberson of the Navy Medical Corps had been ordered by Admiral Sabin "to go ashore to establish the necessary medical and sanitary facilities which would be needed for the refugees and, insofar as possible, to establish good liaison with the French and Vietnamese to expedite the mission." Dooley initially served as an interpreter in meetings with French and Vietnamese health officials in Haiphong, but soon he and his colleagues were absorbed in the wretched suffering of the migrants. Amberson estimated that there were "about 200,000" refugees in Haiphong at the time: "They were living in the most squalid conditions—no sanitary conveniences. The human excreta combined with the presence of enormous numbers of flies were the making of epidemic diseases among these unfortunates . . . the heat was intense. Strong odors permeated the air."[11]

For all of that, Dooley sensed that an extraordinary opportunity was beckoning him. On September 1, 1954, he scribbled a note instructing his mother to reinvest all capital gains from his stock portfolio, because "I don't need cash where I'm going." He also accurately remarked of his new duties, "I don't know much more about it." It seems Tom never fully grasped the true nature of his mission in Vietnam during the next nine months, when his medical intelligence work was subordinated to an emerging role as a uniquely gifted spokesman for a massive political operation. Vietnamese refugees were about to become the bulwark of a new state in the South, led by the Catholic mandarin Ngo Dinh Diem under the scrupulous tutelage of the premier nation-builder of Southeast Asia, Lt. Col. Edward Geary Lansdale, a kind of freelance CIA agent attached for cover to the United States Air Force and charged with running the Saigon Military Mission.[12]

The journalist Neal Sheehan promoted a widely held view of Lansdale's most notorious achievement: "South Vietnam, it can truly be said, was the creation of Edward Lansdale." While some have argued that this assessment is slightly exaggerated, there can be little doubt of the maverick CIA operative's more modest triumph in "discovering" and "inspiring" the Dr. Tom Dooley of myth and legend. For Lansdale, born in Detroit in 1908 and educated at UCLA, engineered Operation Exodus (as it was designated by the United States Operations Mission, or USOM, which implemented foreign aid programs in the field; the navy entitled its own contribution Operation Passage to Freedom, the term later enshrined in Tom Dooley's *Deliver Us from Evil*); in the process, he utilized some of the same skills he had developed while handling the account of Nescafé, America's first powdered coffee, during his career as a San Francisco advertising executive. According to the journalist Evan Thomas, Lansdale was an "iconoclast and a loner," who "preferred to operate on his own" and was given a wide berth by such influential CIA patrons as Desmond Fitzgerald, the acting head of the Far East Division of the CIA's covert action operation, the "blandly named" Office of Policy Coordination. As historian David L. Anderson explained, "Lansdale invented the name Saigon Military Mission [SMM] as a cover designation for his specifically recruited team of Philippine and American agents. . . . The SMM operated with virtually total independence from the regular CIA station in Saigon, and its members engaged in special operations ranging from espionage to propaganda to free medical aid for peasants.[13]

Fitzgerald's "overall responsibilities included the Philippines," where Lansdale had successfully engineered the electoral triumph of Ramon Magsaysay in 1953 and the subsequent neutralization of the leftist Huk rebels. Fitzgerald "was smart enough to see that Lansdale was an original, highly effective on his own, and best left alone," Thomas explained. After Lansdale arrived in Saigon in June 1954 he immediately sensed that Diem's fate was intimately linked to his ability to win public support in the United States. The elderly and maimed refugees Tom Dooley helped load onto LSMs at Baie d'Along were of little immediate use to the new administration in the South, but they proved indispensable to Lansdale's more immediate objective, selling the authoritarian Ngo Dinh Diem to a stateside audience still recovering from a protracted involvement in a Korean "conflict" that did not always seem relevant to America's vital interests.[14]

The solution lay in the refugee pilgrimage for religious freedom, something all Americans could relate to even if the crucifixes that were the sole possession of many of the exiles were not standard equipment in most denominations. But these Asians were at least Christians of a sort, and in one of his many inspired moments Lansdale recognized in Tom Dooley—the young go-getter he kept hearing so much about—an almost too perfect conduit between the suffering Catholic pilgrims and the straight-shooting, wise-cracking American journalists and pundits both in the country and back home who knew a human interest story when it fell into their typewriters.

"Lansdale's SMM worked hard during the evacuation period to ensure a maximum exodus of refugees," recalled Howard Simpson, who contributed to the campaign as an employee of the United States Information Agency [USIA]. "The fine art of 'gray' and 'black' propaganda was used to convince wavering Tonkinese that their salvation lay in the South." Meanwhile, Tom Dooley attacked his work with a newfound fervor. In a highly revealing irony, Dooley would be celebrated for service in Haiphong that he himself mistakenly construed as an elaborate cover for intelligence gathering. "On Facade, to the world, we are doing the DDTing [the refugees were doused in the pesticide DDT sprayed from machines before embarking on U.S. Navy ships] and medical triage to the refugees who are here in such large numbers," he explained to his mother. "The second part of our job, and the real thing is Medical Intelligence." He helped set up an epidemiological laboratory for the study of various indigenous parasites and bacteria, "so if and when we have to fight here the men will know exactly what to expect in the way of disease."[15]

Many months later, in August 1955, after his mother heard that he had been detained by the Viet Minh in Haiphong early in the previous May, Dooley wrote to reassure her:

> I knew all along that you fully realized what my job was for those last six months in Indo China. The Viet Nam government in Saigon had doctors, the U.S. Public Health had doctors who are specialists in Refugees. And dozens of other organizations such as the International Rescue Committee, CARE etc all have doctors to work with refugees all over the world. Yet the Navy saw fit to keep me there, who had no training whatsoever in refugee work. The reasons must have been obvious to anyone. In fact they were, to the Viet Minh.[16]

This crucial letter leads us down many dark roads of inquiry, but it surely confirms Dooley's unfitness for intelligence work. Tom had indeed bragged to Mrs. Dooley about his "cloak and dagger" escapades, in letters sent through ordinary military channels and delivered by the United States

Postal Service to the Dooley home in St. Louis. It would be difficult to imagine an authentic spy broadcasting the details of his intrigues to family members; Lansdale scholars have found nary a scrap in *his* voluminous papers to illuminate the precise workings of his extravagant machinations in Vietnam. The profoundly unassuming father of modern psychological warfare was not likely to recognize a kindred spirit in the young officer, for Dooley was a compulsive talker who ranged on the scales of veracity somewhere between a colorful storytelling wit and an inveterate liar. But Lansdale undoubtedly recognized that Dooley not only viewed the refugee exodus precisely as the CIA man hoped Americans at home would, but also proved a kind of malleable counterpart to Ngo Dinh Diem, the rigid and authoritarian Catholic mandarin. The all-American boy as loose cannon, Dooley was strategically positioned in Haiphong in a military dress rehearsal for campaigns the farsighted Lansdale knew were sure to come.[17]

By late September 1955 Dooley had established the unique blend of showmanship and idealism that marked his peculiar genius, abetted by an immunity from doubt regarding his amorphous roles. From "Camp de la Pagode," the refugee center in Haiphong, he wrote: "This camp sanitation is really part of the facade, but we have to make a good show. There will be a large group of officials out in a few days to see what we are doing . . . We just give them a good show, so that we may continue the real work of medical intelligence unperturbed." He was then invited to brief Admiral Sabin aboard the flagship USS *Estes:* "He quizzed me for intelligence information as to the refugees themselves, their thoughts and beliefs etc. You see, being one of the only four American service men living actually with the refugees we are able to assimilate a great deal of information that the high echelons can never get." Tom was already deeply concerned with "what the world in America is saying about this whole thing." He was confident "the newsreels will show" that he was in good health. "RKO, Pathe, and all the others were photographing our work last week, so please go to the movies. We are really doing a great thing mother in helping these people, and they realize it. Back-see-mao in Viet means 'Good American doctors' and the people keep saying that."[18]

Dooley was grimly fascinated by the many German mercenaries of the French Foreign Legion who suffered the "Dien Bien Phu death march" as prisoners of the Viet Minh: "They are the young movie type of swashbuckling lad full of sound and fury, only unlike the quotation, these signify much." He was puzzled by their motivation, since "it is better and easier to endure something when you understand firmly and believe wholeheartedly for the cause, whatever it may be. These legionnaires have no cause."

Dooley's cause was fueled initially by a disdain for French colonialism, but that animus was eventually dwarfed by his profound contempt for the communist Viet Minh. Although he recognized that Ho Chi Minh had initially sparked the nationalism of the Vietnamese, Ho soon "showed his background in the Kremlin." Dooley's staunch anticommunism was consonant with his education as well as the military mood in the immediate aftermath of the Korean War, to say nothing of the many palpably unsavory aspects of Viet Minh–style Marxism. It is therefore surprising to discover that a lengthy gestation period occurred before his hostility to the French fully give way to his trademark Manichaean depiction of the struggle between Vietnamese Christians and the Reds.[19]

When Hanoi was turned over to the Viet Minh on October 11, the remaining French troops were moved to Haiphong, which served as the last "neutral" site in North Vietnam from which refugees were transplanted to the South. Dooley reserved his greatest anger for French general René Cogny, an "idiot" who insisted on "PARADING into Haiphong. . . . The whole city is turned out for it, and I am quite sure they are turned out to demonstrate at being handed over little cattle for the slaughter."[20]

In early October Dooley began presenting lectures to the enlisted "white hats" aboard the LSMs and other navy vessels at Haiphong. A naval intelligence officer recalled watching as Dooley was transformed from a halting public speaker into a phenomenally charismatic and inspirational performer whose own convictions seemed to grow in response to the sailors' rapt attention. His earliest "history" lessons focused more on the Vietnamese people's struggle against colonialism than on the threat from the Viet Minh, though he also insisted that American aid to the region served as the midwife to democracy. In a letter of September 29 he mentioned for the first time the "fine and independent Priem Diem" and noted correctly that the most pressing threat to Diem's leadership came from "two army generals who are refusing to recognize his authority. The two generals are both pawns of the French, who do not want Viet Nam to have full independence."[21]

Before long Dooley's commodore was fielding requests for " 'that officer so eloquent in the history of the political situation' . . . so I get a free chow on the ship, and a talk. Then the usual questions from the men, which never cease to amaze me." Dooley also made certain the navy brass in Washington were aware of his tireless exploits, as his boundless capacity for self-promotion was now clearly matched by his accomplishments. After the surgeon general of the navy, Rear Adm. Lamont Pugh, learned of Tom's work (from one of Dooley's St. Louis patrons) he wrote: "It is gratifying to know that there remains at least one Service Doctor who appreciates the opportunity of going places and doing things." The admiral concluded that should Dooley one day attain his avowed goal of surgeon generalship of the navy, that office "will be in most worthy and 'can do' hands."[22]

In late October Dooley was named Commander of Task Unit 90.8.6, ostensibly placing him in charge of the remaining preventive medical supplies and DDT dusting equipment in Haiphong. He recruited five of his favorite navy corpsmen and became, in effect, the last American naval officer in Haiphong before it was turned over to the Viet Minh in May 1955. The timing of his new assignment coincided with the events that permanently altered American perceptions of the Vietnamese struggle and set in motion Dooley's ascent to glory. Lansdale had apparently concluded that the refugee exodus needed to be accelerated and dramatized with a bolder focus on the religious dimensions of the campaign. On October 27 Dooley described the evacuation of entire dioceses of North Vietnamese Catholics and confessed his genuine puzzlement over its ruthless efficiency:

> Well just lately, the last three nights the following has happened. Through a "system" which no one will explain, the people around Phat Diem, and Bui Chu (south of Haiphong) are getting out on small rafts and extremely small boats to the seaport village of Van Ly. From here, at some "exact time" they paddle out beyond the 3 mile continental limit and are there met by French LSMs and small craft which bring them up 77 miles to Haiphong and to my camp. This is the first time that we are actually picking them up.[23]

Since under the terms of the Geneva Accords the allies were not permitted to encroach on Viet Minh territory beyond Haiphong, "the refugees now are getting to the mouths of the small rivers, like the one near Van Ly . . . and then at the 'appointed' hour, they paddle out beyond the continental limit, where our vessels pick them up." Tom then posed a rhetorical question; in the answer was found the key to his future: "how do they know exactly at what time they should be at the appointed place?"

> This can be answered without any fear of security risks when you realize the strong Catholic church, and the true meaning of the Church Militant. These old and young Vietnam priests who come to the mission here in Haiphong and go back and forth into their villages (for they are not yet imprisoned) are in laison with us. . . . And the times are appointed. How long we will be able to do this we don't know. However, we now have 12,000 people in the refugee camp (almost at maximum capacity) one night 2650 came up, arriving at 0300. I was called down to the camp to direct traffic . . . and again and again.[24]

Edward G. Lansdale, raised in a Christian Science family, could not speak of the Church Militant. Neither could Dwight D. Eisenhower—who announced in 1952 that "our government makes no sense unless it is founded in a deeply felt religious faith, and I don't care what it is"—nor could Secretary of State John Foster Dulles, the Presbyterian minister's son who was not pleased when his own brilliant son, Avery, entered the Society of Jesus after being wounded in World War II. Francis Cardinal Spellman could roar of the Church's triumphalist mission to destroy world communism, but his image as a belligerent sectarian was just what Lansdale needed to avoid in marketing his Catholic protégé Ngo Dinh Diem as the "George Washington of Vietnam."[25]

Tom Dooley hated communism as most Americans did, and he equated religious with political freedom in simple layperson's terms that gave no scandal to the most militant advocates of strictly separate spheres for church and state, at home as well as abroad. In November 1954 President Eisenhower proclaimed: "We are sunk without a conception of the dignity of man founded on religious freedom." The fervent desire of Diem's American backers to portray South Vietnam as "the first new nation" founded on this model of pluralist democracy led to the positioning of Dooley as the human bridge to Saigon.[26]

Lansdale faced the more immediate challenge of shoring up Diem's fledgling regime against a host of enemies including, as Lansdale saw it, the Viet Minh, powerful local gangsters and the "sects" they controlled, and the emperor, Bao Dai. As a teenager in the early 1930s, Bao Dai had appointed Diem "secretary of a 'commission on reform,'" but French resistance to change prompted his resignation, and Bao Dai, once an "earnest and intelligent" young man, according to historian David L. Anderson, "lapsed into an indolent life of hunting, gambling, and womanizing." By contrast, Diem appeared at first to be someone earnest Americans could identify with. Secretary of State John Foster Dulles "wanted primarily a strong anti-Communist position in the south and was drawn to Diem's ascetic, intransigent anti-Communism." But as biographer Townsend Hoopes added, "Dulles, along with most Americans, was magnificently ignorant of Vietnamese history and culture."[27]

Jean Baptiste Ngo Dinh Diem was born in 1901 near the imperial city of Hue, in central Vietnam. He was a member of a prominent mandarin family who "had also accepted the added discipline, and cross, of Catholicism." The family's religious convictions often placed them at odds with both the French and leftist Vietnamese nationalists: Diem's father was virtually the only member of his family who survived a massacre of Vietnamese Catholics in the 1880s. Most of the Americans who met Diem considered him a mystic; few ever doubted the intensity of his personal devotion to the Church. What they failed to understand, as Denis Warner explained in *The Last Confucian,* was that "Catholicism and Confucianism went hand in hand in the Diem household." Diem's brother Thuc, a "gentle man" as well as a bishop, felt that Diem was "too severe for the Church, too inflexible to perform the duties of a priest among his own people." Whether it is true, as Warner claimed, that "this dogged aspect of his character, his rejection of advice, reflects his Confucian, rather than his Catholic, background," it is surely the case that his key American supporters assumed that just as Catholicism in America was undergoing a dramatic transformation in the 1950s, so too could Diem readily be molded into a "democrat" without surrendering his core convictions. Rarely has one individual been misread by so many, with such devastating consequences.[28]

In addition to being a kind of lay monk (having taken a vow of celibacy), Diem was deeply committed to a free Vietnam: when the French reneged on promises of reform of their colonial administration in 1933, he resigned his post as minister of the interior under Emperor Bao Dai. He spent the next decade leading "the reflective life of a scholar-revolutionist" in Hue. In 1944 he was declared a "subversive" by French officials, who had been permitted by the Japanese to continue administering Indochina. In March 1945, Diem rejected an offer from the Japanese to become prime minister of "an 'independent' government" under Bao Dai in Hanoi. In September of that year, "when Ho Chi Minh seized power in Hanoi, Diem decided, against the advice of his friends, to go back to Hue to warn the people against the new regime." He was promptly arrested by the communist Viet Minh and nearly died of malaria and dysentery at a camp near the Chinese border. Ho Chi Minh had him brought to Hanoi in February 1946; far from repentant, Diem reportedly called Ho a "criminal" for authorizing the murder of his brother Ngo Dinh Khoi the previous year.[29]

Diem's rejection of Ho's overtures was both stubborn and realistic. According to the Italian priest-historian Piero Gheddo, the "enthusiastic and total" support of Vietnamese Catholics in 1946 for Ho's new regime—based largely on a shared hostility to the French—broke down once "Vietnamese Communism made clear the goals it would pursue: undisputed domination of the country through the elimination of the non-Communist resistance forces" (Ho, the product of a "disenfranchised scholar-gentry" family, had written a book in French in 1925 which "portrayed Vietnamese Catholic priests as rapacious land thieves"). Another of Diem's brothers, Ngo Dinh Thuc, the bishop of Vinh Long, had "declined to join the three other Vietnamese bishops in the country when they had initially supported Ho Chi Minh's declaration of independence in the patriotic fervor of 1945."[30]

By 1950, after harassment by the French and death threats from the Viet Minh, Diem went into an exile that included a notorious stay at Maryknoll seminaries in Lakewood, New Jersey, and Ossining, New York, where he mostly "meditated and did some writing," allegedly with the active patronage of Cardinal Spellman, though Chester L. Cooper's assertion that "Spellman paid little attention to him until he became Prime Minister" has yet to be challenged by fact. In Stanley Karnow's version, Diem spent his two years at Maryknoll "washing dishes, scrubbing floors, and praying, like any novice, and he even watched a football game at Princeton." On his occasional forays to New York City or Washington, Diem was introduced to an odd assortment of American political and intellectual figures, many of whom soon championed his bid for authority in South Vietnam. They would all, including the Catholics among them, fatally underestimate the magnitude of this "last confucian's" commitment to an ancient model of rule by divine right that brooked no appeals to such modern innovations as "pluralism" or "tolerance."[31]

Bao Dai anointed Diem the prime minister of the State of Vietnam at a May 14 meeting in Paris, shortly after the fall of Dien Bien Phu, while diplomats in Geneva were settling on a temporary partitioning of the country. Diem initially refused Bao Dai's offer to become prime minister, indicating that "he planned to enter a religious order. He quickly yielded, though, to the emperor's appeal to his patriotic duty. Bao Dai then produced a crucifix and had Diem swear before his God to defend Vietnam against the communists and, if necessary, the French." An aide to a rival candidate believed that Bao Dai had concluded that "the time for the Americans had arrived"; as David L. Anderson explained: "Regardless of what Bao Dai otherwise may have thought of Diem, he was the most likely channel to American aid." On June 18 Diem "formally agreed to head a new government"; he made his distinctly untriumphant return to Vietnam on June 26. "The manner in which he rode into Saigon from the airport on the day of his arrival was characteristic," wrote Neal Sheehan: "He sat in the back of a curtained car. None of the curious Saigonese who had gathered along the route for a glimpse of the new prime minister could see him, and he was not interested in looking out."[32]

On his arrival in Saigon Diem found Lieutenant Colonel Lansdale awaiting him. Lansdale was dispatched to Vietnam after his successful campaign in the Philippines. He had visited Vietnam briefly during the previous year "with a small U.S. group headed by General John W. 'Iron Mike' O'Daniel," to advise the French on their fading prospects for victory over the Viet Minh. On that trip he "became aware of how strikingly different the Vietnamese were from his Filipino friends"—a difference that ensured his successes in the Philippines would not be reprised in this new assignment.[33]

Plans for Lansdale's mission had originated at a January 30, 1954, meeting in Washington of the President's Special Commission on Indochina, when

"Mr. Allen Dulles [Director of Central Intelligence] inquired if an unconventional warfare officer, specifically Colonel Lansdale, could not be added to the group of five liaison officers to which [French] General Navarre had agreed." The State Department was still far from convinced that Ngo Dinh Diem would emerge as the leader of a free Vietnam. Lansdale was simply told to "do what you did in the Philippines."[34]

In the summer of 1954 Lansdale became a constant companion of the besieged leader; he acted swiftly to provide Diem with a constituency in advance of elections mandated for 1956 by the Geneva Conference, though there was little doubt they would never take place. "U.S. officials wanted to make sure that as many persons as possible, particularly the strongly anti-Communist Catholics, relocated in the south. (Four-fifths of the total number of refugees who moved to the south were Catholics, representing about two-thirds of the Catholics in the north.)" Some observers believed that even more souls would have left the North had they not been prevented from fleeing. Lansdale focused on transplanting as many Catholics as he could and deployed one of his legendary psychological warfare ("psywar") campaigns, relying heavily upon his patented repertoire of "black operations," spy talk for "dirty tricks." The historian Bernard Fall, whose background as a French-born American lent a unique perspective to his histories of the Vietnamese wars, offered perhaps the most judicious view of Operation Exodus:

> Although there is no doubt that hundreds of thousands of Vietnamese would have fled Communist domination in any case, the mass flight was admittedly the result of an extremely intensive, well-conducted, and, in terms of its objective, very successful American psychological warfare operation. Propaganda slogans and leaflets appealed to the devout Catholics with such themes as "Christ has gone to the South" and the "Virgin Mary has departed from the North"; and whole bishoprics—Bui Chu and Phat Diem, for example—packed up lock, stock, and barrel, from the bishops to almost the last village priest and faithful.[35]

The provinces of Phat Diem and Bui Chu became the focal points of Catholic resistance to the Viet Minh. The bishop of Phat Diem had "raised a Catholic militia who marched under the yellow-and-white flag of the Vatican state"; once the colonials departed, his forces "could not have done much to shield off the victorious Viet Minh." The bishop of Bui Chu, in a similar position, ordered his parish priests to lead their flocks en masse to the awaiting American vessels. To American Catholics these pilgrimages evoked wrenching images of persecuted refugees in Eastern Europe and tortured missionaries in China. An editorial cartoon entitled "One More Crucifixion" appeared in diocesan newspapers in early August 1954, adding

Vietnamese Catholics to the litany of persecuted brethren in Lithuania, Czechoslovakia, Romania, and China. This time, however, War Relief Services of the National Catholic Welfare Conference (soon to be known as Catholic Relief Services) was prepared to respond with a massive show of support. In July 1954 Premier Diem asked Cardinal Spellman for help: by the end of September 1955, Catholic Relief Services had aided "this greatest mass movement in the history of the world" by providing the resettled refugees with roughly two million pounds of clothing and nearly ten million tons of food, at a combined value of nearly $4.5 million.[36]

In 1971 Harry Haas and the pseudonymous Vietnamese writer Nguyen Bao Cong assigned culpability to the best-known American Catholics involved in the refugee operation. Dr. Tom Dooley, the authors declared, "was a typical exponent of the blind anti-communist attitude of the Americans in general, and of the Catholics among them especially; he does not seem to have been aware of the CIA network in which he became involved. Cardinal Spellman of New York was another one, but of much more influence than Dooley." The author of one of the top-secret studies comprising the *Pentagon Papers* even endorsed this view of Dooley's guilelessness, noting simply that "Dr. Tom Dooley found refugees with a Vietminh pamphlet showing a Hanoi map with three concentric circles of nuclear destruction—conceivably an example of Colonel Lansdale's handiwork." Yet the naval physician's presumptive "innocence" of Lansdale's chicanery only further obscures the nature of Dooley's actual role. In *A Bright Shining Lie,* Neal Sheehan advanced the maximalist interpretation of the lieutenant colonel's nation-building wizardry:

> The French and the U.S. Embassy had dawdled. Lansdale drew up a plan; got Diem, the U.S. military, and the French all working together; arranged for the Navy to provide a Seventh Fleet amphibious task force for sea evacuation (it brought down more than a third of the refugees); and had the French award Civil Air Transport, a CIA airline run by Gen. Claire Chennault from Taiwan, a profitable contract to assist in the air evacuation.[37]

Not all students of the origins of U.S. involvement in Vietnam share Sheehan's assessment of Lansdale's prowess, perhaps because, as David Halberstam wrote, "in person [Lansdale] sometimes appeared to be a curiously disappointing, almost simplistic man," an impression the lieutenant colonel was pleased to encourage. But there is little doubt that Tom Dooley's "preventive medicine" team represented one of the many components in Lansdale's painstaking blueprint for launching a viable Diem regime. In a letter to his mother Dooley alluded to the "illegitimate" nature of his work and described with a slight air of bewilderment his remoteness from official navy operations in the Gulf of Tonkin; this passage supports the view that he had been "loaned" to Lansdale. Operatives of the legendary psywar team (headed by Lucien Conein, a wily commando who remained behind in North Vietnam after the borders were sealed) later reported being aware of Dooley's presence in Haiphong, but they generally dismissed him as a crass opportunist with an idealistic streak who may have simply found himself "in the right place at the right time."[38]

Although Dooley's orders called for him to perform military intelligence work in Laos as well as Vietnam, he never strayed far from Haiphong during Operation Passage to Freedom. He was expected to make himself available for photo opportunities and to provide material for the growing numbers of American journalists covering the campaign. While it is not clear precisely when Lansdale first met Dooley, Tom's reassignment to commander of the preventive medicine unit was possibly timed in anticipation of the evacuation of Bui Chu and Phat Diem. It is thus a distinct likelihood that Dooley's "cover" in Haiphong was designed to situate him for a role that even he believed was secondary, as informal liaison to the press and certain American audiences. In the meantime he was authorized to fancy himself a daring agent of espionage.

Dooley later readily acknowledged his unfitness for epidemiological work but never seems to have questioned his even greater lack of aptitude for spying. He continued to betray a somewhat desperate aim to please his superiors in spite of his notorious disregard for navy protocol. In November 1954 the navy's *Medical News Letter* published a letter he had written and that had made its way to Surgeon General Pugh. Thomas A. Dooley III was now an official morale booster: "Many of the older officers have commented on the fact that it is refreshing to hear someone who isn't complaining about the navy's policies."[39]

Dooley's more immediate function was indicated in a letter of October 29, just days after he became commander of the preventive medicine unit. "Enclosed is something that was sent to me," he wrote to his mother. "It is a write up that a Navy Chaplain sent to some Catholic Paper back in the states. He was on a tour here, and I was asked to show him our setup. Please note the fluent Viet Nam. I can say about twenty stock expressions, and the words for 'don't urinate on the ground, use the toilet.'" As a key source of "inside" information, Dooley supplied intelligence to Patrick O'Connor, a priest from Ireland working in Vietnam who wrote stirring tributes to Diem and the faith of the refugees for the News Service of the National Catholic Welfare Conference. His dispatches were then syndicated to diocesan newspapers across America, where they reached an enormous audience. In early December Gen. J. Lawton Collins, President Eisenhower's special representative charged with determining whether Diem warranted further American support, appeared in Haiphong on an inspection visit and saw Dooley in his white surgical gown "standing knee high in kids . . . General Collins turned to one of his aides and said 'I know this guy's an American, he's Irish.' "[40]

Ngo Dinh Diem's fate rested on the outcome of the conflict between Collins and Lansdale, two men who "were poles apart in their backgrounds and methods." Lansdale had little respect for Collins's judgment or his pre-occupation with "the orderly course of planning" and "the framework of military hierarchy." But Dooley was ecstatic to learn that Collins would be paying a visit to the Haiphong refugee camp. He began to identify himself with an unfolding crusade:

> With the arrival of General J. Lawton Collins, there is much pleasure. We feel here that America is dismally unaware of the seriousness of the situation here. We too realize its pessimistic outlook, for the elections of 1956. But we feel deeply of the propaganda importance of American aid, (NOT INTERVEN-TION) here. To show the free world that the U.S. is willing to help a young and a free, newly free country get on its feet, when there is no direct nor obvious aid going back to the U.S. . . . to show the world this is a good and an important thing.[41]

Dooley dined in Haiphong in late November with Collins and Lt. Gen. John W. O'Daniel, chief of the Military Assistance Advisory Group (MAAG) in Saigon and a Lansdale ally who became one of Diem's most vociferous supporters. O'Daniel was in charge of building an army for South Vietnam; with Lansdale he would have impressed on Dooley the necessity to win Collins over to their camp. By the time Collins returned for an inspection in early January, Dooley's public relations skills had improved to the point where he effortlessly promoted the refugee operation as a symbol of Diem's decisive leadership. Dooley eagerly awaited the visit as an opportunity to "really give him a show. Have ordered twenty coolies for tomorrow and for Tuesday to really give the place a clean up. . . . We'll pour lime into the latrines which makes the odors less distasteful. Will manage to have a few of the Communist-tortured refugees in the hospital tent for Collins to see, rather than distributed throughout the camp."[42]

"Our first refugee camp became the center of attraction for visiting digni-taries," wrote Dooley in *Deliver Us from Evil*. By New Year's Day, 1955, his showcase had become an integral component in the campaign on Diem's behalf, and the dividends began rolling in. "The correspondents are begin-ning to be interested in Indo China I think," he informed his mother. He noted the visits of Joseph Alsop (who "created a good deal of turmoil, but at least came") as well as Homer Bigart of the *New York Herald Tribune*. "All we need now is Maggie Higgins [a flamboyant reporter for the *Herald Tribune*] to come down from Russia," Tom wrote knowingly, albeit with some of the cynicism that occasionally crept into his missives. Homer Bigart was an especially important conduit because the *Herald Tribune* published a prestigious international edition and reached a viscerally conservative audience at home who might disdain other influential papers like the *New York Times.* Bigart was among several correspondents entrusted with assuring favorable press for the refugee operation. In the "Lansdale Team's Report on Covert Saigon Mission in '54 and '55," reprinted in the *Pentagon Papers,* the unidentified author wrote:

> Till and Peg Durdin of the *N.Y. Times,* Hank Lieberman of the *N.Y. Times,* Homer Bigart of the *N.Y. Herald-Tribune,* John Mecklin of *Time-Life,* and John Roderick of Associated Press have been warm friends of SMM [the CIA's Saigon Military Mission] and worked hard to penetrate the fabric of French propaganda and give the U.S. an objective account of events in Vietnam. This group met with us at times to analyze objectives and motives of propaganda known to them, meeting at their own request as U.S. citizens. These mature and responsible news correspondents performed a valuable service for their country.[43]

Where the highly influential syndicated columnist Joseph Alsop had concluded that Diem was "wholly out of contact with reality" and had virtually no chance of success, Bigart wrote from Saigon on December 22, 1954, of "the plucky, honest, mournful little premier" who struggled to rid Saigon of its legendary corruption. On January 1 Bigart covered Diem's greeting of a boatload of refugees, nearly all Catholic, who were assured by the premier that their "arrival will bolster confidence in a government striving for complete independence and liberty." Bigart noted that the refugees appeared revoltingly filthy, but that their spiritual dignity was appreciated by at least one American on the scene: "'These are a noble people, a proud people,' a United States Navy doctor, Lt. Thomas A. Dooley, 3rd, of St. Louis told this correspondent at the Haiphong camps. But he admitted that their nobility was not easily manifest at first glance."[44]

On January 2 Bigart wrote of Vietnamese priests and nuns who had been tortured and imprisoned as spies by the Viet Minh and were now boarding the USS *Howze* with other refugees for the trip south. Bigart reiterated his alarm at the appearance of the pilgrims and the rude conditions aboard ship, but was again reassured "by a young naval officer, Thomas A. Dooley, 3rd, of St. Louis, who told me the sanitation is adequate." Dooley told Bigart that four to five hundred such refugees appeared at Haiphong each day. "Politically ignorant," Bigart concluded, in words that echoed Dooley, "they have been prompted mainly by simple faith. But their faith has enabled them to resist Communist propaganda and to overcome the obstacles the Viet Minh has placed in the way of their departure."[45]

Dooley did not openly participate in the visit of Cardinal Spellman to

Saigon in early January 1955, where the New York prelate conferred his blessing on Diem and the refugees (Spellman made an annual visit to American military bases in the Far East, bearing Notre Dame football highlight films and cigarettes along with rosaries and miraculous medals). Since Dooley's most unique asset resided in the "natural" quality of his faith as an American, his appearance in any sectarian context might have undermined the evolving fiction of a pluralist Vietnamese democracy. In fact, General Collins expressed his concern to John Foster Dulles that a Spellman visit would embolden those Vietnamese who had already charged that Diem was "an American puppet. . . . The fact that both Diem and the Cardinal are Catholic would give opportunity for false propaganda charges that the U.S. is exerting undue influence on Diem." Collins then contradicted himself in noting that a Spellman visit would serve to dramatize "once more the great exodus of refugees from the North, the greater part of whom are Catholics."[46]

Collins's fears exposed a variety of critical issues. Although he was an American Catholic with a long military career behind him, his attempt at a politically realistic appraisal of Diem (he admired the premier's "spiritual qualities" even as he suspected that the "strange anomaly" of his religious identity would lead to his undoing in Vietnam) infuriated Senator Mike Mansfield, a Montana Democrat and influential member of the Foreign Relations Committee. Mansfield, Senator John F. Kennedy, Brooklyn Congresswoman Edna F. Kelly, and other Catholic politicians were among Diem's most ardent supporters, as were several important prelates, most notably Francis Cardinal Spellman. For decades it has been widely suspected that powerful American Catholics exerted undue influence on behalf of Diem: it has even been argued that "America's ethnocentrism mandated support of a devout Catholic over any Buddhist alternative."[47]

Cardinal Spellman was in fact worse than useless as a champion of Diem once he was in office, because his guise as a superpatriot only drew more attention to his prominent role in the universal Church. It was the pope not President Eisenhower who urged Spellman to make a report on the situation in Vietnam. The fiction of a Catholic South Vietnam was one thing, but everyone involved in the campaign for Diem had to recognize the volatility of this religious issue back home, though few beside Lansdale possessed the sophistication to depict effectively the refugees as Christian pilgrims with as few denominational peculiarities as possible. According to Neal Sheehan, "Lansdale thought the Catholic refugees from the North were Vietnamese patriots who had 'fought for their country's freedom from the French' until they discovered they were being hoodwinked in a Communist conspiracy and so were fleeing south to 'Free Vietnam' to create a new life of liberty there." To find the ideal American spokesman for Diem, Lansdale would have to invent a type of American Catholic that had seemingly never existed: a staunchly anticommunist yet theologically low-key ecumenist who could speak across various cultural divides.[48]

By early 1955 Dr. Tom Dooley had not yet fully become that man. The budding crusader's way of seeing was still deeply colored by his religiosity. Dooley's spiritual response to the suffering Vietnamese pilgrims often threatened to subvert the clinically approved rhetoric generated by the Lansdale team, as he struggled between a promise of heroism his secular bosses could authorize or withhold, and a romantic mystical streak that drew him toward a Catholic audience who viewed the refugees' suffering in a very different light from the view of the ex-advertising executive. Catholic anticommunism has often been caricatured or ridiculed by historians, but along with its profoundly moral and spiritual origins and its political appeal, the ideology also provided an effective organizing principle for a disparate religious subculture.[49]

In a letter of November 28, 1954, Dooley had introduced his mother to a genre of reportage on communist atrocities that marked his early published work and exasperated his sponsors. Dooley often traveled to the perimeter of the allied zone in Haiphong to watch the refugees make their way across the river. "They are still shaking with fear and exhaustion from the ordeal of the trip," he wrote. "Seeing an American Doctor is usually quite amazing to them, especially when I don't beat them or whip them." He administered instead penicillin and eye ointments for the trachoma the refugees suffered in epidemic proportions. They were then transported to the camp in Haiphong, "where I see them again, and listen to their stories."[50]

"Mother," he wrote, "I have seen things here that I didn't believe humans capable of doing." One night a Vietnamese priest brought Dooley to see an elderly colleague who had been transported to Haiphong on a raft by eleven children "while they swam kicking softly so that the Viet Minh would not stop them." Two nights earlier, Dooley was told, the priest had been in the village church of Namh Giang when soldiers accused him of preaching lies against the Viet Minh.

Their leader was a "RED CHINESE" officer. He spoke Vietnamese with a heavy chinese accent, this the priest stated firmly. They took this old priest and hung him from a beam overhead in the mission by his feet. They stripped him naked. Then they beat him with short bamboo rods, with the emphasis of the beating of his genitals. Into his head they stuck thorns (so he could be like the Christ of whom he spoke) and then into his ears they rammed chop sticks. They beat him for hours evidently, because when I saw him there was hardly a square inch of flesh that was not swollen and purple, and often split, though not bloody. Being left hanging feet up all night, the vessels in his eye ruptured, leaving him nearly blind.[51]

Since the bamboo rods bruised rather than broke the skin, the priest was "a mass of hematomata, black and blue, and purple and bruised all over . . . I washed him as best as I could. He was in tremendous pain, from the beating, and the hideous condition of his groin. I can't even write of these things without getting all filled up with emotion." Dooley was never the same after this experience, but he quickly learned to channel his lonesome visions into political rhetoric that validated his own ordeal. "I am not writing this to you to nauseate you or make you feel bad," he wrote, "but in hopes you will letter others read this, and understand the nature of the enemy that we are fighting. . . . The conditions here in Indo China directly effect us at home." His mother's role was now transformed into that of model for a future audience. "I don't reread what I write . . . I write as it comes from me, just as though I were speaking to you."[52]

Patrons of the Catholic press in America had been familiar with accounts of tortured priests since the era of the Mexican Revolution, but Dooley's language more closely evoked the sufferings of missionaries in China after the communist victory in 1949. By the time Vietnam came to the attention of American Catholics they were familiar with a paradoxical rhetoric of suffering and triumph that applied to the Church's travail throughout Asia. A Vietnamese priest writing in February 1954 for the Catholic News Service proclaimed: "The Church in Vietnam is passing through the most tragic and yet the most illustrious period of its history . . . a special chapter of glory is being written meanwhile in the Red-dominated area itself where persecution has stimulated rather than diminished the loyalty and devotion of the Catholic faithful."[53]

Dooley's more lurid accounts of tortured priests earned him the permanent devotion of millions of Catholic Americans, but they infuriated functionaries at the United States Information Agency (USIA), who later dismissed the atrocities reported in *Deliver Us from Evil* as groundless. In May 1955, as Operation Passage to Freedom concluded, Dooley provided an Associated Press reporter in Vietnam with claims too explosive for inclusion in even his own book. After lauding Dooley as "a modern Dr. Livingstone," Larry Allen reported Tom's assurance that "there was documented evidence that the Vietminh have brutally tortured young Vietnamese whom they caught attempting to reach American ships. The Reds are also making life difficult for Catholics . . . Dooley added that evidence recently disclosed that the Vietminh burned at the stake a young Viet Namese who led a

Catholic youth movement in Vietminh territory in 1953." In December 1955, the *St. Louis Globe-Democrat* repeated Dooley's allegation that nurses and corpsmen in Haiphong had been "burned alive" by communists in Haiphong the previous May. "I took photos of it from a camera the size of a pencil which the Navy had given me."[54]

Whether these atrocities occurred or not, Dooley had good reason to denounce the Viet Minh for hindering the flight of those Vietnamese who wished to move to south. As a propagandist, he was bound to ignore any nuance in the situation of Northern Catholics. His personal papers contain a copy of a letter from a Haiphong priest reprinted from the *Catholic Patriot*, a communist newspaper published by the National Union of Catholic Peace-Loving Patriots, part of an attempt by the Viet Minh to create a North Vietnamese Church independent of Rome. Father Dominique Pham Quang-Phuoc condemned the refugee campaign, which in his view led to "the destruction of families, the separation of husband and wife, of parents and children. Arriving in the south the young men are put into the Army by force, the young girls, pure children of Notre Dame, are sold to houses of prostitution, boys are being sent out to the rubber plantation." The priest claimed that "I have received a group of Christians who have resisted with energy the restraints and the lies of the Americans and have refused to sign up for the evacuation, and are living now beneath the bells of the churches, christians who have hidden themselves to escape the military mobilization."[55]

In the complex reality between these competing versions of the truth, 680,000 Catholics fled the North. But even in the Phat Diem and Bui Chu dioceses, "almost half the Catholic population stayed at home. They were attached to the soil and many had family obligations." Msgr. John Dooley, the pope's diplomatic representative and an Irish national of no apparent relation to the young St. Louisan, remained behind, as did the French priests of the Foreign Missionary Society. "When Dooley and his assistant, Father Terence O'Driscoll, chose to remain in Hanoi after the 1954 Communist victory," wrote historian Roy P. Domenico, "Ho's government promptly branded the legation as a nest of spies, an accusation with some probable foundation." But the very real suffering and heroic faith of the refugees—translated by the "other" Dooley into the idiom of American Catholicism at a moment of serious concern over their own status at home—provided fertile ground for the launching of his career as spiritual idol.[56]

Tom Dooley's obsession with publicity was originally motivated by an overpowering desire to avenge his medical school humiliation. In February 1955 he wrote his mother: "Please keep as many people informed as to my whereabouts and doings as possible. One of the reasons I am trying so very very hard to be more than average is to shove it in the faces of all those doctors in St. Louis and in the Medical school." Dooley's astonishing energy was legendary throughout the American military in Southeast Asia; his enormous charisma and charm persuaded superiors to overlook his excesses and attracted reporters seeking fresh angles on a complicated story. In a pattern emerging in the months before he became a celebrity, Dooley linked himself so tenaciously with tales of Catholic heroism and communist brutality that his cause assumed a life of its own apart from the goals of his military sponsors. Lansdale and his team could harness the doctor's crusade to serve the immediate needs of Diem's public relations, but as a true believer Dooley could not be switched on and off at will. A real contest was now under way between his mountainous ego, his monumental faith, and those who would dare exploit his gifts for any purpose less than divinely inspired.[57]

By early 1955 Tom Dooley was clearly the most popular American in noncommunist Vietnam. He sent his mother a sound recording from a New Year's Eve party at the Haiphong home of Madame Vu Thi Ngai, a Vietnamese widow who ran an orphanage whose inhabitants were later transported to Saigon by the Lansdale team. Dooley can be heard gently bantering with the children in French and his Vietnamese patois; they jubilantly respond to him as *bac sy my, bac sy Dooley* (American Doctor Dooley). He was genuinely touched and disarmed by the children, and their affection for him is unmistakable. The tone of this recording stands in marked contrast to the staged radio broadcasts he made later from Laos. Here the children sing their new national anthem for Mrs. Dooley; they bravely count in English with Tom's encouragement. A Vietnamese gentleman makes a brief speech that concludes, "We hope we may be together in freedom and liberty for many more years." Dooley tells his mother that he hopes to remain in Vietnam until April when the mission is over; he quietly and repeatedly professes his love for her. Several weeks later on Tom's birthday, the children presented him with "about a half mile of beautiful white Chinese silk to have some shirts made of."[58]

Where Edward G. Lansdale awkwardly tried to teach Ngo Dinh Diem to play Cowboys and Indians in the presidential palace, Dooley made a sincere effort to understand Asian customs, though he naturally gravitated toward the Catholics of Vietnam. His brother Malcolm had been startled in the summer of 1954 when he met Tom on the island of Guam and his brother managed to communicate with the host of a Japanese restaurant in the man's native language. That November Tom asked his mother to contact a family friend and request that she "give you the name of some good books that she used in her course on the Comparative Religions of the Orient."

I am finding this part of the world more and more fascinating . . . for example, the Buddhists are beginning to leave Tonkin, which is considered extraordinary, as theirs is a religion of resignation, and if Buddha has sent the curse of communism to them, they must bow their heads and endure. Then also the Toaist (taoists) have recently done some amazing things in central Viet Nam in reference to a national unity movement in Peiking. I should like to understand more about these religions. So if you could send me some books on these, Buddhism, Coptism, Taoism, Shintoism and Confusciusianism I would appreciate it.[59]

Mrs. Dooley sent him Catholic philosophy books instead. "Smiled at you mother," he wrote on February 12. "I can see you puzzled and concerned for fear I might become an apostate and join the local order of Buddhist bonzes. Have no fear." Dooley enjoyed a real gift for educating Americans about *his* understanding of Asia without undermining their own convictions. He had sent his mother a holy card given to him by an elderly Vietnamese priest. "If you notice, the blessed virgin is depicted as being an oriental, with the typical Vietnamese National dress and shoes . . . with Indo China under her feet. It is quite lovely, so keep it in your prayer book mother."[60]

Even as Dooley helped perpetuate the myth that Vietnam was predominantly Christian, he groped for an understanding of the region that challenged, if only tentatively, the racialist assumptions governing much of American thought and policy in the cold war:

The belief that the oriental people must always be lead, have not the incentive or initiative to great on their own . . . this was thrown to the ground when a small country like Japan nearly conquered us . . . it took us five years and countless thousands of lives to subdue her. The orientals are quiet, soft spoken, and "just rice workers . . . " but in them rests the future, in Koreas, and Indo Chinas, and Indonesais, and Burmas, and the small countries rest the potentialities for a catastrophe whose consequences could alter world history.[61]

Convinced he was present at the birth of a new dispensation, Dooley's letters assumed a tone at once elegiac and ominous as the May 1955 deadline for closing the border of North Vietnam approached ("how this place is dying," he wrote in late January). Among a handful of Americans to remain in Haiphong ("the Embassy has definitely forgotten us"), he cultivated a profound conviction in his unique visionary experience of a noble people's suffering and his healing power as their *bac sy my*. Less than three years earlier Dooley had arrogantly shown up for medical school class in his riding attire; now he rescued tortured priests on the front lines of what looked like the final struggle with world communism. One priest was "so miserably beaten that I had to leave the little hut I had been taken to, and vomited and vomited until my guts turned inside down." That was the first time he had ever been sickened by a medical emergency. "But it wasn't just medical, it was something sort of the soul and heart, and very nature of man."[62]

Suffering and salvation, death and rebirth became the central themes of Dooley's final months in Haiphong, as the drama of his own experience mirrored the tragedy and hope of the Vietnamese Catholics. He continually sought validation of his lonely perspective and became obsessed with reaching his nascent audience in America. He was convinced that decadent colonialism must yield to the fresher spirit he so frenetically embodied. "Some article came out in *Newsweek* (which I've never seen)," he wrote on March 1, "which told the brutal truth . . . the out and out attempts to foil the work of the U.S. in Indochina on the part of the French. The French are bitterly furious about this. Though they are a beaten and defeated race, they are a proud race."[63]

In late March Dooley learned that he was likely to receive a navy commendation for his work in the refugee camps; he especially looked forward to wearing the award in St. Louis. One of his former navy commanders was circulating an article about Dooley among the top brass in Washington. A radio personality in St. Louis broadcast to his audience a letter Dooley had been inspired to write while listening to the radio in Haiphong. Tom was pleased because "that helps sell my Viet Nam." He was already planning his stateside speaking engagements, even as a Filipino production company with a budget of $1.5 million (and close ties to Lieutenant Colonel Lansdale) appeared to make a feature film centering around "a love story taking place during the evacuation." Dooley explained to his mother: "It is good too, because the Philippines were only a few years ago a colony, and now they have their independence."[64]

The young naval officer's genius for self-promotion was abetted by the cultural lag between the kind of spiritual heroism he represented and the conventions of celebrity journalism in the postwar era. Since early March Dooley had been living in the former Hong Kong Bank building, purchased from the British to house the small remaining American contingent. But since his housemates were either MAAG personnel or agents of even vaguer commitments, Tom Dooley was virtually the last American "officially" stationed in Haiphong, purportedly executing last-minute strategies to rescue as many refugees as possible. Yet no one seemed to question the veritable media circus that swirled about him: his idealism and selfless courage appeared so transcendent that the coverage of his feats assumed a naturalistic quality that defied cynicism. Dooley was a celebrity in waiting, and reporters and cameramen seemed drawn to him by some basic instinct of their calling. He exploited this relationship to the breaking point in years to come, but the spring of 1955 found him exquisitely sculpting an image as the freshest American hero since Audie Murphy—an exalted status he achieved without having to kill anyone.[65]

By early May Haiphong finally disintegrated, as various factions scurried about just prior to the deadline for closing the border. As riots broke out Tom asked his mother to send him a series of articles from the *Washington Evening Star* which had presented his point of view, in contrast to that of "insipid asses like Alsop." The series offered "hope for the south, and fully realized the nobility in the misery of the camps." On May 9 he wrote: "We have been so desperately busy. Time & Life and Look all have correspondents and photographers here. There has been one riot after another. We had to close off the house the other afternoon because the tear gas the french had used to break up a riot down the street was drifting in." In his final letter from Haiphong Dooley graphically described the communist's impending takeover in hometown terms: "The Viet Minh have all ready several large areas, like having Forest Park and perhaps Alton, East St. Louis, and the North Side. They are driving around the city in big russian made Molotava trucks. Their uniforms are everywhere. The people in the city (many VM sympathizers) have hauled out the red flag."[66]

On May 11 Tom scrawled a rare handwritten note: "Just arrived in Saigon on an emergency plane and Haiphong is all over." Dooley was about to be confirmed as the symbol of Vietnamese-American friendship in the ongoing struggle to promote the first democracy in Southeast Asia. Nothing Tom had done for the previous nine months would compare in significance with a brief photo opportunity in the presidential palace during his second day in Saigon. "Well so much has happened," he wrote to his mother on May 12, "that I will have to type for several hours just to scratch the surface. So be seated and read, and perhaps you will be proud." He went on to describe the chaotic final days in Haiphong, marked by riots and tear gas in the streets. Dooley's last act in North Vietnam involved the rescue of a five-foot-high statue of Our Lady of Fatima given by the pope to Catholic pilgrims from Haiphong. The statue had "always been the pride of the mission in Haiphong," and as "defying Catholic statues is one of the Communists favorite tricks," Dooley smuggled the icon aboard the emergency flight to Saigon.[67]

He was debriefed at Lieutenant General O'Daniel's home by top MAAG and embassy personnel. Dooley was scheduled to embark for the Philippines en route to Yokosuka, Japan, the following day, but as he was checking out of O'Daniel's office, the general "shouted at me 'Where the hell have you been, I've been hunting all over town for you for two hours.'" Premier Diem, "who had heard that I was in town . . . requested that I come to his palace at

1200 so he could decorate me for what I had done while in Indo China." Without a chance to change his shirt Dooley was ushered into the Cabinet Room where, before assembled dignitaries, the premier read the following citation:

> It gives me great pleasure and it is a honor for me to speak in behalf of my people. They have asked me to award you recognition for the outstanding work you have done for the past ten months in the refugee camps in Northern Viet Nam. You are well known and beloved by my people. In the resettlement areas here in Saigon the name of the "Bac Sy My" Dooley is well known. I have heard it mentioned often by the refugees and by the members of the various committees concerned with the evacuation. In the greatest majority of cases you were the first American that the people of the Tonkin rice fields came in contact with, and by knowing you and loving you they grew to understand the American people. Your medicine and your knowledge has saved many of their lives and brought comfort to their sufferings; but more than this it has shown them the true goodness and the spirit of help and cooperation that America is showing in Viet Nam and in all the countries of the world, who seek and strive to achieve and maintain their freedom. Again Doctor I want to thank you personally and in the name of my people who will long remember their *Bac Sy,* his work, and his love.[68]

Capt. Walter Winn told Dooley "it was extremely unusual for a junior officer to receive a decoration of a foreign country. And to have it personally awarded by the countries president in the middle of the internal strife he has in his country . . . this was most extraordinary." In 1965, in the first "exposé" of Dooley's propagandistic role, Robert Scheer wrote: "It attests to his innocence that he did not know that the choice for the award had been inspired by the CIA's man in Vietnam, Colonel Edward Lansdale." In the 1980s Lansdale told a historian that the citation had come directly from his own typewriter, and that at a subsequent meeting when Dooley waxed characteristically boastful the colonel suggested Tom compare the quality of the citation's typescript with earlier communications produced on his government-issue hardware.[69]

Lansdale also performed a great favor for the navy brass, since they assumed most of the credit for Dooley's good works. Apart from the doctor's own efforts, Operation Passage to Freedom had been a public relations debacle up to that point. In a January 1955 report to the chief of naval operations, the commander of Task Force 90 admitted:

> It is the opinion of CTF 90, based on letters received from parents, wives and friends of the personnel in the task force, that national coverage in the news media was disappointing. It is believed that the Navy's part in this dramatic operation was not fully exploited. . . . The U.S. Ambassador to Indochina personally told CTF 90 that he thought the U.S. Navy was missing a golden

opportunity to tell the people of our country a very gripping and powerful story which would not only redound to the credit of the U.S. Navy but would bring home to the people the efforts of our government in its continued opposition to Communist aggression and in its interest in the principles of humanity and personal freedom.[70]

"A raft of newspaper photographers covered it," wrote Dooley of the award ceremony, "and after the usual delay of several weeks the pictures should be arriving in American papers." The navy had made Dooley available to Lansdale during the pivotal evacuations of Phat Diem and Bui Chu, and he was known for a pragmatic habit of allowing others to take credit for his own strokes of genius. In 1982 Lansdale told an interviewer that the Americans in Saigon were angered to learn that he had arranged Dooley's citation, since Tom was widely viewed by military and embassy personnel alike as an abrasive publicity hound. Lansdale recalled explaining the genuine depth of the young physician's commitment to the refugees and the love they offered him in return. As usual the sleuth saw beyond a superficial reality; he recognized another dimension of Dooley's nature that eluded Tom's many detractors but ensured that he would emerge as the most celebrated and beloved veteran of Operation Passage to Freedom.[71]

The awards ceremony also represented a great triumph for Premier (and soon to be President) Diem and his chief American strategist. Dooley noted that present in the Cabinet Room was "a general from the recently conquered Binh Xuyen." The Binh Xuyen, one of the Vietnamese sects that threatened to subvert Diem's regime in its infancy, had controlled the vice rackets in Saigon-Cholon in collusion with French authorities. On March 29, 1955, their mercenaries had launched an attack on Diem's palace; in the ensuing combat, "various sections of the city were burned." Diem ignored the military advice of General Collins "and that, as far as Collins was concerned, was the last straw."[72]

Collins quickly returned to Washington to urge President Eisenhower and Secretary Dulles to jettison Diem for good. But in late April, just as the U.S. embassy in Saigon was about to be informed of a "compromise" solution in which Diem would retain "figurehead" status in a new government, renewed fighting broke out. This time Lansdale took charge, firing off a memo to Allen Dulles assuring him the Binh Xuyen would be defeated, advising Diem to ignore the emperor as well as the embassy staff, and urging American attachés to get out in the streets and see for themselves. (General O'Daniel was the only American who, in Lansdale's estimation, passed the test of courage on Diem's behalf: "He rode past the Vietnamese troops in his sedan, flying the American flag, and though he wasn't supposed to take sides, he leaned out and gave them the thumbs-up sign, shouting, 'Give 'em hell, boys!' He was a real fighting man.") Lansdale evaded an attempted kidnapping by the Binh Xuyen in time to rally Diem's spirits as well as those of his troops.[73]

Meanwhile, "back in Washington there was total consternation when Lansdale's wire was received indicating that the Binh Xuyen attack was being repulsed. Secretary Dulles immediately telephoned his brother Allen at CIA. Then urgent instructions were cabled to Saigon to disregard the previous long cable containing the new policy statement"; that first cable was promptly burned. Lansdale had orchestrated the defeat of the Binh Xuyen by preventing an alliance between that group and the other leading sects, the Cao Dai and the Hoa Hao, "the traditionalist sects of the south." Founded by civil servants in 1925 when the Cao Dai "revealed itself as the supreme god of the universe," this sect, wrote Frances FitzGerald, "worshiped all the world's religious leaders and placed such figures as Jeanne d'Arc and Victor Hugo along with the Taoist gods in their panoply of minor saints." The sects also had armies, which concerned Lansdale far more than their theological qualities.[74]

Lansdale's biographer claimed that the colonel may have spent up to ten million of the CIA's dollars to purchase the loyalty of such figures as Trinh Minh Thé, the Cao Dai leader who agreed to lead his black-uniformed soldiers into Saigon at the service of Ngo Dinh Diem. Surviving members of Lansdale's team insist that Thé was a great nationalist who needed no bribes to endorse a postcolonial Vietnamese state, but their late boss admitted at least to providing The "'a month's pay' for his troops when The integrated them into the Vietnamese Army." The was killed on May 3, 1955, as he led mop-up exercises against soldiers of the Binh Xuyen, the last sect in Diem's way. The defeated general present at Dooley's award ceremony was a trophy to Lansdale's success; by September the last remnants of the Binh Xuyen were wiped out.[75]

The defeat of the sects ensured what had been almost inconceivable only weeks earlier: the United States was now prepared to fully support the Diem regime. At the same time, French influence over its former colony was effectively eliminated. At tripartite talks in Paris in early May, French prime minister Edgar Faure had declared, in the presence of John Foster Dulles and British officials, that Diem was "not only incapable but mad." On May 10 Diem's nemesis General Collins was removed as U.S. ambassador to South Vietnam. On May 11 Faure grudgingly embraced the Diem regime; his principle request, that Lansdale leave Vietnam, was promptly rejected by the American contingent in Paris. A day later, Dr. Tom Dooley received his citation from the beaming leader of South Vietnam.[76]

"One of Lansdale's advantages during this period," argued Howard Simpson, "was the fact that his cables were vibrant accounts of what he had witnessed himself during the Saigon fighting." As a Lansdale aide recalled: "Ed was low-key but he could always convince people . . . God! The way Ed explained the situation in Vietnam. If we gave up, all of Asia would go down the drain. It was just remarkable. . . . Of course, he was an advertising man, a salesman, very soft-spoken, very quiet, very smooth." Those same talents seized on the figure of young Tom Dooley as an ideal symbol of the nascent Asian democracy. It did not take much of Lansdale's genius to recognize that no one in America could make sense of the war against the sects: perhaps they could understand Diem as an antiracketeer, but how to explain the Cao Dai, which modeled itself after the Catholic Church, right down to its own pope and pantheon of saints? Dooley certainly showed no awareness of the sects' complexities in his writings and was more than willing to focus exclusively on the Viet Minh as the lone source of Diem's woes. Lansdale was so determined to sell this misleading scenario to the American public that he later even helped rewrite the script for the film version of Graham Greene's anti-American novel, *The Quiet American*. In the meantime Dooley found himself on the brink of superstardom. He may also have been in the midst of a nervous breakdown.[77]

Tom Dooley returned to the mammoth naval base at Yokosuka in late May 1955 and was accorded a hero's treatment, particularly from those who were favored with his gripping tale of the final traumatic days in Haiphong. At a cocktail party he met two young fellow naval officers, Silas Spengler and Joe Albanese, a former track star and, like Spengler, a recent Yale graduate. Dooley invited them to accompany him to Tokyo for a dinner engagement; as they drove through bombed-out neighborhoods Tom appeared alternately despondent and giddy, laughing at elderly peddlers sent sprawling with their pushcarts in the wake of his reckless driving. At dinner Dooley broke down in fulsome tears as he finally shared with his new friends an astonishing tale of terror at the hands of Viet Minh agents who, he reported, kidnapped him during the week prior to his triumphant arrival in Saigon. "The story" was never written out in full but it survives in the memory of those who heard Dooley pour out his anguish in a heartbreaking rush of tangled emotions.[78]

The story never entered the official canon of Dooley folklore but remained ever-present along the margins of his legend as an archetype for the perpetual aura of impending crisis and dark intrigue that seemed always to becloud his hard-earned acclaim. Dooley's mother received the most elaborate yet diluted version of the story, and Tom was concerned that his misadventures would only add to the imposing burdens she already bore and treated with ample doses of alcohol. On August 26, 1955, he wrote: "Dear poor mother, who always gets the word second hand and who gets so upset about it . . . almost guilty sometimes. There is absolutely no need to feel bad about anything mother." After acknowledging that his real work in Haiphong had involved intelligence gathering (though he had boasted of this throughout the mission), Dooley tried to clarify the story that Mrs. Dooley had heard from the mother of a St. Louis acquaintance stationed in Yokosuka; this individual had demanded an explanation after hearing Dooley described at the hospital as "our POW."[79]

"Many around here know that there was a period of some silence between the Communists coming in on the 4th [May 1955] . . . and my sudden departure to Saigon on the 11th (a period of one week mother, seven days and eight nights)." Dooley could not disclose the full details of his detention by the communists, but he assured his mother "NOT A HAND WAS LAID ON ME . . . I was saluted, sired, and treated with the utmost respect at all times." He was purportedly held in a building in Haiphong, where "no one missed me as I had no corpsmen." Dooley was concerned that "the story" be minimized in St. Louis circles so as not to provoke undue alarm regarding his well-being. He admitted that he was denied toilet facilities and subjected to humiliating interrogations: " 'Sir, do you own an automobile. And is it not true that this car cost the equivalent of many people's yearly salary?' "[80]

Dooley was especially concerned lest his mother fear he had been "brainwashed" in the manner of American prisoners of the Red Chinese during the Korean War. In fact Tom confided to his navy friends that he was in profound turmoil over the state of his soul, so shaken had been his faith in his God and his Church. Mistaking Joe Albanese for a Catholic, Dooley convulsively wept in his presence for fear of irreparable spiritual damage wrought by his captors. In typically self-contradictory fashion, Tom mailed an innocuous letter to his mother on August 26, the same day ón which he later learned she had heard "the story," prompting his immediate frantic response. In the earlier letter, he had enclosed detailed specifications for the 1955 Oldsmobile 88 Convertible he planned to purchase on his return to St. Louis (concluding with a request that his mother "get me one of those beautiful color charts that show them in their real depth"). He had apparently survived the attempted brainwashing.[81]

In a December 1955 account of Dooley's final days in Haiphong, the *Saint Louis Globe-Democrat* reported that he "was detained by the communists until June and sent to Saigon where he received the highest honor the government gives to a foreigner." This chronologically if not factually inaccurate version of the story was not soon repeated in print. But it was too explosive to fade entirely away. In August 1959 Dooley's friend Robert

Hardy Andrews, a Hollywood screenwriter and devout Catholic, wrote a tribute to the now-famous jungle doctor of Laos in the *Ventura County Star-Free Press*. Andrews reported a recent conversation during which Dooley explained that three years earlier he had undergone a medical procedure by which "the nerves in his leg had to be stripped—to arrest crippling paralysis caused by communist captors who beat his legs with bamboo poles. 'But,' he said, 'that's all in the past,' and we dropped the subject by mutual agreement."[82]

Dooley was livid on learning of the article; officials at MEDICO's New York headquarters fired off a frantic telegram to Andrews telling him never to repeat "the story." But by then Dooley was a best-selling author who had learned a crucial lesson: he who commands the largest audience dictates the authoritative version of any story. And Dr. Tom Dooley was above all a storyteller. Lansdale knew as much and made sure Dooley was pointed in the right direction in the immediate aftermath of Operation Passage to Freedom, "that rocky period when all was over, and so much seemed confusion." Dooley's doctors at Yokosuka thought his writing might prove therapeutic. It is unlikely they suspected he was about to write a book that would help make world history.[83]

☆ 3 ☆

Deliver Us from Dooley

Deliver Us from Evil is the quintessential Tom Dooley text: its genesis shrouded in mystery, its blockbuster appeal rooted in the author's peculiar genius for galvanizing a mass audience while remaining aloof from the sources of his own power. The "book" actually originated as a condensed edition for the *Reader's Digest* and was then "planted" for simultaneous publication in a longer version by the prestigious New York firm of Farrar, Straus and Cudahy. As the April 1956 publication date drew near, some important people decided they wanted a piece of Dooley's action; a few got burned while others scurried to exploit his vulnerability for their own ends. By the close of a winter publicity tour touting the book, Dooley's life had been shattered, and a hasty retreat into obscurity might have represented his last best hope. He went on instead to become America's first celebrity-saint.

Dooley was a far better talker than writer, though his verbal flair occasionally seeped onto the page. Father Doremus, one of his Notre Dame French professors, recalled that Tom's written work as a collegian abounded with "beautiful words and lousy verbs." By 1954 Dooley's skills in English grammar and spelling remained similarly erratic, but he had manifested— during visits to navy ships in Haiphong harbor—a rare talent for highly emotional storytelling, captivating otherwise skeptical hordes of enlisted men while impressing the brass with his impassioned Vietnamese history lessons. Dooley's career as an author was born in "the white light of revelation" which compelled him to lay a proprietary claim on the exile's flight to religious freedom.[1]

Tom had made several faltering efforts to write of his experiences in Vietnam, beginning as early as August 1954 in a manuscript entitled "Passage to Freedom." It is not clear how he visualized his intended readership: the manuscript was filed among reports Dooley prepared for his superior officers, but the story appears to have been written primarily with a stateside civilian audience in mind. Tom was most interested in being remembered by St. Louisans (he sent several reports to the hometown *Post-Dispatch* in the fall of 1954 that the newspaper declined to print), particularly the social and medical elites who had scorned him.

"Passage to Freedom" is mawkish and alternately eloquent and crude, but it conveys a more authentic sympathy for the refugees than do the subsequent, slicker writings. The Vietnamese priests aboard ship in Haiphong harbor, Dooley wrote, "would offer Mass in the various holds. It is poignant to hear these people, plagued by so many years of war, singing softly their praises to God Who seems to have temporarily been looking elsewhere." The simple goodness of rough-hewn sailors represented the apotheosis of America's indomitable spirit: "We are suppose to transport the people, our mission is not to attempt to treat all their illnesses, this would take a decade. However, who is to stop American charity and ingenuity. . . . Nothing is as warming as to see these American sailors caring for the world's oppressed. How fine these boys are. How proud we should be of them, and of their mothers, who made them so."[2]

Dooley's early writings from Haiphong naturally focused on the refugees from the Catholic provinces of the North: his short essay "Bui Chu Means Valiant," published in January 1956 in the *U.S. Naval Institute Proceedings,* provided the core around which the narrative of *Deliver Us from Evil* was later constructed. In an early draft written during the evacuation Dooley explained: "Bui Chu . . . is intensely Catholic, and a militant people. It forms part of the rich rice delta of Tonkin, and in a relative way, the people too are rich. They own thatched homes, small plots of rice fields, a water buffalo or two, maybe some pigs and chickens. And their home life is warm and friendly, simple and joyous. At least prior to the war it was." The natural ease with which Dooley instinctively equated Vietnamese Catholics with republican yeomanry belied the legacy of two centuries of tension back home, but that innocence bolstered his effectiveness as a propagandist. "Then for eight years," he wrote of Bui Chu, "the war tore their land asunder. The war which started as a colonial one, and ended up to be Communism vs Freedom."[3]

Flush with his core idea, Dooley remained—for all his manic self-promotion—woefully naive about the politics of mass communications and oddly detached, even slightly estranged, from the "Tom Dooley" that everyone in Vietnam was beginning to hear about. The most revealing of his early writings is "Liberty in Saigon," an autumn 1954 guide for sailors of the USS *Balduck* (one of the evacuation ships) on liberty in Saigon. The "whitehats" who had listened intently to Dooley's shipboard lectures were now favored by his strikingly comprehensive knowledge of the capital city, from the temples and museums ("you have failed miserably in an attempt to know Indo China if you pass this place up") to the nightclubs and casinos of Cholon. "Here is wickedness," he wrote, adding that "it is great sport to roll dice and not have to worry about the O.D. . . . Another good place is the 'Au Baccara' which has taxi girls, just for dancing, truthfully. The floor show here would make the Bowery blush! At least it use to."[4]

Dooley concluded by gently warning the sailors that since they would be closely watched by "both the Commies and the Viet Nam," their behavior would reflect on the U.S. Navy as a whole: "And no matter what you think of the Navy as a unit, think of it as the guy who racks out next to you. If you make a drunken slob out of yourself antagonise someone, start a fight, or just be an out-and-out ass, then it is your buddy, either now or later, who will suffer from your blasted stupidity."[5]

"Liberty in Saigon" offered a glimpse into the Dooley riddle just months prior to his birth as a public figure. At once haughty and solicitous, the tour guide displayed his wealth of knowledge about the world without revealing the personal experiences, or the person, at its source. Poised uncomfortably between an officers' corps that often scorned his gladhanding and the unsophisticated "whitehats" to whom he lectured on venereal disease as well as dialectical materialism, Dooley's profound loneliness pervaded this seemingly innocuous text. "Have a good time you sons of guns," he concluded, "and drink a beer for me." In counseling sensitivity to the sailors' hosts— "The Vietnamese are so bewildered and confused they don't know what to think"—Dooley projected his own torment on the Asians, as he continued to do.[6]

Throughout his career Tom Dooley was blessed by people who entered his life for a period of time, sensing his vulnerability and compassion where others saw only arrogance and self-absorption. Norton Stevens was a young naval intelligence officer and recent Yale graduate working in Haiphong in the autumn and winter of 1954–55, "trying to find out the bad guys." He often met Tom for a late afternoon drink in Haiphong, when they would exchange intelligence about Viet Minh troop movements; Dooley was particularly enthusiastic about Stevens's cultivation of a local priest who often turned up at Nort's door armed with a pistol.[7]

Nort Stevens came to treasure Dooley as a young man with an "enlarged" view of life that broadened the horizons of everyone he came in contact with. He witnessed Tom's growing mastery of his dramatic gifts on the fantail of ships like the *Estes* and the *Balduck* where, often accompanied by children from the orphanage of Madame Ngai, Dooley produced theatrical renderings of their travails and those of their dead parents, provoking tears from even the most "grizzled old bosuns."[8]

Stevens was sufficiently impressed to propose that Dooley serve as the subject of a book on the boatlift, to be written with the help of a writer working locally on the staff of the Office of Naval Intelligence (ONI). On April 7, 1955, Dooley wrote to Stevens: "Reference the book . . . do with me what you like . . . my pride rises high to think that you anticipate that it may sell. I agree with your plans, and if Dooley is the angle that helps sell the world on realization of the importance of the Indo China sell out . . . then use him to the utmost."[9]

Stevens also offered Dooley's story to the *Reader's Digest* but was turned down, though the magazine soon reconsidered after being contacted by a more experienced author, U.S. Navy Commander William J. Lederer. Lederer provided Dooley with crucial editorial and marketing advice and imparted the spin that propelled the young doctor onto the best-seller lists. He had known Dooley since the autumn of 1954 when, serving in his capacity as public information officer (PIO) under the command of Adm. Felix Stump, commander-in-chief of the Pacific fleet (CINCPAC), Lederer visited Haiphong seeking human interest stories as promotional material for the refugee operation.[10]

Lederer was a remarkable character of whom a friend once remarked, "the incredible guy is pixilated." Born in New York City in 1912, he had gone to work at the age of fifteen for the legendary journalist Heywood Broun, quickly mastering a scene that exalted street smarts over social pedigree and formal education. Lederer then charmed his way into Annapolis and rose quickly through the navy's ranks, until a submarine he commanded had an infelicitous meeting with a wharf at Pearl Harbor. He remained with the Navy, however, serving in such capacities as chief of the magazine branch of the Defense Department. He began writing freelance pieces as well. Lederer's friend Ed Lansdale tersely recalled: "He took up writing and was making dough."[11]

Since Admiral Stump never understood why he needed a PIO, he gave Lederer a wide berth, which is how the latter came to know Tom Dooley in Haiphong late in 1954. After listening to the young Irishman spin some riveting tales of atrocities and heroism, Lederer exclaimed that Dooley had a "helluva book" on his hands, and on noticing "odd stuff" that resembled manuscript fragments in Dooley's room, he urged Tom to keep a journal for the duration of his mission (Lederer was correct about the manuscripts: Dooley informed his mother in early December of the "literally hundreds of typewritten sheets about this operation" that he had compiled, "just individual stories of what is going on; individual declarations from the refugees. One story a week is mimeographed and sent to the two ships now in this area").[12]

An entrepreneurial journalist, Lederer was particularly impressed by Dooley's gift for charming supplies from such civilian concerns as the Charles Pfizer Company, a New York pharmaceuticals firm that provided him with cratefuls of Terramycin (oxytetracycline) tablets for "his" refugees. Lederer, whom Lansdale called "irreverent as hell," sensed in Dooley a kindred spirit for whom he might serve as mentor (he later called Tom a "genius . . . who could squeeze money out of anybody").[13]

Lederer's own literary specialty consisted in applying a light, even humorous touch to such poignant events as the sinking of ships (in 1950 he wrote a memorable story of a submarine disaster—not his own—for the *Saturday Evening Post*). He also understood the vicissitudes of the writing industry to a degree unmatched by anyone serving in the navy. In a lecture to superior officers on literary technique, he once explained: "If we had come in here and found a movie star's dead body on the table, with a note, 'Admiral McJones did it,' that would not be a good magazine story. But it would be a good newspaper story."[14]

Lederer even provided Dooley with an explicit model for writing of the refugee operation. "They'll Remember the Bayfield," published in the March 1955 issue of the *Reader's Digest,* was a first-person narrative of Lederer's journey with two thousand Vietnamese exiles aboard the USS *Bayfield* in August 1954, en route from Haiphong to Saigon. Lederer, a non-Catholic, noted that the refugees mistook American sailors for priests; he reported that after being bathed by an Engineman First Class, one little girl exclaimed to her mother: "Mama, the big American is a priest. First he blessed me and then baptized me an American."[15]

By focusing on the compassion of the enlisted men, those "sea-going ambassadors," Lederer personalized the refugee mission for American readers and effectively contrasted their kindness with the vicious, coldly abstract communists the refugees were fleeing. An introductory note by a *Reader's Digest* editor supplied the political lesson implicit in Lederer's more whimsical story: "When the Reds took over North Vietnam last year, a half million refugees fled southward from their homeland. Most of them were Catholics.

They sacrificed their homes and all their possessions for one precious thing: the right to worship in the religion of their choice."[16]

The tone and texture of *Deliver Us from Evil* were prefigured in "They'll Remember the Bayfield," an article composed at a time when Dooley could scarcely dream of authorship. On May 13, 1955, one day after being decorated by Premier Diem, Dooley was ordered by Capt. Walter Winn to prepare "memorandums on the end of Indo China." His first mention of the project that yielded *Deliver Us from Evil* occurred on June 5, 1955. From aboard the USS *Diachenko,* en route to Yokosuka, Dooley wrote to his mother: "I spent all last night and all today working on the book. Doesn't that sound formidable? But that is just what it is, a book." Three days later he added:

> I know I have been remiss in my letters, but blame the BOOK. It is consuming every free moment of my day. When I finish work in the evening, I start typing and find that I cannot tolerate the least disturbance. It breaks my train of thought and I can't seem to adequately pick it up again. Now I know why authors go to cabins in the north-woods to write a book. The title is still unsettled. What do you think of "Treatment for Terror?" I have definitely rejected "Exodus from Agony." Commander Bill Lederer was certainly right when he said, "giving birth to a baby is a cinch compared to fathering a book." I haven't a finished manuscript to show him yet. Do you like "Trial in Tonkin?" Another possibility is "Bamboo and Blood."[17]

By June 30 Dooley had completed a draft of the book, aided considerably by the use of a dictating machine and a battery of enlisted "secretaries" who typed the manuscript "about as fast as I can talk (and they tell me I'm pretty rapid)." Dooley's literary inexperience was so vast it had not occurred to him (despite his already legendary egotism) that the story could be told most effectively as a first-person narrative organized around his unique experiences. But after receiving advice from several navy friends, he explained:

> It is now being rewritten with emphasis on TAD. That is, it is the story of Indo China, NOT only as TAD saw it, but as TAD lived it. . . . When I speak of the rescue work off the beach, instead of describing them as I was told they exist, I use poetic justice, or license or something, and describe them as though I was sitting on the ship "where we could see just clear stretches of water, no noise, no movement, just the quiet swell of the ocean . . . all quiet on the sandspit." This is supposed to identify the reader with Me, and sort of follow me, through a year in Indo China. . . . Ego-centricity instead of being wrong in writing a book is supposed to be a good thing.[18]

Dooley and Lederer, now stationed in Hawaii, corresponded throughout the spring and summer of 1955. Tom sent the commander a chapter on Bui Chu with the request that "if you think there is any value in this . . . please let me know, or push this a little I write as an exercise to train me to put my thoughts and emotions into a cage of words, succinctly, briefly, and adequately. But the more I can expose this to the happier I am." Lederer agreed to handle security clearances and steer the manuscript through his own literary agent. In September Dooley was awarded the Legion of Merit and was assigned to the U.S. Naval Hospital in Bethesda, Maryland. He finally left Asia on November 19, 1955, and flew to Hawaii, where he briefed Admiral Stump on Vietnam and spent two weeks "holed up" with his literary mentor in the Royal Hawaiian Hotel.[19]

The "Tom Dooley" persona emerged as the focal point of the manuscript during these intensive sessions. Bill Lederer specialized in creating rakish yet lovable characters such as Lt. Hymie O'Toole, who bent navy regulations to the breaking point but proved resourceful, deeply committed, and ultimately indispensable to the service. In "Hymie O'Toole Is Never Wrong" (1950), the first-person narrator and hero is tormented by an officious superior who "griped" that "I chummied around so much with the sailors." Hymie winds up greatly impressing the secretary of the navy during an unlikely encounter and is invited to lunch with both the president and Winston Churchill, to the dismay of O'Toole's commander.[20]

Dooley's insouciance was now readily transmuted into boyish charm to bolster the unassumingly heroic tenor of *Deliver Us from Evil:* "Yes, cocky young Dooley, whom the profs at medical school had ticketed as a future 'society doctor,' was learning things the hard way, but he was learning at last." Like Hymie O'Toole, Dooley's irrepressible spirit and genuine talents (including a knowledge of French) finally won over—at least in the narrative version—superior officers wary of his disregard for hoary naval protocol: where Hymie, in Lederer's yarn, is finally ordained "the finest officer in this ship," Dooley surpassed these "regular guy" credentials in *Deliver Us from Evil* by becoming the first officer ever to receive the USS *Montague's* Shipmate of the Month award.[21]

In Lederer's stories Hymie O'Toole's mother "owned a two-bit Kosher delicatessen in Brooklyn"; his father was "a fightin' Irish bricklayer." Tom Dooley was likewise only half-Irish; in St. Louis, where money and charm counted for nearly as much as pedigree, he had demonstrated little if any genuine interest in his ethnic heritage. Nor was there much to be gained, in the present circumstances, from advertising his mother's membership in the Daughters of the American Revolution. His family had long since traded in their "semi-Irishness" for a staunch identity as American Catholics, a gesture to be adopted by countless others during the 1950s. Yet William Lederer was among a host of World War II–era authors and screenwriters who persistently fielded multiethnic (though decidedly not multiracial) squadrons in their stories of America's bitter struggle against the Aryan-supremacist Nazis.[22]

Now in the midst of a cold war, Dooley and Lederer adapted the ethnic angle for *Deliver Us from Evil*. When the crew of the USS *Montague* elected Tom Shipmate of the Month, "I had a hard time controlling the tears that come so easily to an Irishman's eyes." Later, during the refugee crisis, U.S. Navy Comdr. Wendell Mackey "quietly infused some patience into my Irish breeding which I needed when my mob required a touch of 'diplomacy.'"[23]

Dooley's Irishness conveyed a vaguely nostalgic charm, particularly when invoked to reaffirm his stature as the quintessentially "regular" American, a tough pragmatist with a touch of the poet and a sentimental streak. His Catholicism, however, was a potentially volatile issue, an essential ingredient of his appeal that had to be carefully monitored in his writings and appearances. The *Reader's Digest,* according to its chronicler John Heidenry, traditionally had "as little to do as possible with religions like Catholicism. . . . Appearances by prominent Catholics in the pages of the *Digest* were mostly limited to an occasional anti-Communist tirade by New York's powerful conservative archbishop, Francis Cardinal Spellman." Although Heidenry noted that "another popular Catholic, Tom Dooley, was likewise publicized in the *Digest* only for his anticommunism," he overlooked the crucial distinction between Spellman and Dooley, who as a layman could more readily bridge the enduring gulf between Catholics and other Americans. Dooley soon embodied a vast, ecumenical cold war coalition on which the continued prosperity of the *Digest* would depend.[24]

In *Promises to Keep,* Agnes Dooley noted that, beyond merely helping to reshape her son's manuscript, Lederer "arranged an appointment which was to end Tom's writing problems. He had a date to meet with the editors of *Reader's Digest* back east." Lederer had originally recommended that Dooley submit a chapter to the *Saturday Evening Post,* but that magazine rejected the article in August 1955, turning it over instead "to one of their agents who will try other markets for it, such as Colliers, Look, etc." An editor at the *Post* also agreed to write a cover letter on behalf of the manuscript to Viking Press, where the book-length manuscript was once again rejected.[25]

Dooley's early publishing setbacks must be weighed against a compelling temptation to view the Lederer–*Reader's Digest* connection as part of a larger conspiracy linking Dooley and *Deliver Us from Evil* with elements of the Central Intelligence Agency's propaganda apparatus. Lederer certainly thought Dooley could prove useful to the navy's public relations campaign in the wake of Operation Passage to Freedom, but he may also have borne additional obligations. On May 11, 1955 (one day prior to the Lansdale-orchestrated ceremony honoring Dooley in Saigon), Allen Dulles, director of the CIA, had written to Admiral Stump requesting that Lederer be made available for "special assignment," noting that the commander had recently completed a similar mission for the Agency. Dulles wrote that the need for military personnel to conduct such unspecified "research projects" reflected "an increasingly serious estimate of the threat of Communist expansion by means other than major overt military action."[26]

Deliver Us from Evil was a work of propaganda, pure and relatively simple. It is less clear who authorized Dooley to take singlehanded credit for the success of history's largest refugee operation. Lederer, as noted, was a friend of Lansdale, dating back to the Philippine campaigns (Lederer's wife was a Filipina). The master spy was later immortalized in *The Ugly American,* a runaway 1958 best-seller coauthored by Lederer and Berkeley political scientist Eugene Burdick. The character of Colonel Hillandale was drawn so transparently that Lansdale feared, justifiably, that his cover was blown for good. He shared with Lederer an impatience bordering on contempt for the hidebound bureaucracies dominating the military and intelligence communities. Lansdale broke the world down into categories of intrepid men of action and vision, like himself, and ineffectual functionaries whose blunders crippled American foreign policy in the cold war. He would later squarely place his stamp of approval on Lederer in recalling the days when Bill "was a captain and CINCPAC [Felix Stump] was an Admiral commanding all U.S. forces in the Far East. Lederer would meet me at the airport and drive me to CINCPAC and we'd go by the Admiral's house. He'd yell out the guy's first name and the admiral would look out and yell 'hi.' "[27]

Could the "irreverent as hell" duo of Lansdale and Lederer have engineered a publishing coup that turned their protégé into a celebrity and advanced the goals of the CIA's legendary loose cannon as well as those of Lansdale's client, Ngo Dinh Diem? Dooley explained to his mother on June 15, 1955, that all the publicity he was receiving at home as a result of his Vietnamese medal "was probably Lederer's doing"; since Lansdale had drafted the citation presented to Dooley by Diem, he also undoubtedly advised Lederer regarding maximal visibility for Dooley. On December 16, 1955, the *Reader's Digest's* secretive owner-publisher DeWitt Wallace wrote Lederer in gratitude "for steering Doctor Dooley to the *Digest*" and enclosed a cash token of his appreciation. "Doctor Dooley's book should be the best thing that has come our way since your article, 'They'll Remember the Bayfield.' "[28]

Two days earlier Dooley had appeared before a half-dozen *Reader's Digest* senior editors including James Monahan, a former air force officer best known for his obsessive mission "to bring the American tobacco industry to its knees," despite his own status as a two-pack-a-day man. "Tom Dooley began his rapid fire recital that day even before he sat down at the luncheon table," Monahan later wrote. "Two hours later his listeners were still spell-bound by the story of his adventures in the wretched refugee camps of Haiphong. . . . The *Digest* editors recognized at once that Tom Dooley was a singularly colorful personality with a great story. An agreement was made for its publication." Monahan introduced Tom to Roger W. Straus Jr. of the publishing firm Farrar, Straus and Cudahy; on January 3, 1956, Tom Dooley signed his first book contract.[29]

Writing in the leftist journal *Covert Action* in 1988, Fred Landis accurately noted that "the *Digest* is the world's most widely circulated magazine; it is also the most ignored by intellectuals and journalists." Landis was determined to expose "the worldwide propaganda activities of the CIA and the *Reader's Digest*, and the secret relationship between them," which existed within what he called "an informational 'black hole.'" He produced a long list of "CIA officers, media agents, and friendly correspondents who have written for *Reader's Digest*," but he failed to explain "whether the *Digest* is a straightforward propaganda outlet for the CIA or the relationship is more one of ideological consensus." He even conceded the fascinating possibility that "what looked like CIA propaganda at the *Digest* was more a matter of disgruntled former CIA agents getting the ear of ideologically kindred spirits."[30]

William Lederer continued to work as a contributing editor for the *Reader's Digest* ("an organization," he wrote to DeWitt Wallace in 1958, "having interests completely congruous with my own") following his retirement from the navy, but Wallace had reservations about his flamboyant character and even turned down condensation rights to *The Ugly American*. In 1959 Lederer suggested a story idea on Lansdale to the *Digest*, exclaiming that his life of intrigue would make for "a spectacular article. . . . He can dissemble and camouflage as easily as a ballerina can change her costume." By 1963 Lansdale himself appeared at *Reader's Digest* luncheons in Pleasantville, New York, supplying names of colleagues "who are in today's struggle abroad" and thus worthy of articles "for doing the right thing unselfishly, and who are doing it towards a specific and desirable U.S. goal."[31]

In his massive study of the *Reader's Digest*, John Heidenry argued that the magazine "enjoyed an intimate relationship with the agency perhaps unmatched by any other major American communications giant, with the exception of Time-Life." Yet the *Digest's* condensed version of "Deliver Us from Evil" was more than a CIA plant. If anything, the correspondence between Wallace and Lederer indicated that the powerful editor always enjoyed the upper hand in his relationships with authors: in his empire, journalistic entrepreneurship always prevailed over efforts to make the *Digest* a source of unmediated propaganda.[32]

Those who would subordinate the *Digest* to any government agency grossly underestimate DeWitt Wallace's personal ambitions in the realm of international relations and American business. Critics have generally assumed, like most readers, that the *Digest* merely reprinted articles from other publications. In fact the magazine—founded by Wallace and his wife, Lila, in 1922—has featured original articles since 1933. DeWitt Wallace also inaugurated the practice of "planting" articles conceived and produced by the *Digest* in other magazines, then reprinting them in his own, satisfying his "combined creative and evangelical itch" while promoting the fiction that the *Digest* is primarily a reprint magazine.[33]

Wallace's father was a lay preacher in the Presbyterian Church and a professor at Macalaster College in St. Paul, Minnesota. His maternal grandfather was an ordained minister, as was the father of his wife. Like his more renowned rival Henry Luce, Wallace was powerfully imbued with a sense of America's missionary destiny; the *Digest* came to operate sixteen offices around the world and, by the time *Deliver Us from Evil* was excerpted as a "condensed book" in the April 1956 edition, "Wally" could crow to its young author: "It is no news to you that the condensation from your book 'Deliver Us From Evil' was read by the largest magazine audience in the United States. But I know you will be gratified to learn that, in addition, this excellent piece was reprinted in fourteen (14) of our international editions. Thus you have reached millions of other readers in many lands."[34]

A sensible interpretation of Wallace's phenomenal success would focus not on sinister international intrigue but on the indomitable wedding of profitability and messianic Americanism unabashedly touted in each issue of the *Reader's Digest*. "It is no accident," the Jesuit critic Walter Ong wrote in 1955, "that Mr. and Mrs. DeWitt Wallace, creators and owners of the *Reader's Digest,* optimistic travelling companion of modern commercial voyagers and missioners of a cheery do-goodism, are, together with a rather extraordinary number of their early collaborators, children of Protestant ministers." Ong argued that "the Protestant has tended to carry his optimism away from his religion into the business world." W. A. Swanberg located numerous similarities between the *Digest* and Henry Luce's Time-Life empire (with which Dooley later enjoyed a significant if more complicated relationship), beginning with their founders' profound world-evangelical motivations. Of course the *Digest,* Swanberg sniffed, always appealed to readers "in the lower spectrum of intellectual vigor."[35]

"The secret of *The Reader's Digest* is editing," said Norman Cousins of *Saturday Review.* "I tell my audiences, often to their surprise especially in academic circles, that *The Reader's Digest* is the best edited magazine in

America. Wally himself is the best pencil man, and the result of his tech-nique is clarity—the words lift right off the page into your mind." Wallace understood that no idea could sell without being wrapped in a good story, which accounts for his immediate recognition of the limitless potential in Dooley's homey, one-man crusade for Vietnamese freedom.[36]

The *Reader's Digest* played a central role in each of the incarnations of "Deliver Us from Evil." John Heidenry asserted that the book version was "polished" by *Digest* editor James Monahan and his staff before "the *Digest* excerpted it, Condensed Books published a condensed version, the book itself [Farrar, Straus and Cudahy edition] became a best-seller, and for the first time Americans began to pay attention to a place—formerly a French problem—called Vietnam." A detailed memorandum prepared for Dooley by a *Reader's Digest* editor in early 1956 provides a rare glimpse into the jugger-naut's editorial processes at the height of the Wallace era.[37]

The editor (identified only as "EL," possibly Eleanor Hard Lake of the Condensed Books division) reminded Dooley once again that his own role "was the essence of the story and should not be obscured. . . . At what point was the whole operation unloaded on your shoulder? . . . What we need, in short, is a more dramatic and impressive picture of a young doctor (who had relatively little authority or responsibility in the past) suddenly faced with a colossal job." From his initial desire merely to "explain Bui Chu, and say my piece against Co-Existence" Dooley was now authorized to court the Free World's gratitude for saving "half a million patients" and present himself as the "young MD, almost fresh out of medical school, faced with surgery . . . on a scale and in a variety most doctors don't see in their entire career." William Lederer later called Dooley "a terrible liar," but it is not difficult to see how readily a young man, even one lacking Dooley's titanic ego, could have become swept up in the personal mythology being prepared for him by media experts.[38]

The *Digest's* editor more than prompted the ideological themes as well: "As you make fairly clear, every fugitive was really an escapee. In theory people were free to leave. In practice the Reds used everything from propa-ganda, intimidation to terror to prevent the exodus. Would you spell out for me, in memo. form, what the Communists did to block the tide of flights to freedom?" Dooley gladly obliged; if what he had seen was not sufficiently dramatic he could always exercise "poetic justice, or license" to make up the rest.[39]

The final "condensed" version of "Deliver Us from Evil" was a *Reader's Digest* masterpiece ("a virtual gift from heaven," as Heidenry called it—an "idealistic, devoutly religious American . . . who was single-handedly holding back the Red sea in Southeast Asia with his thumb"). Even though Farrar, Straus and Cudahy rushed the book version into print to coincide with the April issue of the *Digest* (and it went on to sell over half a million copies), the book was overshadowed by the *Digest's* original version, which reached millions of readers around the globe. Where the book begins with a corny tale in which Dooley converts a cynical young ensign to his view that "there is a special power in love" capable of defeating the communists, the *Digest* version opens with a distillation of the book's third chapter, establishing immediately the Dooley persona in the opening lines: "One night last spring I lay sleepless and sweltering in the dying city of Haiphong, North Viet Nam, asking myself the question that has taunted so many young Americans caught in faraway places: 'What in hell am *I* doing here?' "[40]

The story traces Dooley's passage from naïveté to the practical wisdom of one who learned by doing:

> At Notre Dame the priests had tried valiantly to teach me philosophy. But out here in this Communist hellhole I had learned many more profound and practical facts about the true nature of man. I had watched tough U.S. sailors become tender nurses for sick babies and dying old men. I had seen inhuman torture and suffering elevate weak men to lofty heights of spiritual nobility. I knew now why organized godlessness can never kill the divine spark that burns within even the humblest human.[41]

A little more than a year since his first halting performance on the fantail of the USS *Estes,* Dooley had been supplied with his true voice. "Deliver Us from Evil" went on to summarize "the whole sordid story of the refugee camps, the Communist atrocities, the 'Passage to Freedom' and the perilous future of southern Viet Nam," but Tom's vocation and his mission were capsulized in that single paragraph; it also revealed the source of his usefulness to sponsors. Like some young initiate, Tom Dooley had been passed from one guide to the next, from Lansdale to Lederer to DeWitt Wallace, each of whom knew something about the cash nexus of ideas and the power of the word in exporting America's missionary imperative. Theirs was a very different world from that of Catholic St. Louis, or Notre Dame.[42]

Since Dooley was "authorized" in more ways than one by these men to create a work of propaganda, questions regarding the book's veracity became less germane over time. With each new revelation of the CIA's sponsoring role in various cold war "front" activities, *Deliver Us from Evil* was implicitly discredited. Yet even confidential critiques from government agencies must be viewed with some suspicion. The United States Information Agency, for instance, solicited an appraisal of the book in 1956 from, according to an FBI report, "six individuals who were associated with Dooley" and who "did not accept the thesis of the book that the success of the evacuation of the refugees was entirely his work." These individuals also complained that he "tended to discredit the French, who deserved most of the credit for the successful evacuation." A differing account of the original USIA document reported that Dooley's claims of communist atrocities against Catholics were mostly "nonfactual and exaggerated." While these objections were almost certainly valid, it must be remembered that the USIA's predecessor, the International Information Agency, had been dismantled after the G. David Schine–Roy Cohn barnstorming tour of its European libraries in 1953. The newly created USIA did not wish to see a replay of that McCarthyite humiliation; its preparations to discredit Dooley may have represented an insurance policy against a renewed outbreak of anti-internationalism.[43]

Other agencies of the U.S. government similarly treated *Deliver Us from Evil* according to their own needs. The United States Navy, for instance, actively supported the book's account of Operation Passage to Freedom, even in the years after Dooley left the service. But by the middle of the 1970s, as naval historians began to critically examine the Vietnam War from the perspective of American defeat, Dooley's role was reduced from the mythological to the mundane. The official historians of the navy's role in the "Vietnam conflict" noted that "only Lieutenant (jg) Dooley and three corpsmen remained ashore" at Haiphong after October 1954, and they lauded Dooley's "aggressive steps to prevent an epidemic" of smallpox in February of that year. They also cited his talent for soliciting large donations in supplies from American pharmaceutical firms, and concluded their brief discussion of Dooley's work in Vietnam with a reference to the May 12, 1955, award ceremony in Saigon.[44]

In 1989 retired Capt. Julius M. Amberson reduced further the scope and luster of Tom Dooley's performance at Haiphong. Writing in *Navy Medicine*, Amberson, a physician with the Navy Medical Corps whom Dooley professed to admire as a role model, simply named Tom as one of two officers who "served as French and English interpreters" in the early stages of the campaign. A note marked by an asterisk, indicating that "LTJG Dooley went on to write *Deliver Us from Evil*, recounting his experiences in this operation," served only to increase the distance between Dooley's claims and the more authoritative version of a superior officer.[45]

Daniel M. Redmond, another veteran of Operation Passage to Freedom and a former naval intelligence officer, similarly relegated Dooley to the margins of history in his own *Navy Medicine* memoirs. Apart from recounting "several hilarious hours" he spent "with Dooley and a corpsman trying to capture a couple of monkeys in the garden of the Continental Hotel so they could get samples of simian body lice," Redmond noted only that Dooley "later became famous." Numerous participants in the Passage to Freedom later described Dooley as a consummate "bullshit artist." Redmond, along with Dooley's corpsman Pete Kessey and other eyewitnesses, tended to view him—if perhaps only after the fact—as a compulsive self-promoter who grossly exaggerated or even fabricated the details of his contribution to the refugee operation. Dooley's personal peculiarities were remembered far more vividly than his work. Redmond recalled another episode from Haiphong's Hotel Continental, where he was enjoying a drink in the bar with Dooley and several other physicians from the Navy Medical Corps (who are notable for their absence from *Deliver Us from Evil*). A young, nervous-looking sailor approached the men, explaining that he had an appointment with Dr. Dooley, who promptly ordered the serviceman to drop his pants. The sailor was obviously suffering from a venereal disease. As soon as he walked away, the other physicians upbraided Dooley for his callous and unprofessional behavior, whereupon Tom replied that the sailor had earned the humiliation as a result of his sexual impurity. Redmond was an Irish Catholic himself, but he found Dooley's rather punitive moralism an unsavory component of his personality.[46]

Yet like so many others, Redmond recalled as well Dooley's pronounced compassionate streak; he once accompanied Tom on a visit to a "filthy" French hospital in North Vietnam, where Dooley bitterly protested with French doctors who insisted they could do nothing for the scores of Foreign Legionnaires who were dying for lack of better care. Redmond, along with virtually all those who had seen Dooley in action in Vietnam, recognized his supreme dramatic gifts while harboring suspicions of the motivation behind the brilliant performances.[47]

In 1958 William Lederer and Eugene Burdick invented a Jesuit character for their best-seller *The Ugly American* that was likely based in part on the image of Dooley that Lederer had helped to create. "A practical, tough-minded and thoughtful man," Jesuit Father John X. Finian is also a ferocious anticommunist toiling in Southeast Asia who believes above all "when Americans do what is right and necessary, they are also doing what is effective." Dooley was encouraged, in the months after Haiphong, to view himself in this light: though we have no record of his inner feelings as he stood poised on the brink of stardom, he must have felt for the first time that he truly belonged to some powerful inner circle. The ambitions of his debutante era now paling by comparison, he was ready to take his story on the American road, including a stop at Pleasantville, where DeWitt Wallace spoke for the masses who had received the word that winter and spring: "The response was unanimous: your talk was a thriller—truly as impressive a speech as I've heard in a long time. Situated atop that warm Irish heart of yours is a cranial cavity filled with rich and rare gifts." Unfortunately for Tom Dooley, Irishness represented a lesser source of his profound "difference" from the club he ached to join.[48]

Tom Dooley was reassigned to the U.S. Navy surgeon general's office in January 1956 to facilitate a whirlwind lecture tour culminating in the publication of *Deliver Us from Evil.* "He talked to medical societies, sororities, high schools, colleges, grade schools, Rotarians, press clubs, Chambers of Commerce, U.S. Navy stations (including a submarine base), and religious groups of all faiths. He gave TV interviews, radio interviews, and press interviews; he addressed hospital staffs and luncheon clubs. He even spoke at the Willys automobile plant at Toledo. Everywhere he went he told the story of the 'Passage to Freedom.'"[49]

The response of the Denver Rotarians to Dooley's speech on March 8 was typical of the plaudits he grew accustomed to receiving at each appearance: "Outstanding—informative—inspiring—these and other superlatives might well apply to Dr. Dooley's talk entitled 'Passage to Freedom.'" The tour was officially cosponsored by the U.S. Navy and Charles Pfizer and Company, the pharmaceuticals giant that had supplied Dooley with medicines for his refugees. Tom was delighted to perform his dual role of corporate and military spokesman in the tradition of the *Reader's Digest.* "Rest assured," he wrote in *Deliver Us from Evil,* "we continually explained to thousands of refugees, as individuals and in groups, that only in a country which permits companies to grow large could such fabulous charity be found." His priestly role not only transcended denominations, but bridged the gap between East and West: "With every one of the thousands of capsules of terramycin and with every dose of vitamins on a baby's tongue, these words were said: 'Dai La My-Quoc Vien-Tro' (This is American Aid)."[50]

Dooley rarely wrote letters from within the United States or shared his feelings with others; we can only speculate on his response to the power newly bestowed on him. The surgeon general's secretary, Clare Murphy, recalled that Tom was

> the snappiest, best-looking young naval officer I had seen in a long time, and he was blessed with a keen sense of humor and all the charm of his Irish ancestry. . . . Even at 28 he was master of the spoken and written word, and his dictation was perfect and so fascinating you were sorry when he stopped. . . . He was always in a hurry, and the consensus in the Navy Department was that

if Dooley kept up this pace he was headed for a breakdown, either mental or physical. . . . The public relations officers were wild about him, because he was in great demand and always made good copy. They could not get enough of him.[51]

Since all of the published accounts of Dooley's lecture tour confirmed the impression that this gifted young man in navy dress blues was destined for greatness, it is profoundly jarring to compare the public adulation he received in the winter of 1956 with unpublished accounts of his activities, emanating from sources of a very different nature. A navy press officer who attended the doctor's lecture before the King County Medical Society in Seattle on March 15 witnessed a less savory side of Lieutenant Dooley. "While Dr. Dooley's remarks were interesting in general," he noted in a memorandum to the navy's Public Information Office, "it is felt that his presentation on this occasion was a disservice to the Navy." The press officer complained that Dooley resorted to "off color humor" in his talk, including jokes about circumcisions, mention of a "tall flat-chested Navy nurse" to whom he had lent his car during the refugee operation ("when I got back eleven months later, the car had 45,000 miles on it and the Navy Nurse looked like she had about 35 on her"), and such quips as "every time I broke wind [Norman] Baker saluted—we were a sharp outfit."[52]

The press officer objected to Dooley's criticisms of both French and American policies in Indochina. He was also incensed at Dooley's "poor use of Navy terms": Admiral Sabin and his staff "were called the 'heirarchy' [sic]"; Dooley described highly specialized naval craft simply as "boats." Despite Dooley's growing reputation as a sparkling after-dinner speaker, the press officer reported that during the talk, "many of the audience left . . . at the conclusion of the address, forty to fifty people left. Only one question was asked."[53]

The navy had a question of its own for Lieutenant Dooley. The press officer was probably unaware that his report contributed to an ongoing, exhaustive investigation of Dooley's sexual behavior that was to result in his forced resignation from the service, effective March 28, 1956. On January 26 the chief of naval personnel had ordered the director of naval intelligence to initiate an "appropriate investigation" to determine whether Dooley "has homosexual tendencies," and if so, to determine "the extent of his homosexual activities."[54]

The rumors had begun at Yokosuka in the summer of 1954: one of Dooley's closest gay friends even claimed that Tom was assigned to the Vietnam refugee operation in retaliation for seducing the son of an admiral at the base. Dooley was without question a homosexual as well as the victim of a navy witch hunt. Although some of his admirers have sought to place

Tom in the category of people with homosexual "tendencies" who do not necessarily act on their sexuality, he was in fact an extraordinarily active gay man who was considered one of the great underground sex symbols of his era—a figure well-known in sophisticated gay circles as far-flung as Hollywood, Washington, D.C., and the capitals of Southeast Asia.[55]

Dooley's ardent homosexual life had begun amid the dramatic social transformations wrought by World War II, which greatly influenced what the historian John D'Emilio called "the social expression of same-sex eroticism. The war years allowed the almost imperceptible changes of several generations, during which a gay male and lesbian identity had slowly emerged, to coalesce into a qualitatively different form. A sexual and emotional life that gay men and women previously experienced mainly in individual terms suddenly became, for the war generation, a widely shared collective phenomenon."[56]

As a devout Catholic of the 1940s and 1950s, Dooley was expected to suffer for his sexuality; a psychiatrist who briefly lived in Laos (just after Dooley's death) and was apprised of Tom's life style was convinced that he died of guilt manifest as melanoma. Yet there are powerful counterclaims to this conventional narrative. Historian George Chauncey, in his study of gay New York culture between 1890 and 1940, convincingly dispelled what he called the "myths" of "isolation, invisibility, and internalization" that have dominated perceptions of urban gay life in the prewar era. Tom Dooley found a well-established subculture awaiting him when he began acting on his homosexuality in the early 1940s: his sexuality most definitely was not divorced from his social life.[57]

Tom had spent the summer of 1952 as a medical intern at the naval hospital in Bethesda, Maryland. One day he was picked up on a streetcar by a German airline steward who took him directly to the home of one of the leading lights of the Washington gay community. Dooley quickly became a favorite of a group that included theater people and musicians, Rock Hudson's future manager, and a man who went on to become a renowned omelette chef. Dooley was recalled as "a most mesmerizing person" and "one of the most charming people you could ever meet," an emotional, spontaneous young man who brightened his surroundings and the lives of all around him. In that world, where homosexuals referred to each other as "friends of Bertha's" or "friends of Dorothy," or some other variation on the theme, Dooley was considered extremely desirable; according to one of his friends, he offered his sexuality as a gift to those he considered less attractive than himself. This individual recalled with exceptional clarity a conversation in which Dooley bluntly dismissed the Catholic Church's teaching on homosexuality as simply wrong. There was even then a certain mystical quality to

Dooley's sex appeal, with his wild, undisciplined streak and his sparkling presence that friends insist distinguished him from other conventionally attractive men. Dooley would "drink like a fish" while playing the tunes of Gershwin and Porter (occasionally interspersed with darker classical melodies) at elegant rounds of parties.[58]

Yet if he consorted with a cosmopolitan gay elite as part of his ambition, Dooley also allegedly found time to engage in the kind of behavior guaranteed to confirm the navy's equation of homosexuality with criminal behavior. The "joyous way of looking at life" that Tom's friends recalled so vividly of the summer of 1952 is notably absent from the ONI report. The navy's informants portray Tom Dooley as a manipulative, even predatory character. One pickup reported that after they had sex, he suggested they get together again while Dooley was in New York, but Tom's "reply to that was that he was 'not here to make friends.' "[59]

The ONI procured sworn affidavits from several of Dooley's pickups, including a man he met on February 3, 1956, at the Penn Bar of the Hotel Statler in New York. The informant and a friend mistook Dooley (wearing "a Navy blue uniform which had two gold stripes on the cuff") for a hotel employee and asked him for directions to the men's room. The "naval officer became indignant, or pretended to be." As a result of the incident the men began to converse; the informant told a special agent of the ONI that several drinks later ("it was apparent to me at that time that the Naval officer was 'gay' ") Dooley invited him up to his room, at which time "the naval officer told me to take my clothes off, which I did [though Dooley later swore he never chased men while in uniform]. By the time I undressed, the naval officer already had his clothes off and was as naked as a jay-bird. . . . He then groped me, that is he fondled my penis, and he may have kissed me. . . . He then told me that he was married and that his wife blew him every night, which was an indication that he wanted me to do the same. I then blew him by placing his penis in my mouth and sucking him until he came." To establish his credibility, the informant, who never saw Dooley again, testified, "I am homosexual, and in my opinion the naval officer is promiscuous—at least he is not inexperienced in homosexuality."[60]

Agents of the ONI bugged Dooley's phone, stationed officers outside his hotel room door, and followed him throughout the day in the town where he was speaking. Their most intensive efforts were focused on New York City, which had already become, as it would remain, his American base of operations. Agents posted outside his hotel room on February 17 overheard Dooley brag to a companion of his luncheon that day with Francis Cardinal Spellman, Sen. John F. Kennedy and "the senator's brother," presumably Robert. Later, when agents broke into Dooley's Denver hotel room, they found a journal entry describing an earlier luncheon engagement with Spellman and Joseph P. Kennedy, the family patriarch and a booster, with Spellman, of the so-called Vietnam Lobby, an eclectic coalition of Americans devoted to promoting Ngo Dinh Diem's regime at home and abroad.[61]

The report of the navy investigation is unique in providing a glimpse of the private, unguarded Dooley at precisely the moment when the *Reader's Digest* publicity mill was running overtime to package him as a homespun hero. The fascinating multivocal quality of the ONI file merely adds to the welter of conflicting claims regarding Dooley's true nature. Since the ONI was obviously determined to portray Dooley as a pervert, their report must be read with skepticism, but the overall tone confirms the recollections of many of Tom's acquaintances, that for all his charm he was an extraordinarily self-centered individual with a discernible streak of cruelty. He was also naive to the point of self-delusion, perhaps the key to the central Dooley paradox: how could someone so ruthlessly self-promoting have simultaneously been so naive, if not plain self-destructive?[62]

The ONI report includes a transcript of Dooley's part in a telephone conversation with his brother Malcolm from early February 1956. In this barely coherent "narrative," replete with the ONI's penciled corrections on the manuscript, Dooley boasted of six-figure negotiations being conducted with Paramount and RKO for the film rights to *Deliver Us from Evil*, but he added that "I would just as soon run it up their ass," since he had already received $25,000 from *Reader's Digest* and had three television appearances lined up for $5,000 each. He perceptively observed that the film version of his book would probably "have me shacked up with one of my refugees, or they'll have it a sticky, messy doctor hero of Indo-China kind of thing."[63]

Dooley found himself "in hot water" with "Walter Winchell and some of those men" who wanted to scoop his story before the March 22 publication date. "I have to say like the young Virgin 'No, you can't—not yet.'" (In a journal entry purloined by the navy, Dooley less elegantly noted feeling "like an old slut being passed around to be mauled.") In sensing the conflicting interests of the navy, his publishers, gossip columnists, and Charles Pfizer and Company, Tom began to glimpse the commodification of his image and he was bemused, angry, and a bit bewildered, though he never entertained the possibility that he was in over his head. He claimed that a Manhattan publishing executive who was serving as his agent ("a Jew who is so damn clever") would see to it that the demands of his various constituencies were balanced to Dooley's advantage. Yet he was still tempted to say "the hell with the Digest" and his other sponsors, once their checks had arrived. There were "so many eggs in the fire," the "young Virgin" was being pushed to the brink.[64]

The navy was of course concerned less with Dooley's deal-making prowess than his status as a potentially colossal embarrassment. Adm. Arleigh Burke, chief of naval operations, had already praised "the courageous exploits of the young lieutenant" in the foreword to *Deliver Us from Evil*. "It is a story of which the United States Navy is proud," he concluded. A Miami ONI informant claimed that Dooley had told him on January 31 that "the Navy is more interested in the book than he is." Tom also reportedly told the informant that Admiral Burke had "asked" if he could write the foreword, "explaining that as Chief of Naval Operations he had many things to say to the public which could not be said through ordinary mediums." When Dooley agreed, Admiral Burke reportedly "pulled out a prepared manuscript of the preface." Now the navy's greatest public relations asset found himself the subject of a 6-J (navy code for homosexuality) investigation, the purpose of which was to gather enough evidence to prompt a confrontation with Dooley, after which he presumably would resign "for the good of the service" rather than face a court-martial.[65]

The navy's timing was rather curious: Dooley had been suspected of homosexual activity since at least the summer of 1954, but why did the investigation only commence in January 1956, following allegations made by "a confidential informant of unknown reliability"? The leadership may have concluded that Dooley was incapable of discretion and thus represented a scandal waiting to happen. We also cannot entirely discount the possibility that Dooley had had enough of the navy and willingly placed himself in compromising positions. There is a strong hint that he had been tipped off as to the existence of an investigation: ONI agents who opened his mail in Denver on March 8 found letters from a navy friend of Dooley's that discussed an FBI inquiry with Tom as its subject. On March 16 the director of naval intelligence admitted to a district officer that Dooley was probably wise to the investigation; he advised that the source of the leak should be identified before "finalizing plans to interview" Dooley regarding the allegations he faced.[66]

That the navy bungled its investigation was hardly surprising, given their target's repertoire. Dooley was far too complex to play his assigned role in a putatively straightforward inquiry into sexual misconduct. A California ONI agent reported that when Tom was observed at the Alameda Naval Air Station on March 17, "his walk at all times had been very fast and he walked very erect and with a military bearing." But as soon as Dooley arrived at San Francisco International Airport, "subject very strangely developed a severe limp which had definitely not been noticeable prior to his arrival at the airport, and his walk was similar to that of an individual afflicted with a club foot." Dooley had perhaps decided that a civilian airport was a good place to display the "injury" incurred when a Viet Minh officer purportedly slammed a rifle butt into his foot during his "detention" in Haiphong the previous May.[67]

The navy lacked the resources or perhaps the will to keep pace with Dooley's rich stock of story materials. Their agents must have been profoundly befuddled by Tom's assertion—to several civilian audiences—that the only reason he had failed to make the rank of lieutenant commander was because, while at the Sorbonne in the late 1940s, he had led a group that raised funds for Ho Chi Minh. The ONI's Miami informant reported that Dooley had spoken to him in both Polish and Chinese ("subject stated he could speak Chinese as well as he could English"). In early March Tom reported to his mother about a speech before five hundred physicians at Tuckahoe, New York, after which he "drove back [to the Waldorf Astoria] with a psychoanalyst (ugg)." The "psychoanalyst" was actually a "confidential informant of known reliability" who later provided a transcript, from memory, of Dooley's conversation during the ride back to the city. The report is a model of fastidiousness compromised only by the informant's inability to discern that he was being not only seduced but conned by the young physician. After confessing that he had first had "sex in the Navy" at the Great Lakes base in 1944, Dooley told the informant that he had gone to college at the University of Paris during which time he lived with a Frenchman for four years. They had sex three or four times a day at first, "then he began to play around outside and I didn't care because I was, too." Dooley repeated his standard assurance that he refrained from sex on his current speaking tour out of deference to the navy, that in fact "I never carry my civilian clothes on tour and that helps to keep down my sex drive . . . I like the Navy."[68]

In reply to a question from the informant on "the medical aspect of homosexuality," Dooley assured him that "it has nothing whatsoever to do with environment." He cited as proof a famous military leader who "lives and dies for his son" but still found himself the father of "a flower." The informant asked how Dooley knew: "Did you have an affair with him?" "Don't be silly," Dooley replied, "but it takes one to know one." As they neared the Waldorf the informant suddenly told Dooley: "I think I recognize this as a pick-up. But you've got the wrong guy. I am married and have three children." "You son of a bitch," Dooley reportedly responded, "I hope the conversation was entertaining, you son of a bitch, you son of a bitch, you son of a bitch."[69]

Since Dooley's credibility was virtually nonexistent, there was no reason to take reports of his sexual confessions more literally than any of his other fabulations. The ONI was simply another interested party intent on nailing down a definitive Dooley—this time the hero as sex criminal. Tom's vulnerability was certainly evidenced in the conclusion of the "psychoanalyst" informant's report ("the subject's eyes were filled with tears" as he left the car), but he continued to defy expectations: as the ONI investigation neared its conclusion in March 1956, the director warned his agents that "after subject is interrogated he may exhibit suicidal tendencies, whether or not he makes a confession of sexual perversion." There is no record of Dooley's response to the charges (nor are we certain a formal hearing ever took place), but one of his navy roommates, Alden Vaughan—who later became a well-known historian—vividly recalled meeting him on a New York streetcorner in the late spring of 1956. Tom appeared in high spirits and in the middle of their conversation he characteristically darted away to enter a phone booth. When he returned, Tom informed Vaughan that he had decided on the spot to resign from the navy; the purpose of the phone call had been to alert his superiors. Agnes Dooley's account of the resignation similarly stressed its abruptness: "I was waiting for his book to come out, for his change of orders from the Office of the Surgeon General to his residency in orthopedics at Bethesda. Then one evening in February he told me: 'I'm resigning from the Navy, and I'm going to Laos.' It was as simple as that."[70]

A large part of Dooley's appeal was rooted in his ability to convey the refreshing sense that things really were "as simple as that." He saved Vietnam "simply" because it was his job. Later he returned to Southeast Asia "simply" because, as his trusted corpsman Norman Baker was said to have put it, "Aw doc, we just want to help people who ain't got it so good." Dooley's resistance to his own complexity obviously had harmful consequences, but given the circumstances his posture is not difficult to understand. For us the complications are endless. Even the "simple" matter of the timing of Dooley's resignation from the navy is far from clear. Agnes Dooley may "simply" have had her dates confused, since the navy's investigation continued at least until March 14, at which time Tom was still in uniform representing the navy at his lectures. The ONI hoped to conclude its investigation by March 21, at which time they planned to interview Dooley himself and force a confession. The results of that plan are not included in the seven-hundred-page ONI file; Dooley's discharge was dated March 28, 1956.[71]

His character surely housed a surplus of contradictions, and in his "secret life" Dooley was at least as prone to manufacturing multiple selves as he was in his various public guises. But the disparate components at least occasionally met at the borderlands of his soul. An ONI operative on stakeout at the bar of New York's Statler Hotel overheard Dooley ask a young civilian: "Are you a Roman Catholic? Do you go to church often?" Only later, after Dooley became an object of veneration by millions, did he tenuously construct a homoeroticized mysticism which he seems to have shared with some other prominent Catholics. In the short run, however, his spiritual explorations were naturally of no concern to the navy investigators, who sent him unceremoniously packing and presumably were relieved to allow Dooley to slink into the disgrace wrought of his "perversions." They were not the first to underestimate profoundly the resiliency of the Chinese- and Polish-speaking Sorbonne Irishman.[72]

☆ 4 ☆

The Vietnam Lobby

Tom Dooley's navy discharge was dated March 28, 1956. Reviews of *Deliver Us from Evil* began appearing in mid-April, leaving a deluge of praise for the young physician in their wake. Critics lauded in particular the extraordinarily intimate quality of the narrative. A reviewer for the *Des Moines Register* exulted: "You can almost feel Dr. Dooley sobbing with frustration as he writes about seven children whose eardrums were pierced with bamboo slivers because they attended a class in religion." Dooley's favorite review appeared in the *New Yorker*, whose readership spanned the quickly diminishing gulf in sophistication between his midwestern fox-hunt pedigree and a new role as the toast of Manhattan. That august publication praised *Deliver Us from Evil* as "a moving poem of the human spirit victorious."[1]

April 22 found Dooley at the center of a now customary commotion, his base of operations a table with a telephone at the Waldorf Astoria's Peacock Alley lounge. Martha MacGregor of the *New York Post* neatly captured the scene:

> Dr. Dooley was talking rapidly—he seems to do everything rapidly—over the telephone. I caught the words "generosity . . . capitalist America," and then, with the enthusiasm of the propagandist, "It's true!"
> "I can give you until five o'clock," he told me, hanging up. "I'm speaking to the Overseas Press Club tonight. Afterwards I'm going to the warehouse to

autograph 1,000 copies of my book. I have a radio show in the morning." He reeled off a list of engagements. His publicity representative (Dr. Dooley hardly seems to need one) ordered a drink for me and the waiter handed the doctor the telephone. "I don't think I can, Joe," he said. "Overseas Press Club . . . Admiral Byrd Dinner . . . the Surgeon General . . . Knights of Columbus . . . Dutch Treat . . . the National Security Council."[2]

Dooley had honed to perfection the role of wisecracking regular guy first encouraged in his contacts with William Lederer. William Hogan of the *San Francisco Chronicle* called him "a kind of 'Mr. Roberts' of the medical world rather than a saint in the classic tradition," though Hogan would have done even better to liken Dooley to Ensign Pulver, the free-spirited character from Thomas Heggen's best-selling 1946 novel, *Mr. Roberts*. A columnist for the *San Diego Union* called Dooley a "cocky, happy-go-lucky, so-what guy on the surface" whose story "restores your faith in your fellowman, and in the wonderful things individual initiative can accomplish when the need is great."[3]

Lost amid the ballyhoo generated by the publication of *Deliver Us from Evil* was a counternarrative provided by the American Catholic press. Where secular journalists focused on Dooley's breezy personality, Catholic writers tellingly yoked his story of the Vietnam refugee operation to the core of their spiritual identity, in anticipation of tribulations yet to come. In a clerical journal, the *American Ecclesiastical Review,* Father James A. Murphy celebrated *Deliver Us from Evil* for its firsthand account of "the terrible struggle raging between Communism and Christianity . . . the author paints the portrait of Christ crucified in Indo-China. Before the reader's eyes the members of Christ's Mystical Body are called up, here in huddled masses, there in wretched loneliness." Writing in the Carmelite publication *Spiritual Life,* Sister Mary Francille reported that "Doctor Dooley's *Deliver Us From Evil* shocks us into the reality of the application of the doctrine of the Mystical Body as we learn of the Christlike ministrations of American sailors to the persecuted Vietnamese." Following a speech by Dooley at Holy Cross College on April 14, Father William A. Donaghy, the president of the Jesuit school, urged doctors and dentists everywhere to "take care of the Mystical Body of Christ, which is being lacerated all over the world." Turning to Dooley, Father Donaghy proclaimed: "He is my speech. Go thou and do likewise."[4]

Dooley always deflected his plethora of contradictions with a manic industriousness, as though the frenetic pursuit of new challenges prevented the demons from gaining on him. He probably never paused to consider the magnitude of the role his Catholic followers envisioned for him. But little was lost on his postsectarian handlers who, as part of a far-flung campaign to make the world safe for Madison Avenue humanitarianism, conjured a vision of Tom Dooley, jungle doctor. Dooley was in a state of disgrace—at least insofar as the military was concerned—and not likely to resist a flattering offer from professional image-makers. Better still, he was just the kind of Irishman and just the kind of Catholic required to neutralize a brooding mass of Americans who still seethed over the recent downfall of Joe McCarthy—no small order, since the fate of American liberal internationalism hung in the balance.

The rehabilitation of Tom Dooley's image was launched, fittingly, at the University of Notre Dame, where he spoke before more than two thousand students and faculty on April 13, 1956. The *South Bend Tribune* reported the next day that the "young, modern day Dr. Livingstone" had just sold the film rights to *Deliver Us from Evil* to actor Kirk Douglas, who planned to appear as Dooley in a film to be made by Douglas's own production company. Dooley also told his Notre Dame audience that he now planned to return to Southeast Asia to work as "a doctor and missionary on Americanism" in Laos.[5]

Dooley showed remarkable poise at Notre Dame and during the ensuing promotional tour on behalf of his new mission, which had begun just days after the director of naval intelligence warned agents their prey might exhibit suicidal behavior when confronted with evidence of his sexual deviance. There was ample confusion over Dooley's new role in civilian life. The Reverend James E. Norton, vice president for student affairs at Notre Dame, wrote to U.S. Navy Surgeon General Bartholomew W. Hogan on April 23: "It was my pleasure to introduce Dr. Dooley. He wanted me to make it clear that the reason why he was out of uniform was that he wanted to return to Laos in Indo-China to continue his work and that he could return only as a civilian doctor. He gave the impression that he regretted very much having to leave active duty and that he plans to return to uniform in the future."[6]

In his second book, *The Edge of Tomorrow* (1958), Dooley offered a facile cover story for his sudden shift to a civilian vocation. He described a February 1956 dinner with Vietnamese, Cambodian, and Lao officials in Washington during which he had expressed an interest in returning to Southeast Asia; the evening reportedly ended with the Lao ambassador, Ourot Souvannavong, proclaiming, "Dr. Dooley . . . my country would be honored to receive your mission. Will you come to see me at the Embassy in the morning?" Judging from his correspondence, Dooley did not know how to spell *Laos* prior to April 1956. His bugged telephone conversations and purloined mail through March of that year confirmed his interests in Hollywood deal-making and Manhattan nightlife; nowhere is there even a hint of his recognition that a new future was being prepared for him.[7]

The decision to establish a mission in Laos could not possibly have been Dooley's. It could have been made for him, however, by officials of the International Rescue Committee (IRC) who were also key operatives of the notorious Vietnam Lobby, a coalition of Americans with a deep investment in Ngo Dinh Diem's regime who now sought to widen their sphere of influence throughout Southeast Asia. Prior to any evaluation of Dooley's subsequent work in Laos, we must take an excursion into the deep thickets of cold war cultural politics, focusing along the way on the terrain where an emerging American "consensus" was threatened by ethnoreligious strife among white, English-speaking males.

After decades of often ill-informed speculation as to the nature, aims, and very existence of a centralized Vietnam Lobby, historian Joseph G. Morgan's exhaustively detailed study of that group's holding company—the American Friends of Vietnam (AFV)—left little room for doubt that the key figures at the International Rescue Committee: renaissance man–entrepreneur Leo Cherne, patrician-diplomat Angier Biddle Duke, émigré socialist Joseph Buttinger, and publicist Harold Oram effectively constructed an interlocking directorate of pro-Diem activities fronted by the AFV. While the Vietnam Lobby's efficacy is certainly a matter for debate, its role in rehabilitating Dr. Tom Dooley is less difficult to establish.[8]

Leo Cherne was the multimillionaire cofounder of the Research Institute of America (RIA), later dubbed the "CIA for businessmen"; the firm had "provided political and economic information and analyses to America's business, labor and public opinion makers since the mid-Thirties." Roberta Ostroff, the biographer of Dickey Chapelle (a female combat reporter who endured a memorable stint working for the RIA), noted that the firm's "great success hinged on its far-reaching intelligence-gathering capabilities, making it profoundly important—before there was an OSS or a CIA—for predicting the political climates of unstable countries." A *Saturday Evening Post* profile of Cherne and RIA cofounder Carl Hovgard noted that among the institute's "most profitable commodities is prophecy and its batting average has been high."[9]

Leo Cherne has been described as "a flamboyant, brilliant man of action, a product of New York City's 'dead end,' a former poolshark, longshoreman, a pilot, a doer," and was "hailed as a 'Renaissance man' by the *Reader's Digest.*" Cherne was also a sculptor specializing in busts of prominent world figures: among his subjects was Dr. Albert Schweitzer, a personal hero whose example would inspire the creation of an American jungle doctor. In the spring of 1939 Cherne grilled a protégé, William J. Casey: "How do you take a country like ours, stuck in a depression, and convert it into an arsenal? . . . This is an opportunity for the Institute." Cherne and Casey, attorneys both, quickly produced "a thick, squat volume," *The Business and Defense Coordinator,* in which they explained that "war has become a conflict of economics in which financial and material resources are the chief weapons." In the institute's fall 1941 newsletter, they predicted that the United States "is unlikely to get involved in the war in Europe until a triggering event occurs in the Pacific." In the aftermath of their accurate if chilling prediction, wrote Casey's biographer, "the Institute's reputation soared."[10]

A New Deal liberal as well as an entrepreneur of ideas and information, Cherne became deeply involved in the work of the International Rescue Committee in the early 1950s, to a degree that Roberta Ostroff could describe the IRC as the "other arm" of the Research Institute of America. The IRC, the product of a merger between rival leftists groups who made up part of the byzantine revolutionary socialist movement of the 1930s, was descended from the first organized efforts by American socialists and social democrats to rescue European intellectuals from fascism. According to the socialist scholar Eric Chester, the IRC "can only be understood within the context set by segments of the Revolutionary Left in Germany, Austria, and the United States. Small organizations of revolutionary cadre sought to pursue a strategy far more militant than that of the mass social democratic parties, while remaining independent of the erratic path followed by the Communist International and its member parties." Joseph Buttinger had belonged to a "tiny Leninist sect" in addition to leading the Austrian Revolutionary Socialists in the late 1930s. Buttinger married an American heiress, Muriel Gardiner, and moved to the United States in 1940, where he exerted his "enormous moral authority" as an international socialist leader over the Emergency Rescue Committee, an antifascist relief organization.[11]

Buttinger and a fellow émigré, Karl Frank, soon convinced Eleanor Roosevelt to urge her husband to "expedite the granting of visas to antifascist political refugees." According to Chester, "the government looked sympathetically toward refugees coming from socialist organizations whose leaders had already indicated their willingness to cooperate with government agencies in operations both overt and covert . . . most of these recruits soon adapted their politics to the liberal mainstream." In 1942 the IRC merged with the International Relief Association, a group associated with the more conservative labor-movement socialism of David Dubinsky and Jay Lovestone, although their influence in the organization never rivaled that of Joseph Buttinger. By the early 1950s the International Rescue Committee had become a fixture in the American liberal anticommunist firmament, enjoying a role akin to that of European socialists often utilized by the CIA because, as a former agency operative recalled in 1967, they were "the very people whom many Americans thought no better than Communists—[but who] were the only people who gave a damn about fighting Communism." While the IRC was inevitably condemned by New Left critics for "selling out" to American cold war interests, leaders of the IRC did not necessarily perceive a contradiction in the desire to promote democratic socialism abroad while opening new markets for their humanitarian and informational services.[12]

Leo Cherne assumed the chairmanship of the IRC in 1953, in the wake of vitriolic attacks on the group by Vadim Makaroff, a right-wing Russian émigré who "cultivated an extensive network of contacts within ultrareactionary and anti-Semitic political circles." Makaroff convinced such elite supporters of the IRC as Vincent Astor, "heir to one of the nation's largest fortunes," that the organization was a "Marxist-front outfit." "Facing imminent dissolution," the IRC increasingly depended upon Leo Cherne to build bridges to the intelligence community and to members of traditionally conservative constituencies, including American Catholics (Gen. William "Wild Bill" Donovan, former OSS director and a notable Catholic, fulfilled both categories in his capacity as an IRC board member).[13]

Cherne travelled to South Vietnam in the spring of 1954, seeking a role for his organization with the small group of Vietnamese intellectuals who had migrated from the North. Despite his initial concern that Ngo Dinh Diem was an "ascetic" who had assumed power "without a base of popular support in South Vietnam," Cherne quickly became a proponent of American backing for the fledgling regime. He established contacts with key representatives of the foreign aid program and upon his return to New York won approval from the IRC board for an ambitious new program in Vietnam. In October 1954, Joseph Buttinger became the IRC's field representative in Saigon, where Edward G. Lansdale "introduced him to Diem" and he quickly became part of the ruler's "inner circle." He wrote numerous magazine articles on Diem's behalf and urged others to do likewise. Late in 1954 Buttinger "negotiated a memorandum of agreement with a key CIA officer, Samuel Adams, detailing the IRC role in the overall Vietnam program." Adams operated with cover provided by the Foreign Operations Administration, which recognized, with the CIA, that it was "inadvisable for U.S. government agencies to undertake certain projects which a voluntary agency need not hesitate to undertake."[14]

In the spring of 1955, as Ngo Dinh Diem's fate hung in the balance, Joseph Buttinger decided to "form a private organization supporting the Diem regime, the American Friends of Vietnam." According to Joseph Morgan, the most judicious student of the organization, Buttinger authorized publicist

Harold Oram in April of that year to establish the AFV: membership appeals were promptly sent to prominent Americans "under the signature of Angier Biddle Duke," a wealthy patrician and gentleman diplomat who had recently agreed to serve as the president of the IRC. Harold Oram was a socialist who had "won his spurs raising support for the Loyalists in the Spanish Civil War." Oram's successful Madison Avenue firm provided public relations and fund-raising services for a variety of causes to which he was sympathetic, including Planned Parenthood, the American Civil Liberties Union, and the NAACP Legal Defense Fund. Joseph Buttinger flatly informed Oram in late 1954 that Diem was committed to fostering a postcolonial, pro-Western democratic socialist regime in South Vietnam.[15]

"At the same time that he organized the AFV," Morgan noted, "Harold Oram signed a contract with the Diem regime designating him as the government's public relations representative in the United States." Morgan suggested that Leo Cherne had first recommended Oram's firm to Diem in late 1954. Cherne, Duke, Oram, and Buttinger, along with Wesley Fishel of Michigan State University, were the key players at the AFV throughout the remainder of the 1950s. Cherne and Duke, with public relations assistance from Oram and, quite likely, urging from Edward G. Lansdale, also comprised the inner circle of a bold new campaign in Laos, built around a young and charismatic author-physician.[16]

Historians have been properly skeptical regarding the extent of the Vietnam Lobby's actual influence over U.S. policies in Southeast Asia in the 1950s and early 1960s. There is no doubt, however, that Cherne, Duke, and Oram constituted the driving force behind Tom Dooley's stunning metamorphosis from potential sex criminal to secular saint. To their great relief he proved a quick study. Just over three weeks after his outster from the service Dooley was asked by a reporter: "Are you still in the Navy?" "No," he replied, "but next September under the auspices of the International Rescue Committee I'm returning for six months to Laos. . . . Walt Disney has given me a little movie projector that runs on a battery. We're going to take lots of white sailor hats, baseballs, ball-point pens, Sears Roebuck catalogs, yes, Sears Roebuck catalogs, to show these people a little bit of what America is like."[17]

Dooley's relationship with the Vietnam Lobby was highly anomalous despite the starring role he played in what was clearly their most successful public relations coup. As a handsome talking head he stood apart from the sophisticates and intellectuals whose interests he represented, if often precariously. Gentlemen of the establishment were not ordinarily inclined to endanger the nonprofit status of their lives' works though sponsorship of a notorious loose cannon who not only scoffed at their requests for fiscal accountability, but charged his expenditures on rough trade to a Waldorf Astoria tab he demanded the IRC assume. Dooley was a sufficiently rare asset to justify extraordinary tolerance of his antics, yet he remained blissfully unaware that if not for his appeal to American Catholics, he would have been summarily consigned to obscurity.[18]

Tom Dooley's ties to the Vietnam Lobby were first "exposed" in the radical Catholic press several years after his death. The journalists Robert Scheer and Warren Hinckle coined the term *Vietnam Lobby* in a July 1965 *Ramparts* article purporting to uncover the activities of "a small and enthusiastic group of people . . . who maneuvered the Eisenhower administration and the American press into supporting the rootless, unpopular and hopeless regime of a despot and believed it actually was all an exercise in democracy." Scheer and Hinckle described Dooley as a "naive, well-meaning" publicist and pawn of the lobby whose membership included, in addition to Lansdale, Cherne, Oram, and Duke, such well-known Catholics as Sen. Mike Mansfield, Joseph P. Kennedy, his son John, then a Massachusetts junior senator, and their family friend Francis Cardinal Spellman of New York.[19]

It was only fitting that Dooley's defrocking originate in a publication founded as an independent journal of Catholic opinion. The metamorphosis of *Ramparts* into a radical sheet reflected the convulsive aftershocks of the Second Vatican Council (1962–65), whose moment of high promise quickly yielded to the furies. Warren Hinckle assumed command of *Ramparts* in 1964 upon the bankruptcy of its founder, a supposedly wealthy Catholic convert named Ed Keating who had launched the magazine just three years earlier. Hinckle—a 1960 graduate of the Jesuits' University of San Francisco—successfully transformed *Ramparts* "into something more than the Catholic penny dreadful that it was." In a 1974 memoir, Hinckle confessed that his interest in exposing the Vietnam Lobby "began, as with most baptisms of fire at the paper, in an earnest attempt to hang something on the Catholic Church. We set out looking to lay some of the blame for Vietnam at the silken slippers of the Pope; we succeeded only in implicating Cardinal Spellman."[20]

Scheer and Hinckle's pioneering work was indeed marred by their overreliance on New Left folklore concerning the Church's role in bolstering the Diem regime. In "Hang Down Your Head Tom Dooley," yet another *Ramparts* exposé, Scheer assailed "the Tom Dooley–Cardinal Spellman type of myth" about the nature of the Vietnam conflict, and even concluded: "If the war continues, may it not one day be called Cardinal Spellman's final solution to the Vietnam question?" Scheer and Hinckle recognized that Dooley was a pawn of the Vietnam Lobby, but in failing to separate his role from the exaggerated influence of Cardinal Spellman they overlooked the doctor's real significance as a new type of American Catholic, and they underestimated the subtlety of the Vietnam Lobby's image-making machinery. While Dooley's religiosity was central to his appeal, Spellman—the embodiment of sectarian politics—remained the last Catholic that Diem's publicists wanted near their client.[21]

Leo Cherne enjoyed showing visitors to his office at the IRC's Manhattan headquarters a copy of the *Ramparts* article linking him to Spellman as coconspirators in the Vietnam Lobby. Cherne would then persuasively and with good humor insist that he had met Spellman but once in his life. Less convincing was Cherne's recollection of the origins of his relationship with Dr. Tom Dooley. In 1990 he claimed that the IRC grew rather suddenly interested in sponsoring a Dooley mission to Laos because of the great concern shown toward the region by IRC president Angier Biddle Duke. Cherne recalled that he may have first met Dooley in the hectic days when Operation Laos was being constructed, on board a vessel Cherne kept at the Seventy-ninth Street yacht basin. When asked how the mission was arranged so quickly, he asserted that there were fewer bureaucratic obstacles at the time to impede voluntary international aid programs sponsored by groups like the IRC. As Marvin Liebman, who worked on the IRC account for the Oram firm, recalled of the sudden creation in 1952 of a related advocacy group, Aid Refugee Chinese Intellectuals: "Events moved with a speed that caught me by surprise. Looking back, I see that it was government support, including that from the CIA, that helped things move along at such a rapid pace."[22]

In an April 1961 interview taped by Jane Miller of the *Reader's Digest*, Cherne and IRC executive director Richard Salzmann asserted that they had been in touch with Dooley since November 1954, after Tom reportedly contacted the IRC by letter, alerting the group of his refugee work and expressing a desire to go beyond his navy duties to help the IRC in the fight against communism. In November 1955, Dooley told a reporter from the *Honolulu Star-Bulletin* that the IRC had sent "practically a whole shipload" of clothes to Haiphong the previous year, in response to his request. Following the creation of Operation Laos, however, Dooley never again discussed the genesis of his relationship with the IRC.[23]

The IRC had shifted its focus from antifascist to anticommunist rescue operations after World War II: this new orientation certainly meshed with Dooley's limited ideological aims, but otherwise Cherne and Salzmann shared nothing in common with the young naval officer. In their unpublished interview with Jane Miller, they claimed that by the summer of 1955 the framework of a Dooley-IRC mission to Laos was squarely in place, though Tom's vision was clearly fixed at the time on advancement through the ranks of the Navy Medical Corps. In a slightly puzzled tone, Miller asked Cherne and Salzmann whether Dooley was identified as being with the IRC by 1955, to which they replied, "absolutely."[24]

At the time of that interview, Dooley had been dead for ten weeks. Cherne claimed that Tom had grown anxious in his last days for an accurate historical account of his work, a task Cherne now solemnly assumed. The absence of Dooley's own voice from this canned version of history being served up in his honor was grimly fitting, since during his career as a "compromised" pawn of others' designs, the glib, fast-talking Irishman was never able to stand back and reflect on the unlikely circumstances of his election to stardom.

The IRC had never involved itself with the internal affairs of another nation, nor had it ever supported medical activities abroad. There was no precedent for the group's sponsorship of Dooley's Operation Laos. There was even strong resistance to Dooley from within the organization itself. Claiborne Pell, the IRC's chief Washington representative, wrote to Leo Cherne in June 1956 to report that an American ambassador to a Far Eastern country had warned him that Dooley's reputation in the region was at great variance with the impression given in his *Reader's Digest* article. Pell leveled what was to become a familiar charge—that Dooley was primarily a publicity hound—and expressed the fear that Tom might damage the reputation of the IRC. Angier Biddle Duke, for his part, was fully aware of the reasons for Dooley's navy discharge: he recalled phoning Admiral Burke and being assured that although the navy "had had a problem" with Dooley, the IRC could expect to experience no such problems in the future! Before Dooley even left the United States for Asia in August, Duke had to warn Tom that his continued fiscal if not personal irresponsibility could cost the IRC its tax-exempt status. Duke implored him to keep careful records and receipts, only to be told by Dooley that such concerns were so much "chickenshit" as far as he was concerned.[25]

There are several plausible explanations for the IRC's willingness to underwrite Operation Laos. Duke believed that Dooley was a "neo-genius" whose charismatic zeal, so reminiscent of Joan of Arc, might ignite the spark of genuine democracy in Southeast Asia. We must never discount the intensity of the "messianic liberalism" that motivated many of the Vietnam Lobby's key operatives, especially Edward G. Lansdale, and provided the ideological foundation of Dooley's subsequent work. Few Americans in 1954, or 1956, or even 1960 could have predicted the horrors to result from the aggressive campaign of "nation-building" supported by the bipartisan consensus underlying American politics in the cold war. At the same time, few historians, understandably, have been able to fully contextualize the leftist-liberal orientation of some of Diem's most vociferous American supporters, at least not without betraying the special disdain that New Left intellectuals showered on their forebears beginning in the mid-1960s. Yet Diem was in fact lionized, in some circles at least, as a beacon of noncommunist Left internationalism in the 1950s.[26]

A related theory would focus on the well-documented role of the Central Intelligence Agency in supporting "liberal" international organizations such as the IRC in the 1950s. In May 1953 CIA director Allen Dulles responded to Cherne's lobbying efforts on behalf of a closer working relationship between the agency and the IRC. Dulles was "quite familiar" with Cherne's work, having discussed it with IRC board members, including Cherne's protégé Bill Casey. Dulles cautioned Cherne: "I have felt that the work of your committee, while of deep interest and concern to us, was somewhat outside of the scope of our proper activities." Dulles did, however, leave open the possibility of a meeting with Cherne, should he "feel that a conference would be useful." Shortly after Leo Cherne was appointed by President Gerald Ford to the Foreign Intelligence Advisory Board in 1976, the *New York Times* reported that the IRC had received funds from two foundations identified in 1967 as "conduits" for CIA financing of "a number of domestic organizations." Cherne denied any knowledge of CIA involvement in the group he had chaired since 1953. William C. Gibbons, the author of a highly judicious study of the U.S. government and the Vietnam War (sponsored by the Senate Committee on Foreign Relations) stated that the IRC "worked very closely with the U.S. Government, particularly its President, Leo Cherne."[27]

Cherne's legendary persistence must have been rewarded in the case of his entreaties to Dulles, for in 1955 the IRC launched a major fundraising effort with the United States Junior Chamber of Commerce in support of Operation Brotherhood, a CIA program devised in 1954 by Edward G. Lansdale in collaboration with his close associate, Manila businessman Oscar Arellano (in 1956 Tom Dooley was named one of the Ten Most Outstanding Young Men in America by the Jaycees, an award garnered some years earlier by his newfound mentor, Leo Cherne). Operation Brotherhood sent Filipino physicians, nurses, and dentists to South Vietnam to offer medical and political support to the Diem regime ("America gave democracy to the Filipinos," Arellano often intoned in a classic Lansdale cadence: "Now we will give it to Asia"). Tom Dooley was sufficiently guileless, or ignorant, to write breezily in 1958 that the "whole idea" for Operation Laos was "borrowed" from Operation Brotherhood.[28]

"And then we had Operation Brotherhood," Lansdale told Congressional Research Service interviewers in 1983, "Philippine medical teams in Vietnam, so they were going up to Laos, so I got them in to help Dooley get started with his medical work in Laos. So, they all worked together and did it very well, but his activities were not backed at all by CIA." Since Lansdale never identified *himself* as having worked for the CIA, his denial of the agency's involvement with Dooley's work is hardly surprising.[29]

The exact order of events and decisions that resulted in Dooley's charge to provide medical aid to people "who ain't got it so good" will most likely never be recovered. But there was only one truly compelling reason for the Vietnam Lobby to send Dooley to Laos: as a nonideological Catholic, he could fulfill the role created during his ingenue days in Vietnam in late 1954. He could remind America's most militant anticommunists that the struggle in Southeast Asia did not end with Diem's ascendance; more critically, he could provide the lobby with a human buffer against those who might view its central figures—not entirely without cause—as leftist entrepreneurs bent on expanding their markets abroad in the immediate post-McCarthy era. Lansdale, later demonized as a cunning imperialist, fits neatly into this scenario, since he expressed his great disdain for McCarthy and his followers to at least one key publicist of the Vietnam Lobby. As a liberal man of action, he was a hero of the noncommunist Left in the 1950s.[30]

To understand Tom Dooley as a product of the McCarthy era requires an imaginative leap into a world strikingly unlike the United States in the 1990s. The most pronounced cultural tensions in America divided Catholics from "Protestants and Others Americans United for the Separation of Church and State," as the neonativist group fueled by the best-selling works of Paul Blanshard was known (Blanshard was a New England freethinker and eugenics enthusiast, author of such works as *American Freedom and Catholic Power*). The potency of Catholic anticommunism infuriated adherents of a wide variety of liberal and leftist religious and political denominations. The *Brooklyn Tablet,* a militant organ not unrepresentative of conservative Catholicism, proclaimed in June 1950: "The time for being naive about the substance of the McCarthy charges is long past. The presence of close to a hundred perverts in the State Department—even though [Alger] Hiss has been forced out and convicted . . . justify [sic] a complete and thorough search for further evidences of the Communist conspiracy within the departments of our government. That is the avowed objective of Senator McCarthy's efforts." McCarthy was indeed a devout Catholic but he was an even more devoted political opportunist with nary a hint of interest in Catholic social thought, at least initially. While historians have debated the extent of his actual influence over Catholic voters nationwide, there is no question that he was widely believed at the time—to the dismay of liberal Catholics—to enjoy the full blessing and encouragement of the American Church.[31]

Leo Cherne had debated McCarthy twice: on the radio in 1947 (before the senator had turned his anticommunism into a crusade) and with greater fanfare in 1952 during a raucous and singularly unenlightening episode of the television panel show "The Author Meets the Critics." As a representative of the liberal cold war establishment, Cherne sought to delegitimize McCarthy's means, rather than his ends, by accusing him of leveling "thinly veiled charges of treason" against Dwight D. Eisenhower in his book, *Retreat from Victory.* As a staunch product of the New Deal and a wealthy businessman, Cherne enjoyed the strongest establishment credentials of anyone at the IRC other than Angier Biddle Duke; like other liberals of the period he often found himself in the potentially awkward position of launching preemptive strikes against the enemies of his Left-leaning colleagues. It was a thin line to tread, requiring patience as well as fortitude.[32]

For Cherne the stakes were high: the son of a socialist printer, his greatest ideological affinity was perhaps with New York's Liberal Party, "the political arm of two major New York labor unions," the International Ladies' Garment Workers Union (ILGWU) and the Amalgamated Hatters Union. While the Liberal Party was a product of the anticommunist socialism of the ILGWU, publicist Marvin Liebman—who worked briefly on Harold Oram's account with the Liberals—later claimed that the party was in fact "only a bit to the right of the communist-controlled American Labor Party." In 1951 Leo Cherne enthusiastically supported Rudolph Halley, the Liberal candidate for president of the New York City Council and, according to Liebman, the Liberal Party's best hope to one day take "the State House in Albany and ultimately the White House." But Cherne's partisan political agenda was less urgent, in the mid-1950s, than the threat of a renewed outbreak of the irrational passions that had overflowed in the McCarthy era. On William F. Buckley's "Firing Line" program in 1968, Cherne claimed that he had opposed McCarthy initially because the senator "was supported by communists." While this initially appeared to be a bizarre charge, it was consistent with Cherne's experience as an eyewitness to the kind of internecine strife on the Left that had always proved almost perversely counterproductive. From the perspective of liberal anticommunism, the problem with McCarthy was not his ideology so much as the specter of social disorder and even chaos his irrational approach had raised.[33]

Leo Cherne was a realist with good reason for concern over the ideological baggage of key personnel at the IRC. Cold-war liberal anticommunists sought a rational political culture in which ex-radicals and even former communists could earn legitimacy by their deeds. When Marvin Liebman was recommended to Oram for employment in 1951, Liebman "did not lie about my past membership in the Communist party. Impressed that I had confided in him, Oram said that my communist past did not matter so long as I didn't consider myself a Stalinist any longer."[34]

The leftists and liberals of the International Rescue Committee fulfilled a role advocated by sociologist Seymour Martin Lipset in his 1960 work, *Political Man*. Lipset argued that "the leftist intellectual, the trade union leader, and the socialist politician" had a useful role to play abroad, working "with non-Communist revolutionaries in the Orient and Africa." Lipset assumed, as the British author Godfrey Hodgson has noted, that such individuals accepted the fact "that serious ideological controversies have ended at home." Yet Lipset readily acknowledged that Western leftists, "by virtue of the fact that they still represent the tradition of socialism and equalitarianism within their own countries . . . can find an audience among the leaders of the non-Communist left in those nations were socialism and trade unionism cannot be conservative or even gradualist."[35]

Lipset was a product of the legendary Alcove One of the City College of New York lunchroom where, in the 1930s, young Trotskyites did verbal battle with the communists of Alcove Two. Like many of his fellow New York intellectuals, Lipset confirmed his born-again "centrism" in the 1950s by joining the Congress for Cultural Freedom (CCF), a group of elite liberal anticommunists who symbolized—in the minds of younger 1960s radicals like Christopher Lasch—all that was corrupt about cold war culture in America, especially after the CIA's funding of the group was disclosed in 1966. It is somewhat surprising that the CCF has received far greater scrutiny from historians as a bastion of the noncommunist Left than has the International Rescue Committee, given the latter group's socialist leanings and its far greater engagement with U.S. foreign policy, particularly toward Southeast Asia.[36]

Yet from the initial *Ramparts* exposé of the Vietnam Lobby in 1965 to the appearance in 1992 of Joseph G. Morgan's study of the American Friends of Vietnam, the activities of the IRC were largely overlooked by scholars and critics. It was generally taken for granted by historians that ex-radicals and socialists like Joseph Buttinger were mere accomplices to U.S. imperialism. The one notable exception was Hilaire du Berrier's *Background to Betrayal,* an intermittently lucid critique of the Vietnam Lobby from the so-called lunatic fringe of the Right. Du Berrier argued that the IRC was at the heart of a conspiracy to turn Vietnam over to the Reds. In reality, the agents of the IRC, like most cold war leftists, were simply performing a highly characteristic function of postwar Americanism, in applying to "developing nations" what the cultural historian Christopher Shannon has called "a single, universal standard of freedom as self-determination and autonomy from nonconsensual social relations." Joseph Buttinger's scornful attitude toward

American mass culture and its "conformism" was quite common in the 1950s, but no less popular was his conviction that the United States bore the ultimate responsibility in universalizing a view of culture itself, in Shannon's words, "as relative and therefore open to revision in the service of consciously chosen ends."[37]

Since this dominant ideology placed a great premium on such presumably universal values as tolerance and pluralism, it rewarded the flexibility demonstrated by IRC operatives in the field. Buttinger longed for the triumph of democratic socialism in South Vietnam but his agency had recently shifted its focus from antifascism to anticommunism; in the American political culture of the early 1950s appeals to the finer distinctions within leftist politics were now rendered superfluous. Yet in Vietnam, Ngo Dinh Diem's premodern Catholicism became the object of the Vietnam Lobby's most intensive cultural work. If Diem would not become a social democrat, his image could at least be reshaped into that of an American Catholic democrat, like Thomas A. Dooley or the young Massachusetts senator John F. Kennedy, a charter member of the American Friends of Vietnam. Buttinger knew that Diem's much-discussed "Third Force" ideology owed little to traditional socialist thought; it was more accurately an amalgam of the politicized mysticism associated with the French Catholic philosopher Emmanuel Mounier and the group centered around the journal *Esprit*. Diem was purportedly an ardent exponent of Mounier's thought, which rejected both capitalism and communism on behalf of a vision of the human person and a beloved community. Buttinger and the IRC worked to construct an image of Diem that muted the zealotry of his faith; they promoted him instead as a spiritual democrat in the tradition of America's civil religion.

Though it is doubtful that either Diem or his American handlers had kept pace with the evolution of Emmanuel Mounier's thought, the Frenchman had turned sharply to the left between the end of World War II and his untimely death in 1950. In 1963 Bernard Fall noted the irony that "today European personalism is espoused by 'left-wing' Catholics who advocate socialization of industry, a 'third force' policy that Americans usually term 'neutralism,' and a measure of East-West understanding or cooperation that would be tantamount to outright abandonment of the Western system of military alliances." Yet even if this variant of Catholic social thought found favor among socialists, it bore no resemblance to the guiding philosophy of the Diem regime. It was Diem's brother Nhu who truly claimed the mantle of personalism, but he was widely despised by the Americans in Vietnam and shared little in any event with the outlook of the later Mounier. Much too late Buttinger conceded, in quoting Fall, that Diem was "a spiritual son of a fiercely aggressive and militant faith rather than of the easygoing and tolerant approach of Gallic Catholicism." In 1963 Fall wrote: "In light of his concept of divinely appointed leadership, it should hardly be surprising that any Madison Avenue attempt to make a baby-kissing popular leader out of Diem would fail." But since few Americans involved with Vietnam in the 1950s were much troubled by local realities, it seemed a simple matter of public relations to anoint Diem a modern, pluralist Catholic Democrat, while keeping Spellman and other prelates just far enough away to assuage suspicions in the heartland as well as the Ivy League.[38]

Harold Oram tended Diem's image with a $3,000 monthly retainer from the South Vietnamese government, which naturally owed its continuing existence to the taxpayers of the United States. As the publicist for the IRC and the creator of the American Friends of Vietnam, Oram used his firm as the clearinghouse for the interlocking directorate of interests making up the Vietnam Lobby. As 1955 wore on, Oram and the IRC leadership faced a new challenge: not being in the habit of employing practicing Catholics, they suddenly needed to find one to instill confidence in their most important client. In 1956 Tom Dooley practically fell into their laps, but he was never meant to work behind the scenes. Oram initially called instead on a young Harvard graduate named Peter White.[39]

After Diem assumed power in 1954, Peter White recalled that he himself "helped (a lot, I think) getting [Diem] to hire Harold Oram to represent him, and I worked on the account until 1957." White met Tom Dooley only once, but his diligent work for the Vietnam Lobby foreshadowed Dooley's more theatrical contributions in the years to come. White's job was to steer Diem toward the right kind of American Catholics: personalists, internationalists, representatives of the burgeoning spiritual avant-garde, and other "vocal opponents of Senator Joe McCarthy, for whom Cardinal Spellman and powerful Catholics were cheerleaders." White sought "strong contacts" for Diem with all those "whose clout was unimpaired by McCarthy's downfall." He had met Diem in 1950 while doing some freelance work on the Oram firm's account with the Great Books program, whose cofounder, Robert Benton, had been an Oram client as a candidate for the United States Senate from Connecticut. Benton permitted White to use his New York office; there White was introduced to Diem by a Belgian Jesuit missionary, Emmanuel Jacques. Diem was apparently quite impressed with the appointments of the office and suffered from an exaggerated appraisal of Peter White's clout with American media and political elites: when he assumed control in Saigon in 1954 he quickly turned to White for counsel, saying he needed him badly.[40]

Peter White was a grandson of the renowned architect Stanford White. Like many prominent American Catholics of the mid-twentieth century, he came from a convert family with impeccable social credentials. After serving as a lieutenant colonel in World War II, White had returned home to Long Island to begin an eclectic and often precarious career, while he and his wife Jehannie became parents to eleven children. The Whites participated in the fervent Catholic intellectual revival of the postwar years, numbering among their friends the writers Robert and Sally Fitzgerald and Edward Rice, a close friend of the celebrated Trappist monk Thomas Merton and the founding editor of *Jubilee*, a handsome Catholic monthly in which White planted several articles on Diem's behalf.[41]

At a 1950 dinner in Diem's honor in New York City, Peter White was approached by an editor of the radically Catholic *Integrity* magazine who, knowing of his work in public relations, asked if he would be willing to promote Diem as "a Catholic spokesman for the great world outside" (outside, that is, the militantly conservative confines of the New York archdiocese). White believed that the editor in question was Carol Jackson, *Integrity's* cofounder, though she questioned this account. White recalled quite vividly, however, that when Father Emmanuel Jacques brought Diem to see him at Senator Benton's office, White asked the Belgian why he had taken Diem to *Integrity* in the first place, to which Father Jacques replied: "Je savais qu'il y avait là des gens dévoués" (I knew that was where the devout people were).[42]

Integrity and *Jubilee* encompassed the broad spectrum of American Catholic thought in the 1940s and 1950s that was fired by a profoundly countercultural impulse. "Integral" Catholicism sought to restore all things to Christ, including the state. European thinkers provided the inspiration, as usual, since they were accustomed to seeing even their most grandiose spiritual politics translated into action; during the cold war many now shifted their focus to Southeast Asia. In 1953 Father Jacques wrote the article "Opportunities in Vietnam" in Msgr. Fulton J. Sheen's *Worldmission* and proclaimed: "The Church has an excellent chance not only to check temporary Communist victories but to bring her own answers and, in that way to bring the entire country to the whole truth."[43]

For American Catholics in the "lay apostolate," the prospect of translating their religious convictions into foreign policy was both novel and extraordinarily complicated. Catholic radicals such as Dorothy Day had often scorned the reflexive patriotism of their benighted coreligionists, but it was always easier to discern what they were opposed to than what they advocated in the political sphere. *Integrity* generally ignored global politics, the notable exception being a 1951 essay by Edwin Halsey on the Third Force. Halsey began with this startling assertion: "Today the world is split between two murderous ideologies, the communist and the democratic. . . . Each of them preserves the sense of universalism which is properly a prerogative of the highest religion, that is to say, they are each in some degrading way professing Catholicity." Halsey condemned nationalism, called for a revival of the distributist ideology featured in papal social encyclicals, and ominously noted that Catholics, as an American minority group, were "fit subjects for the role of scapegoat in the national loyalty rites."[44]

Disappointed by the quixotic temperament of the Catholic avant-garde, White then turned to the liberals associated with *Commonweal* magazine as the last best haven for Diem's cause in Catholic America. The editors of *Commonweal*—a leading voice of urbane laity since 1924—certainly could sympathize with White's plight. As liberal internationalists they cultivated a lonely stance in opposing the much larger isolationist bloc of American Catholics who, James O'Gara lamented in a 1953 essay, regarded Senator McCarthy as "their knight on a white horse." "Enthusiasm for him," O'Gara continued, "has become identified in their minds with both Americanism and Catholicism, and woe to the man who ventures to criticize." The Jesuits' *America* magazine was the other prominent voice of Catholic internationalism in the 1950s. In late 1955 and early 1956, Angier Biddle Duke and Gilbert Jonas of the Harold Oram firm collaborated with Father Jacques to plant a pro-Diem article (written by Christopher Emmett, an IRC board member) in the magazine.[45]

"Commonweal Catholics," along with a segment of *America*'s readership, opposed McCarthyism but struggled to construct a distinctive alternative. Their dilemma accounted for Peter White's inability to deliver the liberal Catholic power base for Diem in the United States that Harold Oram had desired. White's mission was not enhanced by the imposing cultural barriers separating those who happened to share the same religion but little else. One of the liberals to whom White introduced Diem was Joseph Calderon, a young New York attorney who specialized in Italian affairs and was a follower of Don Luigi Sturzo, the antifascist, anticommunist leader of the Christian Democrats in Italy. Calderon spoke passionately of Sturzo in Diem's presence but, White recalled, "Diem was authoritarian and the lecture didn't take."[46]

Peter White worked in Saigon for Harold Oram on the Diem account in the winter and spring of 1956; on his return to New York he attended meetings of the American Friends of Vietnam and continued to work the Catholic angle. But his role diminished as the International Rescue Committee expanded its operations throughout Southeast Asia. "Leo Cherne, Joseph Buttinger, and Oram's contacts were heavyweights with experience," he recalled, "and I was beyond my depth." With the advent of Operation Laos and the invention of Tom Dooley as the jungle doctor (whose ascendance White likened to that of "the Irishman in the WASP law firm"), the

Vietnam Lobby scored a public relations coup well beyond the scope of Peter White's pioneering work on their behalf.[47]

Tom Dooley's rebirth as missionary for Americanism was rooted in the ethnocultural tensions of the early 1950s. He was uniquely immune from the contentiousness marking interfaith relations at precisely the moment when Americans were being urged to embrace "national brotherhood." Catholics were still prohibited from participating in assemblies of such interfaith groups as the World Council of Churches, whose ecumenical work, Samuel Cardinal Stritch reminded Chicago Catholics in 1954, was "based on the false assumption that Roman Catholics, too, are still searching for the truth of Christ." The Jesuit magazine *America* editorialized in August of that year: "The attitude in recent times of many of the large Protestant bodies in this country towards Catholics has not made it any easier for us to feel interest in or sympathy for their present efforts." The editors alluded as well to the neonativist writings of Paul Blanshard, along with "much shaking of fists over our Catholic school system."[48]

The "culture wars" of the period were fought primarily between Catholics and a rather loosely defined coalition of liberal Protestants, Jews, and assorted secularists who saw the growing Catholic population as a threat to their cherished notions about a wall separating church and state. Since fundamentalist Protestantism was still viewed as a strictly marginal phenomenon, and since the Church appeared monolithic in its authority, Catholicism was generally equated with what would only later be tagged the "religious right." Yet Catholics were often still denied their legitimacy as authentic Americans by such urbane voices of liberal Protestantism as the *Christian Century*, which was "often home," wrote historian Patrick Allitt, "to anti-Catholic sentiments in the 1940s and 1950s."[49]

One of the most widely discussed books of the mid-1950s was Will Herberg's *Protestant-Catholic-Jew*, wherein the author, a Jewish theologian and social critic, explained how Catholicism and Judaism had gained cultural authority in postwar America by subsuming their ethnic constituencies within a model of acculturation that Herberg called the "triple melting pot." In "post-Protestant" America, a term coined at the time by historian Winthrop Hudson, Catholics imagined new opportunities; these in turn generated the deep religiopolitical tensions witnessed in the 1950s, from controversies over birth control to arguments over the propriety of using public subsidies to transport Catholic school students.[50]

At the same time, the congruence of cold war domestic imperatives with Catholic interests in Eastern Europe and Vietnam undermined the traditional isolationism of "white ethnic" Americans, while exacerbating their animosity toward American foreign service personnel and other internationalists, a sentiment brilliantly exploited by McCarthy. Voluntary organizations like the International Rescue Committee depended on favorable public opinion not only for the agency's survival but for the health of related enterprises conducted by its leadership. The IRC was essentially in the business of humanitarianism, with influence and prestige to be measured in donations and a positive relationship with brokers of the U.S. foreign aid program. Its leadership remained highly vulnerable to Catholic critiques from the Right, even after McCarthy's fall. Underlying concerns over a renewed outbreak of anti-Semitism played a role as well, shared alike by the leaders of internationalist groups such as the IRC and Catholic liberals. James O'Gara of *Commonweal* warned in 1954 that "the hard core of Catholic support for McCarthy . . . has the same emotional roots as support for Father Coughlin in the thirties." Though scholars of the period have conclusively demonstrated that McCarthyites reserved their greatest scorn not for Jews but the Anglo elites, the IRC was doubly vulnerable as a group dominated by East Coast aristocrats like Angier Biddle Duke and New York Jews whose politics ranged from New Deal liberalism to involvement with the sectarian Left.[51]

Harold Oram possessed an acute understanding of how American opinion was shaped. He made certain that the National Committee of the American Friends of Vietnam comprised perhaps the most ecumenical coalition of opinion-makers ever witnessed, from military figures (retired Gen. John W. O'Daniel was the first chairman) to distinguished academics like Samuel Eliot Morison and Arthur Schlesinger Jr. to such religious leaders as Msgr. Joseph Harnett, the head of Catholic Relief Services and a close associate of both Cardinal Spellman and President Ngo Dinh Diem. Had Spellman not been fully aware of the high stakes in Diem's future, it is doubtful he would have permitted his representative's name to appear on a masthead adorned by at least one socialist leader, Norman Thomas. The eclectic makeup of the AFV later inspired New Left critics to see a byzantine conspiracy at work linking the Church, the Pentagon, and Madison Avenue. Harold Oram knew the representatives of these institutions would probably never meet, but he also knew that the AFV's extravagantly diverse character would provide insurance against suspicion about the character and motivations of his various clients, including Diem and the IRC.[52]

An incident from the autumn of 1956 testified to the centrality of ethnoreligious issues in the cold war work of the International Rescue Committee. On November 8, the IRC sponsored a mass rally at New York's Madison Square Garden in support of the Hungarian Freedom Fighters. It should have been a triumphant event for the organization; Leo Cherne and Angier Biddle Duke had traveled to Vienna on October 30, just days after Hungarian patriots rose up against Soviet occupation by targeting the secret security police who enforced communist rule. While the Soviets removed their tanks from Budapest, Cherne, along with the IRC's Vienna representative, staged a daring mission to the besieged city in a 1946 Chevrolet "with a Red Cross flag wrapped over its radiator." In Budapest they delivered the "first installment of American aid" ("$200,000 worth of antibiotics contributed by Charles Pfizer Company"). Cherne also "was on hand to greet" Josef Cardinal Mindszenty when he was liberated from eight years in communist captivity. On November 4 the Soviets brutally crushed the Hungarian uprising; on returning to New York, Cherne appeared on Ed Sullivan's television variety show and made an impassioned plea for support that netted $400,000 of the $2.5 million the IRC raised for Hungarian relief.[53]

As Harold Oram later noted, Cherne's decisive action had "captured the Hungarian crisis for the IRC," but the triumph was short-lived. The Madison Square Garden rally was a debacle: the IRC's in-house historian even conceded that it was "a tumultuous, riotous gathering that frequently seemed on the verge of violence." The IRC staff—particularly the executive left in charge while Duke and Cherne were in Europe—had failed to consider the religiopolitical dimensions of the Hungarian uprising, especially as they were felt in the United States. The overwhelming majority of Hungarian Americans attending the Garden rally were Catholics who, in addition to their anticommunism—the one characteristic they shared with the IRC—also harbored profound suspicions of leftist and anticlerical Hungarians of any kind, several of whom were invited to speak at the rally by the IRC.[54]

The crowd at the Garden jeered vociferously at the speech of Anna Kethly, a houseguest of the Joseph Buttinger family who was described in the *New York Times* account of the rally as "leader of the Hungarian Social Democratic party and a member of the ill-fated final Cabinet of Premier Imre Nagy." Leo Cherne pleaded with the booing crowd to permit Kethly to continue speaking. Milton Bracker, a reporter for the *Times* (which regularly ran stories planted by IRC publicists) insisted that Kethly's use of the term *coexistence* was mistranslated in such a way that she seemed to recommend coexistence between the Free World and communism (as opposed to, in Bracker's words, "co-existence between Hungary and her immediate neighbors, including the Soviet Union, on the basis of respect for Hungary's integrity and self-determination," a fine distinction hardly likely to appease Hungarian Americans). Yet a bilingual Hungarian American, Elizabeth Nagy, later wrote to Angier Biddle Duke protesting "the insidious Communist propaganda that Mrs. Kethly was injecting into her speech in Hungarian."

Nagy was confident that had Duke only understood what Kethly was saying, "you personally would have removed her from the rostrum instead of permitting Mr. Cherne to plead with us to listen to her. The Hungarians booed her because although she calls herself 'Social Democrat,' she talks like a Communist." The "Communist closed fist salute" demonstrated by Kethly at the conclusion of her address only served to further antagonize the crowd.[55]

At least one prominent IRC board member doubted that his colleagues fully apprehended the issues involved in the controversy. Christopher Emmet, a passionate advocate of human rights who served on the executive councils of both the IRC and the American Friends of Vietnam, fired off an angry memo to the IRC leadership on November 16, 1956. "Although Emmet was an American," recalled Marvin Liebman, "he came off as a typical, eccentric English don." From an old New York family in gracious decline, Emmet was a cousin of Peter White, the Catholic connection to the Harold Oram firm. Since Emmet's mother was also a Catholic, he was the nearest approximation of a "fellow traveler" to the Church at the IRC. He now accused the IRC executive in charge of the rally with ignorance of and insensitivity to the concerns of the Hungarian Catholics in the audience, the majority of whom, he explained, "were on the emotionally militant and relatively conservative side. Most of the American-Hungarians and refugees belong generally in that category in line with the national tradition. The same is true of many American-Irish and other Catholics."[56]

Emmet reminded the IRC of a delicate truth: "The position and reputation of the IRC (and my own) is a little left of center. Aside from this political handicap in dealing with the nationality groups is the fact that the IRC, while scrupulously and nobly non-sectarian, has a small proportion of Catholics either on its board or among its working personnel." In fact Catholics were such a rarity at liberal, secularist organizations like the IRC prior to the mid-1950s that Leo Cherne claimed, in an October 1954 letter to a member of the U.S. embassy staff in Saigon, that Joseph Buttinger's background as an Austrian Catholic would enhance his value in the field. Yet while Buttinger was born into an impoverished Catholic family, he discovered at the age of fifteen that he "no longer depended on the comfort of religion. This need was gradually replaced by a passion for a world of freedom and equality among all social groups and for lasting peace among all nations." In his subsequent political work Buttinger inevitably allied himself with various anticlerical groups, hardly the ideal credentials for one of the key American "handlers" of the militantly Catholic Ngo Dinh Diem.[57]

The ethnoreligious issues were so vexing to the IRC that Christopher Emmet, having raised them, was unable to propose a solution. Emmet had already invested too heavily in a liberal Hungarian cleric and IRC board member, Msgr. Bela Varga, "the last legally elected Speaker of the Hungarian Parliament." Emmet touted Monsignor Varga as "a bridge" between militant Hungarian American Catholics and liberals, "just as he has always filled the role of a bridge within the Hungarian National Council and the IRC." Emmet was incensed that Varga's name had been stricken from the list of speakers at the rally, only to be restored at the last moment; amid the confusion Varga finally spoke before a "half empty house." In one of the most revealing aspects of the Garden debacle, an internal dispute broke out at the IRC over who was to blame, the Left or the Right. Emmet insisted that Monsignor Varga, as a cleric, could have placated the "emotional" Hungarians at the rally who sensed that the program tilted toward those anti-Catholic leftists who comprised but a tiny fragment of the freedom fighters. Yet an anonymous "Hungarian American" who wrote to Cherne after the rally complained that both Kethly and Varga were "double-crossing turncoats" who had failed to adequately resist communism in their homeland.[58]

Emmet finally conceded that Varga was indeed "a trifle left of center," which was another way of saying he was wholly unacceptable to the masses of American Catholic anticommunists of all ethnic backgrounds. Varga's "unique service to the IRC in combatting smears and ignorant attacks from the right wing" was ultimately of little value since he enjoyed scarcely more credibility on the Right than did the IRC itself. Despite his anger and frustration, Emmet lauded the efforts of Harold Oram to salvage the Garden rally, and he pointedly suggested that had Duke and Cherne been in New York during the planning stages, the disaster would have been averted. Leo Cherne, in particular, was highly sensitive to the "Catholic issue." He kept files on the various controversies that threatened to perpetuate interreligious tensions in America and was a gracious friend to Msgr. Joseph Harnett. To Cherne, such conflicts must have threatened the empire of entrepreneurial humanitarianism he was constructing on a solid foundation of enlightened self-interest.[59]

Leo Cherne aggressively pursued his vision of a world in which the death of colonialism and the quest for freedom would yield enormous markets for his information services, while also providing an outlet for his personal creativity as a humanitarian and artist. The one conviction Cherne and his colleagues shared with nearly all cold war liberals was a belief that cultural freedom, indeed the very notion of culture itself, was a universal value that had achieved its apotheosis in the celebrated pluralism of postwar American life. The two domestic groups that stood outside of and potentially threatened this consensus, Paul Blanshard alleged in 1951, were communists and Roman Catholics. Communism obviously no longer represented an acceptable form of dissent. Unlike Blanshard and other nativists, however, Cherne recognized that many American Catholics were ready to have confirmed through rhetoric and ritual the full legitimacy they had already earned on distant battlefields.[60]

Tom Dooley was constructing his first clinic in Laos at the time of the Hungarian uprising. A young Catholic spokesman for international freedom, he was yoked with none of the baggage of a Monsignor Varga, a fact that clearly endeared him to his sponsors. It is more than plausible to conclude that one of Dooley's missions was to run interference with the American Right—especially the Catholic segment—on behalf of the IRC in order to prevent just that kind of religiopolitical disaster the Hungarian rally represented. Only in America, perhaps, could one find a Catholic who was impossible to locate along the conventional ideological spectrum yet who enjoyed unimpeachable credentials as a cold warrior. Dooley's rare gifts did not go unnoticed by John Fitzgerald Kennedy, a charter member of the American Friends of Vietnam who was just then seeking a way to surmount the tribal bonds that had hindered his father and his father's friend Joe McCarthy. The difficult trick was to break free without alienating the affections of an intensely loyal Catholic constituency, a feat that had never been accomplished as of 1956.

In the summer of that year it would have been extremely difficult to find anyone who could muster an objection to the idea of a medical program in Laos led by Dr. Tom Dooley. His own militant innocence proved a boon to his sponsors. When Oram's associate Gilbert Jonas—holder of a graduate degree in Asian studies—met with Dooley at the Waldorf Astoria for briefings on Lao politics, he was astounded by Dooley's ignorance and lack of curiosity over issues he would surely face in Southeast Asia. Tom assured Jonas that Louisville Sluggers, Sears and Roebuck catalogs, and Walt Disney films would more than suffice in winning the love of his new subjects, a prediction that was fully confirmed in the months to come. In the meantime there was the small problem of Dooley's hotel bills, which contained hefty charges linked to the young men he frequently entertained at the Waldorf, but which were apparently paid as part of the costs of doing business with this one-of-a-kind asset, the newly minted jungle doctor of Laos.[61]

On June 1, 1956, Dr. Tom Dooley spoke at "the first public conference on Vietnam ever held in the United States," a symposium sponsored by the AFV. "I won't speak to you about anything very high level," he began his remarks. "Foreign policy is for the admirals, the generals, and the statesmen. I will tell you something about the refugees of Indochina, the refugees at Haiphong." The following month, the International Rescue Committee issued a prospectus for Operation Laos. The document was written in the first person and featured Dooley's trademark enthusiasm; as Harold Oram remarked in 1986, when it came to day-to-day operations, Dooley never really needed a publicist. Once the young doctor embraced a project it became fully his own, so much that even routine questions about his sponsorship would have seemed irrelevant. The humiliation of his recent navy discharge was not even remotely evident in the manifesto launching Operation Laos. "We want to be on the offensive for America," he wrote, "not just denying what the Communists say about us, but getting there and doing something about it. We shall try to translate the democratic ideals we DO possess into Asian realities they CAN possess."[62]

"But most especially," Dooley concluded, "what will make our mission a success is that we are enthusiastic and anxious to tell these people a little bit about America. We wish to explain it to them on a hand-to-hand basis, at the grass root level." This deceptively simplistic philosophy was the cornerstone of Dooley's work in Laos. As we shall see, this ideology of the "little way" was ideally suited to the propagandistic role he performed for the Vietnam Lobby. But there was something different about Dooley that must have appealed to the artist in Cherne as well. He was becoming noted as a bit of a sculptor for his busts of such world figures as Dr. Albert Schweitzer, Boris Pasternak, Ralph Bunche, and "Wild Bill" Donovan, artworks that enabled him to become acquainted with each of these dignitaries. Like Dooley, Cherne was also a performer. His familiar voice graced the airwaves of New York radio for several decades, where his wit and erudition made him a fixture on popular programs hosted by Martha Deane and Barry Gray, among others. During his long tenure as head of the Research Institute of America, Cherne would make an annual appearance at the Grand Ballroom of the Waldorf Astoria and "predict exactly what was going to happen in the twelve months to come" to an audience composed of "2,000 businessmen, lawyers, accountants and politicos." He boasted of an 80 percent accuracy rate.[63]

In his April 1961 interview with a reporter from the *Reader's Digest,* Cherne made the fascinating claim that the most tragic consequence of Dooley's premature death was that it prevented him from fully developing his talents not as a jungle doctor but as a *writer.* Cherne understood that Dooley's career had really been more about mass communications than humanitarian medical aid. He had worked with other Catholics on refugee programs, particularly Monsignor Harnett, who, Cherne remarked in 1990, was a much more authentic humanitarian than Dooley. But Harnett was an extraordinarily humble, to some even saintly, priest from a working-class Philadelphia Irish background; he shared few interests with Cherne outside his work. The same might be said of Cherne's other Irish American protégé, William J. Casey, who began his career as an attorney for the Research

Thomas A. Dooley III in the early 1930s, St. Louis.

Tom Dooley (*third from left*) with brothers Eddie Mike, Malcolm, and Earle, Green Lake, Wisconsin, mid-1930s.

Graduating from Saint Louis University High School, January 1944.

Navy Corpsman Tom Dooley with Eddie Mike, Malcolm, and Agnes W. Dooley, 1945.

The medical student as horseman: with "Jim Hawkins," ca. 1950.

U.S. Navy Captain Walter Winn (*right*) with Vietnamese "orphan" and unidentified fellow officer, Haiphong, September 1954. Official photograph, U.S. Navy, courtesy Daniel M. Redmond.

Vietnamese refugee and interpreter, Haiphong, September 1954. The refugee was reportedly the 100,000th to be moved South by the U.S. Navy. Official photograph, U.S. Navy, courtesy Daniel M. Redmond.

Lt. Tom Dooley, Father Khue, Capt. Walter Winn, and South Vietnamese prime minister Ngo Dinh Diem, following the ceremony anointing Dooley Officier de l'Ordre National de Vietnam, Saigon, May 12, 1955.

The aspiring surgeon general of the U.S. Navy, winter 1956.

With actor Kirk Douglas at Lucey's restaurant, Hollywood, April 1956.

Promoting Operation Laos, spring 1956.

Operation Laos corpsmen Norman Baker, Peter Kessey, and Dennis Shepard, at Angkor Wat, Cambodia, late summer 1956.

With Corpsman Norman Baker and Operation Brotherhood personnel, South Vietnam, late summer 1956.

With Peter Kessey (*far left*), Norman Baker (*center*), and Bishop Ngo Dinh Thuc of Vinh Long (President Diem's brother), identity of others unknown, South Vietnam, late summer 1956.

Entertaining at Operation Brotherhood facility, South Vietnam, late summer 1956.

In Manila with Ramon Magsaysay, president of the Philippines, December 1956.

Institute (and ended it over forty years later as CIA director during the Reagan administration). While Cherne admired Casey's intellect, he was less impressed with the "moral prejudices of a middle-class Irish Catholic" that pervaded Casey's thought and demeanor. To Cherne, Casey "personified a Yiddish expression of my youth—a *graubyon*, a coarse young fellow."[64]

Cherne told Casey's biographer, Joseph E. Persico, that his erstwhile protégé "was to the right of Attila the Hun. He was one hundred percent for Franco and one hundred percent against the Loyalists. To understand this, you had to understand his Catholicism." In contrast, Tom Dooley was a new kind of Irishman to Cherne, so unlike those he had encountered during the bitter days of the 1930s, when conflicts between the Irish and Jews of New York often turned violent, aggravated by Father Coughlin and the looming cataclysm in Europe which polarized New Yorkers along ethnic lines. Dooley was a smoother, much more cosmopolitan Irish American, in the European cut of his suits and the passion for classical music he shared with Leo Cherne.[65]

The two men also seemed to share a conviction that they were deserving of fuller recognition from those on the "inside." Their respective stature among liberal Jews and conservative Catholics came perhaps almost too easily: both chased some elusive goal that entailed winning the acclaim of cultural and political elites, among whom were found the kind of people always capable of reminding one of one's origins. Those New Left revisionists who condemned Cherne as a CIA insider must have been unaware of the intensive lobbying he directed at Allen Dulles in the early 1950s before the agency was willing to work with the IRC. Though Tom Dooley was not yet as wealthy as Leo Cherne, he boasted the looks and charm that complemented Cherne's knowledge of the business of international humanitarianism; from their mutual need grew an unlikely and sometimes awkward relationship.[66]

Cherne continued to write inspirational letters to Dooley into the final months of the jungle doctor's life, well after the formal relationship between the IRC and Dooley's mission had been rather acrimoniously terminated. Both men possessed attributes the other admired and perhaps even envied, though Dooley's "pretty brilliance," as Sen. Joseph McCarthy had described it in 1956 (at their only meeting), proved far more ephemeral than Cherne's tough-minded humanitarianism. A man who truly did well by doing good, Cherne was pleased to sponsor—in the year that saw "Tailgunner Joe" McCarthy hand over to Dooley the dubious mantle of Catholic folk hero—the flighty yet enchanted young physician on his first errand in the Lao wilderness.[67]

☆ 5 ☆

A Madison Avenue
Schweitzer

Dr. Thomas A. Dooley embarked from San Francisco for his new civilian mission on August 7, 1956. He made lecture stops and social appearances in Hawaii, Japan, and Hong Kong prior to a rendezvous with his team of ex-navy corpsmen in the Philippines. In Manila he met with President Magsaysay and with Oscar Arellano, cofounder of Operation Brotherhood, the Lansdale brainchild which had in turn inspired Operation Laos.[1]

On September 6 Dooley and his team—Norman Baker, Peter Kessey, and Dennis Shepard—arrived in Saigon, where Tom was treated to a returning hero's welcome and flown in President Diem's personal airplane to various refugee resettlement sites. "In each village," he wrote, "we found people we knew in Haiphong during that city's death. Dozens came and said 'look Doctor, my arm is all healed now . . .' or 'Look, Baker, my eyes are better.' It is a tremendous thing to be remembered." By September 28 the team finally arrived in Vientiane, Laos, where Dooley immediately began negotiations with Lao government officials over the nature and location of his first assignment on their nation's behalf.[2]

President Diem arranged for one and one-half tons of equipment to be flown into Laos, materiel originally shipped into Saigon by the United States Navy for Operation Laos. Dooley had acknowledged the contribution in a June 21 cable sent to Adm. Arleigh Burke from a hotel room in Beverly Hills.

Tom had made his customary splash on visits to Hollywood that spring to discuss a film version of *Deliver Us from Evil,* the rights to which were acquired for actor Kirk Douglas by Bryna Studios. At a press luncheon at Lucey's in Hollywood on April 11—just days after learning of his forthcoming role in Operation Laos—Dooley appeared with Douglas to discuss the film and his new project, which, Tom explained (with his characteristic disregard for irrelevant detail), would "be financed by the American Rescue Committee." Though Douglas was slated to play Dooley in the Hollywood version of *Deliver Us from Evil,* Tom told an audience at Holy Cross College on May 3 that he would play himself—with Douglas portraying his trusty sidekick Norman Baker—in a production to be completed in time for a September departure to Laos.[3]

The State Department followed Dooley's lead and viewed the Laos mission as a virtual appendage to the film production of *Deliver Us from Evil.* In a confidential memorandum of June 30 John Foster Dulles alerted the embassies in Vientiane and Saigon that "Department desires insure most favorable results from U.S. point of view are obtained from Dooley medical mission to Laos and motion picture production Viet Nam. To this end any appearance friction between his mission and official U.S. agencies should be avoided."[4]

Dooley's errand in the Lao wilderness evokes Perry Miller's classic metaphor for the Puritan mission to the New World. Was he an "errand boy," playing a prescribed role on behalf of others, or would his work assume a more authentic character as an errand whose meaning unfolded in the encounter of Dooley and his Lao patients? Initially Tom was entirely beholden to his sponsors at the IRC and to less overt but highly useful connections who were in a position to smooth over the customary tensions within the Dooley camp and steer him clear of unsympathetic American officialdom in the region. As the CIA's Edward G. Lansdale recalled in 1984,

> The Americans [in Southeast Asia] were mad at me. They thought Dooley was a blowhard, and I said no, that I had seen him look at the Vietnamese that he's treating and there's a real affection in his emotions and the guy cares. . . . Well, he stayed over and tried to operate in Laos. He had gotten in trouble with his team when he came back into Saigon to take him on up to Laos. He had homosexual tendencies and his team got mad at him personally, and there were fights and I had to straighten that out.[5]

Lansdale arranged for his friend Anne Miller—the wife of United States Information Service (USIS) official Hank Miller, who worked closely with Lansdale for many years—to intervene on Dooley's behalf in Saigon "with a team to straighten out their personal affairs." That Dooley sorely needed such imposing patronage became clear even before he arrived in Southeast

Asia. Tom loved Hawaii and expected a warm welcome during an August stopover, his first visit to the islands since the publication of *Deliver Us from Evil*. A staunch admirer of Dooley, Robert Tollaksen, the pseudonymous Ensign Potts of *Deliver Us from Evil*, was working as a protocol officer for Adm. Felix Stump; he had planned to show Dooley the "red-carpet treatment" in Hawaii until he was tipped off by an agent of the Office of Naval Intelligence that Dooley was a homosexual and had been forced to resign his commission. The protocol officer then informed Admiral Stump, who ordered his personnel to avoid Dooley for the duration of his stay in Hawaii.[6]

A thoughtful man who became deeply interested in religion and philosophy after meeting Dooley, Tollaksen feared he had been a "virtual Judas" for seeming to betray his troubled friend, though his personal decency was no match for the navy's structure of authority. Dooley had given the protocol officer a rare glimpse of his vulnerability in a letter of March 1956, responding to his query over rumors Tom had recently married: "It didn't happen," Tollaksen was informed. "Girl wanted a horse, a dog, and a man." Dooley added that he was "sleeping alone and not particularly liking it," but cryptically assured his friend that he would not "do anything 'im' or 'a' moral."[7]

Tollaksen resented the military's "intimidating ostracism" of Dooley in Hawaii. He recalled that in Honolulu civilians sought to touch Tom as he signed autographs, his gaunt figure draped in leis, lending him the appearance of a prophetic and even Christlike figure. Tollaksen accompanied Dooley to the beach at Barbers Point, where Tom stood up on a surfboard on his first try. While Dooley could be manically rude (he embarrassed a waitress in Honolulu by announcing that he knew she was having her period, a stunt he pulled repeatedly during his public career), he also offered "philosophical stimulation" to those, like his friend, who saw through Tom's celebrity facade. Tollaksen's life was permanently changed by his encounter with Dooley, whom he linked thereafter with the archetypal figures of Joseph Campbell's *Hero with a Thousand Faces*.[8]

In the light of Dooley's recent humiliation, his constant boasts ("the VIP treatment, invitations all over the place") in letters to his mother assume a poignant quality. Of course Dooley *was* being feted throughout his journey by people unaware of his ouster from the navy, and friendly columnists like Louella Parsons continued to promote his unique blend of stardom and selfless humanitarianism. He was also soon authorized yet again to create the official account of his mission in a book. In *The Edge of Tomorrow* (1958), Tom charted the progress of Operation Laos from its shaky beginnings in Vientiane to his triumphant departure from a clinic at Nam Tha, in remote northwest Laos, in the late summer of 1957. The narrative was constructed around the pilgrimage of Dooley and his young team, as they journeyed from the capital to nearby Vang Vieng, where they established a prototype clinic before finally making their way to Nam Tha, just miles from "the rim of the Red hell," the Chinese border.[9]

The Edge of Tomorrow was even more successful than *Deliver Us from Evil;* a best-seller, it also won virtually universal critical acclaim. Much more than accounts of his life's work, Dooley's books defined his image and enabled him to build an intimate relationship with his audience that transcended the relatively limited public relations function originally designed for him at the IRC. Many admirers had written to Dooley after reading *Deliver Us from Evil.* One correspondent was Teresa Gallagher, a devout Irish Catholic and militant anticommunist who in the summer of 1956 was on vacation in the Catskills; after attending Mass she sat down on a bench and wrote to Dooley, now working in a country she had never heard of. "The book made a deep impression on me," she later recalled, "and Dr. Dooley's vivid picture of the frightened refugees remained with me long after I closed the book. His sense of compassion, his deeply rooted faith, his patriotism, his ability to make you see the Vietnamese as real people and suffering human beings who needed help, made me re-read the book again and again."[10]

Dooley's books presented a mythical version of his life's work with the bumps and missteps excised from the permanent record. In *The Edge of Tomorrow* there is no mention of Kirk Douglas or his film project, which was quietly shelved like so many other schemes that briefly commanded Tom's energies. The book opened with a simple yet brilliantly effective litany of contributions made by Americans to Operation Laos, from the Irish nuns of St. John's Hospital in St. Louis to a "little Jewish girl in school in New Jersey [who] says that she prays for me 'frequently.'" All of his supporters were now enlisted into what Tom's official idol, Albert Schweitzer, called "the Fellowship of Those Who Bear the Mark of Pain." "In a very small way," Dooley wrote, "because of my profession, I have found entrance into this Fellowship. I have discovered hundreds of others in it, too."[11]

Tom's editor at Farrar, Straus and Cudahy was Robert Giroux, a distinguished littérateur and devout Catholic who had worked with numerous spiritually inclined authors, including Robert Lowell and Jack Kerouac. The friendship and guidance Dooley received from Giroux and Roger Straus, the firm's coproprietor, were crucial if unpublicized ingredients in his success. *The Edge of Tomorrow* is both an American adventure story and a journal of the spirit that evokes the "little way" of St. Thérèse of Lisieux (a central figure in the Catholic revival of the 1940s and 1950s and the patroness of Dorothy Day, founder of the Catholic Worker movement) and other participants in the "lay apostolate" of the era. Dooley described a conversion experience he had undergone in Vietnam, where "simple, tender, loving care—the crudest kind of medicine inexpertly practiced by mere boys"—had been rewarded by "the white light of revelation." He had discovered who he was and what he was meant to be: "an American doctor who had been privileged to witness the enormous possibilities of *medical aid* in all its Christlike power and simplicity."[12]

Dooley's "simplicity" provided the cover for some pointed critiques of the State Department that intensified as his fame grew. In *The Edge of Tomorrow* he asked whether spiritual barrenness explained why "the foreign aid planners, with their billion-dollar projects, found it difficult to understand" his vision for transforming "the brotherhood of man from an ideal into a reality that plain people could understand." Dooley's naive idealism also perfectly situated him to maintain a flexible posture in the yawning void that was Lao–United States relations in the middle of the 1950s. Unlike neighboring Vietnam, where the cult of Ngo Dinh Diem was being fervently promoted, there was no clear leader of the anticommunist forces in Laos to satisfy American concerns. The State Department remained baffled by this politically and culturally variegated new nation for years to come. In 1960 an American official in Vientiane called his post "the end of nowhere. We can do anything we want here because Washington doesn't seem to know it exists."[13]

Washington knew Laos existed, but U.S. policymakers seemed indifferent at best to actual conditions in the field. The improbable cultural authority Tom Dooley came to enjoy was rooted in his talent for fashioning a simple, compelling narrative of his Lao experience, complete with names and places that remained foreign to most American officials posted there. Laos had only become important to the United States in 1954, when the Geneva Convention partitioned the former constituent of French Indochina according to the Vietnamese model. After Geneva, the leftist forces of the Pathet Lao ("land of Laos"), the ally and client of Ho Chi Minh, regrouped in their stronghold northeastern provinces of Phong Saly and Sam Neua, with national elections "to be held within two years leading to reintegration of those Pathet Lao administered areas into the Kingdom of Laos."[14]

The logical recipient of American support for the leadership of Laos was Prince Souvanna Phouma (1901–84), who with his half-brothers Prince Phetsarath and Prince Souphanouvong had formed a nationalist movement in resistance to renewed French designs on Laos after 1945. By 1950, with Phetsarath in exile in Thailand and Souphanouvong at the head of the newly formed Pathet Lao, the pragmatist Souvanna Phouma yearned for a return "to a reconciled and unified nation, whose independence he felt was drawing near." From the time of Dien Bien Phu well into the 1960s, Souvanna Phouma led a series of Lao governments, which Washington sporadically funded while encouraging pressure from the militarist Right. The Eisenhower administration was banned under the terms of the Geneva settlement from introducing military personnel into Laos, but, as historian Timothy N. Castle explained, "the predicament was solved in December 1955 when the U.S. State Department placed the management of American military assistance to Laos under the control of a thinly disguised, but politically defensible, military aid organization called the Program Evaluations Office (PEO). This decision set the precedent for nearly two decades of covert U.S. military aid to the Royal Lao government." The State Department viewed Souvanna Phouma's quixotic "neutralism" as a euphemism for his willingness to include the Pathet Lao in coalition governments, a move Washington deemed unacceptable and which led to their support for a series of coups, yielding in their turn to counter-coups and a generally chaotic political situation until Laos finally fell to the North Vietnamese in 1975.[15]

The State Department was concerned lest Dooley promote a view of the Pathet Lao as "misunderstood" nationalists, an impression he must have conveyed in a letter to Assistant Secretary of State for Far Eastern Affairs Walter Robertson. Robertson fired back his reply on November 21, 1956, admonishing Dooley not to fall for claims that the Pathet Lao were merely "erring brothers who are anxious only to return peacefully to the fold." Dooley's unique blend of idealistic neutralism and reflexive anticommunism ideally served the flexible internationalists at the IRC. Leo Cherne helped support the humanitarian work of the group with some of the proceeds from his Research Institute of America, the "CIA for businessmen" seeking intelligence about developing overseas markets. Cherne made it his business to maintain close contacts with American personnel in Southeast Asia. In February 1955, Carter de Paul of the United States Operations Mission in Laos (the agency that administered foreign aid in the field for the International Cooperation Administration, or ICA) had cheerily advised him that "the combined Indochina complex should add up to a sizeable chunk of business if the right salesmen are active enough." Since Cherne had worked tirelessly to create networks throughout the developing world he hardly needed to be reminded by de Paul that "it's going to take real on the spot selling out here to break through established patterns—no one is going to get very far by mailing catalogs to the missions or the Embassies." De Paul promised to come "running" to Cherne with tips pertaining to opportunities "in the IRC field."[16]

With patronage from the likes of Cherne and Lansdale, Dooley was able to bypass most of the protocols governing humanitarian aid programs in Southeast Asia. But he was also aided by his own indomitable ambition, an intensely practical if flamboyant nature, the instincts of a smuggler, and not least of all a generous share of physical courage that was tested repeatedly in his newly adopted homeland.

"Like Vietnam," wrote William Prochnau, "Laos had been governed by France until 1954. But where the French exploited Vietnam commercially and trained a Vietnamese bourgeoisie to run the exploitation for them, they treated Laos with languid neglect." Through the course of Dooley's career there Laos remained "an extraordinarily isolated and backward land of deep forests and forbidding mountains, a place locked in by its neighbors—China, Burma, Thailand, Cambodia, and the two Vietnams—like a tiny piece of a jigsaw puzzle. The Land of the Million Elephants, Laos was called, and, if so, that gave it one elephant for every two people. The Westerners drawn there gave it still other names, invariably taken from the fairylands of their youth. Never-Never Land, they called it, and The Land of Oz." Tom Dooley would simply call it home.[17]

In *The Edge of Tomorrow* Dooley claimed that he originally sought to establish a clinic at Nam Tha and that he was "amazed," given the Lao government's emphasis on his independent status, by their request that he first win approval from the American ambassador, J. Graham Parsons. Dooley had actually preferred Muong Sing, a strategically important village in northwestern Laos just five miles from the Chinese border, but in any case he professed bitter disappointment when Parsons strongly urged him to begin his mission at Vang Vieng instead, a village located roughly halfway between Vientiane and the ancient Lao capital of Luang Prabang. Vang Vieng was at greater risk because "this area has been infected by Pathet Lao whereas provincial officials and population at Muong Sing are strongly pro-American." The ambassador concluded that Dooley could be a "definite asset in right place and might do our cause real harm in wrong place."[18]

A CIA report from early October 1956 concluded that Dooley "does not know anything about the political situation in the Muong Sing area because the Embassy and USOM will not brief him on it and no one in Washington would tell him about the political situation in Laos." While the State Department chose to keep Dooley in the dark, an official with the aid program expressed his wish to Carter de Paul that Tom's mission resemble "less of a circus and more of a training and demonstration project in applied medicine." As a Lansdale-style "psywar" project, Operation Laos coexisted uneasily with more conventional programs, even those funded by the "official" CIA. While Dooley conceded in retrospect that he "was humbly grateful to Ambassador Parsons and [Lao Minister of Health] Dr. Oudom [Souvannavong] for insisting upon a 'shakedown cruise' in Vang Vieng," he also charged in *The Edge of Tomorrow* that USOM "promised me a great deal, sincerely and genuinely, but the end result coming from their men on the scene in Laos, turned out to be very little." Such remarks help explain the deep and abiding mutual resentment harbored by Dooley and embassy personnel in Laos throughout his career there.[19]

In the wake of Ambassador Parsons's request that Dooley work at Vang Vieng, the embassy initially sought to placate him, though often in a condescending fashion. In describing a cocktail reception for the members of Operation Laos, a foreign service bureaucrat informed Parsons that "Dooley and his boys were having a high time with the five Embassy belles we had asked along, and the time was for mild high jinks and the usual complement of boasting. Dooley did try to assure me, however, that his brash declarations of independence from the State Department . . . were designed to fool the Commies. He asserted that he really needed our guidance very much and would be lost without it. I said I was glad to hear it." Dooley's nonconformity should not have been the sole cause of his poor reputation among official Americans in Laos: Ambassador Parsons "had to obtain transfers for eight men in the PEO who were chronically drunk or had serious adjustment problems," and an investigator later concluded that the military advisors in Laos comprised "the worst collection of misfits I ever saw."[20]

Even so, in the weeks prior to departing for Vang Vieng, Dooley's antics (he informed, for example, the deputy director of USOM that "whether American officials here liked it or not . . . everything he did was to receive publicity and there was nothing we could do about it") made him the leading "conversation piece" among the Americans in Vietiane, a situation that Ambassador Parsons sought to curtail in a blistering memorandum of October 17. While reiterating official support of Dooley's mission, Parsons noted that "Dr. Dooley's troubles with American officials are of his own making. He has been rude, arrogant and short-tempered . . . he has consistently misrepresented what has been said to him in regard to things which he has wanted but not received." Furthermore, "he complains that no one had offered him a drink or wished him good luck."[21]

Parsons then suggested, as had numerous others in the State Department and at the USIA, that *Deliver Us from Evil* was tainted by Dooley's self-aggrandizing disregard for fairness and accuracy: "On the basis of past performance I expect him to play fast and loose with the truth in print and to be the victim of such distortions." Parsons insisted such threats would not result in his penalizing Dooley, despite his "arrogant, sometimes unreasonable and irresponsible behavior." On the eve of Dooley's departure for Vang Vieng, Parsons summarized his judgment of Operation Laos: "I will, so far as possible, continue to seek to avoid unpleasantness or unnecessary antagonism, but he will have to understand that I cannot discriminate in his favor and against those other private missions here whom I personally think are much more dedicated to the welfare of the Lao people." The ambassador cryptically added: "I would like a better atmosphere too as I do not want there to be trouble for the Department, particularly with the kind of groups who will be more ready to believe Dr. Dooley than to believe us." Parsons was surely referring here to the post-McCarthyite coalition of Catholic and rightist forces who continued to scorn foreign aid programs as the misbegotten domain of Ivy League diplomats.[22]

It is not clear how much Parsons knew about Dooley's support from quieter but more influential Americans. In 1972 the political scientist Charles A. Stevenson quoted an unidentified source who claimed that "the CIA was the arm of policy implementation under Parsons" in Laos. Yet since Edward G. Lansdale's "freewheeling, out of channel procedures" were often camouflaged from the CIA itself, we cannot assume that the ambassador or his staff were fully aware of who was running Operation Laos, or for what reasons. Dooley himself probably did not know. It is hard to distinguish his self-deception from the customary swaggering tone in which he informed his mother that while most Americans in Vientiane were either jealous or obsequious toward him, the people who counted most were solidly in his corner: "The Ambassador and Carter de Paul (head of USOM) have been very kind. They sort of have to because both Admiral Felix Stumpt, and Assist Sec. Defense Perkins McGuire who were here separately last month, have 'ordered' that we be assisted as much as possible, what a fine thing we are doing, and how the eyes of Washington are upon us. . . . So as usual we have the Admirals and Generals on our side, but the Lts. don't particularly like us. The story of my life."[23]

If Dooley's operations were enmeshed within a web of interagency intrigue, as is likely, the source of the tension was never acknowledged and may not even have been apparent to most of the principals, though it is curious that USOM and the embassy in Vientiane were obliged to support publically a mission they disdained. It must have been particularly galling for the gentlemen of the Foreign Service to have to endure Dooley's peculiar blend of mockery and social climbing. In a letter to the head of USOM Laos requesting a favor in June 1956, Dooley had written, "Now dear old Carter, would you do this for me." By that autumn, Carter de Paul must have felt he had done quite a lot for Dooley, who could easily be mistaken at times for a world-class bounder. On October 26 de Paul submitted a bill for $59.75 from the USOM Cooperative Mess for meals he had purchased for the head of Operation Laos. "Needless to say," he informed Ambassador Parsons, "this amount was paid with personal funds. It is regarded as my personal contribution to the success of the Dooley mission, given the fact that to date no offer of reimbursement has been forthcoming."[24]

Having quickly worn out his welcome in Vientiane, Dooley eagerly embraced the challenge of Vang Vieng, where Operation Laos transformed a local dispensary into a village clinic within days of the team's arrival on or around October 15, 1956. The 120-mile northward journey from the capital had consumed two days of jeep travel, over a road Dooley described to his mother as "the worse one will ever find, here or in hell." In *The Edge of Tomorrow* he wrote: "Under blazing sun, we crept and crawled through dense jungle, plowed through monsoon mud, and hit long stretches of suffocating dust. But we also saw some of the most fantastically beautiful scenery on earth."[25]

As a budding nature mystic Dooley had a flair for natural description. When coupled with some polishing in the New York offices of Farrar, Straus and Cudahy the results could be quite stirring: "The setting for Vang Vieng must have been selected by a master artist. It is spectacular. The village rests at the foot of stupendous walls of rock, rising two thousand and three thousand feet into the sky. These mountains have no foothills. There's no gradual rise or slope. Just an absolutely flat plain; then suddenly, abruptly, a staggering wall of rock."[26]

Dooley entrusted the more prosaic job of constructing a clinic to ex-Seabee Norman Baker, who with the aid of "a half-dozen coolies" turned a low, whitewashed building of three rooms into a serviceable if tiny and crude hospital. A kinsman of their Lao translator, Chai (Dooley provided his own spellings for the names of the Lao he met who were other than public figures), offered the team use of a small home he owned at the southern end of the village. This elderly man had also "spread the word that we were white medicine-men bringing powerful remedies to the people. Hence many of the women and children came [to greet them] with gifts of flowers, cucumbers and oranges."[27]

The primitive conditions he found in Vang Vieng appealed to something in Dooley. He wrote to Admiral Burke: "We shall stay here several months treating the hundreds that ooze in every day. Most have never seen a white man, none have ever seen a doctor." Tom was suddenly empowered to bridge the huge gap in worldviews and experiences that separated the Lao from his culture; he was totally in charge, with no meddling authorities to judge his behavior or his uniquely simple practice of medicine. Initially he was "overwhelmed by the horrible health conditions we found in Vang

Vieng. These were yaws, tuberculosis, pneumonia, malaria and diseases far more heartrending. I was appalled by the sight of so many women mutilated and crippled in childbirth, and by the many traumatic injuries long neglected and horribly infected." He encountered leprosy for the first time: "Here the patients who gaped at us were just remnants of human beings, rotted and bloated beyond ordinary shape. In dealing with this loathsome disease I had constantly to suppress the strong urge of nausea."[28]

Dooley quickly established a daily "sick-call" at the clinic in Vang Vieng. In the afternoons Pete Kessey and Denny Shepard often conducted "jeep calls" in the surrounding countryside while Dooley performed surgery at the hospital. Much of the treatment involved dispensing protein powder and injecting vitamins to combat kwashiorkor and other consequences of malnutrition. But "obstetrics, if I may call it that," he wrote, "was our biggest problem from the outset." He estimated that one of five mothers in the village died in childbirth, "and many of those who survived were left horribly mutilated." Dooley set up a midwife training program aimed at "young girls who aspired to the calling." The trainees accompanied him to deliveries and were taught "the principles of modern, aseptic midwifery." After each trainee had delivered twenty-five babies under supervision, she was "graduated" and presented with one of "the wonderful midwife's kits prepared and distributed by CARE."[29]

If Dooley had finally realized at least half of his oft-stated desire to become a "society obstetrician," he came to view his role in Laos as more akin to that of the family practitioner than the specialist. As a "nonpolitical" operative in Laos, Dooley persistently featured the domestic virtues of his mission, especially the power of love to win new friends in a strange land. "Having a coolie, a cook, a houseboy, interpreters and other servants in Laos is a different thing than it is in America," Dooley wrote of his Lao staff. "They dined with us, bathed with us, swam with us, worked with us, and came out on night calls with us. Later they became extremely devoted to us, caring for every aspect of our life, easing the strain whenever they could. We grew to love them all very much."[30]

In return, Dooley and his team showered their patients with "what American nurses call 'T.L.C.,' tender loving care." They were convinced that the genuine concern they felt for the Lao would earn admiration and loyalty not only for themselves but for the distant nation they represented. When the Dooley team entered the hut of a Lao family ("they are just as proud of their homes as we are," Dooley informed his readers) the visitors did not "bleat about the glories of stateside plumbing," but identified themselves only by the American flag attached to their jeep and "the words with which we instructed our interpreters to precede every statement: '*Thanh Mo America pun va* . . . The American doctor says.' We wanted eloquence in deeds, not words."[31]

In the years after Dooley's death there was much controversy about his "deeds" in Laos, as the legitimacy of his medical work in Laos was called into question. Some even dismissed the mission as a "hoax" or a "sham," denying that he provided any but the most superficial of care and then only when the newsreel cameras were rolling or the photojournalists from *Time* and *Life* were present. Yet a valuable eyewitness account of Operation Laos by a young American anthropologist working for USOM, Joel Halpern, suggests that Dooley was every bit as driven and committed to his work as his admirers claimed. During a field trip to Vang Vieng, Halpern accompanied Dooley one day "on his typical routine." The day began at 6:30 A.M. with patients already gathered on the front porch of the Operation Laos compound (or what Halpern called the "Dooley mansion"). From 7:30 to 9:30 Dooley treated patients at the dispensary: "With each patient he would explain to the local nurse . . . how he arrived at his diagnosis and why certain prescriptions were being given."[32]

Halpern accompanied Dooley on a mid-morning round of the village via "Agnes" the jeep (named in honor of Dooley's mother). "In each home," he wrote, Tom was "humble, courteous, understanding, and patient." They then set out for a village eight miles from Vang Vieng:

> As we drove up slowly to the center of the village, the youngsters ran excitedly along the jeep screaming "The American doctor has arrived." Within two minutes, over 150 people had gathered about the car. Mothers pushed their babies into his arms, old women and old men showed him their pains, trachoma patients asked him to cure their partial blindness. With each one he behaved differently, humoring the old ones, cuddling the small ones, joking with the young men and women, never giving them false hope. With each pill or injection the patient was told that this was a gift of the American people. They all were grateful to him; they brought him fruit, and they seemed to like and respect him very much.

After returning to Vang Vieng for a lunch of "glutinous rice," Halpern and the corpsmen rested while Dooley answered mail. The afternoon saw another road trip and another round of writing for Dooley, followed by a dinner of more rice prior to the evening's film screening. At 10:30, after a man arrived to announce that his wife was about to deliver a baby, Tom rode off in "Agnes" with one of the corpsmen and did not return until 2:30 A.M. "The next day," Halpern concluded, "we were *all* up at 7:00 and another similar day began."[33]

Halpern made it clear in his field notes that he would "not comment on Dooley as a social being, since it is in this capacity that most of us know him." And Dooley, for his part, made no effort to ingratiate himself to Halpern, probably because his unerring sense of hierarchy figured Halpern for a sympathetic individual who could add precious little to his prestige in the eyes of people who counted. Halpern's account of Operation Laos was echoed in the dozens of eyewitness reports filed from the site of Dooley's clinics in the months and years to come. When Tom was on location in a village, the work consumed his full attention and left no room, as he saw it, for social niceties that could be readily cultivated in the capitals of Southern Asia. Halpern perceptively caught the measure of Operation Laos in its first incarnation: "It must be said in all fairness and quite objectively speaking, that Dooley and his three young men are doing an excellent job . . . it can be said that he saved some lives, cured some, though perhaps temporarily. However, the most important aspect of this operation is that his reputation is spreading throughout the *muang* [an administrative district, akin to a canton] and if his labors leave no long range effects, it must be said that he will have sold America to 18,000 people who prior to his arrival had never heard of us."[34]

The Dooley that emerged from Halpern's report resembled a dedicated rural family practitioner. This domestic ideology at the heart of Operation Laos was prominently featured in the radio broadcasts Tom began making for St. Louis radio station KMOX in the late summer of 1956. The "little arrangement" that Dooley made with the station—the powerful, 50,000-watt midwestern flagship of the CBS network that William Paley called "the jewel in CBS's crown"—typified the high-pressure tactics Tom and his sponsors utilized to promote the fiction of down-home humility that distinguished Operation Laos from more costly programs emanating from Washington. Apart from being his hometown radio station, KMOX, as the conservative "voice of middle America" with a range covering well over twenty heartland states, guaranteed a wide audience for his Saturday dinner-hour program, "That Free Men May Live."[35]

Dooley's artistry was lauded in a State Department internal memorandum of February 21, 1957. "A large part of these tapes," wrote the bureaucrat assigned to monitor the program,

> is devoted to accounts, spiced with anecdotes, of the homely housekeeping routine of Dr. Dooley and his group—how they live, what they eat, who cooks their food and in what fashion, and the reactions of various members of the group to these conditions of life (including the cooking). Despite their folksy and casual tone, these talks have a certain calculated literary style and could easily be put together in book form.

The reports were made on Dooley's battery-operated tape recorder and shipped to St. Louis at irregular intervals. In place of specific discussions of fleeting political issues in Laos, Dooley provided his listeners with a feel for everyday life in rural Laos and urged all Americans to consider the commonalities they shared with these heretofore unknown peoples. "The political, social, and economic motives which make Asians behave as they do are the same which make Missourians act as we do," he proclaimed, in solidifying his own middle-American credentials. "I believe," he explained in a subsequent broadcast, "that if we want to show Asia and the world what America believes in that it's going to have to be done at the level of the villagers, by individuals like you and me who get down there and sweat and talk and explain."[36]

The KMOX program also enabled Dooley to domesticate his religiosity in a fashion sure to appeal to a midwestern audience. In his first broadcast he reminded his listeners of the six hundred thousand Vietnamese refugees who were "determined to live in an area where they could freely and openly worship in Jesus Christ." There were precious few Christians in Laos and Dooley never failed to assure his various audiences that there was no place for proselytizing in his mission other than of the red-blooded Americanist variety. He was particularly concerned lest non-Catholics at home mistake him for a priest, as many were doing in addressing mail to "Tom Dooley, S.J." But the "family rosary" he said aloud each night represented a simple, unthreatening affirmation of his Christian faith, and he could even disarmingly joke that the Protestant Pete Kessey complained, "Seems you can hardly get to sleep at night, up there in the jungle, what with the Catholics clicking their beads all the time."[37]

The broadcasts represented a turning point in Dooley's career; their success proved beyond any doubt that his appeal transcended the politics of anticommunism. He was an enormously gifted communicator who reached into the hearts of his audience with a rare power. In *The Edge of Tomorrow* he wrote of the broadcasts: "One time I commented, 'I certainly wish I had some hot chocolate.' I should have known better; the response by mail, air freight and other modes of transportation was overwhelming and we received hundreds upon hundreds of cans of hot chocolate."[38]

In April 1956 Dooley had sat in a suite at the Waldorf Astoria, listening distractedly to a lecture on Lao politics from IRC publicist Gilbert Jonas. By that fall it was clear that the IRC's best strategy was to "let Dooley be Dooley." At times Tom could sound remarkably insightful in ways that bolstered the flexible neutralism favored at the IRC. In a broadcast from September 1957, Dooley warned his listeners that when "Asians dislike us," it is because "we seem to be hypnotized . . . by fear of communism and its products . . .

[they] claim we blame everything on the communists." The Lao, he continued, "dislike being a buffer state . . . fear we'll drag them into war . . . establish new economic imperialism or colonialism over them."[39]

Yet if Dooley occasionally catered to his sponsors, they could be equally certain that his American constituency had little concern for their interests in Southeast Asia. He proved to be a highly unmanageable spokesman for the IRC and his other patrons, because he knew that his relationship with a rapidly growing, intensely loyal audience enjoyed a life of its own. Dooley was nobody's idea of an organization man, and he meant it when he told his KMOX listeners: "We'll try to project the more generous and kindly aspects of the American individual's impulses rather than the cooler but equally needed impersonal aspects of the bundle marked foreign aid." Those individual impulses were mediated not by any private or governmental agency, but by a highly personal spirituality and a mystical vision of an extended family, Dooley's beloved community, which increasingly consisted of people whose names he never knew.[40]

Few of his listeners were likely to have noticed the homoerotic dimensions of Dooley's family ideology. Tom presided over his mission with a blend of paternalism and military discipline. He recreated the "man's world" he had known in the navy minus the officious regulations he had either ignored or evaded. Dooley's corpsmen were invariably young men, collegians or working-class youths like Norman Baker, who was introduced in *The Edge of Tomorrow* as "200-pound barrel-chested Baker (flexing his muscles, as always)." There was an unfinished quality about Tom's "boys," who were naive about Southeast Asian politics and kept in the dark by Dooley regarding his own knowledge of Lao affairs. In later years several of the corpsmen recalled passes made at them by Dooley—suggestive pats on the leg or comments he made that seemed less inappropriate at the time. He backed off after the men showed no interest in or awareness of his overtures.[41]

When Pete Kessey was recruited by Dooley for Operation Laos in April 1956, he was struggling to remain academically afloat at a Texas pharmacy school. Kessey, like Baker and Shepard, had served as a corpsman under Dooley at Haiphong in 1954. He recalled that Dooley had already "acted like a celebrity" during the refugee operation, and though Kessey suspected Tom was "a big bullshitter," he was impressed when Dooley called him to report that he was about to launch a program in Laos modeled after Operation Brotherhood and needed Pete's help. Denny Shepard was from a small town in Oregon and halfway through his premedical training at Oregon State when he was recruited for Operation Laos. He too had been impressed by Dooley's commanding presence and social skills ("he knew where the forks went," Shepard recalled) and welcomed the opportunity to gain valuable medical experience while serving his country in Laos. Only later did the men begin to question the nature of Dooley's character as well as his mission. While in Laos they did as they were told and asked few questions; they were there, Shepard recalled, "to do a job."[42]

A number of the corpsmen who worked with Dooley in Laos between 1956 and 1960 were married, and several of their wives gave birth to children in the United States while their husbands worked with Dooley halfway around the globe. One of the corpsmen in Vang Vieng "missed his wife terribly," Dooley wrote in *The Edge of Tomorrow*, "and spent his odd moments composing lengthy letters." In a letter to his mother Dooley cruelly denounced this woman as "worthless. . . . She should realize that she has a part in the operation too . . . her job is at home, like Milton said, 'to stand and wait.' "[43]

Dooley's attitudes toward women may not have differed that greatly from those of many American men of the 1950s. In later years when he was often hospitalized, he refused treatment from female physicians (sending one away by calling her "Miss"). But his only serious relationship with a woman—his mother—was both intense and tormented. He greatly preferred communicating with Agnes Dooley through devoted daily correspondence over a distance of eight or ten thousand miles to dealing with her in person.

Dooley quickly became part of a lively, international gay community centered in the larger cities of Southeast Asia. He frequently visited the home of James H. W. Thompson, a rather mysterious former OSS officer and silk merchant whose Bangkok homes—featuring his celebrated collection of Asian art—were gathering places for travelers of many persuasions, but especially gay men (in 1959 Dooley informed his mother that Thompson, "my good friend," was the model for John Colvin, the sympathetic "powdered milk man" featured in *The Ugly American*). Dooley's intimate relationships with men were fleeting and erratic. An American employee of a large relief agency working in Laos spent a considerable amount of time with Dooley in 1956. One evening at a Vientiane bar called Dirty Dan's, Dooley kissed the man on the lips; later at a hotel the man made a sexual overture to Tom but was rebuffed because, Dooley explained, he was "in a state of grace and couldn't do that anymore." Ted Werner, who later became Dooley's pilot and was among his few confidants, recalled that Dooley conducted ongoing sexual relationships with Thai employees of Bangkok's Erawan Hotel, which quickly became his home away from Laos. According to Werner, Dooley also had relationships with several American marines assigned to the embassy in Vientiane.[44]

Werner and several other of Dooley's associates believed that Tom enjoyed one lasting emotional relationship in Laos: with Chai, his "interpreter." In *The Edge of Tomorrow* Dooley described Chai as "a short, husky lad with beautifully modeled features, wide-set eyes, clear bronze skin, and jet black hair. He wore the native sarong, knotted at the waist, an immaculate white shirt with French cuffs (the colonial influence) and, of course, no shoes." Chai slept on a mat next to Dooley in the Vang Vieng compound. He later accompanied Dooley to his next clinic in the village of Nam Tha; when Tom returned to Laos in 1958 to establish a hospital at Muong Sing he immediately had a house built at the back of the compound for Chai, who was by then married. "Chai was the most important member of our mission," wrote Dooley, "along with his phantoms, ghosts, and spirits, with whom we learned to live in peaceful coexistence."[45]

It is highly likely that Dooley viewed Southeast Asia as had numerous voyagers of various sexual persuasions: as a place where judgments on his "difference" so prevalent at home no longer applied. For an earlier generation of gay men, the lure of Orientalism originated along the Eastern frontiers of Asia. "Perhaps nowhere else," wrote literary scholar Joseph A. Boone, "are the sexual politics of colonial narrative so explicitly thematized as in those voyages to the Near East recorded or imagined by Western men."[46]

Dooley's sexual odyssey certainly recalls the experiences of such renowned Orientalists as T. E. Lawrence, who projected onto a fourteen-year-old Arab water boy with whom he grew infatuated "an idealized vision of the Arab race as pure, simple, and untainted by Western culture." Dooley's reputation has been long haunted by charges—not likely to be verified—of pederasty involving young Asian boys. His companion Chai, though young-looking, was probably in his early twenties when he first met Dooley. More important than his age is the role he played as a translator not just of language but of an entire culture Dooley found irresistible. Tom met Chai while viewing a "love court" in Vientiane: "I had often heard of this unique Lao entertainment which chants the art of courtship. It is sheer poetry, improvised on the spot. The boy extols the beauty, grace, virtue of the courted maiden; the girl sings of the boy's nobility charm, bravery." Dooley had always stood apart from other boys in St. Louis for his indifference to sports, but in Laos, at this romantic ceremony that he found deeply pleasing, "the audience listens raptly, applauding an inspired passage with an enthusiasm that Americans reserve for touchdowns or home runs." It was at that moment he decided he needed a translator. " 'What is this performance?' " I asked loudly in French. " 'What is the meaning of these words and gestures?' The people turned and stared at me. Then a voice said: 'Moi parler français, monsieur.' He introduced himself as Chai, and proceeded to interpret the love poetry into passable French."[47]

Chai's mediation of Lao culture through the French language added another romantic dimension to his appeal for Dooley, who continued to brag about his "education" at the Sorbonne. Yet if Dooley's sexuality colored his attitude toward the Lao, it coexisted easily with dominant cold war ideas about America's responsibility to developing nations. Far from affecting the "desert drag" of T. E. Lawrence, in Vang Vieng Dooley sported crisply pressed khakis and outdoor wear acquired in Manhattan at Abercrombie and Fitch. He was addressed as "Sir" by his corpsmen as well as the Lao crew members, and he always forbade his American employees to grow beards lest they be mistaken for French colonialists. Operation Laos blended military discipline with a middle-class American family ideology of hard work, loyalty, and sensible religiosity. Dooley even sent his mother a floorplan of the team's living quarters, with the "rackspace" of each member designated by name along a far wall. His mat was indicated alongside that of Chai in a corner of the room, in what could very well have been a chaste arrangement so long as Tom enjoyed continued access to urban hideaways like Bangkok's Erawan Hotel.[48]

It is difficult to compare Dooley's sexuality with that of other gay adventurers in developing nations because we cannot definitively characterize his own self-identity, depicted as it was in such wildly variegated colors by many people who claimed to know him well. He clearly enjoyed greater personal freedom in Southeast Asia than in the United States, and the region may well have represented to him a liberated zone from the bonds of homophobia that had wrecked his military career. Yet it is also true that if Laos proved to be Dooley's "sanctuary for gay men," his experience raises moral issues not unlike those faced by Lawrence and others in the Near East, where "certain historical and economic factors of Western colonialism allowed a level of exploitation potentially as objectionable as the experience of marginalization and harassment that sent these Western voyagers abroad in the first place."[49]

While Dooley may have idealized or objectified the Lao, there is evidence that many of them found Tom to be as peculiar and difficult as many of his fellow Americans did, especially compared with his easygoing corpsmen. One of Dooley's Lao translators recalled that the clinic always ran more smoothly when Tom was away. Dooley's sexual difference thus comprised but one element of a most unusual personality. To find a precedent for his unique appeal we might do well to turn from the brooding figure of T. E. Lawrence to the zany American adventurer Richard Halliburton (like Dooley a "confirmed bachelor") whose 1925 *Royal Road to Romance* chronicled the winsome Princeton graduate's retracing of Ulysses' journey in Homer's *Odyssey*. Halliburton was even better known as an itinerant lecturer;

his "rapid-fire delivery, wild gesticulations and pantomime with a high-pitched voice that vibrated with enthusiasm" neatly anticipated Dooley's performative self by several decades.[50]

From its inception, Operation Laos freely embraced the show business dimension of modern humanitarianism. Dooley courted the brokers of his celebrity from deep in the "jungle": had it not been for the medical work that was conducted almost in spite of his hectic public relations schedule, Dooley might readily be dismissed as a high-camp chorus boy with a stethoscope. Yet the months in Vang Vieng generated an undeniable personal power, rooted in Tom's ability to communicate his profound need to serve, both to the Lao and to his American audience. At times his radio broadcasts verged on messianic Hollywood madness, as when he described an evening's entertainment in the village, courtesy of Operation Laos:

> My boys love to sit with me on the porch and look into the faces of the hundreds of kids who sit on their haunches as close to the screen as they can get. The light reflected into their eyes is wonderful. There is fascination and charm, poignancy and yes, sadness too. You can see it in their eyes as they watch the world of wonder that our movies show them. We have decided against explaining some of the 16 millimeter stories to them, those that don't have a Laotian soundtrack. We do not translate but let the children build their own little delusional castles. And how they must dream, after they see the fantasy of love and lollipops, the sugarcane world of Disneyland.[51]

The Lao watched the movies from both sides of a sheet that doubled as a screen. Their dreams went unrecorded, as did those of their lonely guest, while his humiliations receded into distant memory and he found himself reanointed the people's choice as spokesman for America's crusade against godless Asian communism.

During the autumn of Tom Dooley's first tour in Laos the accolades and awards began pouring in. In late November (not "late winter" as he wrote in *The Edge of Tomorrow*) he "received a letter that made me feel like a village priest elevated to the Cardinalate. It informed me that the Junior Chamber of Commerce of the United States had voted me as one of their ten outstanding young men of 1956." The award also bestowed on Dooley membership in the Jaycees of Laos, an outfit in "its formative stages" which in 1958 provided the nucleus for the Committee for the Defense of National Interests (CDNI), an elite cadre of young anti-communist bureaucrats designed to supplant the ineffectual Lao aristocracy in governing the country. The CDNI, which scholar Len Ackland termed "no more than a U.S. front organization," played a key role in undermining efforts at coalition governments. In *The Edge of Tomorrow* Dooley exulted: "The Jaycees asked what they could do to help my mission. I had come here to help the Lao and the Lao in turn were offering their help to me."[52]

The Junior Chamber of Commerce made for a rather benign "front organization," which is probably why it had appealed to Edward G. Lansdale as he cast about, in the late summer of 1954, for yet another "psyops" angle to aid his refugee operation. He created Operation Brotherhood in collaboration with Oscar Arellano, president of the Southeast Asia Jaycees. Filipino medical teams went to Vietnam to provide "Asian-to-Asian" care for the refugees while gathering intelligence on the side. Lansdale later explained that the "CIA backing was part of U.S. support I had urged for a number of undertakings where 'people's wars' were raging and the misfortunes of countryfolk were so exploitable."[53]

Lansdale exerted a powerful influence over numerous prominent Filipinos. Where Arellano was lionized in the U.S. Catholic press as the paragon of an emerging Christian culture in Asia, Lansdale biographer Cecil B. Currey described a scene in which a despondent Arellano talked of killing himself. "Ed plied him with whiskey and sat down at his typewriter to write a long glowing eulogy about Oscar. . . . When he finished, he handed the eulogy and a .38 caliber pistol to Arellano and told him to read the paper before he shot himself. 'He read the letter, wept whiskey tears over all the nice things I'd said about him, and handed me back the gun.' "[54]

Since the Southeast Asian Jaycees organization was hardly a well-oiled fundraising machine, its American counterpart was quickly enlisted into the campaign for Operation Brotherhood, with an assist from the International Rescue Committee. On March 10, 1955, Harold Oram's public relations firm issued a press release on behalf of the American Jaycees and their president, E. Lamar Buckner, who pledged the full support of his 2,750 chapters for Operation Brotherhood. Leo Cherne informed Premier Diem on March 18 that the million-dollar campaign would support Filipino medical teams working in Vietnam. On May 8 the IRC sent an "urgent telegram" to its donors requesting they "send immediate contribution which within hours after receipt will be transmitted front line freedom in Vietnam."[55]

In an October 1955 letter to Gene Gregory, an administrator with the Jaycees International in Saigon (and the publisher of *The Times of Vietnam*, Diem's English-language mouthpiece), Leo Cherne expressed his preference for private initiatives like Operation Brotherhood to governmental aid programs. In January 1956 Cherne informed Diem that his brief service in Vietnam on Diem's behalf had inspired him to shift the IRC away from its exclusive focus on European refugees. Operation Laos was molded in the image of the Filipino program, but with the focus on a charismatic individual. When private support for Operation Brotherhood virtually collapsed in

1956, the IRC firmly hitched its declining fortunes to the jungle doctor's star. In the meantime, Dooley's selection as one of the ten outstanding men of 1956 was well timed to publicize the IRC's dual programs in Southeast Asia.[56]

Dooley had actually preceded Operation Brotherhood into Laos and could even claim to have provided material support for that mission, which, he informed his mother in April 1957, "is having a rough time getting started" despite the program's great success in Vietnam. In June he told his radio audience that Angier Biddle Duke of the IRC had personally delivered to him a check for $15,000, which Tom was to then present to Operation Brotherhood. Yet he had told his mother that the money was originally intended as "a gift to my mission": only after Tom told Duke he did not need the funds was it offered to the Filipinos. In either case the gift represented a typical instance of the Vietnam Lobby's talent for recirculating funds through their various front organizations as a means of avoiding any suspicions of governmental involvement.[57]

Operation Brotherhood had in fact been a Lansdale program from the start, in Laos as in Vietnam. The Lao version was supervised by Rufus Phillips, a former Yale football player, trusted Lansdale aide, and veteran of the Vietnam refugee campaign of 1954. The notion of a Lao Junior Chamber of Commerce sponsoring Operation Brotherhood represented one of the more audacious fictions of the cold war, as American donors were encouraged to picture earnest young Asian businessmen meeting for luncheons in bustling downtown Vientiane. When Dooley arrived in Laos in 1956 there was exactly one physician in the entire country, with a population estimated at between two and three million people. Laos was one of the poorest, most underdeveloped lands on earth, with no railroads, a handful of working telephones, virtually no electricity outside of the fitful service found in the capital and in Luang Prabang, and no coherent identity as a nation-state. (The U.S. infused staggering quantities of money and equipment into Laos beginning in 1955: by 1963 the expenditures exceeded $480 million, or $192 per capita, the highest in Southeast Asia. The per capita income of the Lao people has yet to surpass that figure.)[58]

Operation Brotherhood was perhaps the most cost-effective aid program administered in Laos. In 1959 D. C. Lavergne, the new director of USOM Laos, informed the U.S. ambassador that "it must be considered as one of the maximum political impact activities in the country." But in an ominous if cryptic foreshadowing of the scandals later to be exposed by American journalists, Phillips conceded in an April 1958 report that the "RLG [Royal Lao Government] has been reluctant from the beginning to provide counterpart funding for the project and has on several occasions diverted Operation Brotherhood funds for other purposes," such purposes tending toward the care and feeding of the opulent lifestyles numerous Lao officials had grown accustomed to, at the expense of U.S. taxpayers.[59]

Dooley's kinship with Operation Brotherhood implicated his own mission in a much closer relationship with the American government than was ever acknowledged. As early as July 1956, Milton Esman of the State Department had informed Carter de Paul of USOM that the IRC, "at our request, is exploring the possibility of developing local sponsorship [of Operation Laos] through the Vientiane Jaycees, which may provide some valuable local support for the entire undertaking." Yet while USOM documents clearly reveal ongoing U.S. financing and direction of Operation Brotherhood, Operation Laos was treated at a greater distance. In September 1956 Dooley told a CIA informant in Laos that he had been approached in Saigon on behalf of Operation Brotherhood by an unnamed "third person," who relayed a request that he travel to Sam Neua and Phong Saly—Pathet Lao strongholds in northeastern Laos—"to show the people that the agreement between the Royal Government and the Pathet Lao was sincere." Dooley reportedly declined the request on the grounds that "he did not wish to get involved in politics and wanted to know more of what was going on before making such a move."[60]

Dooley's characteristic bluster obscured the true nature of his relationship with Operation Brotherhood. From its inception in Vietnam in 1954, explained former CIA agent Joseph Burkholder Smith, the program depended heavily on the "cover" provided by "Catholic relief organizations, which, unlike the Operation Brotherhood activity in 1954, did not require complete funding from the CIA budget." "Thanks to the private efforts of the Catholic relief groups," wrote Smith (a participant in the "psyops" dimension of the refugee campaign), "it was possible to make Operation Brotherhood appear like another legitimate effort of humanitarian concern for brother Asians." Amid the work of such official agencies as Catholic Relief Services, Dooley had been groomed in Haiphong as a kind of postsectarian medical missionary. His time had now come: in non-Christian Laos any form of Church-related activity would be viewed with the deepest suspicion. He genuinely embraced Oscar Arellano's conviction that "it is time that Asians helped Asians."[61]

In fact Dooley understood the situation better than the Filipinos themselves. Miguel Bernad, the Filipino Jesuit historian of Operation Brotherhood, noted that "both in Laos and in Viet Nam the relations between Dooley and the OB personnel were most cordial. This was perhaps because, besides working for the same ends, they had a common bond in their religion." Bernad reported that while touring Operation Brotherhood facilities in Vietnam in September 1956, Dooley impressed his Filipino guides by arising early each morning to attend Mass; he cabled a Jaycee official in Manila that "the 'fine work' he had seen in Viet Nam gave him 'added inspiration' for his forthcoming crusade in Laos." But Dooley's view of his "crusade" was different from that of his Filipino coreligionists, who wore their Catholicism in a militant fashion Tom found unseemly in the post-colonial contest between communism and a spiritual yet distinctly nondenominational vision of messianic liberal Americanism. The Lao embraced Dooley's message of love while often resenting the Filipinos, as had the Vietnamese before them. Ngo Dinh Diem told Lansdale that "the Vietnamese didn't need the help of a bunch . . . of nightclub musicians (most of the dance bands in Asia at the time were made up of Filipinos)." Joseph Burkholder Smith believed the Filipinos "simply had been associated with Americans too long"; as a Chinese observer explained: "They have brown faces but they wear the same Hawaiian sports shirts the Americans do."[62]

Dooley genuinely believed that "the brotherhood of man transcends the sovereignty of nations." Whether the notion meant anything to his patients or not, there is no question that by January 1957, when Operation Laos departed Vang Vieng for a new project at Nam Tha, Dooley and his team enjoyed a relationship with the Lao unmatched by any other white men in the region. The villagers gave them an elaborate *baci,* "a ritualistic ceremony, climaxed by a grand feast, which the Lao hold to celebrate a birth, a marriage, a soldier's return from the war, or the departure of cherished friends." In his painstaking explication of the local theology to his readers, Dooley evoked the medieval scholasticism that reigned over his own, perhaps not so remote tradition. "The Lao tribes feel that the soul is a vagabond, and must be recalled to the body from time to time," he explained. After a "sorcerer" implored each of the souls corresponding to the thirty-two parts of the body to make their return, the ceremony ended with cotton strings affixed to the wrists of the honorees, one for each of the wishes bestowed on them by the sorcerer (for example, "May you always be strong against the tusks of elephants," "May you always carry with you our love"). Tom Dooley must have truly meant it when he told a friend that, in Laos at least, he resided in a state of grace.[63]

On December 28, 1956, Prince Souvanna Phouma revealed that the Royal Lao Government and the Pathet Lao had reached an agreement to form a coalition government and bring the northern provinces of Sam Neua and Phong Saly—held by the Pathet Lao since 1954—under the administration of the RLG. Although this decision had been mandated at Geneva in 1954, the United States continued to resist any cooperation between the RLG and the Pathet Lao; they were deeply suspicious of Souvanna Phouma's avowed "neutralism" and they sent him a message by temporarily suspending American aid in December.[64]

During this routine crisis Dooley reported meeting with Souvanna Phouma in early January 1957. He repeated a claim he had previously made to a CIA informant, but now added that the prime minister himself had "broached the subject I feared he would . . . would we go into the Red provinces as a Royal Lao govt delegation of Medical aid to the reds." Tom had "invited the American Ambassador to go with me [to the meeting], so I would not goof up." Dooley reported telling the prince that he was there to help the Lao, "but in no way did I want to become a political 'thing.'" Ambassador Parsons reportedly echoed Dooley's concerns and urged Souvanna to send Dooley to, in Tom's words, "those provinces who had shown alligience to the country the doctor called home," meaning anywhere other than Sam Neua or Phong Saly.[65]

Dooley knew that the embassy would have to approve any offers made by the Lao government, yet in his customary fashion he managed to further alienate Ambassador Parsons, who was still seething from a recent report that Dooley had "expressed serious criticisms of official Americans in Vientiane" in a conversation with an embassy staff member. Parsons was particularly incensed by Dooley's threat that "it was well known that he had a large audience back home and his treatment here would be made known to them." When Dooley learned that Parsons had been informed of the conversation, he fired off a memorandum on January 10 informing Parsons of his belief that it was "a miserable shame" that a government employee "has nothing else to do in Laos but to write gossip columns on official memoranda concerning my personal conversations." He also rehearsed some familiar complaints over the lack of promised support from USOM in shipping equipment from Vietnam to Laos and informed Parsons, "I haven't time for such mistakes or gobblygook."[66]

Parsons could be stuffy and officious, but Dooley's tantrums would have tried the patience of a saint; by any standard of decorum he had clearly earned himself a one-way ticket back to St. Louis. Instead, he received a calm reply from Parsons on January 12—just days after their meeting with Souvanna Phouma—in which the ambassador expressed his regret at the various misunderstandings that plagued the relationship between the embassy and Operation Laos. It was during this same period that Nam Tha was chosen and approved as the site of a new Operation Brotherhood hospital, presumably a safe locale for Dooley as well. The embassy's opinion of Dooley had certainly not improved: Parsons dubbed him "the Madison Avenue Schweitzer" in a January 16 letter to the acting director of the State

Department's Office of Southeast Asian Affairs, while Carter de Paul, in writing to a regional director of the International Cooperation Administration, referred to the "Dooley show" as a success only within "its very limited objective of bringing American medical care to certain segments of the Laotian population." But Dooley could still count on his angels as well as his growing legion of admirers. "Praise coming from around the world," he cabled his mother on the eve of the move to Nam Tha. According to the final line of the telegram, he was "most of all grateful to God you are my much beloved mother abounding especially in patience and understanding."[67]

Agnes Dooley's patience and understanding were about to be sorely tested. Dooley proceeded to Nam Tha in late January 1957. Though located in northwestern Laos not far from the border of communist China, the village was neither particularly vulnerable nor strategically significant. It appeared to provide an ideal locale for maximizing Dooley's public relations function while separating him by a mountain range from the more critical provinces to the east.

Of the original Operation Laos corpsmen, Norman Baker had already left the country and Dennis Shepard departed shortly after helping establish the clinic at Nam Tha. Through Erma Konya, a trusted friend who worked in the dining service at Notre Dame, Dooley recruited a pair of twenty-year-old undergraduates, John deVitry and Robert Waters, to replace Baker and Shepard. Before leaving South Bend, however, one of the men received an anonymous telephone call, apparently placed from Florida, explaining the circumstances of Dooley's resignation from the navy and warning him, as Dooley put it in a letter to a former navy friend, that he "was a no good character."[68]

In the flurry of letters and telegrams that ensued, Dooley never used the word *homosexuality* or any of its equivalents to describe the charges leveled against him, which quickly made their way to the Dooley home in St. Louis. As Tom's Saint Louis University High School classmate Michael Harrington explained years later, for Catholics of that era homosexuality was something that "only happened in hell," if it was imagined at all as a form of human behavior. Yet Dooley had to respond lest his career disintegrate for the second time, and he wasted no time in constructing a time-honored defense. "Know full story," he cabled his mother on February 11. "Was warned on this sort of attach. Mechanism awaiting my word." Three days later he penned a rambling letter to his mother—with copies for Clare Murphy, his former secretary, and Erma Konya—in which he made a startling announcement. "Senator McCarthy," he informed them, "whose politics I have no great point of view, called me in for several sessions while in D.C. and warned me of such an attack that may sometime come."[69]

Dooley had never before referred in writing to McCarthy, whom he had succeeded as a Catholic anticommunist folk hero. Now he recounted the grim prophecy McCarthy had offered him. The discredited senator had explained that there were two kinds of people who created public opinion in America, the "professionals" like Walter Winchell and the Alsop brothers, who were immune from personal attacks due to their permanent access to the media of mass communications. Then there were the "nonprofessionals" like Dooley himself, "who flash in the pan, have pretty brilliance for a while, and they are heard no more. . . . Senator McC says the latter are the really powerful as they are fresh and wholesome . . . and they are the most susceptible to attack as they have neither professional immunity, or adequate knowledge on how to cope with the problem."[70]

The memory of McCarthy's warning perhaps inspired Dooley to elaborate his conviction that unnamed communists were behind his latest ordeal. He had "mechanisms set up in top level bureaus in D.C. who will investigate" the rumors as part of a pattern of slander against Americans doing valiant work throughout the developing world. "It was on such a conglomeration of small little individual slanders (though horribly large to the individual) that the great Hiss's have been discovered." Considering the stress Dooley was undergoing, his conspiracy theory was relatively lucid for the times and circumstances. At least he had finally created a more imposing personal enemy than the medical faculty at Saint Louis University or jealous factotums in the navy or at the State Department. His suffering could now be squarely "offered up," in Catholic parlance, in the global struggle against godless communism.[71]

As to the specific, unnameable charge, Dooley reassured his mother: "In a man's world, on ships, in the service, these things float around all the time, landing sometimes giving a shadow varying in intensity." His faith would provide the strength he needed to persevere, for "religion gives me the weapon to conquer any such pettiness as this." As for worries his reputation would be sullied at his beloved alma mater, Dooley insisted: "I am not in the least concerned about it at Notre Dame. Neither is our Lady in the Grotto." Millions of Catholics around the world turned to Mary for consolation in times of suffering. The Blessed Virgin had also, since the visions at Fatima in 1917, served as the patroness of the struggle against international communism. Dooley had no doubt of his leadership role in a climactic stage of that campaign. Rather than passively cultivate his suffering, as many Catholics were inclined to do, he fought back, convinced that his was a divinely inspired "mission that will help free people all over the world take heart and erase this scourge from the face of the earth."[72]

By late February, with the new team settled at Nam Tha, Dooley was desperately anxious for all concerned to forget the scandal and move forward. "I pray to God," he wrote to his mother, "you have done as I have asked and dropped the whole dirty affair." But just as the monsoons came early to Laos that spring, Dooley was enshrouded in a storm generated by his own arrogance, denial, and bitter sense of humiliation. Even the journalists he had manipulated for three years now appeared as threats to his fragile equilibrium. A *Time* magazine reporter visiting Nam Tha with Angier Biddle Duke of the IRC "will probably write a stupid article on me, get me in trouble with RD [*Reader's Digest*] and frighten you [Agnes]." He even claimed he "couldn't care less" if the great Edward R. Murrow brought a crew to Nam Tha, as planned. "I work from dawn to dusk," he explained, "a 17 hour day every day. If photographers want to photograph it okay. I'll not go out of my way for them, nor will I arrange anything special."[73]

For the first time, signs of wear began to show in Dooley's relationship with his mother, as though her unwitting involvement in his recent humiliation tainted the unconditional approval he expected from her. By this time Agnes Dooley had developed a serious drinking problem, and in her growing concern for Tom's well-being she began making erratic inquiries to personnel at KMOX, sensing that her son did not provide her with a complete account of his problems in Laos. When a scheduled tape recording was late in arriving, the station contacted the State Department on behalf of Mrs. Dooley. When Tom found out about it he flew into a rage, accusing KMOX of caring only about "the holy buck" and scornfully telling Agnes, "They are still talking in Vientiane about how 'Dr. Tom is so busy with his slant eyes that he doesn't write his mommy.' "[74]

In response to his mother's lament that she was "having to learn to cut You out of my life," Dooley angrily wrote: "Why in hell do you choose to cut? Because I am working in Laos longer than originally intended?" Dooley must have initially been grateful for the opportunity to rehabilitate himself through service to Operation Laos. Now he was beginning to glimpse his future as a full-time jungle doctor, and those who failed to appreciate this special calling—even his mother—would have to learn to share him with a grandiose unfolding destiny. After complaining in a letter about the mud and insects of Nam Tha, he concluded, "I assure you mother, were it not for my 'mislead and misdirected' sense of duty I'd get the hell out of this stinking hole."[75]

By May 1957, while still confessing to some uncertainty about his future, Dooley left little doubt that he was determined to grasp whatever grandeur might be bestowed on him. After admitting to his mother that some nights, after a hike through the rain forests, he longed for "Jim Hawkins [his show horse], Park Plaza apartments, and a small general practice in Clayton," he added quickly, "I think this would make me a common man, and I do not choose to be a common man . . . I seek opportunity—not security." He described himself as "the kind of man that must take the calculated risk; to dream and to build. The joy of building my own hospital is boundless." A touch of messianism crept into the letter, as Dooley sought to distance himself further from the "dull man's role" others willingly assumed. "It is my heritage as an American," he lectured his mother, "to think and act for myself, to enjoy the benefit of my creations, and to face the world boldly and say, 'this I have done.' Realizing my duties to God and to man is the only levelling rule I must heed."[76]

Although his letters were often rehearsals for books yet to be written, they also show how Dooley was beginning to separate himself from even his mother, his most intimate human connection. While her son's kingdom was at least of this world, that was small consolation to Agnes Dooley, who never adjusted to life as a celebrity mother, her duty to share her son with the inhabitants of a kingdom halfway around the globe. For Tom Dooley, the Lao provided that unconditional love and approval he no longer sought from his fellow compatriots. He was certain the ruling elites of Laos admired and appreciated him. During yet another crisis in U.S.-Lao relations, he wrote that "my buddy Souvanna Phouma resigned as Prime Minister," but added: "The two possibilities are Katay and Phetserath . . . both more pro Dooley than even Souvanna Phouma. While in Vientiane everybody from the Ambassador down told me that Phetserath talks about no American save Dooley."[77]

Of even greater importance was the response of the montagnard people in the Nam Tha area to Dooley's new mission. Where his patients in Vang Vieng had been, for the most part, ethnically "Lao," in Nam Tha, he wrote, "there were many different tribes, each with their own ethnic characteristics. We now met such people as Yao, Thai Dam, Thai Neua, Lolo, Lan Ten, Meo, Lu, Chinese and Kha." In his radio broadcasts Dooley loved to intone the names of these groups in a voice eerily inflected with Southeast Asian tonalities. As an amateur anthropologist, his participant-observer view of ethnic interaction in Laos set him dramatically apart from American officialdom there, including even the small community of social scientists employed by USOM. In May he was visited once again by Joel and Barbara Halpern, anthropologists stationed in the ancient capital of Luang Prabang. Joel Halpern steadfastly defended Dooley against his critics, contending that Tom was "doing a remarkable job. Perhaps the thing that impressed me most was his boundless energy and enthusiasm for his work." Dooley did not always return the praise. In a letter to his mother Dooley complained that the Halperns had humiliated some villagers in bargaining for Lao costumes they hoped to donate to the Museum of Natural History in New York. "When I voice objection," he complained, "they say that the people enjoy the argument (I know a bit better) or that the thing is not of any more value (no standard by which to judge)."[78]

In reporting that the Halperns "embarrassed me, humiliated the old [Lao] man," Dooley identified himself emotionally with his hosts and patients, as he would do with increasing fervor over the next few years. In explaining to his mother why the Lao government had expelled all voluntary agencies save his from the country as a means of preserving neutrality, Dooley placed himself outside of the orbit of the colonial or imperialist mentalities no longer welcome in Southeast Asia. "They owe allegiance only to themselves," he lectured. "If, to the western mind, this chauvinism looks as though they are cutting off the head to spite the face . . . it must be remembered, that is only TO THE WESTERN mind. To them it is not." His anger toward the Halperns owed as much to a sense that they had violated his proprietary relationship with the Lao as to any concern for Lao autonomy. On June 30, Dooley wrote to the couple offering to sell them his tape recorder as well as to serve as middle-man for a pair of Yao pants the Halperns were interested in acquiring. Tom's attitude toward visiting whites was determined largely by how much respect they showed for "his Laotians."[79]

Dooley's "difference" was dramatically recast in northern Laos, as close to a state of nature as he was likely to find. There were few authorities of a civil or ecclesiastical nature, there appeared to be no judgments placed on sexual variations, nor was there a dominant ethnic or religious group. In *The Edge of Tomorrow* he described an unscheduled visit to Nam Tha by a pair of Seventh-Day Adventist missionaries stationed in Bangkok. While they were eating an Easter Sunday lunch Dooley suddenly remembered a promise he had made to circumcize "a few of the Pakistani boys in our village" on that day which, he explained, happened to be a "felicitous" one according to "the Islam calendar." Later than night Dooley "crawled back to the house and just collapsed. Only to hear Pastor Currie laughing loudly. 'Think of it,' he said, 'Irish Catholics eating lunch with Seventh Day Adventists, on Easter Sunday, performing an ancient Hebrew rite on Moslem children in the Buddhist Kingdom of Laos!' "[80]

Playful as it sounds, Dooley's story offered an important message to his audiences about ecumenism and interethnic harmony, notions that continued to encounter resistance at home even in the age of sociologist Will

Herberg's "triple melting pot." Primitive Laos ironically offered Dooley more "progressive" social conditions than he had found in the States. In viewing his religion and ethnicity in relative terms ("there are more spirits and phantoms in Laos," he wrote, "than there are fairies and leprechauns in Ireland"), Tom was able to surmount the tendency of many American Catholics to equate their faith with the nation's destiny. His actual experience in Laos had almost nothing to do with fighting communism, though he kept a ready supply of rhetorical materials on hand to sustain an audience who envisioned him rescuing freedom fighters from jungle battlegrounds.[81]

Dooley spent a great deal more time battling with his own demons than he did fighting communism. The months at Nam Tha witnessed a maturation in Tom's response to his own experience. He was even able to admit that "I personally lived to a certain extent in a state of fear all the time I was in Laos. Fear of isolation, fear of loneliness, and fear of the great and ominous rain forest." He was growing sufficiently comfortable with his interfaith appeal to remind his readers that "John, Bob and I are Catholics. In the isolation of the north there are no priests, though on two occasions during our time at work, an Oblate missionary came to visit us. It was good to have our hut of a house transformed into a church of God during the thirty minutes that the priest offered holy Mass." But Laos itself provided the sources of a postdenominational mysticism that scarcely cloaked Dooley's pointed critiques of American materialism and even, to some extent, the compromised situation of his own religious tradition in America:

> In college we were taught the ubiquity of God. But to see God in all things when you are plunged into bleating materialism is sometimes hard. I certainly cannot see God when I look at a Mercedes Benz convertible. But in the jungle it is easier. Here we can know God a little better. Perhaps it is because of the solitude. We can see God in the tropic rain, in the monsoon mud, in the tangy sweet smell of the earth that comes upon us as we walk amongst the mountains.[82]

He now convinced himself that the gulf separating himself from the "otherness" of the Lao had been bridged. "We were Americans, our skins were white, our speech and manners and habits were different. But we weren't curiosities or strangers any more. We 'belonged.'" Because he was Tom Dooley, his new insights were often cut with the familiar language of wise-cracking cultural imperialism he could have acquired from the "road" films of Bob Hope and Bing Crosby or any number of other sources. The local "witch doctors" with whom he competed in Nam Tha were dubbed "Old Joe" and "Maggie," a "snaggle-toothed old crone, and the dirtiest woman in the village, dressed in a ragged western-style blouse and skirt with a filthy towel around her head. Maggie shaved her head regularly, but she never washed her hands." Yet the methods Dooley employed to placate the shamans were likely, as he put it, to "raise the hackles of the American Medical Association." He began to treat them "as 'colleagues in the healing arts' who practiced a somewhat different discipline of medicine with which we disagreed yet respected" (and since he was certain they were "getting paid by the Reds," he also paid them "so much a month").[83]

More than a calculated ploy, Dooley's cooperation with Lao traditions reflected a more intimate turn toward a different way of knowing the world. In the summer of 1957 Nam Tha was suddenly gripped with "something called *kia atomique* (atomic fever) which can be roughly translated as atomic flu!" Dooley explained that opponents of his mission, of whose identity he was uncertain, had spread rumors of an American counterpart to the Asian flu then spreading across the United States, borne not by germs but by atomic particles presumably in circulation since the bombings of Hiroshima and Nagasaki in 1945. In *The Edge of Tomorrow* he called it "a masterpiece of subtle propaganda—and a telling blow at the White-Man's medicine which, apparently, was getting to be too popular in Nam Tha." But in writing to his mother on July 2 Tom admitted that, while he believed the witch doctors were responsible for the panic, he "had over 150 at sick call this morning, with bizarre symptoms. Don't know if I'm getting brainwashed . . . but sometimes I wonder about that bomb."[84]

Like the early settlers of America, who were at times viewed by Europeans as having assumed some of the putative characteristics of Indians, Dooley believed that his relationship with the Lao had generated a new identity which immunized him from charges of neocolonialism. He explained that the northern Lao peoples had no ideological orientation but were susceptible to communist propaganda directed "against the white man." But the word for white foreigner, *farange,* was actually "the Lao corruption of the word français or French." It was not Dooley but his Lao interpreters who "told the people that I was not farange, and should be called *Thanh Mo American* or simply *Thanh Mo.*" He therefore felt empowered in name and deed to claim for himself a wholly unique encounter with the Lao, and to interpret their desires to the outside world as well as to heal their bodies.[85]

As the time grew near for Operation Laos to phase out of Nam Tha, corpsman John deVitry suggested to Dooley that they make the first leg of their journey to Vientiane via pirogues, or dugout canoes, stopping at villages along the way to conduct sick-call. Against the warnings of a local Lao official that "the people in the isolated villages were hostile to white men," they embarked in mid-July on a two-week journey to Luang Prabang. The "great float" provided ideal material for the concluding section of *The Edge of Tomorrow,* deepening the tone of spiritual pilgrimage just prior to Dooley's triumphal return to civilization. This section of the narrative features the most self-consciously literary writing Dooley was capable of, and the result was a stirring travelogue of a high order, a kind of medical missionary's Southeast Asian version of *Life on the Mississippi.*[86]

Even his polemics were lent a unique authority when tested in the wilderness. "These villagers have no concept of what happened in the political field," he wrote. "They understand nothing about the two camps of ideas, the God-loving men and the Godless men. They have no idea of what America is and certainly no idea of where it is located." As Dooley was writing this passage in St. Louis in the autumn of 1957, Jack Kerouac's novel *On the Road* became the season's literary sensation, despite having been composed nearly a decade earlier. Late in the novel Kerouac describes the encounter of "Sal Paradise" and "Dean Moriarty" with Mexican peasants in the Sierra Madre Oriental: "All had their hands outstretched. They had come down from the back mountains and higher places to hold forth their hands for something they thought civilization could offer, and they never dreamed the poor broken delusion of it. They didn't know that a bomb had come that could crack all our bridges and roads and reduce them to jumbles, and we would be as poor as they someday, and stretching out our hands in the same, same way."[87]

Unlike Kerouac, Dooley was certain he had much to offer the peasants of Laos, who greeted him not merely with outstretched hands but with gifts: "We were usually met at the river's edge by some elder of the village with a small bowl containing some flowers, candles and other offerings of welcome to the visitors." Just as his patients at Nam Tha were expected to pay for medical services with chickens or fruit, the villagers along the river partook of what Dooley construed as a ritual exchange of offerings that ennobled both parties. Yet he was as solicitous as Kerouac of these "fellaheen" peoples in their blessed ignorance of a world that threatened to destroy their timeless idyll. Tom Dooley was more willing to incant the Manichaean dualism of cold war rhetoric, but he knew by now how little that meant to anyone in northern Laos or, for that matter, southern China, which occasionally supplied him with patients who were as little concerned with his politics as were the Lao.[88]

By the end of "the great float," Dooley knew that he had embarked on a journey much grander than a crusade against godless communism. "We really had taken American humanity into the most unknown, untouched hinterlands. We felt as though we had done some service in the name of our country, our fellow man and our God." A cable to Agnes Dooley testified to the magnitude of his achievement and proclaimed his fitness for challenges sure to come: "Arrived Luang Prabang completing two weeks river trip by dugout pirogue from chinas border. Reached thousands who have never seen doctor not white man distributed half ton medicines excellent health."[89]

★ 6 ★

Jungle Doctor for a
New Age

Tom Dooley began his long journey home in August 1957 with a working vacation in Hong Kong, where he labored over the manuscript that became *The Edge of Tomorrow* and held court poolside at the Peninsula Hotel. In typically humble fashion he had planned an itinerary that included a visit with his role model, Dr. Albert Schweitzer, in Lambaréné, French Equatorial Africa (present-day Gabon). Next came a rendezvous with his mother in Rome where, he later told a friend, he was "given a Papal decoration" (he was actually made an honorary member of a missionary order, the Oblates of Mary Immaculate, who supplied all thirty-five of the priests then serving in Laos). In early October Tom and Agnes Dooley sailed out of Naples for New York aboard the USS *Independence:* "We are first class," he reminded her, "so bring your jewels."[1]

Reporting from Hong Kong for the *New York Times* on August 31, 1957, Greg MacGregor wrote that Dooley "was on his way to the clinic of Dr. Albert Schweitzer in French Equatorial Africa." The story could not have been more effective had it been written—like so many other accounts of Dooley's work appearing in the *Times*—by a member of the Harold Oram public relations firm. MacGregor reported that Dooley stressed the differences in philosophy between Schweitzer, a missionary, and his own postcolonial approach. " 'Religion has often been the avant-garde for colonialism, and the people of Asia know it only too well,' he said. 'I am simply a medical practitioner trying to help my fellow men.'" He acknowledged, however, the practical assistance Schweitzer had offered in his correspondence, "especially in dealing with witch doctors. 'Dr. Schweitzer told me to win them over, so I gave them each 50 cents a week,' Dr. Dooley said."[2]

Regardless of the differences between the two men, a meeting with the great Dr. Schweitzer was essential for aspiring jungle doctors, especially so for Dooley, since he had cited the Alsatian Nobel laureate as the primary inspiration for Operation Laos. The two physicians made for a fascinating study in contrasts. The eighty-two-year-old Schweitzer had been working as a missionary doctor in Africa since 1913. He was a renowned Protestant theologian and philosopher from a family that had also produced Jean-Paul Sartre, a younger cousin. Tom Dooley liked to drop the names of philosophers but had learned to deftly change the subject when it turned out he knew nothing about the thinker just cited, as when he told admirers in a crowded Bangkok hotel lobby that Spinoza was one of his favorites.[3]

Schweitzer was a virtuouso organist and organ builder, a Bach scholar and preservationist of whom it was written: "To the extent that there is good music today in churches and good organ music at concerts, we are greatly indebted to Schweitzer." Dooley knew that the Paris Bach Society had presented Schweitzer with "a zinc-lined piano equipped with organ pedals so that he could continue playing, and practicing, in the humid African jungle where no normal organ could survive." En route to Laos in August 1958, Tom stopped in Hong Kong to purchase a zinc-lined piano with funds provided by the Wilson Club of Bridgeport, Connecticut, in response to his stated desire to "take Chopin to North Laos." He told a friend in Bangkok that Schweitzer had personally ordered the piano for him; if so, the eminent missionary was responsible for introducing cocktail music to the Golden Triangle.[4]

There is an irresistible quality to the contrast between Schweitzer's profound engagement with the civilizing missionary values of nineteenth-century, high-culture Europe and Dooley's embodiment of gladhanding American hucksterism unleashed in the developing world. Yet Schweitzer was no less implicated in the "culture of personality" than the young Irish American he outlived, despite having been born more than a half-century before Dooley. Like Dooley he possessed what we would call tremendous charisma; a friend of Schweitzer referred to the "total presence" that made him, like Dooley, especially attractive to women. "Besides all this," wrote Schweitzer's biographer of his early adult years, "he was becoming something of a dandy—so he himself related in old age to Mrs. Erica Anderson, the documentary filmmaker whose film about him won an Oscar in 1958 and who became a close friend" (Anderson later traveled to Laos to film a documentary on Dooley in action at Muong Sing).[5]

Dooley traveled to Lambaréné in "the days when the appearance of a camera was the cue to strike a pose—a habit he [Schweitzer] never entirely grew out of." Befitting a true celebrity, Schweitzer had even received his first serious dose of the kind of negative publicity that plagued Dooley throughout his career. In late 1953 a British journalist described the hospital compound at Lambaréné as a squalid slum and concluded: "The hospital today exists for him rather than he for it. Here it is: deliberately archaic and primitive, deliberately part of the jungle around it, a background of his own creation which probably means a good deal more philosophically than it does medically." Schweitzer was further criticized for harboring paternalist, racist views toward his African clients ("Democracy is meaningless to children!" he was reported to have bellowed), which, while fully representative of his era, seemed to tarnish the halo that his disciples had been polishing for decades.[6]

The encounter in Lambaréné would have thus provided Dooley with a rare opportunity not only to observe his idol at work but to glean the master's wisdom about the special frustrations of their shared vocation. The meeting assumed its rightful stature within Dooley lore. In *The Edge of Tomorrow* Dooley called their time together his "biggest thrill." "It is difficult to describe him," he continued. "He has sensitiveness and forcefulness at one and the same time. He is both tender and majestic. His grizzly old face is wonderful to see." To his friend Dolf Droge, a USIS operative in Laos, Dooley described his "time with Schweitzer. His hospital is somewhat frightening but the man is absolutely magnificent. His talk is like a long, splendid carol and surge of thought, that bathes one from head to foot or swings you quite free from your moorings. When I talked with him and listened to him it was like watching lights play on a fountain. The man actually sparkles."[7]

While Dooley's powers of description appeared as sharp and sure as ever, the actual circumstances of his initial meeting with Dr. Schweitzer are anything but clear. For starters, Tom could not possibly have been in Africa with Schweitzer in the late summer of 1957. In June of that year Ali Silver, one of several women who devoted their lives to Schweitzer's work, wrote to Dooley in Laos inviting him on behalf of the master to visit Lambaréné during the coming months. Silver informed him that Schweitzer was too busy to write personally and she warned that he "may not be here" when Tom arrived, but he was welcome to come just the same. Schweitzer surely had more important things on his mind, particularly the death of his wife on May 30, just three days prior to Ali Silver's letter to Dooley. Although Hélène and Albert Schweitzer had grown apart, he now faced—in addition to the emotional burdens he kept hidden from view—a lengthy trip to Europe "to clear up Hélène's affairs." On August 1 Dooley informed his mother that "there is a slight chance" that Schweitzer "might be called to Gunsbach in Alsace." Schweitzer's departure for Europe was reported in the international press on August 1; he did not return to Africa until December.[8]

Tom Dooley told at least a part of the truth to a priest, a missionary of the Oblates of Mary Immaculate. In a letter of August 4 to a Father Joseph R. Birch, an Oblate priest, he noted that Schweitzer "is in Alsace at the moment, but I can see his life's work." Yet since he could never tell a simple story, Dooley also claimed that Schweitzer had invited him to consider working in Lambaréné for one year, but that he had "no intentions of the latter, mainly because it is a missionary hospital." In letters to his mother from Laos Dooley hedged about his travel plans but he did indicate one scenario by which he might visit with Schweitzer in Europe: "Dr. Schweitzer wrote that he will be in either Gunsbach, Alsace, Zurich Switzerland, or Rome . . . and we are to go wherever he will be." In *Promises to Keep* Agnes Dooley simply reported that Tom "stopped over in Lambaréné . . . at the invitation of Dr. Albert Schweitzer." Since she met her son in Rome, Agnes presumably would have known about any meetings with Schweitzer in Europe, but she had also learned not to ask too many questions lest she fulfill her great fear of being cut out of Tom's life.[9]

The mystery is only compounded when viewed from the perspective of Schweitzer's biography. By the 1950s, according to James Brabazon, "more and more people could claim to have met Schweitzer, but very few of those could claim to know him." The surviving letters he wrote to Dooley, several brief notes between 1958 and 1960, give no indication that they had met or were connected in any way other than through their shared vocation. Tom received friendlier notes from his assistants Ali Silver and Mathilde Kottman, who may have also written the letters signed in Schweitzer's name; their handwriting "came to look almost identical with his own. Mathilde Kottman's in particular was said to have been seen by handwriting experts and pronounced indistinguishable from Schweitzer's." Finally and perhaps strangest of all there is an undated letter from Schweitzer to Agnes Dooley, apparently written shortly after Tom's death, in which he not only acknowledged having made "his acquaintance when he came to see me at Lambaréné," but claimed that they had "subsequently met twice more," once in Alsace and again in Lambaréné. "Dear Madame, your son was one of the great personalities that have appeared in the world."[10]

Our suspicions, however, are quickly revived by the letter's final line: "Knowing your sadness I send you these lines through Dr. Comanduras." Peter Comanduras was a Washington surgeon who along with Dooley had cofounded MEDICO, the successor to Operation Laos launched in 1958; it immediately became a generous financial supporter of Schweitzer's program, often over Dooley's objections. It is entirely possible that Schweitzer had agreed, perhaps after some urging, to authorize a letter of condolence to Dooley's mother embellishing the extent of his friendship with her departed son. Dooley probably visited Lambaréné in September 1957, and he may even have met briefly with Schweitzer in Gunsbach en route to Rome later that month. From the perspective of public relations it hardly mattered whether Dooley and Schweitzer ever came face to face, so long as Schweitzer offered his imprimatur to the younger, more controversial jungle doctor. The nonrelationship the two men enjoyed was emblematic of the culture of celebrity they both claimed to transcend in differing ways.[11]

While we might call Dooley a liar for placing Schweitzer in Lambaréné when he was actually in Europe, amid the prevaricating he characteristically managed to wrest some useful distinctions between Schweitzer's stubborn antimodernism and his own more pragmatic if less principled attitudes. "There are many things about his hospital I do not like," he told Dolf Droge, citing especially the willfully primitive atmosphere and the resistance to technology that Dooley viewed as counterproductive. "He is a stubborn old Kraut," he concluded in a colorful if ethnically imprecise flourish, "a crusty old Bismarck but as someone once wrote he has a heart of gold."[12]

Soon after arriving in New York on October 17, 1957, Dooley checked into the Waldorf Astoria to revise the manuscript of *The Edge of Tomorrow* on the urging of James Monahan and Robert Giroux, his respective editors at the *Reader's Digest* and Farrar, Straus and Cudahy. He was told to "re-write the whole book again with a few very basic fundamental changes in its philosophy." Until then he had worked on the manuscript for just a few weeks while in Hong Kong and later aboard the *Independence*, where he had conscripted "a group of USIS girls going home from Rome who were delighted to have an opportunity to earn $50 and did not mind typing a few hours each day." Within a few weeks an entirely new version had been produced, reflecting the wishes of his editors: "Rather than be Dooley and his boys in conflict with a foreign aid program the idea had to be changed to Dooley and his boys in conflict with a savage jungle, a distant kingdom, loneliness and the monotony of misery. I quite agree it reads much better this way than the former."[13]

These changes were important if Dooley hoped to work again in Southeast Asia, since any new program similar to Operation Laos would receive even more scrutiny from the State Department as the region's political situation grew more vexing, at least from the American viewpoint. Virtually everyone *but* Dooley had been troubled by an aspect of Operation Laos that had not been adequately addressed in the planning stages: what would become of clinics like the one in Vang Vieng after his team departed for a new adventure? In a November 1956 letter scolding Dooley for viewing the Pathet Lao as merely "misunderstood," Assistant Secretary of State Walter S. Robertson had applauded Operation Laos for rendering a "much-needed service both to Laos and Lao-American relations." But he also expressed his concern that "something can be done to assure continuity after the departure of you and your team-mates; newly awakened demands impose an insistent burden upon the Lao Government for their continued satisfaction." In late January 1957, USOM chief Carter de Paul had conceded to an official of the ICA: "We are still facing the question of what happens in a Dooley penetrated area after his departure."[14]

Even sympathetic observers like the USOM anthropologists Joel Halpern and Howard Kaufman were concerned about the long-term effects of a program that raised the expectations of a local population, only to suddenly disappear with no trace other than an abandoned clinic and such "trainees" as were willing to take up the mission without *Thanh Mo America* at the helm. Kaufman placed the blame not on Dooley but on the character of the Lao "doctor" being trained to carry on the work at Vang Vieng; he was characterized as "lazy" and "prejudiced against minority group peoples who come to the dispensary."[15]

Dooley knew that the man Kaufman referred to as a "Lao doctor" was what the Lao elite called *médecins indochinois,* the equivalent of junior high school graduates "who have had a little medical training." Tom had given no thought to sustaining the clinics after his departure. The original prospectus for Operation Laos had called for the team to work for no more than a week in one area followed by a "return to the capital to get a hot shower, clean up, re-stock, and then go to another tribe. In no way shall we satiate one group of people." Later the clinics were turned over to the Lao Public Health Service, but the facilities at Vang Vieng and Nam Tha quickly deteriorated and were barely functional by the time Dooley returned to Laos in the late summer of 1958. In *Promises to Keep* Agnes Dooley blamed the fiasco at Nam Tha on the "young medical student who had two years of training in Cambodia," chosen by Dooley to run the clinic. "Unfortunately," she sanctimoniously wrote, "the young man in charge was a source of future disappointment for Tom."[16]

Tom Dooley was a white-hot commodity in late 1957, but to sustain his career as a jungle doctor he still needed the ballast only an established humanitarian agency could provide. The International Rescue Committee again mobilized its good offices on his behalf, creating a new program unveiled in February 1958 as MEDICO (Medical International Cooperation Organization), a voluntary agency with which Dooley was intimately associated for the remainder of his life. As early as April 1957 Tom had written to his mother of an offer tendered by the IRC's Angier Biddle Duke during his visit to Nam Tha. "He wants me to return," he explained, "go on the IRC payroll, form a medical team, and return to threatened areas of the world for a year here, or there. He has in mind just now, places like Vienna, Terahan, Africa, Morocco, etc."[17]

During the months since the IRC presented Dooley with a chance for redemption in Laos, a discernible shift in the power balance of his relationship with the agency had occurred, as he noted in a May 1957 letter to his mother: "IRC is absolutely voracious to get their hands on me 'totally' so they can claim me in their publicity etc. . . . Ambassador Duke told me he was at a dinner where Ed Sullivan was, and Duke said 'Why don't you interview me when I return from my visit to the Orient?' Sullivan said 'where are you going?' Duke answered 'to visit Ngo Dinh Diem, and Dr. Dooley.' With this Sullivan said, 'Sorry, got all the politics, and diplomacy I need, but if you can get Dr. Dooley to come here, then we'll give you $5,000 for his mission."[18]

The only personal quality Tom Dooley could scarcely have exaggerated was his prodigious gift for attracting goods, services, and cash to any enterprise with which he was associated. The IRC had witnessed the lavish support showered on Dooley by both individuals and corporations in the early days of Operation Laos; as a group that retained a professional fundraiser, its leaders must have been astonished to discover that he employed no particular technique but simply assumed that people would naturally wish to contribute to his exalted mission. Despite the IRC leadership's reservations about Dooley as a person, he represented the most dependable meal ticket they were likely to find.

The International Rescue Committee was not faring very well in the early days of 1958. In fact the organization had been struggling for years, partly because of its complex ideological baggage, but mainly because the American public could not be counted on to maintain a steady interest in the fate of refugees from strange lands. Harold Oram addressed the IRC's quandary with painful clarity at a meeting on March 27, 1958. "This is an organization," he wrote in a draft statement presented to IRC officers, "that cannot get money for its appeal on a stable basis because people in the U.S. are not interested in refugees per se. They are only interested when they have political significance." As one of the prime architects of a new program centered around Dooley, Oram insisted that MEDICO offered "an element of stability which no refugee program can have" and predicted it would bring in "a million dollars a year," three times what the IRC had raised in 1957, a relatively good year due to the lingering interest in Hungarian refugees.[19]

The IRC was in the business of doing good works. While its leaders were genuine humanitarians, they operated in a competitive environment whose stakes entailed personal prestige as well as greater profitability for other concerns with which they were associated. Harold Oram's assertion that decisive action in 1956 had "captured the Hungarian crisis for the IRC" set the tone for the group's aggressive fundraising strategy, especially at a time, as he put it, when "you are in the downtrod." Several IRC officers had assumed $40,000 of the agency's debt in the early 1950s. When the extraordinarily well-connected and wealthy Angier Biddle Duke was named president in 1954, "they figured he would be the 'open sesame' but it didn't work out that way. It was not as simple a problem as we had assumed." Even the IRC's highly touted partnership with the Junior Chamber of Commerce on behalf of Operation Brotherhood had produced less than $300,000 over a two-year period.[20]

In July 1958 a report commissioned by the National Information Bureau, a watchdog organization concerned with nonprofit agencies, accused the IRC of periodically issuing "fund-raising appeals that are excessively exaggerated or subject to misinterpretation by prospective contributors." The report concluded that "the IRC has not as yet qualified as meeting the minimum standards of your bureau." While the IRC could challenge the political motivation behind such charges, it could scarcely contest a charge that the organization "has not yet defined its political objectives in sufficiently clear and precise terms." The IRC was in an almost impossible bind: vulnerable to attacks from the Right, it was also deeply involved in aiding a key segment of the U.S. intelligence community, whether or not all of its officers and staff were aware of the Lansdale connection.[21]

As long as the leaders of the IRC remained at the helm of the Vietnam Lobby, the organization's activities and goals could never be fully disclosed to donors. In May 1957 Harold Oram's firm had handled the publicity and written the speeches for Ngo Dinh Diem during his "triumphal" visit to the United States in pursuit of greater support from the Eisenhower administration. Diem continued to receive his money's worth: at a Waldorf Astoria luncheon he movingly compared his refugee constituents with "the pilgrims and immigrants who, in past centuries, landed on these shores for a better life in the framework of Freedom." At a dinner at New York's Ambassador Hotel, cosponsored by the IRC and the American Friends of Vietnam, Angier Biddle Duke presented Diem with the Adm. Richard E. Byrd Memorial Award. The dinner program proclaimed: "History will note that the largest single contribution received by any voluntary agency for Hungarian aid came from the Republic of Vietnam. In a gesture which at once strengthened the cause of human liberty and the brotherhood of free nations, President Ngo Dinh Diem, on behalf of the people of Vietnam, contributed $100,000 through the IRC to aid the European victims of world communism." This "gesture" represented yet another instance of the Vietnam Lobby's interlocking directorate transferring funds from one of its programs to another, with the goal of "capturing" one crisis while making another client look good, all at no cost to anyone save American taxpayers. It failed, however, to inspire a significant upsurge in private donations to the IRC.[22]

The problem with the leadership of the Vietnam Lobby—and the key to Dooley's attractiveness—was that they inevitably gravitated to Left-liberals to front their anticommunist campaigns, whether their heart was in the job or not. The most notable example of the Vietnam Lobby's ill-fated "cultural work" was its role in the film adaptation of Graham Greene's 1955 Vietnam novel, *The Quiet American*. The renowned director Joseph L. Mankiewicz acquired the rights to the project in the latter part of 1955. In May 1956, not long after returning from a location-scouting trip to Vietnam (a free-lance publicist working with Harold Oram on the project exulted, of Mankiewicz: "He fell in love with Vietnam and the Vietnamese and I think we have a very important ally"), he became a member of the IRC board. Despite Mankiewicz's lofty artistic credentials, the screen version of *The Quiet American* was essentially a costly, if jumbled advertisement for Diem and his American handlers.[23]

Edward G. Lansdale, who has for years been "cast" by scholars as the model for Greene's inscrutable "quiet American" (a wholly inaccurate surmise which has nevertheless been ritually repeated in scores of books), met with Mankiewicz in Saigon to help the director transform Greene's anti-American novel into an anticommunist film. In a remarkable letter to Mankiewicz, Lansdale even suggested in March 1956 that the main character, Alden Pyle, be portrayed not as an American intelligence agent but as an individual in Vietnam "on a foundation grant from some U.S. foundation," that is, a figure not unlike a representative of the IRC. In several cities the film's 1958 premiere doubled as an IRC fund-raiser, another costly gesture that backfired, since the film was an abject failure both critically and commercially. In its desire to profit from a rousing anticommunist, pro-American action film, the IRC might have done better than to cultivate a director who would later call Los Angeles "the true threat to the American spirit and the American mind . . . a place where I think it is still against the law to teach your children that the United Nations exists." While a member of *The Quiet American* production staff later claimed that Mankiewicz was "brainwashed by prominent Friends of the Diem regime [sic], among them Angier Biddle Duke," the ambivalence the director felt about American anticommunism was clearly shared by elite figures at the Vietnam Lobby, whose propagandistic artistry was often as muddled as the cinematic version of *The Quiet American*.[24]

The debacle only enhanced, however, the image of Edward G. Lansdale at the IRC. Gilbert Jonas of the Harold Oram firm—which continued to represent the Diem regime as well as the IRC and the American Friends of Vietnam—had contacted the State Department for script approval (since *The Quiet American* was to be filmed in part on location in Vietnam), only to be rebuffed by Assistant Secretary of State Walter Robertson on the grounds that Graham Greene was a suspected communist. Jonas then contacted Lansdale and the State Department soon relented, leaving Jonas with the impression that Lansdale, besides being one astute individual, enjoyed ready access to President Eisenhower himself. He also grew impressed during their conversation by Lansdale's denunciation of McCarthyism and the genuineness of his convictions regarding insurgent democracy in the developing world. But Lansdale could not of course play himself, either in a movie or in a real-life publicity campaign on behalf of freedom in Southeast Asia. The casting of war-hero-turned-wooden-actor Audie Murphy in the title role, though, was intended to capture the spirit of the affable Americans Joseph Mankiewicz had witnessed building a nation in Vietnam—"an idealistic bunch of kids . . . who couldn't set off a firecracker on the Fourth of July."[25]

Audie Murphy was not a method actor: he kept a .45 pistol and five hundred rounds of ammunition handy on location in Saigon, lest he be killed or kidnapped by the Asians his character was dedicated to saving. His performance as Alden Pyle showed how ineffective the vaunted psywar techniques of Lansdale—and the public relations experts—could prove in the absence of sincere convictions of the type Tom Dooley projected in abundance. Dooley would in fact exult, in a 1959 radio broadcast: "What makes Americans loved by the people around the world, who do love us, is the fact we're just really a bunch of overgrown kids. We go to movies, we go to drive-ins, we get a little drunk, and everybody has a great time." Tom would continue to exasperate his sponsors by a stunning indifference to basic geopolitical data, but if he was an embarrassment in most settings, his performances in early 1958 on the "Today" show were undeniably brilliant. He now stood poised to become the first great idealist-hero of the television era.[26]

MEDICO was formally launched at a press conference held at the Overseas Press Club in New York on February 4, 1958. Dooley boasted to Anne and

Hank Miller of USIS that at an IRC board meeting late in the previous year, he had convinced the members to amend the group's charter ("to protect, aid, and give financial help to the refugees of totalitarian oppression"), after "talking like grease lightening." A prospectus for MEDICO, "all drawn up in legal flim flam," was then enthusiastically approved. "Under MEDICO," declared IRC president Angier Biddle Duke at the press conference, "a newly created division of the IRC, teams of doctors and medically trained assistants will be sent into 'underdeveloped' areas of the world where they will build, equip and staff medical clinics and small hospitals. Working in remote village areas, recommended by host governments, these doctors will train indigenous staffs, and after eighteen months to two years, withdraw, leaving behind all their equipment and self-sufficient local staffs." In addition to a new program in Laos under "the inspired leadership of Dr. Thomas A. Dooley," MEDICO would "support the work of the legendary Burma Surgeon, Dr. Gordon Seagrave in his hospital at Nankham, Burma."[27]

Four generations of Seagraves had worked as missionaries in Burma. After studying medicine at Johns Hopkins University and marrying an American woman, Dr. Gordon Seagrave (1897–1965) returned to the Karenni State of Burma in 1922 to operate a hospital under the auspices of the American Baptist Foreign Mission. During World War II he led a surgical unit serving the Chinese armies in Burma under the command of American Lt. Gen. Joseph W. Stilwell, fulfilling his desire "to do some little bit that would help the America I loved and called my own even though most of my life had been spent in a foreign country." Barbara Tuchman described Seagrave as "unorthodox, uncompromising, outspoken, and dedicated, with something of Stilwell's caustic character and hatred of pretensions."[28]

Seagrave had indeed confessed in his 1943 autobiography that "as a missionary I was a most unorthodox pain in the neck. As a doctor also I was decidedly unorthodox." In late November 1957 Dooley informed the Millers that Seagrave "has broken with the church and is no longer proseyltizing," and was therefore eligible for MEDICO support. Dooley's professed disdain for missionaries accounted for his ambivalence toward Schweitzer's operation in Lambaréné and bolstered his credentials as an enlightened postcolonialist. He told the Millers that MEDICO would be "publically admitted to be modeled from the Asian Filippino Idea" behind Operation Brotherhood, and added: "I think it behooves we immaculately conceived Americans to copy some ideas from our Asian brothers."[29]

Dooley's hasty judgments on the religiosity of others may have deflected potential concerns about his own commitments. Schweitzer's Protestant theology, after all, was far more "modern" than Dooley's much simpler faith; the venerable Alsatian was "a skeptic—a doubting Thomas" regarding such issues as the Resurrection, and he essentially argued, in such works as *The Quest of the Historical Jesus,* that the scientific method had rendered useless any effort to reconcile the life of Christ with Christianity. Schweitzer called himself an "undogmatic" Christian, one who "follows Jesus and accepts none of the doctrines laid down by the early Church or any other Church."[30]

Schweitzer and Seagrave enjoyed an advantage Dooley seems never to have considered: as Protestants, their missionary activities would rarely be viewed as problematic by the civilizations they represented; they were free to innovate theologically as well as medically. Rather than viewing his manic Americanism as either a public surrogate for Catholicism or a sign of contradiction to it, Dooley believed that his brand of postdenominational humanitarianism signaled a new age. Unlike some Catholics who felt constrained to demonstrate their loyalty, Dooley's ardent patriotism seemed a wholly natural extension of his faith. Dr. Schweitzer was not impressed by this dimension of Tom's mission. Dooley admitted to Anne and Hank Miller that "he does not like my chauvinism, claiming that nationalities should have nothing to do with it, and we should not restrict our selves, nor the phillipine operation, to the areas where the freedom-knowing people are in need."[31]

The IRC had decided that Schweitzer's imprimatur was essential for ensuring the credibility of MEDICO with the humanitarian aid establishment. They dispatched Leo Cherne to Lambaréné in early 1958, accompanied by Peter Comanduras, a fifty-year-old professor of gastroenterology at the George Washington University Medical School who had been recruited by Harold Oram to serve as the secretary general of MEDICO. Comanduras had developed an interest in medical aid to developing nations during a trip to the Caribbean on behalf of the China Board Foundation in 1955, but his role with MEDICO was to administer the program from New York and recruit physicians for new projects as the organization grew. Cherne was such a fervent admirer of Schweitzer that he had just completed "a heroic-size bust of the great humanitarian." Unlike Dooley's "visit" with Schweitzer the previous fall, the journey of Cherne and Comanduras was fully documented with photographs and, more important, a dramatic telegram from the men to Dooley in New York, in which Schweitzer joined them in hailing the announcement of "the formation of MEDICO with which we are privileged to be associated."[32]

Schweitzer observed a strict policy of forbidding his name from being linked to any causes or charities, so it was a great coup for the IRC to persuade him to serve as "Honorary Patron" of MEDICO, though he rarely spoke or wrote of the organization by name. MEDICO established a dental clinic at Lambaréné under the direction of Dr. Frederick Franck; the fledgling operation also provided Schweitzer with "a very large quantity of drugs." Tom Dooley now had ample reason to embellish the details of his visit to Africa, since, as Dr. Howard A. Rusk wrote in the *New York Times* of March 9, 1958, "although Medico is patterned after the work of Dr. Dooley and Dr. Seagrave, it derives its inspiration for [sic] the philosophy of Dr. Albert Schweitzer and his world famous hospital." Rusk was a distinguished physician known as the "father of modern rehabilitative medicine" and a MEDICO board member. The numerous articles on behalf of the organization that appeared under his byline were primarily the work of Gilbert Jonas of the Harold Oram firm. In the weeks subsequent to the launching of MEDICO, the IRC generated a publicity blizzard in pursuit of $1 million in donations from "the American public and American industry."[33]

Since there was no substitute for Dooley's personal power, he was immediately dispatched to the lecture circuit for a five-month tour that saw him make 188 speeches in seventy-nine cities. "Tom was one helluva fund raiser," recalled the former executive director of CARE, a massive relief agency that collaborated with MEDICO on certain projects. "He'd walk in the room and you'd have to hide your gold teeth." Dooley quickly mastered the medium of television in a transitional era; the flamboyant theatricality he embodied had not yet succumbed to the cooler imperatives of the small screen. "A single impassioned appearance" on Dave Garroway's "Today" show netted $10,000 for MEDICO.[34]

In order to maximize Dooley's fundraising potential, the IRC renegotiated his contract with the *Reader's Digest,* which had acquired the rights to his image and likeness in return for the $25,000 the magazine provided Operation Laos in 1956. Dooley chafed under the arrangement, through which the obsessively secretive DeWitt Wallace had apparently forbidden Tom even from serving as the *subject* of articles in other publications without obtaining clearance from headquarters in Pleasantville. In January 1957 Dooley had complained that a pictorial spread scheduled for *Life* had been postponed due to Wallace's objections. Henry Luce's Time-Life empire represented a threat to Wallace less for its circulation figures, which never rivaled those of the *Reader's Digest,* than for its proprietor's capacity to set the agenda for America's cultural mission to the world. So long as Wallace held the exclusive rights to Dooley's persona, he could forestall the total hegemony of Time-Life, a goal he surrendered in negotiations whose details never escaped the fortress of privacy Wallace erected around himself.[35]

In the end, the *Reader's Digest* kept the reprint rights to Dooley's books, while *Life* inaugurated its relationship with the "Do-It-Yourself Samaritan" in an illustrated profile for the issue of March 17, 1958. The magazine reported that Dooley was doing "his own money-raising—$850,000 so far in cash and drugs." Yet Tom continued to insist that "peace demands person-to-person action more than dollar-to-dollar programs. My people in Laos have not learned about America from huge aid programs but from Americans." *Life* highlighted Dooley's regular-guy appeal with a shot of him at the piano in a St. Louis nightclub he had frequented in his medical school days. "Heck," he was reported as confessing, "I really don't want to spend the rest of my life rotting in the jungle. I want to drive snappy convertibles, pinch pretty girls and drink bourbon on the rocks."[36]

In April Tom's byline appeared over a thoughtful essay in the *New York Times Magazine* entitled "Foreign Aid—The Human Touch." The previous May he had been approached by the *Times* to write an article on the foreign aid program in Laos but had declined because, in addition to posing a conflict with the *Reader's Digest,* the proposed essay was a "very erudite esoteric type thing" that was therefore "out of my line." Dooley's impeccable sense of timing was rewarded once again when "Foreign Aid—The Human Touch" appeared at the peak of MEDICO's fundraising effort. The essay, written in collaboration with staffers at the Oram firm, featured a calm, judicious tone designed to appeal to the liberal realists presumed to comprise the paper's readership. "In the field of foreign aid," he wrote, "medicine has a unique role. It has a role in human destiny, far above the give and take of national rivalries. It rises above the fears of colonialism or of domination by selfish foreign interests. At the same time, medicine affords American doctors an opportunity for service to all mankind while serving their own nation."[37]

While the dramatic step up in class from the *Reader's Digest* to the *Times* and Time-Life publications was crucial to MEDICO's fundraising strategy, it also exposed Dooley to a more competitive celebrity marketplace than he had previously experienced. His lecture tour now assumed the character of what historian Daniel Boorstin called "pseudo-events," series of staged exercises designed primarily for maximum impact in various media, from gossip columns to local television news programs to the glossy national magazines specializing in celebrity photojournalism. It was such a heady experience that there is little doubt Dooley forgot Senator McCarthy's warnings about his lack of "professional immunity" from the whims of fashion that would later see him fall hard from grace, especially with the gods at Time-Life. Yet Tom was so good at what he did that Boorstin actually singled him out as an exception to the inexorable declension from hero to celebrity that marked the age of the "human pseudo-event." Dooley's appropriation of the Schweitzer legend had not gone in vain, for as Boorstin wrote in 1961: "There are still, of course, rare exceptions—a Dr. Albert Schweitzer or a Dr. Tom Dooley—whose heroism is intelligible. But these only illustrate that intelligible heroism now occurs almost exclusively on the field of sainthood or martyrdom."[38]

Boorstin extricated Dooley from the debilitating logic of contemporary history by virtue of the jungle doctor's solitary effort, but the real credit belonged to his worshipful Catholic audience who provided an immovable counterweight to a fickle, if not faithless, secular mass communications industry. Dooley's appearances before Catholic groups in the spring of 1958—far more numerous, more spontaneous, and much less publicized than his carefully staged media events—generated a spiritual fervor usually associated with religious revivals. A female student at a Catholic high school where Dooley lectured in February 1958 wrote that, as accustomed as she and her friends had become to "dry speeches from withered old instructors," Dooley provoked "complete bafflement that such a tremendous faith and love of humanity could exist in one man." The girl confided her doubt that she could ever perform heroic work as he did, but she promised that "we'll remember you and today's lesson in Catholic living. For those of us who are not overly religious, you opened up a new idea. For those of us who have the belief in God, you made it stronger, for we saw God's goodness and compassion in the form of a young doctor with unbelievable spirit."[39]

After Dooley spoke at Barat Hall, the St. Louis grammar school he had attended in the 1930s, a Sacred Heart nun reported to Agnes Dooley that "the children were electrified! I really felt he was like a Pied Piper, and they would all have followed him out the front door if we had not directed them elsewhere!" The devotional practices of the students had been altered in the wake of Dooley's visit. "Every morning when the Barat Hall boys make their chapel visit," the nun wrote, "they include this ejaculation: 'Sacred Heart of Jesus, help and protect Dr. Dooley!' "[40]

Dooley's appeal to Catholic youth was greatly appreciated, at a time when the Church appeared to be losing its battle for the souls of young people to a consumerist mass culture. A journalist for *Tidings*, the diocesan newspaper in Los Angeles, told Agnes Dooley: "It all adds up to this: Everywhere he talks all over America, Dr. Dooley is waking up our young people. This is an age when youngsters don't impress easily, but your son is impressing them. This is an age when heroes have gone out of vogue. But your son is a hero to these kids. He is giving them back their birthright, as young Americans, as young Christians."[41]

Adult Catholics had their own good reasons to appreciate Dooley and his message. He offered them a much more compelling, balanced, and sophisticated view of the challenges they faced than any of the numerous self-appointed crusaders against godless communism who were prominently featured in the Catholic media. Historians and memoirists have often ridiculed the maudlin apocalyptic tone of this discourse, evident in such popular works as Harold W. Rigney's *Four Years in a Red Hell,* the captivity narrative of a Divine Word missionary imprisoned in Red China, or in the genre's foundational text, *God's Underground,* the story of "Father George," a Croatian priest who, according to a validating foreword by Msgr. Fulton J. Sheen, spent eighteen months "incognito as an officer attached to the Red Army, six of these traveling inside Russia itself."[42]

Sheen often referred to the Soviet Union as "the Mystical Body of Satan," a view that was probably shared by most Americans regardless of their familiarity with the quip's theological source. Yet Catholics have been routinely singled out by historians for the ferocity of their anticommunism in the first decade of the cold war. According to the British author David Caute, "the rapid spread of Communist hegemony in Eastern Europe only intensified the traditional fear and loathing of atheistic communism. The diocesan papers were full of the sufferings of the East European Catholics." Dooley was often described as the naive embodiment of anticommunist hysteria: by the 1960s even some quasi-Catholic publications dismissed him as an embarrassing relic. Robert Scheer proclaimed in *Ramparts* that "Dooley's simple hostility to Communist 'devilry' was matched by an equally simple respect for American goodness," while Nicholas von Hoffman wrote in the *Critic* (a publication of liberal Chicago Catholics) in 1969 that Dooley's "politics were more primitive than the southeast Asian witch doctory and folk medicine that he fought against," not surprising for one who "had a touch of the American Catholic urban peasant about him."[43]

Yet Dooley appealed to many Catholics in the 1950s precisely because his relative sophistication afforded them a glimpse of a richer milieu than the culture of the urban parish could offer. His unchallenged credentials as a Catholic icon empowered him to present a more complicated portrait of international politics than was provided by the diocesan press. An unidentified reporter for the *Oblate Digest,* journal of the missionary order of which Tom had become an honorary member, explained in March 1958 that he "does not try to convert Asians either to Catholicism or to U.S. ideas. His group simply lets the Asians see what Americans are like, and selflessly offers them medical aid." This religiously ecumenical, politically pluralist view was indeed a central component of Dooley's evolving vision, but it appeared so jarring in the cold war context that the author reassured his readers, without benefit of quotations from the source, that "Dr. Dooley hopes, of course, that the result of Medico's mobilization will be a better regard for America and democracy and the Catholic faith. Even though the organization is not directly under the Church's aegis, Her designs of Christian charity are still directly furthered."[44]

Dooley's relationship with American Catholicism was marked by this exquisite dialectic for the rest of his life. He often appeared to work through his own contradictions by first testing ideas before Catholic audiences, who in turn provided the approval that emboldened him to move forward. In a May 1958 speech at Loras College, a diocesan school in Dubuque, Iowa, he revisited the lurid accounts of tortured Christians that pervaded *Deliver Us from Evil,* but he introduced a newer theme that soon became familiar to his readers. "The doctor said America's materialistic approach won't work," reported the *Dubuque Telegraph-Herald.* "He said that if the people of Asia are given a loving, co-operative, direct approach, they will respond," a signal of Dooley's shifting focus from the external evil of communism to the need for spiritual renewal through service to the world's poor.[45]

A few months earlier Dooley had admitted to his friend Anne Miller that he knew she did not care for his first book. Miller was a sophisticated non-Catholic, a sister of the renowned documentary filmmaker Pare Lorentz, and an integral part of the USIS team her husband led in Vientiane. She was very fond of Dooley; her reservations about his character were expressed more in terms of concern than reproach. She was also one of the few people whom Tom was utterly incapable of conning. Dooley ascribed to the Millers those qualities that he found especially desirable: personal and aesthetic integrity rooted in a version of self-possession more balanced than his customary flights from egotism to self-abasement. Hank Miller was celebrated in a *Life* profile as a "genial, gangling giant of an American" whose "relaxed informality" made him a highly effective representative of the United States in Laos: "His attractive family mixes unself-consciously with their neighbors." The Lao affectionately called him "'Brpet,' the name of a genie who is 'tall as a coconut tree.'" Dooley was fascinated by worldly yet unaffected non-Catholics and sought their patronage without ever abandoning his own intimate community. He told the students at Loras College that Albert Schweitzer had reminded him that it was more important "what people shall do and where they shall go than what they've done or where they've been." While the Protestant saint may not actually have favored the rakish Irishman with these words, Dooley surely believed that their apparent source lent great authority to his own desire to lead the exodus from the immigrant church, for as he liked to say, "the times are appointed."[46]

As a testimony to his rising standards Dooley complained to the Millers that *The Edge of Tomorrow* was being viewed strictly as a commodity by his publishers: "In fact, the bastards would have printed the first drivel just to sell it at Christmas sales, on name, rather than on any inherent quality." Yet when the book was released in April there was little doubt it represented a great improvement stylistically over *Deliver Us from Evil;* for all its simplicity it appealed to secular readers as well as Catholics across a widening spectrum of sensibilities. It was a book that Dooley's editor, Robert Giroux, would not have been ashamed to present to friends such as Thomas Merton, the Trappist monk whose best-selling spiritual reflections still bore the slightly stuffy air of his Ivy League conversion. In addition to his core readership of ethnic anticommunists, Dooley was finding an audience among a new type of 1950s liberal Catholic, described by Garry Wills as "a kind of honorary convert. He tried, for quite understandable reasons, to cast himself out of the ghetto of his upbringing and come back at the church from some entirely new direction." To liberal Catholics, the mentality of the immigrant Church was now associated with treacly devotionalism and the lurid mysticism of *Four Years in a Red Hell*.[47]

The smartly packaged *Edge of Tomorrow* was acclaimed by secular and religious critics alike in a manner attesting to the book's crossover appeal. Reviewers from the non-Catholic press were especially impressed by the lightheartedness Dooley sported in the midst of suffering and danger. William Hogan of the *San Francisco Chronicle* called it "a wonderfully human [book] presented in a curiously jaunty, or boyish fashion. The tall, good-looking, idealistic Tom Dooley emerges a kind of 'Mister Roberts' of the medical world rather than a saint in the classic tradition. He is a good guy with a good cause—and the privately financed cause is working." Charles Poore of the *New York Times* described the author as "a wild young Irishman" who "cannot play Bach as well as Albert Schweitzer" but "shares with that illustrious humanitarian a dedication to the establishment of harmony in the unquiet spirit of man." Poore lauded *The Edge of Tomorrow* as "a breezy and remarkably compelling narrative of his adventures in the kingdom of Laos." The Vietnam Lobby's easy access to the *Times* was reconfirmed by a second review in September 1958, wherein Ed Lansdale's friend Peggy Durdin praised Tom's "Irish gift for the felicitous phrase"; she also paid tribute to Operation Brotherhood for inspiring "Dr. Dooley to work in a world so tragic that most Americans refuse to visualize it clearly or to *feel* it."[48]

Catholic critics were equally effusive if more attentive to Dooley's faith than to his stylized ethnicity (one reviewer applauded the book's "refreshing neglect of the sex angle"). The editors of the popular devotional magazine *Ave Maria* exclaimed: "To read this book is a humbling, edifying—and almost spiritually necessary—experience for all men of good will." The *Critic* published two reviews: arguing in the negative, Albert H. Miller accused Dooley of "a naive belief in the power of medicine" to halt the spread of communism, and he invoked American Catholic missionaries persecuted in China, including Father Rigney, "who could hardly share Dr. Dooley's confidence that his medical aid will prevent acceptance of 'anti-American' propaganda.'" Rare as it was, such criticism could only have bolstered Dooley's standing with his most faithful admirers, urban Catholics anxious to step beyond the borders of their ethnoreligious enclave but who needed a hero to guide them.[49]

The real impact of Dooley's example to Catholics is found not in the pages of religious periodicals but in the thousands of letters he received each month. From one such letter grew a relationship with the person he came to rely on and trust more than anyone else in the United States: Teresa Gallagher, an Irish American from Queens, New York, who worked as a secretary at the Manhattan headquarters of the Metropolitan Life Insurance Company. Gallagher was a single woman several years older than Dooley and a product of the elaborate devotional culture of working-class New York Irish Catholicism. In the summer of 1956 she had sent a fan letter to Dooley in Laos. He responded in writing the following January; by that spring Gallagher and a coworker had founded the Dr. Dooley Aid Club at "the Met." "I never could tolerate indifference and apathy," Gallagher wrote in *Give Joy to My Youth,* her 1965 memoir. "I now suddenly became aware of a great need in the world. Dr. Dooley's book and his letters not only taught me that there were far too many 'have nots' in Southeast Asia, but they also showed me how dangerous this situation was to the peace of the world." Teresa Gallagher was an extraordinarily well-organized individual who, like numerous talented women of her generation and social background, handled responsibilities far beyond her job description, yet still had sufficient energy to become a virtual full-time volunteer secretary to Dooley in the early months of MEDICO's existence. He was highly appreciative of Teresa's toughness and drive: on learning of her sales campaign on behalf of his first book among the Met's multitude of employees, he wrote: "It is especially pleasing to this 'practical' thinking Irishman to read that you are so passionate about pushing *Deliver Us From Evil.*"[50]

Shared bonds of ethnicity and religion provided the emotional basis for their relationship, but these were continually renegotiated in a fashion that mirrored Dooley's broader engagement with his American Catholic audience. The first meeting between members of the Dr. Dooley Aid Club (whose rolls were dominated by such Irish surnames as McInerny, McCann, O'Brien, O'Connor, and Connell) and their champion took place in November 1957 at Connelly's restaurant, an Irish American establishment located midway between the IRC's office and the Met's colossal headquarters. The geography of Manhattan provided an apt metaphor for Dooley's willingness to meet adoring throngs of Irish Americans "halfway": they were brushed by Tom's grandeur while he subtly broadened their cultural perspective, secure in the knowledge they would never abandon him or his cause. The day after the meeting "Tom was called 'Mr. Wonderful' on 23rd Street," Gallagher wrote, adding that her coworkers exulted: "'He's genuine, witty, and spiritual as well.' 'He's so Ivy Leaguish and so young to be doing so much.'"[51]

On February 4, 1958, Teresa Gallagher was invited to attend an IRC dinner in Tom's honor held at Manhattan's River Club. In describing the event in a letter to Agnes Dooley in St. Louis, Gallagher noted that "there were about 71 people there, including Father James Keller, of the Christophers. I'm not sure what I had to dine on, I guess it was a duck, but it could have been a chicken." In drawing on a familiar Irish American discourse that saluted the clergy while confirming her own humility before such exalted company, Gallagher expressed her tribal solidarity with the mother of the dashing Irish American icon. "I feel as though I know you very well," she wrote. "I know your name is Agnes, and that you come from Limerick, Ireland. Did Father Denis O'Brien, a dear Maryknoll friend of mind [sic] from Texas and just back from a junket to Limerick where his father hails from, drop in to see you recently?"[52]

In her reply Mrs. Dooley gently reminded Teresa that "it was my husband's family that came from Limerick Ireland . . . I am just plain American, from way back when." Gallagher was not likely to have met many wealthy converts in her Queens parish, nor was she accustomed to the upper-class tone that suffused Mrs. Dooley's letters, as evidenced in her description of a recent photo session with *Life*. "The [Lao] Ambassador was here, and our local Radio Station decided it would be just ducky to have a broadcast from MY dining room—SOooo we had engineers, plus miles of cable, as well as an announcer. I live in an apartment—a rather large one—but certainly not equipped for such an occasion." In a subsequent letter she again reminded Teresa of her son's difference from the working-class Catholics of Brooklyn and Queens who comprised the Dr. Dooley Aid Club: "Tom's genes are definitely Irish . . . but every once in a while his calm, almost cold, American executive and business judgment amazes people . . . [as] not quite Irish."[53]

Class distinctions among the American Irish would explain little of Dooley's relationship with his core following had they not assumed social and political significance as well. On the morning of his departure from New York en route to Laos, June 23, 1958, Dooley had scheduled a breakfast meeting with members of the Aid Club, who met him in the lobby of the Waldorf Astoria and were told their destination was Eighty-fourth Street. "What's there?" he was asked. "Sy Spengler's," he replied. "I never heard of any such restaurant." Spengler was a Jewish friend of Dooley's, an ex-naval officer who had helped console Tom in the troubled days at Yokosuka following the end of his mission in Haiphong. Dooley apparently departed for the airport from Spengler's home by himself, leaving his friend behind with the women of the Aid Club. "The girls sent Sy a thank you note. We hope he got over the shock of the harem that poured forth on him that quiet Sunday morning," Gallagher later wrote to Dooley. "We also wound up discussing McCarthy and almost missed the cab to the airport. Didn't we find out that Sy didn't like McCarthy and there were Kathleen and I drinking toasts to Wisconsin and our old friend UP THERE [the senator had died in 1957]. Poor Sy, worse yet, Poor You. They will wonder where you ever dug us up!"[54]

According to Dooley's pilot and confidant Ted Werner, it was during this interlude in Manhattan that Tom enjoyed a quiet dinner at the Waldorf with Sen. John F. Kennedy and his young wife, Jacqueline. The senator's father had been a staunch admirer of Dooley in the era of *Deliver Us from Evil*, which must now have seemed like the remote past. For by 1958 the kind of militant, sectarian anticommunism fostered by Joseph P. Kennedy and Joe McCarthy was of little use to Catholic politicians with aspirations to national office or Catholic folk heroes seeking to win the hearts of Lao Buddhists and American sophisticates alike. A new era was dawning for a breed of jet-set postghetto Catholics, wonderfully symbolized in the gift to Dooley of an air travel card ("that would take him any place at any time by air") with the compliments of George Skakel, heir to an industrial fortune and the brother of John F. Kennedy's sister-in-law Ethel Skakel Kennedy.[55]

The members of the Dr. Dooley Aid Club found Dooley personally irresistible ("he was gifted in so many ways," wrote Teresa Gallagher, "as author, lecturer, pianist, doctor. Each of these gifts require very special talents, and Tom used these God-given talents to the utmost"), but they also responded in more subtle ways to his political and theological innovations. The *Catholic Digest* reported in October 1958 that Dooley "would like very much to be a priest. If I felt I was halfway worthy, I would be one tomorrow." In lieu of ordination he generated a personal spirituality that encouraged Catholic lay people to examine their own traditions in bold new ways, offering himself as a mediator of their explorations. Writing in the archconservative *Brooklyn Tablet* in May 1959, Teresa Gallagher wrote that Dooley "says he can almost see God there in Laos, playing with the children, walking in the clouds, and in the bodies of his sick. He knows the meaning of the Mystical Body." Rather than binding Catholics together in suffering with a Christ crucified yet again by communists—the vision of the Mystical Body commonly evoked in the cold war—Gallagher's generous new interpretation called on Catholics to share in Dooley's hopes that "his and our work will bring 'this corner of Asia a brighter dawn.'"[56]

The gender dynamics of Teresa Gallagher's relationship with Dooley can be read in numerous ways. As a single woman roughly a decade older than Dooley who devoted her life to his cause while asking little in return (she was delighted when he named a MEDICO jeep "Teresa" and had it painted kelly green in her honor), Gallagher acceded to the myth of the self-sacrificing "valiant woman" exalted by many Catholics of the era, especially intellectuals drawn to the various lay apostolates. Yet at the same time Dooley's nonclerical vocation opened up new spaces within the Church's culture of service; his rakish celebrityhood challenged the ethic of self-mortification so prevalent within Irish American Catholicism. Teresa Gallagher already knew plenty of priests and missionaries, but thanks to Dooley she now met a variety of show business luminaries and political leaders who bridged the gulf of cultures between which she and her coreligionists had traditionally been forced to choose. While Dooley railed against American materialism, Teresa was equally impressed by "his exquisite taste, particularly in jewelry," and enjoyed his "quick, keen observations about people's appearances," which transgressed the gospel of humility.[57]

In later years Teresa Gallagher deflected questions about Dooley's sexuality, which, she insisted, occupied a "gray area" beyond her understanding. Yet it was precisely within that area, between the extremes of rigid orthodoxy and bitter apostasy, that Dooley's mystique evolved. Unmarried Catholic women beyond their childbearing years were commonly referred to in those days as "maiden ladies" by the Irish American businessmen for whom they often worked in mid-level corporate offices. The warm rapport that grew between Dooley and his "disc girls"—the battalion of volunteer New York secretaries who transcribed the correspondence he dictated onto green Soundscriber discs in Laos—thrived on an irreverent banter that encouraged the women to communicate with Dooley in a manner far different from that expected of them on their day jobs. He was no advocate of gender equity, but his own vulnerability emboldened the disc girls to a protective role whose full significance remained unspoken. After "Do-It-Yourself Samaritan" appeared in *Life,* Teresa Gallagher described for Agnes Dooley the pleasure "the girls" had taken in reading "Tom's comments on pinching pretty girls!" In running interference, even if unconsciously, for Dooley's sexual "difference," the disc girls may have been a party to their own exploitation, but it is just as likely that, at least for some of them, the jungle doctor's "conservative nonconformity" inspired less conspicuous varieties of personal innovation along their own new frontiers of sexuality, ethnicity, and religion.[58]

Amid the excitement generated by his first MEDICO publicity tour, Tom Dooley faced the sobering necessity of choosing a new team to staff the Lao clinic he planned to build at Muong Sing, a site he had coveted since the autumn of 1956. In addition to the $2 million in medical supplies and $300,000 in cash Dooley had raised, MEDICO was besieged by applications from six hundred prospective corpsmen, nurses, and physicians. He summarily rejected "religious fanatics" and sought only those who could help him convince skeptics in both Laos and the United States that "I am *not* a Jesuit in disguise, *not* out to make an imperialistic colony of them, not a member of the C.I.A., etc."[59]

He settled on a pair of twenty-six-year-old premedical students at the University of Texas, Dwight Davis and Earl Rhine, ex-servicemen who had been so impressed by *Life*'s coverage of Dooley's work that they not only wrote to him but also phoned his mother to express their interest in MED-ICO. Dooley met with Davis and Rhine at the Shamrock Hotel in Houston and decided to hire them during a four-hour conversation in which he discerned that "their idealism was balanced by a sense of realism because, in their overseas' duties they had seen the stink and misery in which idealism must rub its nose." They were healthy and had "superb medical technician training." They were also married; shortly before Earl Rhine departed for Laos his wife learned that she was pregnant, but "he had a valiant little gal for a wife who said that she would take care of herself and their child while Earl was out taking care of thousands of kids in Asia. Indeed, she did."[60]

Davis and Rhine were both more experienced and less starstruck than Dooley's former corpsmen: "They had an obvious amount of admiration for Tom Dooley, yet neither was too full of hero worship," he later wrote, providing both an accurate assessment of their views and an affirmation of his own desire to separate the vital work of MEDICO from the sources of his public adulation. Yet like their predecessors, Davis and Rhine were kept at a great emotional distance by their boss, who expected his corpsmen to embody those attributes he viewed as quintessentially American, in particular an unswerving loyalty and quiet dutifulness. These qualities, which Davis and Rhine possessed in abundance, sheltered Dooley from the emotional storms that periodically threatened to destroy MEDICO. He had initially hoped to bring to Asia a man who was more familiar than most MEDICO personnel with Dooley's other lives: the candidate was welcomed into Teresa Gallagher's MEDICO support circle and was scheduled to depart for Laos in August, but he was abruptly dropped from the team without explanation. In an uncharacteristic display of hurt Dooley wrote to Teresa from Saigon in August: "I guess you have heard that Ted is not joining us. I do not know the full particulars yet but I'm quite upset because so much was dependent upon him. It is bad leadership to ever have a program in which one man is indispensible, however, Ted came very close to being that one man."[61]

The principals in this debacle corresponded in awkward tones that barely concealed the emotional cost exacted by the denials, coverups, and reconstructions necessary for Dooley to remain afloat. "Ted" had written a haunting memo in late July to Teresa Gallagher and "all our friends from Mother Met," apologizing for his evasions, offering his mother's illness as an excuse, and concluding with a wish that they "could have at least one 'Last Supper' " before his departure, though he surely knew by then he was not going to Asia. In September Teresa wrote to Dooley informing him that Ted was now "living on 21st St. and 8th Avenue. You know, Tom, I haven't kept in touch with Ted. . . . We were never able to quite understand what happened but it was just a series of little things that left us puzzled." Everyone who was ever close to Dooley was expected to know which of his associates were in or out of grace with him at any given time; since they could never pursue the reasons why, they became either paranoid, like his mother, or aggressively protective, like Teresa Gallagher. Keeping their stories straight was often simply too taxing: in separate published accounts of Tom's summer 1958 journey to Laos, his mother, Teresa Gallagher, and Dooley himself presented conflicting itineraries and dates of arrival at various waystations along the road to Laos, which he reached, depending on the source, between July 21 and mid-September.[62]

None of the accounts of his first MEDICO journey placed him in Los Angeles in early July 1958, although local gossip columnists noted his stopover in their city. Dooley routinely courted the attentions of such journalists as Barbara Cox of the *Los Angeles Times,* who had reassured his fans in February that he remained "a highly eligible bachelor with a confessed envy of friends who have 'a convertible and a few girl friends.' " Writing in the same paper on July 14, Gene Sherman reported that a doorman at the Beverly Hills Hilton recognized Dooley as the physician who " 'took my tonsils out in the Pacific during the war,' " a dubious claim, since Dooley had not served in any wars and his surgical practice on servicemen had been confined, by his own admission, to "emergency circumcisions." But Sherman had definitely seen Dooley in Beverly Hills, because he also reported that "all during his stay last week no one at the hotel would allow Dooley to tip."[63]

It is possible that he was being briefed by intelligence operatives during some of the missing days between late June and mid-July, but it is more likely that Dooley immersed himself in a final round of socializing, primarily in southern California, where he arranged for Earl Rhine and Dwight Davis to tour the set of "Gunsmoke" while he pursued more rarified amusements. When he finally arrived in Hawaii, Tom revisited the unique pattern that marked his stopovers on the islands—relaxation followed by intensive preparation for his reentry into Asian culture—prior to the inevitable round of fundraising appearances. "Especially grand to me was a small group of young men and women called the Junior Chinese Catholic Club and their leader, Fred Luning," he wrote of the high school student who quickly became one of MEDICO's most ardent volunteers. According to his correspondence, Dooley left Hawaii on July 27, stopping in Tokyo before a ten-day visit to Hong Kong, where he was met by a cable from Agnes Dooley demanding to know if he had been secretly married, as reported by a gossip columnist. In reassuring his mother, he launched a preemptive strike as well against swirling rumors linking him romantically with Marilyn Monroe.[64]

In Hong Kong he stayed in the "fabulous" apartment of Ed Lansdale's friend Tillman Durdin of the *New York Times* and spent time "with all the old group that I knew so well before," including Travis Fletcher (head of the Hong Kong office of Aid Refugee Chinese Intellectuals, a CIA front and Oram client) and other fellow travelers of the Vietnam Lobby. Then it was on to Saigon and a visit with his old friend Madame Ngai at the An Lac Orphanage, followed by a jeep trip to Cambodia, where MEDICO hoped to open a clinic. As a special treat Dooley took Earl and Dwight for a "swim at midnight in the pool behind the courtyard of the Leper King, deep within the ruins of the 12th century Ankor. It was a wonderful thrill . . . even tingled my old and slightly jaded bones." Tom Dooley was only thirty-one years old and still in apparent good health, but an obsession with aging was already becoming evident in his writings. From Cambodia they went on to Bangkok and finally, after a two-day drive across Thailand, on September 14, 1958, the heart and soul of MEDICO arrived, in the words of Agnes Dooley, "home again in Laos."[65]

☆ 7 ☆

The Handsome American

In the late autumn of 1957 Dr. Tom Dooley's editors had insisted that he revise the manuscript of *The Edge of Tomorrow* lest it be read as the struggle of "Dooley and his boys in conflict with a foreign aid program." If such advice was extended during the preparation of his third and final (and most successful) book, *The Night They Burned the Mountain* (1960), it went un-heeded. In describing the nonreception he experienced on his return to Vientiane in September 1958, Dooley noted that Hank and Anne Miller of USIS, "probably my closest friends in all Asia," were on home-leave in the United States at the time; their surrogate could do no better than to arrive at the airport as Dooley was claiming his baggage. "This official said to me, 'Good heavens! Your plane came in on time. Planes never come in on time. We usually don't come out until much later.' I immediately flushed with anger at this haughty attitude of the white man toward the Asians and their efforts at running an airline. I asked him, 'Did you notify the Lao govern-ment of the time of my arrival?' He replied, 'Oh, I intended to, but I'm awfully sorry, I never had a chance.' "[1]

In writing to his mother of the trip to Vientiane, Dooley had made it clear that he and his assistants arrived via "a passing jeep" that they flagged down after ferrying their equipment across the Mekong from Thailand. The fic-tional version presented in *The Night They Burned the Mountain* was of course typical of Dooley, but in fabricating an altercation with American officials in Laos, he served notice that the time for reconciliation was long past. The morning following the airport incident, by the book's account, Dooley simply walked into the offices of the prime minister and asked to see him. "His secretary beamed excitement, and within five minutes I was sitting near my good friend, Premier Phoui Sananikone. He expressed regret that no one had met me at the airlines. He knew I was en route back to my 'second home' and said, 'We are very unhappy that we did not have a chance to extend to you the warm welcome and the affection that all of us hold for you, our *Thanh Mo America*.' How good to hear my old title again, 'Doctor America.'"[2]

Dooley's ego had swelled beyond its already mammoth proportions during his 1958 fundraising tour, but there was another explanation for his cocky dismissal of American officialdom in *The Night They Burned the Mountain* and his bold claim that he alone discerned the will of the Lao. During the stopover of his MEDICO team in Hong Kong in August 1958, Tom had shown corpsman Dwight Davis a manuscript copy of *The Ugly American*, a novel coauthored by Tom's friends William Lederer and Eugene Burdick, who later became a MEDICO board member. After reading the novel Davis asked Dooley for assurance that it was not based on fact, only to be informed that the book did indeed tell the unvarnished truth about the dangerous ineptitude of American foreign service personnel in Southeast Asia. With the publication of the novel in September, Lederer and Burdick became controversial overnight celebrities after the fashion of Dooley himself, whose writing career had been launched with a boost from Lederer in the summer of 1955. ("Yes Lederer is Captain Bill Lederer of whom I spoke in [*Deliver Us from Evil*]," Dooley scribbled in a note to his mother in October 1958. "I saw a lot of him in Hawaii—Read the galleys on the book— great!!")[3]

The Ugly American recast the debate over American foreign policy so dramatically that it could very nearly be described as the *Uncle Tom's Cabin* of the cold war. The book spent seventy-eight weeks on the *New York Times* best-seller list; final sales figures exceeded four million copies. As one of the intended by-products of the book's popularity, Lederer and Burdick wholeheartedly endorsed the work being performed in Laos by Dr. Tom Dooley, whom they cited as a prototype for the next generation of American foreign aid providers. The book also articulated the kind of populist internationalism that appealed to much of Dooley's audience, but since they owed nothing to members of the Vietnam Lobby (apart from Lederer's friend Edward G. Lansdale, who was a silent partner at any rate), Lederer and Burdick helped to upset the delicate balance that had made allies, at least on paper, of Catholics and socialists. After 1958 it was much harder for Left-liberals to justify their support of Dooley; both the jungle doctor and MED-ICO were finally cut loose by the International Rescue Committee in September 1959. By that time Dooley faced a life-threatening disease that, in a macabre twist, enabled him once again to upstage politics. This was all a year in the distance as Dooley prepared to launch a new clinic at Muong Sing in September 1958, the season of *The Ugly American*.

William Lederer and Eugene Burdick first met at the Bread Loaf Writers' Conference in Vermont in the late 1940s, then renewed their friendship in 1957 when Burdick visited Honolulu, where Lederer had settled in anticipation of his imminent retirement from the navy. While "waiting for a wave" from atop their surfboards the two decided to coauthor a nonfiction exposé designed to shame or cajole the State Department into providing better training for its overseas personnel, who all too often lacked the "cultural sensitivity" essential for cold warriors. They were primarily concerned with reinvigorating those dormant aspects of the American character that would guarantee victory in the cold war: egalitarianism, common sense, spontaneity, and the "can-do spirit" of pioneer entrepreneurs. A working knowledge of modern advertising and psychological warfare would also help, especially as the Soviets had gained a head start in the developing world through deployment of their own crude psywar techniques.[4]

Following Burdick's return to his teaching post at Berkeley, he and Lederer collaborated on the project for over a year via the mails and on disc recordings not unlike those Dooley utilized for his own correspondence. A veteran *Reader's Digest* contributor, Lederer's stock had dramatically risen at Pleasantville after he "delivered" Tom Dooley to the magazine in 1955, but an editor at the *Digest* rejected the manuscript of "The Ugly American" just the same, to the subsequent chagrin of DeWitt Wallace—at least in Lederer's version of the story. The property was soon acquired by W. W. Norton and was slated as well for serialization in *The Saturday Evening Post*. While surfing with their editor in Hawaii just prior to the manuscript's publication, Lederer and Burdick suddenly concluded that the book would be more effective as a novel since, by their logic, readers were more likely to be provoked toward action by a highly dramatic *fictional* account of misdeeds performed on their behalf in a Southeast Asian nation now to be called "Sarkhan." Over beers the coauthors burned every copy of the manuscript; the following morning they outlined a novel drawing on their nonfiction material and six days later—thanks to "a battery of dictating machines and stenographers" and the authors' rejuvenating afternoon swims—they had their new book. "The way it was transcribed from the machines to paper is approximately the way it was published," Lederer explained. "One chapter describing the sex methods of a Red Chinese spy was deleted."[5]

The Ugly American is less a "novel" than a loosely connected series of vignettes organized around the conflict between comically indolent and incompetent U.S. foreign service personnel in Sarkhan and the small group of independent American operatives who represent the last hope for victory over Soviet communism in Southeast Asia. The "ugly American" of the title is one of the book's heroes, Homer Atkins, a homely "heavy construction man" who has come to Southeast Asia to advise in the building of dams and military roads, only to conclude that such simple devices as water pumps for farmers are much more badly needed. Atkins is among the few Americans in the novel blessed with common sense and the courage to bypass diplomatic protocols to serve Asians at the village level, attributes he shares with Edwin B. Hillandale of the U.S. Air Force, a psychological warfare expert known in the region as "the ragtime kid."[6]

The harmonica-playing Hillandale is so clearly modeled after Edward G. Lansdale that literary historians have been spared the detective work that still engages students of Greene's *Quiet American*. Lederer and Lansdale were long-time friends; in 1959 the former told an editor at the *Reader's Digest:* "I know Lansdale well: and he is a superb operator . . . in fact the first Colonel Hillandale story in *The Ugly American* is sort of based on Ed. . . . He has limitless courage and patience. He is sort of a combination of Colonel House and Cicero (the German one)."[7]

Lederer was a playful sort who grew so tired of Lansdale's burgeoning posthumous celebrity that in 1991, in reply to yet another question about Ed's resemblance to Hillandale, he thundered, "Bullshit, the character's about *me!*" Lansdale was comfortable in the shadows, but admirers tended to blend his characteristics into their own personae, as though to preserve the light of inspiration that might otherwise flicker under his anonymity. He indeed later claimed that "Bill Lederer once told me apologetically that he had me and himself in mind while creating the Hillandale character . . . and would urge me to make use of magic tricks and necromancy—as he said he did—in dealing with Asians. Nor did I ride a motorcycle as the character did." Constructed around the more flamboyant elements of Lansdale mythology, the portrayal of Hillandale in *The Ugly American* inspired numerous imitators among American advisors in Vietnam who learned the harmonica and roared through the countryside on motorcycles to little effect, lamented Lansdale, "except to wind up dead or captured by the enemy."[8]

In late 1959 Lederer and Burdick paid tribute in *Life* to some "non-ugly Americans," who had undoubtedly served as role models for the few admirable characters found in the novel. Although Lansdale blamed the book for helping to blow his cover in Southeast Asia, the authors could still not openly salute his work, but they did laud the efforts of Eugene Hoops and Paul Rusch, agriculture experts who together might well have provided the inspiration for the character of Homer Atkins. They also profiled their friend Tom Dooley, a "Doctor of Democracy." After becoming aware that "the Russians, quietly and without fanfare, are sending medical and surgical teams through Asia," they wrote, "Dr. Dooley responded in the only way he knew," organizing voluntary medical programs of his own "in the Laotian back country, caring for the sick and training native workers to treat the more common diseases."[9]

Dooley was a partial inspiration for a character in *The Ugly American,* the cunning Jesuit missionary John X. Finian, a former navy chaplain and a "practical, tough-minded, and thoughtful man" who mastered communist doctrine as preparation for service overseeing the order's missions in Burma. Finian uses "all his training as a Jesuit, all his alertness, every available trick and wile" to attract a cadre of Burmese allies willing to fight with him for "a country where any man may worship and live as he wishes." The priest employs a classic psywar misinformation campaign to undermine the local communists before departing from Burma for Sarkhan, a fictional nation in many ways resembling Tom Dooley's Laos, though it has usually been identified by critics as Vietnam. "When Americans do what is right and necessary," concludes Father Finian, "they are also doing what is effective."[10]

William Lederer's actual view of Tom Dooley was far too complicated to be wholly grafted into the cartoonish idiom of *The Ugly American.* In 1991 Lederer claimed that he had decided Dooley was a liar after reading *The Edge of Tomorrow,* which appeared prior to the "novelization" of his own book. Only then did Lederer realize that the lurid tales of tortured priests he had helped Dooley compose for *Deliver Us from Evil* were probably fabrications. Lederer now blamed the refugee exodus on North Vietnamese priests who broke up families by ordering the adults to go south where, he claimed, any atrocities occurred under the supervision of the French. In suggesting that "Saint and Devil" represented the most appropriate title for a biography of Dooley, Lederer articulated the powerfully ambivalent feelings of Tom's former friends, who had survived not only his death but the political cataclysm of the Vietnam War era. He could express unbridled anger, as in a 1986 letter castigating Dooley as "a terrible liar, a homosexual, and . . . despite his extraordinary charm, a devilishly egocentric person." Yet Lederer also recalled Tom's vulnerability, noting that in the absence of the emotional "backstop" customarily provided by a loved one, he may have become Dooley's best friend by default, at least in the months following his outster from the navy. Lederer had met Dooley at the airport in Honolulu during Tom's Hawaiian stopover in August 1956, despite orders that the doctor be shunned by all naval personnel. A young navy chaplain warned him: "Don't you know this is an evil wolf in sheep's clothing?" Lederer recalled asking the cleric: "Padre, would Jesus meet him or not?"[11]

Since Tom Dooley was far too strange for fiction, Lederer and Burdick drew on more conventional sources in creating Father Finian; he resembles in various ways Msgr. Joseph Harnett of Catholic Relief Services; the tough labor priest played by Karl Malden in *On the Waterfront;* and such anticommunist priest-intellectuals as Father John Cronin, a labor activist and a key advisor to Richard M. Nixon in the late 1940s and 1950s. As a boy, wrote Lederer and Burdick, Finian "had delivered ice, hauled crates at the Railroad Express, picked over tons of coal looking for the grey gleam of slate; when he was at Oxford he had rowed on the Merton crew and was recognized as the best stroke they had ever had." In constructing an ultramasculine representative of the clergy, Burdick and Lederer exploited a popular cold war image of the American priesthood; they also perhaps overcompensated for presumed deficits in Tom Dooley's character which rendered him a much more difficult subject for hagiography. Yet his spirit as well as his personality pervade *The Ugly American.* One reviewer even wrote in November 1958 that "Burdick and Lederer do find some hope in the work of a few Americans like Dr. Tom Dooley and the couple they call Emma and Homer Atkins in their book," though Dooley is never mentioned in the novel by name, and *Life's* "Salute to Deeds of Non-Ugly Americans" did not appear until the following year.[12]

Dooley ultimately saw himself as a beneficiary of the trouble Lederer and Burdick caused the State Department. In a February 1960 letter thanking Lederer for the *Life* profile, he joked that "you make life difficult for me amongst our friends . . . the Government type that you wrote about." He continued, in a rare, disarming tone of sincere gratitude: "Much of the difficulty that I had in the past, however, no longer exists, Bill, and I think in some ways the Ugly American has been a great service to this cause. It has given a new awareness to Americans about the caliber of their representatives overseas." In exposing the foreign service as a hostage to hereditary elites and electoral spoils, the authors neutralized criticism of Dooley's alleged unprofessional and undiplomatic conduct; they even made a virtue of brashness exhibited in a just cause and were pleased to cite themselves as role models.[13]

The Ugly American was initially misread as a polemic against the very idea of foreign aid. "We were astounded and dismayed," Lederer and Burdick wrote in *Life,* that "it was now being used as a weapon to destroy foreign aid entirely. Canceling the foreign aid programs now on the ground that they contain weaknesses would be as illogical as throwing away a rifle because it sometimes jams—just when the enemy is about to attack." Lederer and Burdick, like their most vociferous critics, were liberal anticommunists, but they disdained career diplomats and championed "do-it-yourself Samaritans" like Dooley, whose genius at circumventing protocol in the service of humanity reminded Lederer of his own scrappy younger self. Dooley's connection with the IRC was of course never mentioned in "Salute to Deeds of Non-Ugly Americans," just as Tom's privileged background was never discussed in his own writings for fear, he told his mother, that others less fortunate than he would regard his vocation as being limited to the rich.[14]

Lederer and Burdick promoted a nascent ideology of foreign aid that valued spontaneity and emotion over pedigree and bureaucracy. As John Hellmann noted, "In the moral scheme of *The Ugly American,* bureaucracy, the pervasive new force in government and business transforming American society after the New Deal and the war, is simply a modern form of aristocracy." When Lederer and Burdick appeared on a television program in California to debate a former State Department official, they were asked about their proficiency in Asian languages. Burdick admitted they did not know any, but Lederer, who was afflicted with a stammer, replied that they possessed a talent for music and dance that represented a more valuable tool for intercultural communication. In response to a demand by the foreign aid professional that they demonstrate some familiarity with the culture of Nepal, Burdick began drumming on a tabletop while Lederer swayed gracefully about the studio in a highly impressionistic rendering of a Nepalese folk dance.[15]

Several years later, while on an evaluation mission for the Peace Corps, Lederer and Burdick were accused by *Time* magazine of having "dumped some fuel on a fire they themselves ignited. Sashaying toward the Champagne Room of the Manila Hotel in the Philippines, Eugene Burdick, 43, and William J. Lederer, 50, authors of *The Ugly American,* were refused entry because they were wearing Bermuda shorts. Squawked Lederer: Bermuda shorts are the national costume of his homeland—Hawaii." When the hotel's assistant manager replied that he thought Hawaii belonged to the United States, where shorts were not part of the national costume, Lederer threatened to write a letter of protest to the Philippine foreign office. On seeing the piece in *Time,* DeWitt Wallace wrote to Lederer asking, "Surely the incident does not enhance your prestige as a writer?" He added, in a scribbled note: "that is, help the sale of your books?"[16]

Wallace characteristically boiled the issue down to its essential ingredient, but Lederer and Burdick had already sold enough books to last a lifetime. *The Ugly American* had brought wealth and no small cultural authority to its authors at the expense of foreign service insiders who had endured the McCarthy era and now found themselves charged with a wider range of sins than mere disloyalty: arrogance, greed, sloth, and a weakness for European-style luxury. The antidote to this crisis is clearly articulated in the novel by Filipino leader Ramon Magsaysay, who makes a cameo appearance to plead for more American representatives like "the Rag-Time Kid—Colonel Hillandale. He can do anything." For Magsaysay, in his fictional guise, "the simple fact" was that "average Americans, in their natural state, if you will excuse the expression, are the best ambassadors a country can have . . . get an unaffected American, sir, and you have an asset." As John Hellmann noted, these virtues carried "special resonance for Americans from their frontier heritage." The few "natural" Americans portrayed in the novel—including a Roman Catholic priest—"walked into the novel's Indochina straight out of the American mythos." It was only shortly after the appearance of the novel that Tom Dooley began to speak of "ordinary" Americans like himself who performed "extraordinary deeds" when fueled by the sense of divine mission that he inherited by virtue of both nature and his nation.[17]

In identifying a decadent transplanted bureaucracy as the main source of America's failure to save developing nations from communism, Lederer and Burdick vindicated Dooley against critics whose identities he had concealed in *The Edge of Tomorrow.* At the top of the list was the American ambassador to Laos, J. Graham Parsons, described by an ex–foreign service officer as a "New Englander with a standoffish personality." The same observer recalled that the "most obvious" American intelligence officer in Laos at that time was "a Yalesman who affected an accent and manners that were terribly, terribly British." An employee of CARE in Laos reported in 1959 that in the early days of the U.S. mission there, "seventy-eight per cent of the American population was Princetonian." Two years later the Pulitzer Prize–winning journalist Keyes Beech informed readers of the *Saturday Evening Post* that the United States was on the verge of losing Laos, in part due to CIA agents like the one who "affected a cover that included a manufactured British accent, a luxuriant mustache, elaborately casual but expensive clothes, and a cane with a secret compartment that held—not a sword—but brandy."[18]

The Ugly American empowered Tom Dooley, as "an ordinary American," to take the offensive in a new stage of his career. Yet a jeremiad is only as good as the anxiety it spawns not just in the bosom of its targeted audience but in its beneficiaries as well. Lest Dooley became too "autonomous," he needed only to recall the circumstances of his discharge from the navy, or the pink riding jacket he had earned chasing foxes at the Bridlespur Hunt Club, to keep his balance amid the rising tide of discontent with the character of American foreign service personnel. He *could* take some comfort in his immunity to charges of conformism, the great pseudo-concern accompanying the discovery of mass culture in the late 1950s and a theme of *The Ugly American* as well. In an era of great scholarly interest in defining "the American national character," Dooley represented a fascinating hybrid, the likes of which had never before been witnessed. As a female admirer exclaimed, he embodied "a mixture of 'The Man in the Grey Flannel Suit' and Mother Cabrini."[19]

When journalists probed his unique composition, Dooley would brusquely insist that he had a job to do at Muong Sing and in so doing effectively rebuff charges that he was carefully tailoring his image as a populist humanitarian. Laos had saved him from personal as well as professional tragedy and the debt was repaid each day with gusto, though we will never know how close he came to completely fulfilling the terms of his original errand into the Lao wilderness.

In 1991 the *Los Angeles Times Magazine* published an article that charged: "Much of Dooley's Vientiane clinic project was a sham. Dooley's assistants were untrained and unqualified to give him the kind of help he would need to operate a legitimate clinic." The piece made explicit allegations that had circulated through constant innuendo during Dooley's lifetime, when his immense vulnerability emboldened many observers to hint that his work was strictly show business, with Tom cast as the Bob Hope of jungle doctors. Dooley often provided his critics with plenty of reasons to doubt his legitimacy. Yet during the first year of the MEDICO clinic established at Muong Sing in September 1958, a small miracle began to unfold.[20]

Dooley was never more generous than in his praise of MEDICO corpsmen Dwight Davis and Earl Rhine, who were responsible for the daily operation of the clinic and bore greater burdens than any of his previous aides. Lederer and Burdick had stressed the value of a positive American image in the region. In *The Night They Burned the Mountain* Dooley wrote that "the image of Americans in the eyes of thousands of people in Muong Sing is the image of the gentility, compassion, and love of Dwight Davis and Earl Rhine." In marked contrast to the functionaries skewered in *The Ugly American,* Davis and Rhine could boast of a total immersion in Lao peasant culture. Dooley described flying the pair into Muong Sing for the first time in September 1958. Since he was scheduled to return immediately to Vientiane to handle "the formalities with customs and the government," they were left to their own devices. "Here they were," he wrote, "twenty-six and twenty-seven years old, more than half a world away from their wives, out beyond the beyond. They were sitting on a primitive landing strip in an ancient land, just a few miles from the hostile frontier of Red China. When the plane took off, there would be no further transportation into this valley until I returned. Here were two young men who did not speak the native dialect, relying on interpreters whose English was highly inadequate. Here were two very brave Americans."[21]

In reality Davis and Rhine flourished at Muong Sing precisely because they did not act like "brave Americans" but rather as unassuming guests. Since for eighteen months the village comprised their entire world (apart from occasional forays to Hong Kong for "rest and relaxation"), they resolved to quietly make themselves at home. While Dooley acted like a demigod, medical warrior, statesman, and movie star, Davis and Rhine established easygoing personal relationships with their Lao hosts; they flowed with the vast differences rather than pretending to overcome them. They went to Laos as premedical students eager for some hands-on training, but their time in Muong Sing may have prepared them even better for the work they later performed in rural America on behalf of federal antipoverty programs. When the Lao asked Davis where his village was located, he initially tried elaborate explanations involving thousands of miles of oceans and mountain ranges; the Lao would just laugh as though Davis was putting them on.[22]

Davis and Rhine found that the response of the Lao to Western technology was not simply one of awe; it reflected their prior experiences and the expectations those engendered. Once when Davis began taking some photographs with a standard camera, a Lao demanded to know when he planned to take the picture out of the box, because he had previously seen a visitor with a Polaroid camera. On another occasion Davis and Rhine decided to bring a record player to a tiny village near Muong Sing where they had recently made a sick call. They informed a man in the village that they planned to throw a big dance party and that all the local women should be encouraged to attend. The Lao assured them he would make the arrangements, but he would not be made to look foolish by the Americans and their outlandish claims about music from a crate: when Davis and Rhine appeared in the village at the appointed time they found an empty village. They also discovered that the men in the region were highly enamored of both firearms and military-style uniforms. On announcing they were soon to travel to Hong Kong, they were besieged by requests for rifle parts and uniforms with matching parts, something the Royal Lao Army had proven unable to supply to its own regulars, despite massive infusions of American aid earmarked for the military.[23]

According to Ngoan van Hoang—the "Black Tai" youth Dooley discovered at a Baha'i center in Vientiane and subsequently brought to Muong Sing as a translator—the clinic functioned much more smoothly in the doctor's absence, since his demanding nature conflicted not only with Lao mores but with the temperaments of his American assistants. They viewed their mission in less dramatic terms than Dooley did, but they provided authentic medical aid, keeping charts and careful records of their patients' symptoms and the medications Dooley authorized for them. A critic later claimed that "his medicine chest was full of pills and elixirs that had been donated by Pfizer, a drug manufacturer, because they had expired and were no longer legal to sell in the United States," though the medications remained potent after their expiration dates and Dooley, in any case, received drugs from numerous pharmaceutical companies under a variety of circumstances.[24]

Davis and Rhine recalled that upper respiratory infections—readily treatable with antibiotics—were the ailments most commonly presented at sick-calls. Davis felt that Dooley had exaggerated the risks involved for Lao women in childbearing: he was more impressed with the communal character of the event, which saw the entire family in attendance, than with the silver nitrate Dooley administered as a precaution against infant blindness.

In a region where opium was widely used as a painkiller and addiction was common, many of the Lao developed a taste for the Americans' cherry-flavored cough medicine and some, according to Dwight Davis, persistently manufactured symptoms in order to obtain more of the syrup. In his view the inhabitants of Muong Sing and environs truly enjoyed the attention they received as the hosts of *Thanh Mo America* and his assistants, but far from being simply exploited for publicity, they "knew how to work the system"; they were after all on home turf and they understood that the Americans would not be with them for long. Rather than make elaborate efforts to ingratiate themselves to the Lao, Davis and Rhine casually dubbed children in the village "Tex" or "Mr. Bigger-eyes-than-mine." For all his egotism Dooley too had displayed a rare gift for connecting intimately with the Lao, but he still resorted to histrionics as though every procedure he performed be suitable for reproduction on film. Davis and Rhine provided a valuable counterpoint to the flashy antics of their boss; during their time in Muong Sing patients at the clinic received decent medical care and the citizenry witnessed two young Americans genuinely concerned for their well-being, qualities that Tom Dooley knew were not exhibited by many Westerners in Laos. Thanks to the character and the effort of Dwight Davis and Earl Rhine, Dooley could now add to his colorful résumé a stint as chief executive officer of a model program in voluntary humanitarian aid.[25]

Dooley insisted on running a tight ship. He explained: "Our relationship as a team was such as would exist on a ship with an officer who was liked but was nevertheless the Commanding Officer. Earl and Dwight always referred to me as 'Dr. Dooley,' and there was a 'sir' at the end of every sentence." Davis and Rhine built a small den in the hospital as an "inviolate cloister" for refuge from what Dooley called his "hyperthyroid totalitarianism." While Davis and Rhine remained entirely outside the political orbit of MEDICO, they formed their own opinions after observing various events in the Muong Sing area. Of the two, Earl Rhine was more concerned with the threat of communism as locally represented by the Pathet Lao (who were still based primarily to the east in the provinces of Sam Neua and Phong Saly), while Davis, at least in retrospect, believed that fears of imminent victory by the Pathet Lao over the Royal Lao Army (RLA) were aroused largely for propaganda purposes. Rhine was convinced that the Pathet Lao had murdered a female dependent of the RLA and her infant child whom they had helped to deliver. Davis recalled that the murders quickly became embroiled in the wider conflict, with supporters of the Pathet Lao alleging they were committed by an enraged soldier in the RLA. He was not certain the murders were part of a larger pattern of Pathet Lao terrorism nor did he recall fearing for his own safety, though Earl Rhine clearly recalled at least one ambush in which a child and her parents were shot execution-style by members of the Pathet Lao on a road near Muong Sing.[26]

The slight but significant differences in perception between Davis and Rhine show how even intimate observers of Laos's unstable political and military climate could disagree about the meaning of events they had witnessed firsthand. They did readily agree, however, that the overall situation was far more complex than cold war propagandists of all persuasions could ever have admitted, including their boss. In Muong Sing alone could be found a Royal Lao Army unit (housed in an ancient French fortress), an ever-changing contingent of Nationalist Chinese irregulars of the Kuomintang (KMT)—regrouped in northern Laos and equipped with startling quantities of international currency as well as the latest wristwatches from Hong Kong—the occasional foray by Pathet Lao guerrillas, and rather conspicuous "covert" operatives of the CIA.

By the end of 1958 this diverse cast shared a common interest in the lucrative opium trade in the Golden Triangle encompassing northwestern Laos, northeast Burma, and northern Thailand. While the Muong Sing area became a primary opium center only in the mid-1960s, it was already in Dooley's time "a center for local opium trade managed by resident Chinese shopkeepers." According to Alfred W. McCoy, a scholar who spent two decades exploring the CIA's relationship with the heroin business, "every spring these Chinese merchants loaded their horses or mules with salt, thread, iron bars, silver coins, and assorted odds and ends and rode into the surrounding hills to barter with hundreds of hill tribe farmers for their bundles of raw opium." At the end of the harvest season, aircraft belonging to the Corsican Mafia's Air Laos Commerciale—of which President Diem's brother Ngo Dinh Nhu was a silent partner—would land near a village (in the case of Muong Sing, at the same tiny airstrip used by MEDICO) to transport the opium to storage warehouses in Vientiane, "until a buyer in Saigon, Singapore, or Indonesia placed an order."[27]

In the early 1960s the opium trade played a key role in financing the "secret army" of Hmong tribespeople the CIA employed to counter North Vietnamese–backed Pathet Lao insurgencies in northern Laos (the Pathet Lao of course ran their own opium business). As of 1958, however, the KMT troops found in Muong Sing were leftovers from a disastrous 1952 CIA operation in which opium-funded KMT units in Burma had launched an invasion against southern Yunnan province, failing to gain even a foothold in China's most fertile opium-producing region. In subsequent years, "the KMT guerilla operations continued to create problems for both the Burmese and Chinese governments," particularly the former, where entire regions were occupied by KMT drug lords who shipped opium out of the country on the CIA's "Air America" (Civil Air Transport, or CAT) in exchange for weapons.[28]

To gather intelligence regarding "Chinese troop movements in Yunnan's border areas," the CIA recruited U Ba Thien, a Christian leader of an independence movement in the Shan states, the area bordering northwestern Laos that had merged with "the newly independent union of Burma" in 1947, only to suffer oppression from the Burmese authorities. U Ba Thien had worked for British intelligence in World War II but his anti-Burmese activities resulted in his exile to Muong Sing in 1958. It was there, according to McCoy, that "he contacted Dr. Tom Dooley, an independent American humanitarian who was operating a free clinic for the hill tribes in nearby Nam Tha [sic], and asked him to get aid for the Shans from the U.S. embassy or the CIA. Although Dr. Dooley was becoming an icon of America's anti-Communist crusade in Southeast Asia, he was no gunrunner."[29]

Dooley was, however, running medical supplies for his own good cause, so it was probably inevitable—in the absence of their own aircraft—that MEDICO would engage CAT to deliver supplies to Muong Sing. Some have speculated that these planes returned to Vientiane laden with Golden Triangle opium, but that was no concern of Dooley's, nor is it likely, as some have suggested, that he stored large caches of weapons in the MEDICO compound at Muong Sing. No one in Southeast Asia believed that Dooley was primarily or even substantially involved in espionage or covert activities; as his many critics have noted, he was hardly equipped for the work. But Tom's obligation to spare his American audience the fascinating details of life at Muong Sing, while not personally difficult to honor, lent a truly surreal cast to his broadcasts and writings at a moment when the situation in Laos was constantly changing, yet his audience's taste for anticommunist melodrama presumably remained constant. During this time the outlines of Dooley's role as propagandist became harder than ever to discern.

Prince Souvanna Phouma, Laos's neutralist prime minister, must have believed Dooley's public assessment of his own clout with U.S. policymakers. During an "unofficial" visit to Washington in January 1958, the prince had been informed by John Foster Dulles that, as national elections loomed, he must abandon his strategy of inclusion toward the Pathet Lao, lest "a great gulf between us" result. According to a record of the meeting prepared by his office, Dulles conceded that the prime minister brought "certain qualifications by which to judge the matter as a result of his intimate knowledge of the situation in Laos," but he reminded the prince of his own expertise, "from our world-wide experience in the way international Communism operates, in the subtlety of its means and the disguising of its purposes until too late." By the time Dulles finished lecturing him, Souvanna Phouma had no need to consult advisors in crosscultural communications to discern the secretary of state's message: exclude the Pathet Lao from elections and from the ruling coalition or prepare to lose all American economic aid to Laos.[30]

Souvanna Phouma patiently reminded Dulles and his assembled deputies that "it was necessary to see the situation through Lao eyes. Dr. Dooley," he went on, "who had lived in the villages, could tell the United States that Laos could not become Communist because of its faith in the old traditions." This was not a great moment in the checkered history of Souvanna Phouma's relations with the U.S. government, for in the room alongside Dulles sat Walter S. Robertson, assistant secretary for Far Eastern Affairs; J. Graham Parsons, the American ambassador to Laos; Kenneth T. Young, director of the Office of Southeast Asian Affairs; and Eric Kocher, deputy director, Office of Southeast Asian Affairs. None of these men was in the habit of soliciting Dooley's advice and counsel regarding Lao political affairs: it would be no exaggeration to describe their collective attitude toward Thomas A. Dooley, in early 1958, as one of disdain, cynicism, disgust, and even contempt, feelings tempered only occasionally by bemusement at the jungle doctor's flourishing celebrity among those Americans whose home furnishings were adorned by copies of the *Reader's Digest*.[31]

In his rejoinder to the prince, Secretary Dulles made no mention of Dr. Dooley's unique perspective on Lao society. But Souvanna Phouma had offered yet another testimonial to the ex-naval officer's tenacious appeal.

Though Dooley was a disgrace in the eyes of the State Department's personnel in Southeast Asia, his stature as an independent force in Laos had assumed a life of its own and there was little they could do about it. Ambassador Parsons certainly could not publicly announce that in 1956 Dooley had demanded passage on charter flights of the CIA's Air America, or that he had used the address of USOM's Carter de Paul to collect donations and personal mail. Nor could Parsons discuss any of the dozens of ways in which Dooley relied on the good offices of the U.S. State Department for a wide range of support services that would be made available as a matter of course to an American celebrity in a developing country. Parsons and nearly every American in Laos knew the circumstances of Dooley's ouster from the navy; they also shared the latest gossip of Dooley's antics in Saigon, Bangkok, and Hong Kong, which reportedly included brushes with the law over his fairly conspicuous homosexual carousings.

The visit of the prince occurred just prior to the public unveiling of MEDICO. While Parsons and his colleagues were quickly losing faith in Souvanna Phouma's ability or willingness to keep the Pathet Lao out of his government, they could hardly object to a humanitarian program which, by steering clear of Lao politics, would promote the appearance of U.S. tolerance for a genuinely neutralist state. Even if they had objected, the CIA, which "was the arm of policy implementation under Parsons," according to one source, enjoyed an even greater role in Laos after he was replaced as U.S. ambassador by Horace Smith in March 1958. This time around the agency achieved "a virtual coup d'etat in Vientiane," whose victim was the ambassador himself, though he kept his post, since "CIA was satisfied because it was able to act unhindered in Laos." Smith's "subordinates on the country team could make end runs to Washington with impunity."[32]

It was no secret that so long as Tom Dooley enjoyed the patronage of Hank Miller of USIS he remained vitally connected to the Lansdale network—whether freelance or regular CIA—whose influence was evident in the elaborate public relations and psywar campaigns Miller administered from Vientiane. One of those campaigns was conducted on behalf of the Committee for the Defense of National Interests (CDNI), also known as the "Young Ones," a group of right-wing bureaucrats and military officers inspired into being by the CIA in June 1958 following the supplementary election debacle in which members of the Pathet Lao or their supporters won thirteen of the twenty-one additional seats in the Lao Assembly. The elections sealed Souvanna's fate, at least in this chapter of his lengthy saga with the Americans: U.S. economic aid was suspended in June in order to force his resignation. In the meantime Secretary Dulles ordered an "intensive search" for "new faces" in Laos "with whom people [are] not disillusioned and who have energy and courage to carry struggle into remote villages and minority tribal areas." The figures Dulles had in mind belonged to a youthful cadre of pro-American Lao that Dooley socialized with and greatly admired: their leaders included Col. Oudone Sananikone (who was technically Dooley's boss as the minister of public welfare and health) and Sisouk Na Champassak, the minister of youth who had come to know Dooley quite well during a stint in New York at the United Nations.[33]

The ascendance of the CDNI, whose power base was the seemingly ubiquitous Vientiane Junior Chamber of Commerce, coincided with the establishment of the first MEDICO clinic at Muong Sing and strengthened Dooley's hand, especially in the wake of *The Ugly American*. "They helped to abolish the former sloth and old corruption," he wrote in *The Night They Burned the Mountain*. "They established rural self-help programs, village school programs, civic action programs, and made it their task to see that the young people became aware of their duties as citizens of the Kingdom of Laos." These "young men," as Dooley never tired of calling them, not only "hold the future of the Kingdom in their capable hands," but "they need more assurance of the fact that the young men of the Western World will also respond to their challenge. They need our hands, our hearts, our economic support, and our diplomatic prestige." The beauty of the CDNI in the eyes of the Americans was that, while they were staunch Lao nationalists, they were also dedicated modernists who would spare their patrons the lectures on Asian tradition that had grown so tiresome to the backers of Ngo Dinh Diem. The public opinion poll conducted by USIS on behalf of the CDNI asked a cross-section of Lao citizens such questions as: "What's the most important problem for you personally?" and "Would you say you're better off, worse off or about the same as you were two years ago?" Unlike Vietnam, the Americans found in Laos the blank slate on which they might build the first modern Asian nation, one in which the aggressive meritocrats of the CDNI might even learn to view the Lao peasantry from the new perspective of "cultural pluralism."[34]

Shortly before Dooley arrived at Muong Sing in September 1958, Phoui Sananikone, "a pro-Western diplomat," succeeded Souvanna Phouma and quickly appointed four members of the CDNI to a new cabinet which included his nephew, Oudone, and Sisouk Na Champassak. American aid to Laos was restored in October. With Dooley's closest Lao allies in command, he became a genuine political asset since, regardless of what the State Department thought of him personally, they recognized the fragility of a government that wholly excluded representatives of the Pathet Lao. He could help their cause in the United States with his broadcasts and *Reader's Digest* articles while they extolled him as a model of cost-effective yet visionary U.S.-Lao cooperation.

The attitude of some officers in the foreign aid program toward Dooley even began to change. Daly C. Lavergne, the new head of USOM Laos, suggested to Tom in the autumn of 1958 that the U.S. foreign aid program might consider "an agreement or contract with MEDICO for about four more teams" like the one in place at Muong Sing. Lavergne told his boss in Washington, Raymond T. Moyer of the International Cooperation Administration (or ICA, which had replaced the Foreign Operations Administration in 1955 as provider of foreign economic aid; ICA was in turn renamed the Agency for International Development, or AID, in 1961), that while Dooley had expressed "some fears that associating their operation with any ICA financing might be the 'kiss of death,' he does agree that the activity is highly desirable." Lavergne reported that Dooley was communicating his views to MEDICO's New York headquarters; in the meantime Tom assured him that he could readily staff and supply four new clinics in Laos but would need an additional $35,000 and a two-year commitment from USOM. Lavergne wrote to Moyer: "It seems to me this could be a valuable contribution and one which we should consider financing."[35]

Lavergne was determined to enhance USOM's image as well as its performance in light of *The Ugly American* and "constant criticism we get in the press at this late date based upon deficiencies which existed a year ago or longer, many of which no longer exist." The foreign aid program in Laos had begun to generate bad publicity even before the novel was published. Hearings held before the House Committee on Foreign Affairs in May 1958 revealed that USOM Laos had failed to establish methods to account for the disposition of U.S. aid imported into that country. In November 1958, on the heels of *The Ugly American*'s appearance, a disgruntled former USOM end-use auditor published a detailed exposé of the program's corruption in the *Reporter.* Haynes Miller revealed a pattern of corruption in USOM's dealings with American contractors such as the Universal Construction Company, an outfit that cornered the market for road-building equipment in Laos soon after the firm was hastily established in Bangkok.[36]

In the spring of 1959, hearings of a subcommittee of the House Committee on Government Operations revealed that USOM's public works director had accepted bribes of $13,000 from Universal in return for his help in securing lucrative contracts; he had then turned a blind eye while 40 percent of Universal's heavy equipment was being damaged within six months by the untrained operators the company provided. The hearings uncovered a story that was already well known in the foreign aid community as an allegory for its own hubris: Carter de Paul, the former director of USOM Laos, had sold his rotting 1947 Cadillac for a grossly inflated sum to the head of Universal, who proceeded to display the inoperable vehicle in front of his Vientiane office until "it became the subject of scornful amusement by Lao and American alike." It was de Paul who had promised to keep Leo Cherne apprised of business opportunities in Laos when the U.S. mission had first been established there. In better days Tom Dooley had often toured the Lao capital as a passenger in de Paul's Cadillac; by the time Dooley returned to Laos for his second mission the automobile had been chopped into pieces and dumped in a local well.[37]

By 1958 USOM had a serious personnel crisis on its hands: the agency's files from the period are replete with case histories of individuals brought to Laos and placed in sensitive positions yet whose liabilities included previous convictions for forgery, confinements in mental institutions, and episodes of alcoholic psychosis, confirming the judgment of Lederer and Burdick that Southeast Asia had indeed become a dumping ground for troubled employees of the foreign service.

In this light Tom Dooley's peccadilloes appeared significantly less disturbing, especially since, unlike many USOM employees, his personal life had generally been held apart from his work; in fact his vocation as a jungle doctor had kept many of his problems at bay. As his friend Anne Miller told her daughter in Vientiane, "He *is* what he *does.*" D. C. Lavergne was thus justifiably confident that the ICA in Washington would approve his proposal for U.S. sponsorship of new MEDICO teams in Laos. He told Raymond Moyer that "I have a feeling from reading material distributed to ICA from time to time that a good many people consider Laos simply as a problem child and that it is a hopeless situation. I usually feel that way by evening, but each morning I start out anew in the firm belief that we are making progress." His enthusiastic recommendation that the foreign aid program finance MEDICO teams through USOM Laos seemed to represent an important step in the right direction.[38]

Washington, especially in the person of veteran Dooley-watcher Raymond Moyer of ICA, was much less sanguine about a partnership with MEDICO. He cautioned Lavergne that "certain difficulties may be involved," particularly "the question of the relationship between these teams and Operation Brotherhood." Moyer cited the "danger of overlapping or of possible conflict between the two." Regarding Dooley's legendary "insistence on a free hand" coupled with his demanding nature, Moyer hinted at "problems of this kind" during Operation Laos in 1956–57. "On the other hand," he conceded, "I recognize the high quality of the service which he has been able to perform and his extraordinary spirit of service." Returning to the cautionary vein, he concluded: "There might be some questions about the project in the minds of Public Health officers here. If so, I imagine the questions would relate to a considerable extent to what would come out of these efforts in the long run, whether they simply are a flash of good will for a short time leaving nothing permanent."[39]

The sorry state of the clinic at Nam Tha—which had deteriorated with predictable alacrity following Dooley's departure in September 1957—"furnished my critics," Tom wrote, "a chance to find grist for their mills . . . the USOM representatives who handle American foreign aid told me with delight and glee how inadequate the médecin indochinois [French for poorly trained Lao medic] was, how poorly the hospital was being run, and how only 30 or so patients were being seen a day." The "USOM types" urged Dooley to return to Nam Tha but he refused, citing his status as "an invited guest in this foreign land." He claimed with little justification that the situation had improved after "the Minister of Social Welfare and Health, Colonel Sananikone, called me and said, 'Thanh Mo America, what is the trouble up at Nam Tha?'" In the end he could "only say what I always say: 'In America doctors run 20th century hospitals. In Asia I run a 19th century hospital. Upon my departure the hospital may drop to the 18th century. This is fine, because previously the tribes in the high valleys lived, medically speaking, in the 15th century.'"[40]

In his request for direct USOM funding for MEDICO, D. C. Lavergne had conceded that "I don't think my suggestion would be received with any particular enthusiasm by certain Public Health officers and perhaps, not too enthusiastically viewed by representatives of another agency." Lavergne's anxiety over encroaching on the turf of "another agency" was a natural reaction among embassy personnel in Laos, where, "as elsewhere, each organization with the embassy developed its own friends and clients in the host country." But as Charles A. Stevenson explained, "Special circumstances in 1958 and 1959 made the embassy in Vientiane more fragmented than unusual." A major conflict was developing there between Horace Smith, the new U.S. ambassador, and Henry Hecksher, the CIA's abrasive yet highly resourceful station chief in Laos. Since USOM Laos ran Operation Brotherhood at the behest of the CIA, Moyer's warning to Lavergne about potential conflicts between that program and a USOM-sponsored expansion of MEDICO was perhaps intended to spare his subordinate the wrath of "the company."[41]

It is impossible to say whether Moyer was aware that Operation Brotherhood was at the heart of the Lansdale party's covert operations network, which had a hand in MEDICO as well and interacted with but was not wholly controlled by the "regular" CIA in country. Lansdale's admirers and critics alike have almost entirely neglected to consider the enormous influence he exerted in Laos, even as his power in Vietnam apparently waned. Historian William C. Gibbons suggested that Lansdale was opposed by "Far Eastern personnel of the State Department and some elements of the CIA" who succeeded, despite "his personal appeal to the Dulles brothers," in forcing his departure from Vietnam in 1956. But while he was physically removed to Washington, his spirit made the much shorter trip to Laos. Rufus Phillips, perhaps his most trusted subordinate from the days of the Vietnam refugee operation, was the chief officer in the field for the Lao Civic Action program, a faithful replica of Lansdale's Vietnamese original. Phillips had reported in April 1957 that he was "using all the psywar I can muster" in the new assignment. Lansdale himself had first visited Laos in 1953, while inspecting French efforts to repel the Viet Minh from the Plain of Jars. His interest in the montagnard people of Laos was renewed in 1961 when he advised President Kennedy on the CIA's training of Hmong tribesmen, who were soon fighting a "secret war" with the communists.[42]

Civic Action was designed by the CIA as the Lao conduit through which Operation Brotherhood could be administered as though it were under local control. A 1958 report of a covert operative noted that "the Civic Action compound houses the Operation Brotherhood offices, the Lao Jaycee offices and is where the Lao Jaycees hold their meetings" (Operation Brotherhood "was requested to come to Laos by the Lao Jaycees" in 1956). Civic Action was obviously designed as a political/financial power base for the CDNI, which comprised the nucleus of the Vientiane Jaycees: a 1958 report indicated that U.S. expenditures on Civic Action totaled $1.5 million by August of that year. The report also noted that Civic Action "has been, and is, as much as anything, the reflection of one man, Col. Sananikone," a key figure in the CDNI as well as the nephew of Phoui Sananikone, the successor to Souvanna Phouma as Lao prime minister (the report's author dismissed Souvanna as being "not capable of thinking in terms of political action").[43]

Colonel Sananikone was the Lao chief of Civic Action as well as the minister of public welfare and health. In *The Night They Burned the Mountain* Tom Dooley explained: "This made him my boss, and an excellent boss he was. He gave me a free hand in the running of my hospital, yet he seemed to know every aspect of administration involved. He had visited my hospital twice in the past. As a Colonel, he was the most interested in our army training program." Part of Dooley's job naturally entailed boosting the public image of Sananikone and the CDNI. After describing a meeting with Sananikone where he learned of the progress of both civilian and military

Civic Action programs operating throughout Laos, Dooley exulted: "I left the Colonel pleased and proud to be working hand in hand with a government such as his."[44]

In May 1957, Rufus Phillips had arranged for heads of Vietnamese ministries to take "a number of young Lao visitors" on a tour of their offices "to show them how they operated." In September of that year he outlined, in a memorandum to the director of USOM Laos, the origins of Civic Action and Operation Brotherhood as programs in Vietnam designed to "perform positive work in the villages which would win over the population to the Government." He concluded his report by asserting that the lessons of Vietnam must be heeded "here in Laos" because of "the paramount fact, that the Laos of 1957 is remarkably similar in many respects to the Vietnam of 1955."[45]

The U.S. military must have agreed, because in February 1958, Adm. Felix B. Stump, commander of U.S. forces in the Pacific, wired the chief of naval operations affirming his support for a "crash program" to prevent a communist victory in the May elections (the program was to be known as "Operation Booster Shot"). He further recommended that immediate action be taken so that an "Individual qualified in psychological aspects of political campaigning against Communists be made available . . . during pre-election period. Col. Lansdale, USAF assigned DOD meets those qualifications. Recommend that he or individual of similar qualifications be assigned temporary duty Laos."[46]

Yet according to biographer Cecil Currey, Lansdale did not return to Southeast Asia until January 1959, as a member of a subcommittee of the Draper Commission, charged by President Eisenhower to investigate allegations made in *The Ugly American*—the very work that had presumably blown his cover. Currey did suggest that traveling openly as a member of a visiting delegation (Lansdale signed a guest registry, for instance, while touring the temples of Ankor Wat) may have provided the cover for "a secret and covert agenda" involving activities in Cambodia and, we might infer, in Laos. In Vientiane he visited with his close friends Anne and Hank Miller, who undoubtedly filled him in on Tom Dooley's recent activities upcountry. Lansdale urged all of the military officials he met on the trip to visit Vietnam "to see how Diem's government had handled a number of civic action programs similar to their own. Many took his advice."[47]

By this point Operation Brotherhood must have seemed like a primitive psyops to Lansdale. In any case, the CIA's Covert Action Staff, that is, the dreaded bureaucracy, had been directing the program, via a USOM cover, since the summer of 1958. Covert action funneled $600,000 from its own budget into the field and dictated to USOM officers that their contribution for fiscal year 1959 would amount to over $440,000, the funds to be administered through "whatever USOM Division found most convenient to preserve its [Operation Brotherhood] political character and probably it should continue to be attached to Civic Action." As an embassy staff member glumly complained to D. C. Lavergne, the director of USOM Laos, "It is disturbing to note that this project is being programmed in Washington rather than in the Mission and we are requested to concur in amount without knowledge as to the proposal's substance, details or directions."[48]

The CIA's "coup" in the Laos foreign aid program was thus confirmed. Yet Ed Lansdale enjoyed only creating covert operations; he left their administration to CIA colleagues of more bureaucratic temperaments. In 1958, with Operation Brotherhood functioning in Laos as a rather conventional psywar vehicle, a Filipino businessman named "Frisco" Johnny San Juan opened a Lao branch of his Eastern Construction Company. San Juan was a Lansdale client who had previously run Freedom Company, described by his sponsor as a "mechanism to permit the deployment of Filipino personnel in other Asian countries, for unconventional operations, under cover of a public service organization." The "technicians" and other employees of the Eastern Construction Company comprised, wrote historian Timothy Castle, "a 'third country' element which would remain an important part of the U.S. military aid program to Laos for many years to come."[49]

The hegemony of the Lansdale party in Laos between 1956 and 1959 may validate the following conclusions. Tom Dooley's Operation Laos was brokered by the International Rescue Committee, in a manner akin to the role it played on behalf of the U.S. Jaycees' sponsorship of Operation Brotherhood the year before. While that program had represented yet another financial bust for the IRC, Tom Dooley offered something new and different as a charismatic humanitarian and celebrity fundraiser. Since few in the United States would ever hear of Operation Brotherhood, *that* program could focus on actual intelligence gathering and counterinsurgency, in addition to its medical programs, while Dooley was encouraged to publicize the private, nonsectarian quality of charity practiced by Operation Laos and, later, MEDICO's dedicated teams. Dooley remained squarely in the camp of Lansdale and the Vietnam Lobby (the sobriquet was of course bestowed on the group after U.S. ground forces had been committed to Vietnam; in the late 1950s "Indochina Lobby" would have been a more accurate term) and actively promoted the anti-French, anti–"old guard" strategies designed to elevate the CDNI's "young ones" to power in Laos. The Jaycees connection remained intact, while the Lansdale party had its bidding done by USOM personnel, who remained vulnerable to rhetoric that associated the foreign aid program with decadent, un-American forces of colonialism in the region. The fact that Dooley believed in this work and devoted his entire being to it proved irresistible not only to the CIA's messianic liberals but also to large segments of the foreign service community: as Henry Cabot Lodge, U.S. ambassador to the United Nations (and a future ambassador to Vietnam) exclaimed in 1960, the year he served as Richard M. Nixon's running mate, "One feels that if there were an unlimited number of Dr. Dooleys, this country would have practically no foreign relations problems."[50]

The triumph of the communist Pathet Lao in the May 1958 elections had paved the way for this mini-coup by members of the Lansdale party, who quickly convinced the Dulles brothers to back those "new faces" (the CDNI). Dulles named Col. Oudone Sananikone, a CDNI linchpin and major Dooley supporter, as part of the "nucleus of group with whom we could work." With the ascendance in August 1958 of Phoui Sananikone, the colonel's uncle, Lansdale and his surrogates in Laos must have believed that they had achieved a major step toward their ultimate goal: "In sharing our ideology, while making others strong enough to embrace and hold it for their own, the American people strive toward a millenium when the world will be free and wars will be past." Phoui failed, however, to satisfy a less supple contingent of Americans in Laos and at the State Department who sought a more reliable leader. As would happen time and again throughout the cold war, a local general—in this case Phoumi Nosavan—was soon placed in charge, effectively undermining the subtle fictions that Dooley's mission served.[51]

Lansdale later insisted that Dooley's "activities were not backed at all by CIA"; far from settling the issue, however, his denials only confirmed his skill at "misdirection," the term favored by his biographer. "Disinformation" is the more familiar label for his method, for while hardly anyone would believe Lansdale's disclaimer, he still managed to reorient the question of the CIA's relationship with Dooley from the only real issue—was he exploited or perhaps even blackmailed—to a simple question of CIA support for MEDICO. In 1979 a flurry of indignation broke out in the American press when, in the course of preliminary investigations into Dooley's fitness for canonization as a saint of the Church, his "CIA connections" were revealed. The issue was immediately framed in such simplistic terms— Dooley's cold war patriotism versus his putative Christian obligation to remain "pure" of such worldly taint—that his "defenders," including the priest spearheading the canonization drive, had an easy time in arguing that Dooley did what was expected of any red-blooded American of his era. Tom Braden, a columnist who as a CIA agent in the early 1950s had designed the strategy of utilizing "cultural front" organizations to fight communism, argued that if Dooley had indeed advised "the CIA on Laotian troop movements," his reputation should only be enhanced.[52]

Tom Dooley may have learned something from Lansdale about dealing with critics. *The Night They Burned the Mountain* featured Dooley's most sophisticated writing in the subtle, almost Zenlike genre of propaganda favored by the master of pyschological warfare. In one passage Tom reproduced a partial transcript of a Radio Hanoi broadcast that had condemned him:

> "The Lao authorities have been acting in collusion with secret agents and organizations . . . permitting them to use the Muong Sing area of Laos to carry out espionage and sabotage activities against China. They have taken advantage of trade across the border to send special agents into China repeatedly to collect information, spread rumors and create disturbances. . . . The above mentioned provocations by Lao authorities . . . in the region of Muong Sing and Nam Tha . . . in the last six months . . . are being done under the guise of a medical team."

In a brilliant gesture, Dooley responded to the charges with a seeming non sequitur:

> The greatest problem that we had to put up with in our kind of work was loneliness. There was loneliness in Laos, but not of a bitter kind; not the loneliness of dead friendships or lost awareness. Rather we had that strange kind of loneliness that men have who find themselves swinging out beyond the boundaries of normal existence, who find that there suddenly bursts upon their view a fleeting moment of almost devastating awareness. We felt as though we were standing on the mountain peak and had, just for a quick moment, a tremendous view of all the world. This kind of loneliness was a good thing, for it made us more aware, and there was no exhaustion of the spirit.[53]

The communists of Radio Hanoi were thus dismissed in the same spirit with which Dooley had brushed aside his critics in the United States government. Spiritually dead, they resorted to petty charges in order to diminish Tom's grandeur, but only succeeded in confirming their own impoverishment, the result of a mutual cynicism that was the sine qua non of cold war bureaucracies, East and West alike. As late as 1984 Lansdale was still pleased to invoke an essentially miraculous interpretation of Dooley's power which reaffirmed the founding charisma of his mission. Far from being a CIA operation, Dooley's was, Lansdale opined, "an individual effort, very much, and volunteers. . . . And his mother, I know, put a lot of money in to help his mission, and I believe the family did, but later a lot of school

children and everything contributed to helping him out. He did some very
fine work there, too. Regardless of his character at all, he had great sensitivity towards the Asians out there and they responded to him. They could
sense his feelings about them as being quite genuine."[54]

The year-long tour of duty at Muong Sing represented a shining moment in
Tom Dooley's personal life as well as in his career as a jungle doctor. The
longer he was away from the United States and from members of his family,
the more balanced and centered he seemed to become; in turn he willingly
shared the insights of a growing maturity with his mother and brothers. By
late 1958 both Agnes and her son Edward Dooley (Tom's youngest brother,
known to the family as Eddie Mike) were in the throes of differing varieties
of alcoholism. Tom's mother drank heavily in the lonely confines of her
elegant and spacious penthouse apartment. She attempted to maintain appearances as the mother of a celebrity but was becoming increasingly accident prone and subject to fits of great despair. Eddie Mike was well down the
road toward his final destination as a skid-row drunk; his short and bitter
life ended at age thirty-one, in a one-car accident in New Orleans in 1965.
Following a brief stint in the military in the mid-1950s, he severed ties with
his family apart from sporadic requests for cash; he was particularly scornful of his eldest surviving brother, whom he dismissed as a "pansy" and a
glory-hound.

In response to his mother's incessant complaints of neglect by her children, Dooley counseled her repeatedly to take pleasure in the growing family of her middle son, Malcolm, and his wife, Gabrielle, who were raising a
rapidly growing family in the Detroit area while Malcolm struggled to establish himself as a stockbroker. For the first time in his life Tom tried to level
with his mother, at least insofar as family matters were concerned: "Mother,
I try so hard to be a good son to you," he wrote in October 1958.

> I know Eddie is being a perfect bastard. I know Malcolm is a family man with
> many responsibilities. And with the millions of things I have to do, the tremen-
> dous pressures on me from all sides, above and below, the travelling around,
> the endless writing, the propaganda against me, the fear I live under, the
> pressure of knowing that so many watch my every move . . . with all this I try
> to be a good son to you whom I love very much . . . and you know it. Yet
> almost every letter I get from you has some bitterness in it, some woe, some
> unhappiness.

With the royalties pouring in from *The Edge of Tomorrow,* Dooley found
himself in a position to help his brothers financially, thus reducing another
source of his mother's anxiety (the wealth the family enjoyed during the
1940s had steadily faded, perhaps due to a lack of financial acumen on his

father's part, though Agnes Dooley was far from poor). He pleaded with her to remember that "I am an extremely fortunate, well endowed, relatively rich young man, with world acclaim. Can't you find some joy in that? Please do."[55]

Several of Dooley's acquaintances—using language not available during his own lifetime—later likened his behavior to that commonly ascribed to many adult children of alcoholics, including the compulsive drive to please others and an eagerness to control situations beyond an ordinary human capacity. While Dooley certainly exhibited these characteristics, he could just as readily be viewed as a "people dis-pleaser." Although he had turned his back on a youthful life of profligate socializing that featured vast quantities of alcohol, he remained a notably inconsiderate adult capable of throwing wastepaper into a half-full glass of beer belonging to MEDICO's pilot and registering shock when he was told off for the deed. Dooley obviously believed the world revolved around him, but while this may have reflected the grandiosity of a child accustomed to rescuing one of his parents, it scarcely begins to account for the many contradictory elements of his personality, or his unique gifts, or indeed the remarkable poise and even serenity he achieved during the first year at Muong Sing.

He discovered above all that he loved being Tom Dooley, the jungle doctor of Laos. As he wrote in *The Night They Burned the Mountain*, "This kind of medicine is my salvation, my hold on life. It is my means of expression . . . I must treat patients with my own hands, reach out and give personal help every day." He exulted: "I realized that I had become more aware of myself and my life's adventure in the material of Asian life." The poignant tone of the book, which Dooley himself found so moving, was greatly enhanced by the dramatic juxtaposition of his mystical ascent to self-knowledge and the account of his discovery that he had been afflicted with a grave illness. *The Night They Burned the Mountain* is framed by an account of his cancer: the book begins with a description of his receipt of an urgent telegram from Peter Comanduras in New York instructing him to return immediately to the United States.[56]

Earl Rhine and Dwight Davis knew the reason for the telegram: a visiting surgeon from California had excised a cyst from Dooley's chest in July 1959 and preserved a sample which, when tested by a pathology lab in Thailand, indicated that Dooley had contracted malignant melanoma, a lethal, rapidly spreading form of skin cancer. Davis and Rhine concealed the results from Dooley for fear he would refuse to abandon the hospital at Muong Sing; they were certain he was fully prepared to die in Laos. Only after Dooley traveled to Vientiane—anxious to learn why he was being recalled to New York—did his friend Hank Miller reveal the diagnosis.[57]

The bulk of *The Night They Burned the Mountain* essentially comprises a lengthy flashback to the triumphant period beginning with the formation of MEDICO in February 1958. The final chapters interweave an account of growing political turmoil in Laos with the first ominous signs of the invasion of his own body by disease. Yet the literary method was ultimately rendered ineffective because Dooley could not candidly explain why his friend, Premier Phoui Sananikone, had been ousted by a militant faction of CDNI members (as the book went to press in early 1960 Dooley awkwardly attached a postscript on the political situation in which he charged that "Prince Sananikone reversed his anti-communism in favor of 'neutralism'"). In the past, Dooley's suggestion that his own self-sacrifice absorbed much of the force of communist aggression was uniquely compelling, especially in the American Catholic folk economy of suffering. But now that his self-mortifications had begun to take on a literal meaning, the cynical uses to which his faith had been employed seemed to exact their toll on his spirit.[58]

In *The Night They Burned the Mountain* Dooley reprinted, in a revised version, a long letter written to his mother on August 8 and 9, 1959, in which he confessed to twin fears over the state of his health and "the shadows, rumors" of an imminent Pathet Lao incursion in northwest Laos. But while the published version concludes, "I am scared. Scared," the original wording was "I am scared. Scared bored. Bored scared." He was actually angry more than anything else, unleashing a torrent of indignation at the demands made on him by ambassadors, publishers, priests, KMOX radio, and the recipient of his letter. "I want you to stop thinking of me," he scolded his mother, "as your infant son who you believe doesn't love you enough." "I am a doctor," he bellowed, repeating the central theme of the letter. "The book of me, the root of the tree, the foundation of the building, the heart of it all is, *I am a doctor.* . . . It was a hard fight, a humiliating fight to become a doctor. Now I am a doctor."[59]

Above all he was a jungle doctor, even if "mountain valley" represented the more precise topographical description of his venue. In the months to come, treated with the most advanced medical technologies available to American practitioners, this physician attempted to aid in his own healing by conjuring "the mountains of my beloved northern Laos, its gulfs and gorges, the hosts of billowing clouds that roll off the slopes of the high rainforest. . . . The waterlogged sodden land of Laos buried beneath the rains of heaven." Shortly after returning to New York for surgery, he dreamed "that I was walking up a steep trail, leading across my valley floor and weaving its way through the high rain forest onto the mountaintop just east of us. My boys were with me, and some of my Lao students. And in the vivid flash of the moment, in my dream, I saw a century-old pagoda that nestles on this mountain slope. The pagoda is made of mud stones and is crowned by a high spire. Hanging from the spire are long white banners, the streamers of Buddhist prayers."[60]

Dooley had seen the pagoda before, but "in the dream I reconstructed it even more lucidly." Since he saw "tiny insignificant little figures of men" planting new rice seedlings "into the burnt soil," "the month of my dream must have been May, the time of lilacs at my beloved Notre Dame. But in Laos, May is a time when the season is driest. These are the nights that they burn the mountain." Dr. Tom Dooley

> knew the meaning of my dream. From my hospital bed in New York, with the same white light of revelation I had known once several years before, I saw what I must do . . . my God and my dream commanded me. I must, into the burnt soil of my personal mountain of sadness, plant the new seedlings of my life—I must continue to live. I must cultivate my fields of flood, to feed those who cannot feed themselves. . . . The jagged, ugly cancer scar went no deeper than my flesh. There was no cancer in my spirit. The Lord saw to that.[61]

☆ **8** ☆

This Is Your Life

On September 1, 1959, Teresa Gallagher drafted a MEDICO press release proclaiming that

> a world-wide crusade of prayer to St. Thérèse, the Little Flower, is in progress for Doctor Tom Dooley, young jungle physician stricken with cancer. Thousands of people all over the world—in every State of the Union and in eight foreign countries—started the prayer crusade on Friday, August 28, and will end on Tuesday, September 8, Feast of Our Blessed Mother. Doctor Dooley, who has set up three jungle hospitals (under the auspices of Medico, a voluntary, non-profit organization which he helped to found) in the beleaguered little Southeast kingdom of Laos, had a cancerous growth removed from his chest at the beginning of August by a physician visiting his hospital five miles from the Red China border.[1]

The draft statement went on to explain that the type of cancer afflicting Dooley, malignant melanoma, was so virulent that surgeons at the famed Memorial Hospital in New York City "were reluctant even to perform an operation on the selfless young doctor, feeling that he had only a short time to live and that the operation with its attendant pain would prolong his life a mere few months." But according to the press release no spread of the cancer had been found following surgery: Dooley's convalescence "has been termed 'startling' by those who have watched his progress in the hospital." It was further reported that just five days after his surgery—which involved not only a radical excision of the cancer from his chest wall but also extensive skin grafts—Dooley had taken "a four-block walk to East River Drive with a hospital orderly." *Our Sunday Visitor*, a national Catholic weekly newspaper, reported on October 11 that on the eighth day after his surgery, "Dr. Dooley hobbled out of the hospital, hunched up and walking on a cane, to attend Mass at St. Patrick's cathedral unaware of the concluding novena" offered as part of the prayer crusade on his behalf. "As he moved slowly and quietly down the aisle, a group of women taking part in the novena spotted him. He said he could see their mouths forming words as if to say 'a miracle.' "[2]

Before the statement was released, MEDICO's secretary general Peter Comanduras made numerous changes in the text, a routine gesture for a chief executive officer whose organization was about to receive unprecedented media scrutiny. Yet the revisions indicated as well an abiding conflict in perceptions of Dooley's mission and character. Where Teresa Gallagher's version of the statement resembled a miracle text, Comanduras sought to restore its secular orientation by substituting "excellent" for "startling" to characterize Dooley's early recovery and by deleting the account of Dooley's walk because he was "not sure [it was an] accomplished fact." Left untouched by Comanduras was the prayer to St. Thérèse being offered for Dooley's cure, perhaps because it evoked a devotional subculture so alien that it was better left alone. The prayer, which Gallagher assured the press bore the imprimatur of the Church, read as follows:

> Dearest Little Flower of Jesus, great wonderworker in every necessity, I humbly implore thy powerful intercession with Christ our King, through Mary our Queen, the Mediatrix of All Graces. I trust as a little child to the boundless love and goodness of God. Obedient to the admonition of Jesus, I implore this grace from the Heavenly Father in the name of Jesus Christ, and I am absolutely confident to obtain my urgent request, if such is for His greater honor and glory and our real good. As proof of my deep gratitude, I promise to make the rose obtained through thy intercession known to others, and to enter upon the little Way of spiritual childhood.[3]

It did not take long for Teresa Gallagher to begin alluding to "Blessed Thomas of Laos." Others shared Comanduras's skepticism about the supernatural dimensions of Dooley's recovery, while certain government officials quickly expressed confidential doubts that Dooley was sick at all but had orchestrated his "surgery" for publicity purposes. In later years at least one physician suggested that Dooley had suffered from AIDS. As for the thirty-two-year-old human being who faced a terminal illness in the late summer of 1959, Tom Dooley once again conjured that familiar, "cloudy out-of-touchness with everything" and "pleasant disembodiment from my own self" that had served him so well in the past. "My mind put me somewhere else where I could look back at the body of Tom Dooley." He was joined there by millions of other Americans who gazed on the body of Tom Dooley while he lay on the operating table as part of a CBS Reports documentary, "Biography of a Cancer," in which the human pseudo-event known as "the jungle doctor" used his own diseased body as a billboard for MEDICO and as a template for all the world's sick and suffering.[4]

In "Biography of a Cancer," first aired on April 21, 1960, and in *The Night They Burned the Mountain,* the publication of which was timed to coincide with the television program, Dooley explored both the etiology and, more important, the teleology of his illness. Although Memorial Hospital's clinical director, Dr. Henry T. Randall, told CBS Reports that melanoma "takes its origin from a pigmented mole in the skin" and denied that "Dr. Dooley's fall down a village embankment in February caused his disease," Tom continued to focus on "this pivotal point in my life" because it linked the cancer to his dangerous work and even to the fate of a free Laos, whose tribulations so neatly paralleled Dooley's. Since Dooley knew that "there is only one tumor that is jet black," his decision not to seek immediate treatment once Dr. Bill Van Valin had excised a black mass from his chest in July gave rise to speculation that Tom harbored a death wish and welcomed a jungle martyrdom. His trusted corpsman Dwight Davis confirmed that he conspired with Earl Rhine and others in an elaborate ruse to conceal the diagnosis of melanoma, lest Dooley ignore MEDICO's vague yet urgent command that he return to New York. Davis felt that Dooley was prepared to die in Laos. Seymour Cholst, a New York psychiatrist who never met Dooley but heard many stories about him while living in Vientiane in the mid-1960s, bluntly expressed in correspondence what numerous others have implied—that Dooley was so wracked by guilt over his homosexuality he willed his own illness. Cholst argued that Dooley's egotism and compulsive good works sprang from a futile desire to overcome the self-loathing wrought of his sexual behavior.[5]

While psychological interpretations of Dooley's illness are by their nature inadequate, they at least accept the diagnosis of melanoma as a starting point, which is more than some government officials were willing to do at the time. An internal memorandum of February 1, 1960, from the CIA's security office noted a report from an agency informant, or "asset," who claimed that "the widely circulated story that Dr. Dooley is suffering from the malignant chest condition is untrue and that the operation supposed to have been performed in connection therewith is a myth." As with many documents of this kind, it is impossible to establish the context of the report since so many passages are blacked out (and the reproduction was "copied from nearly illegible original"), but just prior to this discussion of Dooley's medical condition it was reported that he "is alleged to be a homosexual." Dooley's sexual deviance thus sufficed to undermine any credibility he may have earned from the intelligence community, so that even the authenticity of his illness was subject to question. As yet another obscure document revealed, members of the intelligence community feared that if he was ever "brought out into the public light for what he is," he would "not give up gracefully," but "would scratch and kick in typical style peculiar to his breed, when cornered."[6]

In the late 1980s, after Dooley's homosexuality became public knowledge, it was perhaps inevitable that some commentators would speculate he may have died from AIDS rather than melanoma. While the theory initially seemed preposterous because of the twenty-year lag between the time of his death and the earliest reported diagnoses of the disease, microbiologists at Washington University had reported in 1973 on "a curious clinical syndrome in a native-born American" they first saw in 1968 who by 1988 appeared to these same scientists to have "fulfilled the diagnostic criteria for AIDS." The individual in question was a "fifteen year old black male, born and raised in Saint Louis," prompting a physician in Hawaii to suggest the possibility of a link to Dooley. While the boy was not even born until two years after Dooley's death, the possibility he had AIDS suggested an earlier appearance of the disease in the United States than had been previously believed. The physician also suggested that Dooley's experiences at Albert Schweitzer's hospital in Africa be investigated but the circumstances of his visit to Lambaréné, if indeed there was one, remain obscure.[7]

The facts about Dooley's illness are less spectacular but in their own way more dramatic than the speculations. In December 1957 Dr. Charles Doyle, a prominent St. Louis surgeon, had operated on Dooley at St. Mary's hospital for varicose veins in his legs. Dooley had written to Dr. Doyle from New York earlier that autumn—following his return from Nam Tha—complaining of "bilateral varicosities" that were making it painful for him to stand "on lecture platforms with no moss underfoot"; he also reported undergoing "a constant struggle with an insidious hepatitis" while in Laos and attached a note imploring Dr. Doyle to discuss "nothing but the most innocuous things with my mother." Prior to the procedure, performed under local anesthetic, the surgeon noticed a mole on the lower right portion of Dooley's chest that was described as a "benign, junctional nevus mole." He "took a good whack at it" and preserved a section in a parafin block, but although pathology tests were performed, multiple sections of the sample were not cut for examination, thus limiting the validity of the tests. After Dooley returned to the

United States for surgery in 1959, he asked Dr. Doyle to perform the operation but was referred instead to Memorial Hospital in New York, the nation's leading facility for cancer treatment. Dr. Doyle then carefully reexamined the section preserved from the chest lesion and found "areas of invasion" that indicated a malignancy as of 1957.[8]

The tests also revealed, however, that the cancer had developed far beyond the point at which it might have been prevented from spreading (once a melanoma grows thicker than one-eighth of an inch—the thickness of a dime—it has most likely already metastasized, or spread to other parts of the body through the blood or, in Dooley's case, the lymph system). Doyle believed that it was therefore already too late to treat Dooley's cancer effectively. He later rejected as mere propaganda Dooley's claim that his cancer had been "caused by a fall" in Laos; he insisted that, as a physician, Tom would have known better. Doyle also doubted that exposure to the sun was a cause of the disease. While that finding might be challenged by some skin cancer specialists, few would claim that Dooley's exposure to the tropical sun of Southeast Asia could have produced a melanoma in less than three years, though sun-related damage incurred during Dooley's childhood could certainly have been a factor in the origins of his disease.[9]

The documentary telecast of Dooley's surgery, "Biography of a Cancer," represented a genuine breakthrough in coverage of the disease: the program earned the Albert and Mary Lasker Medical Journalism Award as the outstanding medical television feature of 1960. For several years the legendary producer Fred Friendly had sought a vehicle for a television documentary that would "present to the American public, truthfully and graphically, the facts about cancer." As soon as Friendly learned of the imminent surgery he contacted Dooley in St. Louis, where Tom was hurriedly visiting with his mother en route to New York. Once the approval of Memorial Hospital and the American Cancer Society was obtained, CBS Reports mobilized for an "unrehearsed" documentary on Dooley's surgery and his prospects for recovery.[10]

The documentary opened with Dooley imploring of a cancer specialist, "How long it's going to take for you before you have a real breakthrough in cancer. How long? How much longer must we wait?" Following an evasive reply by the specialist, Dooley was asked by reporter Howard K. Smith if he was afraid of the impending operation. "My fear of surgery tomorrow—no," Dooley replies. "My fear of the future—after surgery—just a certain amount of fear. But a great deal of hope and faith—yes." Smith later pointedly asked Dooley if he is not "a bad advertisement for cancer research" for failing to respond more promptly to early symptoms of the disease, to which Tom replied that he "really never gave it much thought" until he began his journey home. He quickly regained the offensive by telling Smith, "You know, I'm scared to death of this thing becoming maudlin. I'm scared to death of somebody saying a clutching, agonizing sort of a thing. Sure, anybody who's got cancer has got some discomfort. I don't want anyone to get sloppy over this . . . I don't like anything that says—a dying doctor's anguish bit. That's—that's stupid." He then explained that he agreed to have his surgery filmed so that "maybe in some small way, people who will watch this show, and who know that Dooley's got this—maybe, in a small way, I can use this as a method of pointing out to Americans that they need not have as much fear over the word 'cancer' . . . as there has been in the past."[11]

Dooley was a brilliant actor as well as a highly effective teacher; in "Biography of a Cancer" he combined these gifts into one of the most moving real-life performances of his career. In addition to educating the public, he was given ample time to plug MEDICO. He seized the "chance to talk to some twenty, twenty-five million Americans about the work of MEDICO—about the work that we have in trying to send doctors and nurses and corpsmen to the furthest outposts of the world to take care of people who are sick, simply because they 'ain't got it so good.'" More than three years had passed since Dooley had shown enormous grace under fire in the days following his ouster from the navy. He had deftly handled questions about his civilian attire while ardently promoting an Operation Laos program hatched only days earlier along Madison Avenue. Now, in the late summer of 1959, he demonstrated the same qualities as he faced the likelihood of a premature death. But there was even more on his mind than the surgeons and television reporters could discern, for in the days and hours leading up to his surgery and beyond, MEDICO was jettisoned by the International Rescue Committee and the splintering forces that comprised the beleaguered Vietnam Lobby. Even as he awoke from surgery Dooley had to wonder how his vision of humanitarian medicine could endure when stripped down to the core of his unique charisma.[12]

The official explanation applied to the "friendly divorce" of MEDICO from the IRC was typically contradictory and raised more issues than could be resolved by even the costliest public relations experts. Tom Dooley alone seemed to understand that, where his career was concerned, there was little to be gained by elaborate explanations of his shifting fortunes: he simply told stories appropriate to the occasion. The split was not without acrimony. Harold Oram had brought Dr. Peter Comanduras together with Leo Cherne and Angier Biddle Duke in the autumn of 1957 in order to build a medical program that would exploit Dooley's appeal to raise funds as well as the IRC's profile in Washington, building on a political foundation established through support of Operation Brotherhood and Operation Laos. But by November 1958 Oram had grown disgusted with Comanduras, evidenced by a memo to Cherne in which he expressed fears that Comanduras's shortcomings in administration and leadership spelled doom for MEDICO.[13]

Comanduras was no visionary, but Oram's wrath also reflected his own embarrassment that MEDICO had fallen far short of the financial goals established by the IRC as a rationale for sponsoring the program. Tom Dooley was a fundraising machine, to be sure, but *only* when he was touring the United States in support of a book. While in Laos he presided over costly and growing programs that were of little use to the IRC unless they were constantly trumpeted before the American public. Leo Cherne later admitted that MEDICO was a drain on the IRC's precarious finances while Dooley was abroad, but he also suggested that Dooley's illness made him vulnerable to Comanduras's desire to establish a new MEDICO board without representation from the IRC. Cherne also acknowledged that everyone expected Dooley to die quickly in August of 1959, including Dr. Howard Rusk, an associate of Cherne and Oram (it was Rusk who urged Fred Friendly to contact Dooley about the cancer documentary, in hopes that the film would serve as a fitting memorial). Comanduras later told an executive at CARE that he had visited Dooley at the hospital to inform Tom that he wished to get "out from under" the IRC, which he felt was not doing enough for MEDICO. As he left Dooley's room, Leo Cherne arrived: after Cherne emerged two and one-half hours later, Comanduras returned to be told by Dooley ("much to Peter's surprise"), "I'm with you!" The story is reminiscent of earlier face-saving gestures Dooley had made while facing similar pressures.[14]

The timing of the announcement raises several questions, among which is why, with MEDICO rapidly expanding and the United States government showing an increasing interest, would the IRC back out just because MEDICO had not yet fulfilled its financial promise? The IRC's greater willingness to participate in the covert activities of the U.S. intelligence community may have played a role. At a March 1959 MEDICO Executive Committee Medical Advisory Council meeting, plans for a joint MEDICO-ICA hospital project in Vietnam were enthusiastically discussed, although an IRC officer insisted that the investment of the U.S. foreign aid program must remain "covert." The same officer had concluded, in a March 6 memorandum to Peter Comanduras: "The less Asians know that MEDICO has a United States government contract, the better." The issue of secrecy and the possible negative publicity attending to an overt MEDICO relationship with ICA was clearly divisive, especially at a time when the Vietnam Lobby was undergoing internal dissension.[15]

One thing is certain: Dooley was no more involved in the IRC's decision to drop his program than he had been in the creation of Operation Laos in 1956. In fact, with his surgery dominating the headlines, few observers even noticed a seemingly insignificant bureaucratic shift in his sponsorship. Even fewer could have imagined that shifts in the fortunes of the Vietnam Lobby itself may have rendered Dooley vulnerable on both strategic and ideological grounds. The radically ecumenical character of American support for Ngo Dinh Diem had eroded substantially by 1959. In 1955 the American Friends of Vietnam had forcefully mirrored the broad consensus enshrined in postwar American ideology. In that setting only a publicist would have noticed that Tom Dooley's meteoric rise to prominence provided an insurance policy against a renewal of the sectarian hostilities liberals associated with McCarthyism. Along with the rising generation of Kennedys and other Catholic politicians, such as Sen. Mike Mansfield of Montana, Dooley offered to redirect the visceral isolationism of his religious subculture beyond crude anticommunism and into the light of enlightened mainstream thought.

But the furor attending *The Ugly American* gravely undermined the fiction of a classless, de-ethnicized polity united behind the liberal internationalist wing of the cold war consensus. The American Friends of Vietnam had represented a political manifestation of Will Herberg's theory that ancient conflicts between groups were sublimated on behalf of the American Way of Life, a development that Herberg and others alternately celebrated and deplored. The power of ecumenical lobbies like the AFV resided in their seemingly effortless, natural quality: only in America could representatives of the Catholic hierarchy share space on a masthead with socialists and Texas oil magnates.

The Ugly American accused the diplomatic establishment not of communism but arrogance, sloth, wastefulness, and a moral softness that threatened to deliver Southeast Asia to the Reds with nary a shot being fired. Taxpayers of all persuasions were outraged by the scandalous conduct of the foreign aid program, detailed not only by Lederer and Burdick but by a growing chorus of journalists who exploited the populist discontent stirred by the novel. When the dust settled, a fundamental realignment of the Vietnam Lobby occurred, along the same ideological fault lines that Diem's liberal American allies had struggled to erase. The noncommunist Left now rallied around the elite gentlemen of the foreign service who, besieged yet again, took solace in the summer of 1959 from "Fact and Fiction on Foreign Aid," a lengthy critique of *The Ugly American* authored by Joseph Buttinger for *Dissent*. Buttinger and his wife were financial backers of Irving Howe's social democratic journal; in a prefatory note Howe lauded the essay as "an example of a genre which in America has been inadequately cultivated: the criticism of mass culture in the field of politics. For what Mr. Buttinger is doing here is showing how the catchwords and conceptions of liberalism can be appropriated by sensationalistic writers for the popular market and thereby put to quite illiberal uses." Howe recognized that the likes of Lederer and Burdick were more threatening to the Left than McCarthy precisely because they were both liberals *and* popular authors with ready access to the marketplace of ideas so thoroughly tainted by "mass culture." In fact Howe summarized Buttinger's lamentation so neatly there was scant reason to print the essay itself, a tendentious and haughty exercise that aimed to restore the hegemony of foreign aid elites but succeeded only in making *The Ugly American* appear even more prescient.[16]

Buttinger condemned the book for "the flagrant manner in which it distorts, ignores, or contradicts what in respect to our aid and diplomacy I have learned to regard as the essential facts," but rather than reporting those facts he assailed the mass production of ideas in an open society and the gullible citizenry that consumed such artifacts as *The Ugly American*. Incredibly, he even devoted considerable effort to proving that the book was not even "good fiction." He established his own expert credentials by ridiculing the claim of the authors that Vietnamese communists had become "a strong contender for power in the South." Thanks to unnamed voluntary and governmental American aid programs, Buttinger assured his readers, the communists had "lost all hope of a victory which five years ago not even our most consistent optimists had the courage to doubt." In dismissing as fallacious the distinction Lederer and Burdick had drawn between "small projects" of foreign aid and those "big" ones they derided as counterproductive, Buttinger affirmed by implication the intimate link that existed between a group like his own IRC and the State Department, a connection Tom Dooley never tired of denying.[17]

Historians of the cold war, who have persistently argued that the anticommunist and antiradical "hysteria" of the period cast its long shadow over the entire decade of the 1950s, would be hard-pressed to account for the outpouring of gratitude bestowed on Buttinger by high-ranking employees of the State Department who showed no fear in writing to a socialist author on United States government letterhead. C. Alphonso Smith, the State Department's acting special assistant for mutual security information, offered "congratulations and thanks" for a "devastating" and "beautifully documented job." Loy Henderson, deputy undersecretary for administration, informed Buttinger in June 1959 that the Public Affairs Bureau "has already initiated steps to secure additional copies of your preprint with an effort to provide wider dissemination within the Department of State with your thoughtful analysis. I am sure that many of our other officers, who have smarted under

With Harold Oram in President Ngo Dinh Diem's Saigon office, December 1956. On Diem's desk is a copy of *Hungary's Fight for Freedom*, a special report by the editors of *Life* magazine from November 1956, proceeds from which went to the International Rescue Committee. *Photo courtesy of Ruth Lilly, Special Collections and Archives, Indiana University-Purdue University Indianapolis.*

Dr. Dooley with Operation Laos corpsmen John deVitry, Peter Kessey, unknown man, and Robert Waters, northern Laos, spring 1957.

Administering vitamin solution to Lao child, near Nam Tha, Laos, spring 1957.

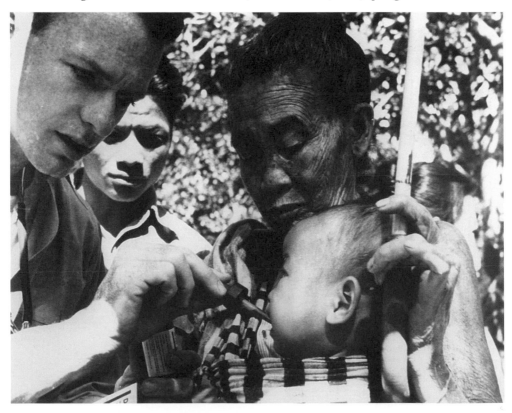

In northern Laos, ca. 1957.

With Robert Waters, John deVitry, and Lao assistants, about to be "bagged" with CARE midwife kits, Nam Tha, spring 1957.

Father Leo Deschatelets, superior general, Oblates of Mary Immaculate, conferring honorary oblate award on Dr. Tom Dooley, as Father Joseph Birch, O.M.I., looks on, Rome, October 1957.

With American female admirers during MEDICO fund-raising tour, spring 1958.

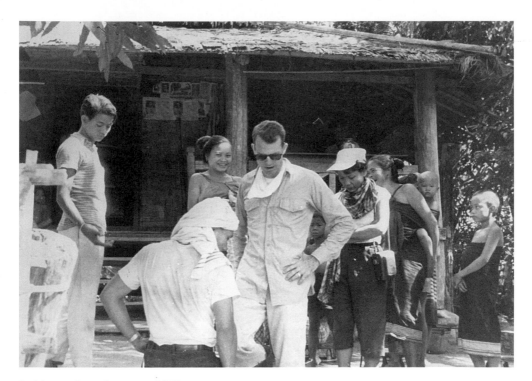

In Muong Sing, Laos, ca. 1958.

MEDICO Corpsman Earl Rhine
with patient in Muong Sing,
ca. 1959.

With Dwight Davis and Earl Rhine, MEDICO compound, Muong Sing, 1959.

USIS officer and Dooley friend Dolf Droge with Prince Phetsarath, Laos, ca. 1958.

With Vice-President Richard M. Nixon, ca. 1959.

Teaching Lao greeting to American schoolchildren, autumn 1959.

With Madame Vu Thi Ngai and Agnes W. Dooley, at taping of "This Is Your Life" program, Los Angeles, November 1959.

With friend and advisor Paul Hellmuth in 1960.

At Notre Dame graduation, June 1960, with fellow honorees, including President Dwight D. Eisenhower (*third from left, front row*) and Giovanni Cardinal Montini, later Pope Paul VI (*second from right, front row*). Between them stands Notre Dame president Theodore M. Hesburgh, C.S.C.

During final visit to Hawaii, July 1960.

the unfair attacks of 'The Ugly American,' will be encouraged to carry on their dedicated services by your spirited defense." As a former member of a blueblooded group of Dean Acheson protégés that included Alger Hiss, Henderson had ample incentive to disseminate Buttinger's essay. United States Ambassador to South Vietnam Elbridge Durbrow expressed his regret that the essay "will not reach the general public. Perhaps someone, some day, will manage to get a book on the best-seller list which portrays the opposite side of the coin."[18]

The Ugly American had engendered a new populist internationalism: far from scorning foreign affairs, its authors urged ordinary Americans to demand more from their appointed representatives abroad. As Tom Dooley became increasingly identified with this point of view (Lederer and Burdick's "Salute to Deeds of Non-Ugly Americans" in *Life* coincided with the publication of Buttinger's essay in *Dissent*), elitist liberals had less reason than ever to support him. Joseph Buttinger was an ideologue, if an indecisive one; since marrying a wealthy heiress he had blended his European disdain for American culture with the scornful attitudes common to members of the upper class, especially in their views toward the very business civilization that had generated their inherited wealth. W. W. Norton and Company, publishers of *The Ugly American,* capitalized on Buttinger's sneering remark that the book was "still defying its destiny, which is to drop into the ocean of public indifference where it will lie until Hollywood announces its resurrection." In an advertisement Norton gleefully retorted: "Hollywood *has* made the announcement—sales are still up—THE UGLY AMERICAN is Destiny's tot." As long as Buttinger remained a left-wing anticommunist, his unpopular views could only further endear him to members of the diplomatic corps: for them, his aspirations for democratic socialism in South Vietnam represented the kind of flexible, sophisticated, "cultured" approach whose absence they now mourned as among the victims of the Red Scare.[19]

Alone among the key figures within the IRC-AFV network, Buttinger had shown no public interest in Tom Dooley; it is easy to imagine his distaste for the jungle doctor's blend of Madison Avenue and middle American antiintellectualism. But Angier Biddle Duke had invested deeply of his social capital in Dooley's work. His defection from the Vietnam Lobby (he had resigned as head of the AFV's executive committee in 1958) was an early warning signal of the internal conflicts that finally wrecked the coalition. Duke shared Buttinger's disdain for retired Gen. John O'Daniel, who as president of the AFV had promoted the Diem regime's military security at the expense of the social agenda favored by Duke and his allies. "It seemed to me," Duke told historian Joseph G. Morgan in 1989, "that the organization was moving away from its 'liberal' roots in the world of Wolf Ladejinsky [a controversial land reform consultant to the Diem regime and close ally of Cherne and Fishel] and Joe Buttinger and was losing the broad spectrum of support that it enjoyed when the refugees were pouring out of North Vietnam." Duke had perhaps grown tired as well of defending Diem against attacks by fellow Protestants of his own social class, including the wife of New York's Anglican bishop James Pike, who in March 1958 forwarded to Duke an anti-Catholic diatribe from an unidentified source who asked: "I wonder if you are aware of the fact that the present government of Vietnam is completely the handiwork of Cardinal Spellman . . . there he has in effect a virtual gestapo." Duke could only reply that Diem had actually proven "disappointing to the Roman Catholic Church" for failing to "help further his religion in Vietnam." Either way, the "religious issue" had failed to dissolve despite the efforts of some of the best talent on Madison Avenue. At a May 12, 1959, meeting of the Advisory Council of MEDICO's Executive Committee, it became clear that the efforts of Duke and others to attract new trustees to MEDICO—by drawing on the IRC's traditional constituencies—were doomed to failure.[20]

Though Duke's position on the AFV's Executive Committee was assumed temporarily by Buttinger, the latter was privately even more concerned with the militarization of the Diem regime: it had been a long time since anyone could have believed democratic socialism was coming to South Vietnam. While Tom Dooley's future surely ranked as a low priority among these weighty issues, Duke's disillusionment was ominous because the tobacco scion had been the one elite figure solidly in the doctor's corner, even when fellow patricians like Claiborne Pell pleaded with the IRC board to eschew Dooley as an unsavory character in 1956. The first fault line to appear in the Vietnam Lobby pitted liberal internationalists—who expected political reforms in the Southeast Asian regimes they supported—against militant anti-communists whose membership in the AFV was designed to bolster the appearance of broad consensus. For all his personal quirks Dooley was intended to symbolize this unity; its slow disintegration undermined his viability both as fact and as symbol.

Things only got worse for the Vietnam Lobby. The runaway success enjoyed by *The Ugly American* quickly spawned imitations, most notably in the form of a journalistic exposé of the U.S. foreign aid program in Southeast Asia authored by Albert Colegrove, a veteran Scripps-Howard reporter. In a lengthy series appearing in the busy summer of 1959, Colegrove alleged that the "stupidity and arrogance of the people who represent our government in Viet Nam may be losing friends for America faster than aid dollars can gain them." While Colegrove's reports added little to the litany of charges made by Lederer and Burdick (and Vietnam Lobby insiders sneered that Colegrove's firsthand experience of the region during his ten-day visit was acquired mainly in barrooms), the factual tone of the series led to congressional hearings on the foreign aid program and prompted the resignations of two of the most conservative members of the AFV, Gov. J. Bracken Lee of Utah and Rep. William Jennings Bryan Dorn of South Carolina.[21]

At the same time, Diem's American Catholic adherents, including Father Raymond de Jaegher and Wisconsin congressman Clement Zablocki, grew more vocal in their support, as amid a weakening consensus all manner of ancient sectarian and ideological animosities threatened to erupt. The summer of 1959 marked the end of an era. Historian Joseph G. Morgan argued that the "appearance of Colegrove's stories and the congressional hearings which followed marked the end of a period when the American Friends of Vietnam enjoyed considerable success in portraying Ngo Dinh Diem's regime as a government worthy of America's support." Since the fate of Laos was now viewed practically in tandem with that of Vietnam, there was no safe haven for Tom Dooley, whose illness served as a stark metaphor for the state of his sponsor's ambitions.[22]

By 1960 Buttinger, Cherne, Duke, and Oram had grown deeply disenchanted with Diem, if in varying degrees. Many observers believed that Diem took Leo Cherne's advice more seriously than that of any other American save perhaps Lansdale, which is why, during a Southeast Asian "tiger hunt" in February 1960, Cherne "spent nearly four days with Diem outlining the problems of the regime, especially the 'deleterious' influence which Ngo Dinh Nhu exercised over the administration." Cherne then boldly told the president's brother that he had to go: when Nhu seemed to agree, word of Cherne's "miracle" spread quickly through Saigon, but Diem promptly ignored Cherne's advice. E. G. Lansdale was extremely reluctant to give up on Diem. Along with retired Gen. John O'Daniel, Lansdale lost faith in the "Madison Avenue eggheads," as he later characterized Cherne, Oram, and company. In September 1960 he urgently lobbied Diem to find himself a new public relations firm; Harold Oram was convinced that the CIA had instigated his firing by Diem in 1961. In August 1963 Lansdale commiserated with O'Daniel over his "long, hard struggle" with the left wing of the Vietnam Lobby. "Knowing the principles for which you have long stood, it gets me mad as hell to have a group of dilettantes confuse what sounds cute at a cocktail party with the reality of needs today in Vietnam."[23]

The "Madison Avenue eggheads" won the battle when Diem was overthrown and assassinated, along with his brother Ngo Dinh Nhu, in early November 1963: hardly a cause for celebration. It was left to President Kennedy, a charter member of the AFV who had been too distracted by other events to exert a firm hand over U.S. policy in Vietnam, to authorize, grimly if tacitly, the removal of Diem. Five years had already passed since the vision of a postsectarian, intercultural network of support for Diem had begun to unravel. Though it went unnoticed at the time, the Vietnam Lobby—in supplying the cultural foundation for American acceptance of a Catholic president of "the first new nation" of Southeast Asia—had performed crucial work for Kennedy as well. While his own assassin may have acted out of random lunacy, the calculated liquidation of the Ngos represented the real end of a generation's hopes for the reign of liberal Americanism throughout the world.

The relationship between Tom Dooley and Leo Cherne was marked by a critical distinction: while they were both "talents" from the perspective of television, radio, and the gossip columns, Cherne was an agent and manager as well who could claim Dooley as his discovery and client. Though the business was humanitarianism, it was a business just the same and the creation of MEDICO had revealed the limits of Dooley's ability to finance an expanded medical program solely on the basis of charismatic appeals. With Harold Oram urging him to disentangle the IRC from the administrative morass they blamed on MEDICO's Peter Comanduras, and with political shifts undermining the Vietnam Lobby, Cherne may have felt that in light of Dooley's illness it was time to act, difficult though it must have been to officially part company with the Madison Avenue Schweitzer. It was probably just an oversight, but when Dooley asked Cherne from his hospital bed for a bust he had sculpted depicting their mutual inspiration, Cherne's office initially sent over a head not of Schweitzer but of Abraham Lincoln, a figure for someone else's movie script.[24]

The IRC's split with MEDICO took months to finalize, but in the days following Dooley's surgery the contrast between his immediate past and his uncertain future was best symbolized by the 1950 Hudson automobile his Catholic disciples used to transport Tom and his belongings from Memorial Hospital to his room at the Waldorf. He always stayed at New York's most elegant hotel, but as he bounced along in Teresa Gallagher's aging vehicle, his right arm in a black silk sling, he must have wondered how MEDICO would survive without the backing from Washington and Madison Avenue that his IRC connections had provided. He still had his faith: in the days to come both his private spirituality and his public image as a Catholic crusader bestowed on him new and unexpected blessings.[25]

Dooley grew ever more dependent on Teresa Gallagher, not only for the secretarial services that were now paid for by the Metropolitan Life Insurance Company as a gift to MEDICO, but also for her unshakable faith that his work was divinely inspired. She was soon joined by an equally devout

Catholic attorney from Boston, Paul Hellmuth, who together with Teresa created a support system to guide Dooley through the final passage of his career. In being returned to the care of his coreligionists, Tom's unprecedented cultural orbit was completed.

In addition to his distinguished legal career, Paul Hellmuth had other commitments that invite yet another scenario to account for the divorce of MEDICO from the IRC. A wealthy managing partner in the powerful Boston firm of Hale and Dorr, as well as an alumnus (1940) and influential trustee of the University of Notre Dame, Hellmuth rather suddenly, according to Teresa Gallagher, "became interested in MEDICO," just as it was being cut loose by the IRC. "One day he came in [to MEDICO's tiny new office in the Graybar Building on Lexington Avenue] and sat in the waiting room, surrounded by mail sacks, crates of pharmaceuticals, filing cases, and cardboard boxes containing dolls and toys and clothing for the kids in Laos. Mr. Hellmuth agreed with Dr. Comanduras that Medico would have to acquire more floor space and reorganize the office force. He helped us find a larger suite of offices on the fourth floor of the Graybar Building." Soon Hellmuth also provided MEDICO with a thermofax duplicating machine and office furniture, donations he billed to the J. Frederick Brown Foundation in Boston.[26]

Hellmuth's interest in office equipment became a footnote to the Watergate affair in 1974, when it was revealed that he had served until the previous year as president of Anderson Security Consultants, Inc., a firm described by John Marks (a former State Department intelligence analyst and the coauthor, with Victor Marchetti, of *The CIA and the Cult of Intelligence*) as "a CIA front company. There is no pretense of private ownership here. The CIA owns it and runs it." Hellmuth's links to the CIA were noted because James D. St. Clair, a fellow Hale and Dorr partner, had relinquished that position to become President Richard M. Nixon's lawyer in December 1973. Anderson Security specialized in debugging offices and shredding sensitive documents for defense contractors. In addition to the claims made by Marks, former White House special counsel Charles W. Colson was captured on tape telling a private investigator that the firm was owned by the CIA. According to the *Boston Globe*, Hellmuth "never denied the report and refused to discuss the matter. 'It's an area I can't comment on,' he said at the time. 'I draw a blank.' "[27]

Hellmuth's ties to the CIA had been exposed as early as 1967, in a celebrated *Ramparts* article that detailed the agency's control of a liberal group, the National Student Association, or NSA. Hellmuth, the story revealed, was the sole trustee of the J. Frederick Brown Foundation and a cotrustee of the Independence Foundation, the main conduits for CIA funding of the NSA and presumably other liberal fronts. In 1962 alone the Independence Foundation had received nearly $230,000 from *other* foundations, monies that Hellmuth (at the CIA's behest) funneled into programs sponsored by the NSA. In 1974 investigative reporter Jack Anderson reiterated the charge that the two Boston foundations "were used as conduits for the CIA's clandestine funding of the National Student Association." Revelations of CIA backing of the NSA had rocked the student movement and the New Left in 1967, leading to renewed attacks on cold war liberalism by Christopher Lasch and others who assumed that the CIA had coopted all of the leftist and liberal causes it had supported since the late 1940s. The J. Frederick Brown Foundation had previously been utilized as a funding source for at least one cause whose ideological orientation was difficult to assess: Tom Dooley's MEDICO, in its short-lived, post-IRC stage.[28]

Newsweek reported in 1975 that Paul Hellmuth admitted both to helping to "set up Anderson Security as a CIA proprietary" in 1961 and to heading two charitable organizations (including the J. Frederick Brown Foundation) that were "used to channel CIA funds." But Hellmuth was apparently not asked, prior to his death in 1986, about the CIA's role in his precipitous ascent as a MEDICO consultant. In the autumn of 1959, Hellmuth became Dooley's personal attorney and most trusted confidant, just weeks after their first meeting, the setting and circumstances of which remain obscure. Teresa Gallagher recalled that Hellmuth had been invited to attend a "Splendid American Award" dinner in Boston honoring Dooley but was unable to attend (Dooley had recently been dubbed "The Splendid American" in response to the ongoing clamor over Lederer and Burdick's best-seller). Hellmuth had missed quite a show: at the dinner Boston sportsman Billy Sullivan presented Dooley with a large sterling silver tray. Turning dramatically toward the audience Sullivan said, "Now let's cover it," whereupon the dinner guests rushed to the dais, their fists clutching bills of large denominations. After reading of the event in the newspaper, Hellmuth, according to Gallagher, flew to New York the same evening to meet Dooley at yet another benefit dinner. "They both had plans to travel to Washington, so they made arrangements to fly down together. It was the beginning of a great friendship."[29]

The "Splendid American" dinner was held in Boston on November 1, 1959. Yet in a letter of November 11 extolling Dooley's virtues to Notre Dame president Theodore Hesburgh, Hellmuth wrote: "I, myself have not had the good fortune to meet him yet, but I hope this may take place in New York within the next month or so before he returns to Southeast Asia." Hellmuth explained that he wished to convey to Hesburgh some thoughts about "one of Notre Dame's truly remarkable younger graduates." Hesburgh was already a Dooley admirer (on the formation of MEDICO in February 1958, Hesburgh had written to Dooley lauding "this truly inspirational plan"), but Hellmuth had more ambitious plans for "tying in more closely Dr. Dooley's great and well directed enthusiasm and imagination, and his love of his Alma Mater, with the ever widening Notre Dame picture as you see it unfolding." These plans came to fruition in 1960, but in the meantime Hellmuth urged Hesburgh "to consider appointing him to membership on one of the Advisory Councils, and we certainly would be happy and proud to have him on the Law Council."[30]

This is a perplexing letter: if Hellmuth had first met Dooley just ten days earlier, as is likely, why would he deny knowing him to Hesburgh? If he was telling the truth, the letter takes on an even stranger cast, since there is no disputing that Hellmuth had become a leading benefactor and major presence at MEDICO by early November at the latest. "All we had to do was indicate a need," wrote Teresa Gallagher, "and somehow he found a way to fill it. It will no doubt embarrass Paul to read here that all of us considered him our Prince Charming, and still do." If he had not in fact met Dooley by that time, by what authority had Hellmuth become MEDICO's leading patron? Why would Hellmuth, not a starry-eyed booster but a prominent university trustee, mislead Hesburgh as to his own role at MEDICO and urge him to bestow cherished and meaningful honors on someone he claimed he did not even know?[31]

In many respects Hellmuth was already the Tom Dooley of Boston society, tirelessly exploiting his connections with the Brahmin elite to raise funds for a host of charities including the Children's Hospital Medical Center and the Boys' Clubs of Boston. But in distinct contrast to Dooley, Hellmuth was an understated insider who, according to one associate, "never came on strong. He was not a high pressure guy." The same colleague recalled: "In some ways he was an unusual person. Some say he should have been a priest." As an unmarried man, Hellmuth explained to Hesburgh in early 1960, "I perhaps have more time than the normal person who is married and raising a family, to devote to educational and charitable projects." Dooley himself had convinced a *Catholic Digest* reporter in 1958 that "he has been mulling over a religious vocation for years. 'I'd very much like to be a priest,' he says. 'If I felt I was halfway worthy, I would be one tomorrow.'" Whether he was worthy or not, Dooley, like Paul Hellmuth, flourished at the dawn of American Catholicism's first true "Era of the Layman." Notre Dame priest-historian Thomas T. McAvoy wrote in 1962 that the persistent suspicion of the priesthood in the United States offered "special work for the Catholic layman to defend and perhaps extend the Catholic faith and culture where the clergyman is unwelcome."[32]

Dooley and Hellmuth bore their shared lay vocation unto the world of secular affairs: as Hellmuth explained to Hesburgh, Dooley's work showed "what great contributions one individual can make when Christian charity and determination are brought into focus on a great ideal." Yet as laymen they operated largely outside of the powerful institutional machinery of the Church that reached its peak in the 1950s. This may help explain why both Dooley and Hellmuth were vulnerable to imprecations from worldly agencies all too willing to exploit their spiritual commitments as well as, perhaps, their human frailties. A CIA document from the spring of 1960 reported an agency asset's conversation with Dooley in which "Dr. Dooley rpt Dooley said a lawyer named Paul Hellmuth rpt Hellmuth, of the firm Hale and Hale [sic], Boston, told him a 'contact in CIA' had told him that top agency authority wanted to get him the word that (A) we approved of his work, and (B) warn him that a Washington and St. Louis source were 'out to get him.' "[33]

It is impossible to determine precisely by what authority Paul Hellmuth spoke to Dooley on behalf of the CIA, but the mere fact the agency was in any way an intermediary in their communications accounts for the melancholic underside of their relationship and, indeed, much of the work they did together for MEDICO after October 1959. Again questions surrounding the MEDICO-IRC breakup surface. Hellmuth's sudden appearance on the scene is reminiscent of the overnight genesis of Operation Laos back in April 1956. The most plausible hypothesis is that elements within the CIA decided to take a more direct involvement in MEDICO at the time of Dooley's illness by planting one of their assets within the leadership of MEDICO. Internecine strife within the Vietnam Lobby may have caused elements within the intelligence community to lose faith in the ability of left-leaning groups to "front" their interests in Southeast Asia.

It is ironic and perhaps fitting that the covert dimensions of MEDICO's sponsorship should prove so difficult to trace, since it was Tom Dooley's special genius to convince audiences that there was no "behind the scenes" where his mission was concerned. His gift for impassioned oratory in service of a heroic cause reached its apotheosis in a seven-week tour beginning in October 1959 that brought him to thirty-seven cities for forty-nine speeches and numerous appearances on radio and television. With a book not due out until the following spring, Dooley devoted all his prodigious energies to selling himself and a vision that, when all the receipts were tallied, was good for a million dollars.

The frenzied response of his audiences was repeated time after time, from Holyoke, Massachusetts, to Hollywood. At an appearance before the Missouri State Teachers' Association in the hometown he had long deemed provincial (largely because it failed to recognize the magnitude of his achievement) Dooley told the educators: "You must arouse in your students a sense of duty toward all men of the world, not just those of your local community." The *St. Louis Post-Dispatch* reported that in a "spontaneous demonstration following his talk, convention delegates went to the speaker's rostrum and threw money on the platform. Dr. Dooley's medical mission in Laos received $1,600 from the unsolicited shower." Dooley aide Crawford King recalled scurrying around the stage with Tom, stuffing bills and coins into their pockets and paper bags. Later, as they went looking for the nearest bank, Dooley darted through downtown traffic, holding out his arm to announce to startled motorists: "It's me!" After hearing Dooley speak at a stag dinner at Manhattan's Lotos Club, a new admirer wrote out a check for $1,000 on the spot (Dooley had given MEDICO's New York office workers "an Oriental gong with a clapper. Every time a check for $1,000 was received in the mail, the gong was sounded and a happy cheer went up from the staff"). Vice-President Richard M. Nixon contributed $500. An employee at General Motors saw Dooley plead for "cold cash" during an appearance on Jack Paar's "Tonight Show"; she solicited donations from coworkers and shipped the proceeds to New York packed in dry ice. At a hundred-dollar-per-plate dinner in Los Angeles, hotelier Conrad Hilton presented Dooley with a check for $25,000 toward the purchase of an airplane: "This will give you the wings to carry on your errands of mercy."[34]

Tens of millions of Americans saw Dooley on their television screens in the autumn of 1959. On November 10, he accepted the prestigious Mutual of Omaha Criss Award in a ceremony telecast live on ABC. In a lengthy speech he dramatically recapped his career before insisting: "We are not missionaries. I despise the term 'missionary.' I am not a medical missionary. I am a doctor taking care of people who are sick." In an ABC News documentary, "The Splendid American," the jungle doctor was lionized as a potent antidote to the "ugly American" syndrome that had become by then a national obsession. As he lounged on a mat before a wall covered by a tigerskin rug in the compound at Muong Sing, Dooley remarked to producer Chad Northshield that he knew a much greater, "more quiet sort of happiness" than his medical school classmates, a happiness not attainable, he added, through bourbon on the rocks or flashy convertibles (two of his own favorite youthful pursuits). "Working amidst primitive people is a very heartwarming thing," he explained: "We have no desire to make them air-conditioned chrome-plated Americans." In the most affecting scene in the documentary, Dooley was shown holding a sick-call in which rather than treating the assembled villagers he engaged in a spirited banter, utilizing gestures and the evidently passable Lao dialect he had learned with his musician's ear for intonation.[35]

Dooley showed his acute aesthetic judgment in rejecting "The Splendid American" for distribution as MEDICO publicity. "It stinks," he told Teresa Gallagher, and indeed John Daly's droning narration and propagandic excesses (while Dooley could perhaps have gotten away with calling China the "monstrous neighbor" of Laos, Daly's mock-apocalyptic tone lent the program just the sort of lugubrious quality Tom hated) flattened the buoyant spirit of MEDICO projected by Dooley himself. James Monahan of the *Reader's Digest* claimed that Tom "had the naive notion that any and all publicity was good publicity so long as it mentioned MEDICO and Tom Dooley," while Bob Copenhaver, a Mutual of Omaha publicist loaned to Dooley for the duration of his postoperative autumn tour, remarked more colloquially that when it came to dealing with the media, he was "as willing and as eager as a round-heeled gal in a Navy port of call." Though Dooley himself possessed a sharp visual sensibility, he simply had no say in the postproduction stage of the many television programs in which he starred. Tom was a most cooperative subject who, unlike Dr. Schweitzer, expressed no disdain for the requisites of modern celebrity. Just days following surgery, while he recuperated in Memorial Hospital, an elderly visitor was "horrified to see Tom Dooley being wheeled out toward the operating room on a stretcher. Dooley recognized the visitor and laughed: 'Don't let them scare you, Daddy-O! This is just a retake for the television film we're making.'"[36]

Dooley certainly asserted his desires in planning his appearance on Ralph Edwards's highly popular "This Is Your Life" television program. Before learning of his illness, he had arranged through friends in Hollywood to appear on the program during a scheduled visit to the United States in November 1959. From Laos he instructed his mother to make sure that "civilian must rule supreme" on the program since he was "already accused by Peking of being a Navy spy." His friend Madame Ngai was "a must"; he also wanted to include appearances by Ngoan, his young interpreter, and Pete Kessey and Norman Baker of his old crew, since the others were "less at ease on a stage." "For God's sake," he reminded Agnes Dooley, "no love affairs, old girls, horses, or anything that smacks of my being a rich man's son. I am. But I do not wish the world to know I've a rich widow mother, a substantial bank account, and no financial worries . . . lest lots of young kids say 'I couldn't do what he does, look at the wealth behind him.'"[37]

Madame Ngai, Ngoan, Kessey, Baker, Shepard (the one corpsman who was able to complete his medical studies in the United States), and Agnes Dooley all appeared on the program that aired in November 1959. The gaunt yet beaming Dooley did a masterful job in portraying his "surprise" on being brought into the television studio and seeing his life presented before him via still photographs and oral testimonials. Marshall McLuhan, the Canadian scholar whose celebrated ideas about mass communications were developed during the years he taught at Saint Louis University, characterized television as a "cool" medium, for which "intense, emotional personalities were ill-suited." Yet it would be hard to imagine a less cool customer than the jungle doctor of Laos, who bounced around manically on Edwards's studio couch, constantly subverting the host's carefully prepared script with wisecracks Edwards struggled to ignore. As each of the corpsmen was brought onto the stage Dooley bounded to his feet, tapped their chests in imitation of a medical examination, and mugged and swooned before the cameras like some stage Irishman in the throes of performing "Casey at the Bat."[38]

Journalist Randy Shilts wrote that though the jungle doctor was "a stirring speaker, Dooley was, in private, extraordinarily effeminate." His campy antics on "This Is Your Life," however, undermined the theory of Shilts and others that, as a victim of homophobia, Dooley was driven by fear of exposure to present a false persona as a manly cold warrior. While Shilts, a gay writer, resorted to essentialist language for polemical reasons, most contemporary theorists of gender roles reject a simplistic dichotomy between the public and private "performances" of sexual identity, even by an individual so presumably "closeted" as Tom Dooley. When the brawny ex-corpsman Norman Baker was brought into the studio, Dooley leered, "I've got anemic crews, don't I."[39]

The cold war era has been depicted as watershed in American homophobia, but Dooley may have benefited from the taboo nature of homosexuality as a topic for open discussion. Contemporary viewers of videotape copies of "This Is Your Life" are often distracted by Dooley's flamboyant domination of the proceedings, an effect heightened by the contrast between his pale visage and the eye shadow he sported for the occasion. But in late 1959 few if any Americans demonstrated open concern for his deviation from a purported masculine ideal. They saw instead an extraordinarily animated young man blessed with the ability to project an enormous emotional range. After the lengthy introduction, during which Edwards repeatedly lauded Tom's willingness to "volunteer" for dangerous medical duty in Haiphong harbor, Dooley quietly replied, "I'm a doctor," powerfully conveying both the spiritual foundation of his life's work as well as his great sense of timing. When modesty was called for, Dooley could deliver it as quickly as any mood. It was real, it was acting: it bore witness to the experience of both Thomas A. Dooley and the "jungle doctor of Laos," whose mantle he wore with grace but always at a jaunty angle.[40]

A feature film on Tom Dooley and his adventures was never produced, but not for lack of discussion over the casting of the lead role, a challenge greatly exacerbated by Dooley's own movie-star grandiosity. Ever since Kirk Douglas had abandoned his Dooley film project in 1956, talk of a movie had been confined to the gossip columns. But in late 1959, with Twentieth Century–Fox committed to producing the Dooley story, the drumbeats quickened in intensity as one performer after another was proposed for the role. Over a period of several months the names of such performers as Fabian, Jack Lemmon, Bradford Dillman, and Anthony Perkins emerged as contenders. The pop crooner Pat Boone allowed that he was interested in portraying the jungle doctor on the screen. One of the most compelling candidates was Art Carney, a brilliant Irish American actor whose incandescent physical comedy in the role of Ed Norton had offered the perfect foil to Jackie Gleason's blustering Ralph Kramden in "The Honeymooners." The darkly brooding Montgomery Clift was perhaps the best fit among those touted for the part, but the whiff of danger suffusing his persona would likely have scared off producers more inclined toward an Andy-Hardy-goes-to-the-jungle treatment of Dooley's exploits.[41]

Jack Paar briefly pursued the role despite not having acted since spending three years "bored to death" at RKO in Hollywood in the late 1940s. But Dooley's spectacular appearances on his top-rated late night television program sparked his interest in portraying this "charming man," whom Paar recalled as "very handsome in an androgynous sort of way. I remember that his looks were rather a surprise considering the danger of some of his exploits. He naturally was enjoying his fame and wanted very much to be on television with me. We all liked him very much and the drama of his undertaking appealed to my sense of real theater." Dooley had become such a hot commodity by late 1959 that when CBS refused permission for his appearance as the mystery guest on "What's My Line"—because MEDICO had not yet gained approval as a charity by the Advertising Council—the show's host, John Daly, huffed: "No Dooley, no Daly!" The network relented and Dooley made yet another memorable television appearance.[42]

In the months after undergoing surgery Dooley became an object of veneration for a multitude of American Catholics, who increasingly came to view him not as some remote celebrity but an intimate friend and cherished spiritual guide. Many believed that by sharing in Dooley's suffering and praying ardently for his recovery they experienced a more intimate contact with the Mystical Body of Christ, the prevailing theological metaphor within Catholicism in the 1950s. One woman informed Dooley in October 1959: "I give you a Spiritual Bouquet, which is nearly completed now. 10

Masses, 10 Communions, 5 Rosaries, 100 Ejaculations, and hardest of all, 5 times of doing each of my brother's dishes." "I had never thought of all those suffering people until I read your books," wrote a fourteen-year-old girl. Now his own agony was wedded to that of his patients in Laos and all those suffering under the yoke of communism and disease. In describing his illness as having been acquired through a fall in the jungle, Dooley implied that he had offered up his own body to the contagions that plagued his adopted land and threatened to spread to the Free World. A young woman wrote: "You say you are not out to convert anybody but you are. You have converted me from a mediocre Catholic to one who wants to act, to love, to bring Christ into the world as you are doing by the free giving of yourself."[43]

The rich symbolism inherent in his sickness was embraced not just by "ordinary" Catholics but the whole subculture. On November 2, 1959, Tom was genuinely surprised to receive an honorary doctorate of science before delivering a scheduled address to the undergraduates at Holy Cross College in Worcester, Massachusetts, a Jesuit institution. The school's president, the Very Reverend William A. Donaghy, S.J., invoked the Mystical Body of Christ in contrasting Dooley with

> the typically modern man [who] has lost the old concept of pain as a sacramental mystery, a participation in the Passion, a means whereby the member can become more like the thorn-crowned Head. In the Christian scheme of things pain was not merely to be anesthetized but canonized; it was not only a cause of misery but a chance for merit; saints prayed for it with resignation and even rejoicing in the dear, ingenuous days before aspirin, anacin and bufferin (which works, according to the Madison Avenue prophets, twice as fast) so largely supplanted aspiration.[44]

With the "Madison Avenue prophets" of the IRC now out of the picture, Dooley's image as well as his spirit were tended by Catholics who shared the views of Father Donaghy. MEDICO administrative assistant Gloria Sassano, told Tom's friend, the Catholic screenwriter Robert Hardy Andrews: "It's really wonderful to be away from the IRC and I know once we get our offices attractively arranged we'll enjoy it even more." Even in Hollywood Dooley inspired a tribal loyalty among the film colony's most conspicuous Catholics, including Andrews and actresses Jeanette MacDonald and Eleanor Powell, all of whom were present when Dooley gave a memorable address sponsored by Immaculate Heart College in Los Angeles on November 16, 1959. Since the small woman's college lacked a large enough lecture hall to accommodate even a fraction of Dooley's fans, the speech was moved to the Hollywood High School auditorium. Running slightly late as usual at the start of a hectic visit that included the taping of "This Is Your Life" and a testimonial dinner at the Crystal Room of the Beverly Hills Hotel, Dooley burst into the auditorium to confess that he would not have made it at all if not for "the glory of God, St. Teresa, the good fortune of Mrs. Murphy, and the luck of the Irish."[45]

With the overwhelmingly Catholic audience now securely in his hip pocket, Dooley quickly got to the point: "We are not interested in conversions," he explained of his work in Laos. "We are not proselytizers. We are not evangelizing. I have no desire, dear Sister," he quipped with a glance toward the president of the college, "to make any of my happy little Buddhist monks into mackerel-snapping Irish Catholics." The crowd roared in shock and delight, as though Dooley had just told a bawdy joke and gotten away with it. Throughout the cold war, American Catholics were consistently urged to pray not just for the conversion of Russia but the "pagans" of Asia as well, especially those in communist countries where missionary priests were often imprisoned and allegedly tortured after the manner Dooley had described in *Deliver Us from Evil*.[46]

He posed a real challenge to those Catholics who sought to contain his appeal within the tight boundaries of cold war piety. Dooley's transcendent popularity suggests that his audience was ready for a different message, especially since their devotion to him compromised none of their intense loyalty to the Church. It was a role Dooley was made for: while he enjoyed his freedom to banter garrulously with the Catholic staff at MEDICO, he also knew that they were committed to discerning the wisdom in his fabled unpredictability. Though he could condemn the "materialism" of America with more conviction than could the Catholic journalists who made a living at it (a cohort lampooned by Wilfrid Sheed in his 1963 novel *The Hack*), Dooley was unwilling to renounce all that he learned from the non-Catholic "prophets" at the IRC. "If you're gonna be a humanitarian today," he testified in his own defense, "you've gotta run it like a business. You've gotta have Madison Avenue, press relations, TV, radio . . . and of course you get condemned for being a publicity seeker for it. But from '54 to '58, I took care of 100 people a day. Now MEDICO treats 2,000 people a day."[47]

The loquacious boy from Saint Louis University High School had become Dr. Tom Dooley, international superstar. The Kingston Trio might have had more record albums in the Top Ten at one time than any group in history, but on a historic early December night in the Gateway City, they willingly deferred to the jungle doctor, in honoring his request for an all-night jam session as a special treat to young Prince Souphan. On returning to Laos, Souphan must have informed other members of the royal family that Dooley's star shone just as brightly above the valley of the Mississippi as in the Kingdom of a Million Elephants.

☆ 9 ☆

Where Are the Serpents?

Tom Dooley spent the last day of 1959 alone in his room at Bangkok's Erawan Hotel. "This year, strangely enough," he wrote, "I haven't the slightest desire to 'ring out the old, ring in the new.'" His apprehensions were justified: MEDICO was in disarray and there was grave doubt that he would live to see another New Year's Eve. At the same time, he was overwhelmed by the burdens of fame, an estate he had once vigorously courted but which now felt vaguely surreal to him. His brother Malcolm, who had given up his job as a stockbroker to work for MEDICO in New York, had sent Tom a clipping on the Gallup Poll's latest ranking of the world's most admired men, which listed two jungle doctors among the top ten. "This staggers me, and frightens me," he dictated into his Soundscriber machine. "They keep pushing me higher and higher. When will people begin to think of Medico, and not of Tom Dooley? How many people know—or care—who started the Red Cross, and yet isn't the Red Cross itself all that matters?"[1]

Dooley's fears were realistic in light of his uncertain prognosis, but his rhetoric was disingenuous for more reasons than egotism alone. He had not in fact "started" MEDICO but had been selected to front the program because he boasted what later would be described as "name recognition." Since he was already a commodity or brand name at the time MEDICO was formed, the new agency essentially franchised the "Tom Dooley" approach

225

to village medicine—complete with an "endorsement" by Dr. Schweitzer—to other developing nations. The arrangements varied, but each MEDICO program was expected to adhere to the personalist model of grassroots medicine so strongly identified with Dooley. The world's third-best-known jungle doctor, Gordon Seagrave of Burma, was "signed" by MEDICO, while Dooley was permitted to choose new sites in his own sphere of influence, the former Indochina. New programs were launched in places such as Kenya and Haiti, of which neither Dooley nor anyone at MEDICO had any knowledge or experience. Everyone understood that Dooley's charisma and his fundraising prowess were the twin engines on which the growing agency depended: though he entertained a "wish for the quiet anonymity of just being a jungle doctor in a village called Vang Vieng," he knew that if he suddenly grew humble, suffering people on three continents would lose the care MEDICO programs offered, meager though it was.[2]

When Dooley, in his mother's words, "accepted advice" while hospitalized that "suggested separating Medico from the International Rescue Committee," he was assured as part of this fait accompli that his role in the agency would expand into the realms of planning and administration. These new responsibilities, coupled with his illness, meant that his career as a practicing jungle doctor was effectively over by the time he returned to Laos in December 1959. He immediately set out instead to shore up morale at various MEDICO sites, beginning with a visit to Dr. Seagrave in Burma. Dooley reported in a memo to Peter Comanduras that Seagrave had been complaining to reporters from the region's English-language newspapers that "he is getting absolutely no support from anybody. Once again no mention of MEDICO." Dooley planned to present Seagrave with a check for $2,000 "plus the offer of more medicine pointing out that 'we don't care about the public relations problems of Harold Oram sir, we are only interested in helping you take care of people who are sick . . . that is MEDICO's goal.'"[3]

Harold Oram's public relations firm remained under contract with MEDICO after its departure from the IRC, an agency with whom Oram did not always have the smoothest of working relationships. Oram was now relegated to promoting MEDICO's lesser-known programs, though he readily conceded that Dooley did not require a professional image-tender. Whatever the source of Seagrave's problems with MEDICO, Dooley's stated hope that a cash donation and a pep talk would "get him back, I think, in our camp" indicated the extent to which intra-agency dissension and personal rivalries continued to plague MEDICO. Oram was openly disdainful of Comanduras, but the secretary general enjoyed only limited authority apart from his role as liaison to the American medical establishment. Paul Hellmuth might have been expected to exert his influence on the organization's behalf, but he remained aloof from MEDICO activities not directly involving his client and new friend.

The lack of coordinated leadership at MEDICO was a recipe for disaster; in addition, Dooley confessed to Comanduras that his physical condition made him "feel as though I am losing my grip." He insisted that MEDICO "must find for me a young doctor to replace me" at Muong Sing while he supervised the construction of a new clinic at Ban Houei Sai, Laos. Dooley stressed that his successor need possess only the experience obtained during "a good rotating internship," since "he must be willing to accept the kind of medicine that I practice which is a long way from a million dollar American clinical medicine." Above all he sought "a guy that will put up with my personality who doesn't mind being second fiddle and always basking in a reflected kind of light until he can let his own candle shine brightly." For someone who was "losing his grip," Dooley demonstrated here, as he did repeatedly in 1960, a soundness of judgment that had been overlooked in the years when his life was not entirely his own. Yet at the same time he faced growing threats of "exposure" that only intensified a profound loneliness his fragile support network was unable to assuage, even as he devoted all of his remaining energies to making MEDICO "a living thriving thing for ever and ever and ever."[4]

Dooley had made a brief appearance at Muong Sing on Christmas Day to find that, as he expected, "everything is just the same as I left it," apart from some improvements made to the facility in his absence by Earl Rhine and Dwight Davis. "The boys have done a magnificent job," he reported to the MEDICO office. "Earl and Dwight are very brave men and very fine men." Dooley was untroubled by criticism that his corpsmen were unqualified to operate a village hospital, even in Laos where, as he never tired of reminding people, medical practices resembled those of the fifteenth century. He rightly pointed out that the nineteenth-century medicine offered by MEDICO represented a dramatic improvement in local health care. He also knew that Earl and Dwight were better equipped to work as jungle doctors than were most licensed physicians. In November 1959 he had written to his friend Dolf Droge of USIS that "Earl and Dwight are there now running the fortress very well, probably not even missing me except when it comes time to do those emergency circumcisions."[5]

While Muong Sing was tranquil, the political situation in Laos was more volatile than ever as the new decade loomed. As Dooley recovered from surgery in early September, newspaper headlines cried out that Laos had been invaded by the Reds of North Vietnam. Although William Lederer wrote in a 1961 sequel to *The Ugly American* that "the entire affair was a fraud" concocted by the Lao government at a time of congressional scrutiny of the scandal-ridden foreign aid program, the State Department was not fooled. While the United States did support Laos's September 4, 1959, appeal to the United Nations for "an emergency force to resist Viet Minh aggression," it refused to risk military intervention in this phantom conflict: by December Premier Phoui Sananikone had been replaced by Gen. Phoumi Nosavan, the choice of the CIA's Vientiane station chief, Henry Hecksher.[6]

Phoui's downfall began when he shifted Foreign Minister Khamphan Panya to a lesser cabinet post in December 1959. Panya was a member of the CIA-backed CDNI who had recently made his first appearance on U.S. television by proclaiming "This is your life" to Dr. Tom Dooley at the outset of the November telecast. Dooley initially reacted to the coup by quipping that it was "just another case of the youngsters trying to kick out the oldsters." He accurately predicted that he could get along with any new regime, since he knew there would be no representation of the Pathet Lao (and if it came to it, he privately felt he could get along with them as well: he had spoken cordially in the past with Prince Souphanouvong and he knew that the Pathet Lao never intended to harm him or his mission). In early August he had assured his mother that "our present 'war' will be over" by the time she received the letter, and he reminded her of how remote Muong Sing was from the fighting in the northeastern provinces of Sam Neua and Phong Saly. He even defended Chinese refugees who had been arrested by the Lao military commandant in Muong Sing: "One has a dressing on from where I dug some lead out of his back. Commandant claims he has irrefutable proof they are espionage agents. Hard for me to believe."[7]

Although Dooley could still produce fiery anticommunist rhetoric on demand, the growing political role of the Lao military and the open support it received from the United States undermined his much more subtle propagandistic function. Tom admired Gen. Phoumi Nosavan, but he was not in Laos to bolster a military dictatorship. Ironically, the new government's renunciation of neutralism only strengthened the Pathet Lao and made it easier for Ho Chi Minh to foment discontent in the northeastern provinces, while his military hacked the supply trail that would bear his name through Lao territory. In late 1959, the North Vietnamese dramatically increased their military aid to the Pathet Lao and instilled a more intensive blend of armed struggle and political indoctrination within the Pathet Lao. Just as Dooley's role in the Vietnam Lobby had been compromised by internecine strife, so too did the shift by the warring factions in Laos from strategies of persuasion to military confrontation threaten to make him a mere spectator—if not a casualty—of a revolutionary tide that could swamp his tiny outposts.[8]

Dooley responded to the political turmoil by increasing the tempo of MEDICO activities throughout all of Southeast Asia, both at existing clinics and in the planning of new facilities. In early February he flew to Kratie, Cambodia, to visit the MEDICO clinic run by Dr. Emmanuel Voulgaropoulos, a young Greek American physician. He learned from Dr. Voulgaropoulos that his relationship with the Cambodian government was excellent; MEDICO's New York office, however, had completely failed to meet its obligations to the clinic. They had not even responded to Voulgaropoulos's desperate pleas for medications to refurbish his depleted supplies: only the intervention of a Chinese representative of American drug firms—who was about to be expelled from the country and wanted to unload his stock—spared the clinic from disaster.[9]

After listening to Voulgaropoulos's complaints, Dooley informed the MEDICO office that the young doctor was "extremely honest" and was merely stating the facts of the case. He suggested that communications could be improved through dissemination of regular reports from the home office to clinics in the field. He also noted that Voulgaropoulos was "extremely anxious" to meet Paul Hellmuth during his upcoming visit to the region, an indication perhaps that Dooley had communicated to Voulgaropoulos some of Hellmuth's abilities to get things done outside of MEDICO's normal channels. But not even Hellmuth could solve a problem Voulgaropoulos shared with all of his MEDICO colleagues save one: his name was not Dr. Tom Dooley. The jungle doctor had exploited his own image to browbeat customs officials and local bureaucrats throughout Southeast Asia, and while many resented the "old smuggler's" high-handed manner, all agreed that Dooley's talent for blitzing through red tape was rare indeed. But that did not mean Voulgaropoulos and MEDICO's other doctors could mimic his nerve; if anything they needed to show excessive humility to avoid an anti-Dooley backlash. Voulgaropolous later absolved Dooley of responsibility for his plight, in noting that each hospital was autonomous and dealt "directly with New York." Yet in the winter of 1960, knowing that his reputation was at stake, Dooley intensified his demands on MEDICO for greater accountability.[10]

His frustration over MEDICO's inability to find a doctor to replace him at Muong Sing became heightened as the tenure of Dwight Davis and Earl Rhine drew to a close. During his recent lecture tour Dooley had recruited their successors at Muong Sing: a twenty-two-year-old, French-speaking devout Catholic named Tom Kirby and Alan Rommel, a twenty-seven-year-old former army medic from Evansville, Indiana, who was enrolled at the local university. When his Russian professor had learned that Rommel was interested in Dooley's work, he took him along on a visit to the home of Dan Snively, a fervent supporter of MEDICO from his post at Mead Johnson, a large pharmaceuticals concern. When Rommel telephoned Snively's home the next day Dooley answered, posing as Snively's butler; he then promptly invited Rommel to interview for a position with MEDICO. While Tom Kirby's fervent anticommunist piety recalled a younger Dooley, the more seasoned Rommel appealed to Dooley's pragmatic side. Rommel assumed most of the medical responsibilities at Muong Sing, even after an interim replacement physician was finally located, an elderly gentleman (described by Rommel as a "misanthrope") whom Dooley eventually fired—just one in a series of personnel disasters that plagued MEDICO for the remainder of its existence.[11]

In late February Dooley met Paul Hellmuth in Bangkok. They spent the next month together, traveling to proposed MEDICO sites and meeting with officials throughout the region. Ever since returning to Laos Dooley had been "most anxious to meet Paul to discuss a lot of business ideas." By this time Hellmuth had become the most important person at MEDICO besides Dooley himself: shortly after his arrival he flew with Dooley to Saigon "to start negotiations with the V.N. government for a hospital there." Dooley had hoped for some time to establish a clinic along the seventeenth parallel just below the border of North Vietnam, but he was overruled and a site was chosen roughly 150 miles to the south, at Quang Ngai. In fact an agreement had already been made between President Diem and someone other than Dooley; by the time he and Hellmuth arrived in Saigon work was already under way on the Quang Ngai hospital.[12]

Just as he had in 1956, Dooley adapted immediately to the new conditions of his mission, giving no indication in his correspondence or in his meetings with the ever-growing roster of American visitors to Laos that MEDICO had been coopted by a silent partner. Dooley must have known that Hellmuth represented the last best hope to salvage his legacy in the region. Hellmuth was not some ex-leftist or an advertising executive whose loyalty to Dooley might waver under pressure; he was a Notre Dame man, as devout a Catholic as Dooley himself, and a loyal companion who not only prayed with Dooley but indulged his taste for expensive jewelry as well. He shared information that Tom had never gotten from Leo Cherne or Angier Biddle Duke, including word that a top CIA official wanted him to know that the agency approved of his work, as well as a warning that sources in Washington and St. Louis "were out to get him." Since the CIA asset who reported on this conversation had assured Dooley that the threats were "probably fictitious," it is possible that Hellmuth was simply reminding him of the generally perilous situation someone with his past confronted at all times, providing further incentive for Tom to adhere carefully to his personal attorney's advice and counsel.[13]

In early March Hellmuth wrote to Teresa Gallagher from the Erawan Hotel in Bangkok, where he and Dooley were spending much of their time together. "Tom and I are having a wonderful series of talks on many different matters. . . . You really can't appreciate, Tess, how much all your work and help to Tom mean to him and how deeply he is thankful for same to you. This is a tremendous experience in my life and I hope it will mean great benefits to Medico, and to Tom in his own personal life. Somehow or other I feel it surely will." Hellmuth and Gallagher were bound by an intimate connection to Dooley that was more intense than any he had ever known. Yet as one of his few friends among the Americans in Laos later explained, "He could sway people with his oratory, but he could not communicate his inner feelings to anyone. I once told him that, for this very reason, he would make some woman the world's worst husband." Though he could not verbally express his feelings for Gallagher and Hellmuth, their communication with each other was always suffused with a sense of Dooley's powerful presence. Profoundly devout Catholics, they exemplified many of the ideals of the lay apostolate promoted by the postwar Church and embraced Tom's cause as a special opportunity to immerse themselves in service to others.[14]

They also enjoyed deeply personal spiritual lives that were enriched through their witness of Tom Dooley's gifts. By 1960 a large segment of the American Catholic populace had come to view him with the reverence usually reserved for the saints in heaven. Even as Dooley fervently stressed the postdenominational character of his highly "modern" humanitarianism, his fan mail grew more devotional in nature than ever before. He received thousands of letters each week, many of them bearing the initials "J.M.J." (Jesus, Mary, and Joseph) above the salutation, as was common in Catholic correspondence of that era. A nun from Tulsa, Oklahoma, wished Dooley to know that

> I shall make a special memento in my Mass every morning that our Dear Lord will give you the strength and courage to continue your labors among the unfortunate members of the Mystical Body. You can be certain that when you reach the end of the road you will hear the words of welcome from Our Divine Savior Himself, "Come you blessed one and possess the kingdom of heaven for I was hungry and you gave me to eat . . . sick and you took care of me . . . " May he bless you always for your generous spirit and your life of sacrifice.[15]

The solidarity of Dooley, his admirers, and his suffering patients within the Mystical Body of Christ was a recurrent theme in much of the correspondence he received. Since his own illness had dissolved the boundary between doctor and patient, his travail resonated deeply within the transpersonal spirit of the Mystical Body. His own spiritual body was now extended as a bridge to provide an intimate link between American Christians and those "pagan" peoples who experienced Christ through the intercession of the jungle doctor, or "Blessed Thomas of Laos," as he was occasionally called. Members of the sixth-grade class at Our Lady of Victory Academy in Tarrytown, New York, informed Dooley that in addition to their contribution to MEDICO, they were "adopting" a child through Catholic overseas missions. "Our first pagan baby is named Thomas Anthony," they informed the child's namesake. Dooley gently responded: "I hope he grows up to be an Irish pagan baby that will be able to say he's living in a world of peace because the Sixth Graders at Our Lady of Victory School put their shoulders to the wheel and helped launch a program called MEDICO." A third grader wrote simply: "You are just like Jesus."[16]

He tried to dictate at least a brief reply to each letter from the staggering pile that MEDICO pilot Jerry Euster, and later Ted Werner, dropped off on each of his flights into Muong Sing. Ever since his adolescence, when he befriended a girl afflicted with crippling rheumatoid arthritis, Dooley had shown extraordinary empathy toward people burdened with physical deformities and chronic pain. He offered to them a theology of suffering in the Mystical Body that bore the mark of his own pain. He had always been vain: long before becoming ill, while barely past thirty, Dooley had begun to worry about aging and the loss of his sexual appeal. The mortification of his own flesh in disfiguring surgery recalled the confused adolescence he had vanquished with manic sociability, then later hard work, making him the perfect symbol for a Catholic subculture of suffering.[17]

But he could not always face the overwhelming pain others asked him to both absorb and console. A young woman from Brooklyn wrote that due to "a faulty pituitary gland, my bone structure is sadly misshaped." Due to her "grotesque figure" she avoided the company of others but had come to "sincerely believe that you may be able to show me how to accept my lot in life." Six weeks later, having failed to receive an answer, she wrote again, lamenting her lack of "the gift of genius" that Dooley obviously possessed. "How I wish I were blessed with a spark of divine understanding. . . . Please, Doctor Dooley, help me to help myself!" She even made a donation "to enable you to carry on your noble work," but Dooley could not bring himself to reply in writing, though after repeated pleading by Teresa Gallagher he finally telephoned the woman in October 1960, four months after she had written to him for the second time.[18]

It was not always that difficult for him to offer advice to strangers. An ex-seminarian from the Netherlands wrote an admiring letter but added that he was no longer a practicing Catholic, a fact that greatly displeased Dooley. Being a "fallen-away Catholic," he wrote, "must add much unhappiness to your life—I know it would to mine. My hope to you is not for health or happiness; my hope to you is that you will come back to our faith." He went on to affirm his own vocation: "Life out here is a deep and moving thing, and there seem to be no shadows in our days. I am very lucky to have this chance to serve . . . and in this, the stench of our work, we can see the beauty that is called 'the Mystical Body of Christ.' "[19]

It was easy for Dooley to convince his disciples that he was an ordinary Catholic, but he reserved a separate place where his own spirituality could spill over the boundaries that still contained most American Catholics. He often seemed freer and more at ease among worldly, non-Catholic sophisticates who shared what Dooley's old navy friend Norton Stevens called his "enlarged" view of life and the spirit. While undergoing tests at Memorial Hospital Dooley had interviewed Carl Wiedermann, a young physician who later worked at Quang Ngai in South Vietnam. Wiedermann asked Dooley why, given his medical prognosis, he did not retire to a place like "the Isle of Capri, where I lived years ago." Tom's response startled Wiedermann. "He asked me about a certain dancer and about a number of people in the international set on Capri. Did I know them? Then he spoke quite familiarly about people who travel in this fast crowd, a group you can only meet in places like Capri. I looked at him with surprise. He was a completely new person."[20]

In March Dooley's friend the actor Eddie Albert organized "a half-hour of group prayer for your recovery" to be held at the "meditation room" of the United Nations building in New York. "All religions will be represented," Albert wrote, "and if you can figure out what time that is in your part of the world—we invite you to join us at that moment." In his response Dooley jokingly requested that, during his impending visit to New York, Albert "sneak me a back door ticket" for the Broadway production of the *The Music Man,* in which Albert was appearing at the time. "As long as I have people like you behind my work," he concluded in a more somber tone, "how can I possibly but succeed."[21]

This intersection of show business and mysticism occupied the space where Tom Dooley was perhaps most at home. His readings in Saint Augustine were now complemented by Kahlil Gibran's *The Prophet,* a work beginning to make the rounds in Hollywood circles in the late 1950s. He remained a conservative nonconformist who offered American Catholics a surrogate adventure to glamorous spiritual locales: while it was not meant for them—he routinely dismissed applications from Catholic zealots eager to serve in MEDICO—they could support his cause financially and squeeze the most from lives he assured them were charged with possibility. In this way he assumed a priestly role as intermediary between a vision that had consumed him and the multitudes of simpler folk eager for even a glimpse of the radiance he deflected their way in the line of his duty, as one specially chosen for an exalted vocation.

The world seemed much smaller in 1960 than in 1956, when Dooley had introduced millions of American readers to a remote place called Vietnam. While Laos remained forbiddingly exotic to his core constituency—many of whom were still wrestling with the idea of making the bold leap from urban-ethnic enclaves to postwar suburbia—there were now plenty of others with the means and motivation to witness the jungle doctor on location in Laos. During the spring of 1960 Dooley was visited at Muong Sing by his benefactor George Skakel; by several prominent American surgeons; by Arnold Enker, a young professor from an Israeli law school who stayed in Muong Sing long enough to build a playground and help deliver a baby; several wealthy St. Louisans; and the usual revolving cohort of reporters, photographers, and documentarians who ensured that any news from northwestern Laos would reach the United States as quickly as local conditions would allow. In April Arthur Godfrey, an immensely popular if ornery radio and television personality and yet another sponsor of Dooley's airplane, taped a broadcast from Muong Sing that featured a lesson in Lao dialect courtesy of his gregarious host and beneficiary.[22]

Paul Hellmuth, who witnessed the parade of visitors during his three-week stay with Dooley, later reported that he grew concerned over Tom's "over-eager co-operation" with Scot Leavitt and Don Cravens of *Life,* in Muong Sing to prepare a lavish photo essay on Dooley. According to James Monahan of the *Reader's Digest,* Hellmuth "expressed misgivings" to his friend before returning to the United States, but "Tom brushed Hellmuth's fears aside: 'I never worry about such things—they always take care of themselves.'" Dooley knew Cravens from a previous assignment and was confident that "he will take some good pictures" and "it will make a good story, but I just hope it doesn't come out before the *Reader's Digest.* You know how touchy they are." Ever since DeWitt Wallace had grudgingly given Dooley permission to appear in other publications, he had enjoyed an unbroken string of promotional triumphs courtesy of America's most prestigious magazines.[23]

This time it would be different. He may have forgotten that DeWitt Wallace was the only media magnate who had backed his faith in Dooley's appeal with cash donations. The *Life* story appeared on April 18, 1960, replete with the glossy photographs neither *Reader's Digest* nor any other magazine of the day could match. But the lead paragraph of Scot Leavitt's brief accompanying text signaled the end of Dooley's immunity from published criticism: "The fact that Dr. Tom Dooley is a controversial figure in southeast Asia astonishes most American visitors. The fact that he is not controversial in the U.S. astonishes their compatriots in southeast Asia."[24]

Leavitt provided a catalog of Dooley's personal shortcomings, especially his rudeness and egotism (which Leavitt conceded was mitigated by a sense of humor: he reported that at a recent Saigon party Dooley had "cut short a woman in mid-anecdote by announcing that there was 'room for only one extrovert at this party'"). On the more sensitive issue of Dooley's actual performance, Leavitt cited unnamed medical figures who condemned Dooley's "hit and run" methods, his frequent absences from Muong Sing, and the deplorable conditions now found at the Nam Tha clinic he had abandoned in 1957. Leavitt stopped just short of calling Dooley a fraud, noting that in preparation for a visit of touring American physicians, he had "drafted a military-style order to his forces at Muong Sing. It included such items as 'Make sure the hospital wards are full' and 'Have the bear-mauling man around.' The bear-mauling man is a hill tribesman who several years ago lost much of his face to a wounded bear. Dooley likes to display him to visitors as a spectacular and horrible exhibit."[25]

Immediately after the article appeared, Agnes Dooley informed Teresa Gallagher that, according to Paul Hellmuth, her son was being punished by *Life* for not "backing 'The Great White Fleet,'" a proposal for a flotilla of hospital ships *Life* had unveiled with great fanfare in its issue of July 27, 1959. Mrs. Dooley's conclusion that "there may be more to this than meets the eye" indicated more than her customary paranoia; the lucrative marketplace in cold war propaganda had grown so competitive that the Luce outlets had ample reason to undermine DeWitt Wallace's prized commodity. Dooley was loudly scornful of the Great White Fleet and its prototype, *Project Hope,* a privately funded medical ship that made its gaudy appearance in the ports of underdeveloped nations, bearing physicians who stayed only as long as it took to deliver supplies and rudimentary care to the assembled "natives." Compared to the blueprint for the Great White Fleet, MEDICO programs were models of sound voluntary aid and were certain to produce much greater political dividends in the long run.[26]

The *Life* article was not intended to stimulate philosophical discussion about foreign aid but to pierce Dooley's halo. Now it was open season for sniping at American jungle doctors. Bernard Fall, the French-born Vietnam scholar then teaching at Howard University, congratulated *Life* for "displaying rare courage—deflating the Tom Dooley myth." Since he had been to Muong Sing, Fall assured the editors that "I can vouch for all the assertions you make about Dr. Dooley's record." Fall claimed that Dooley lacked most of all "one basic ingredient which allows the valiant Dr. Seagrave to carry on in Burma without all that public relations *schmaltz:* simple human charity and consideration for other people's feelings."[27]

It would not have been difficult for Dooley's supporters to dismiss Fall's criticisms: he was both openly hostile to U.S. policy in the region and something of a glory-hound himself; another scholar who worked in Southeast Asia recalled that Fall always seemed to travel with a briefcase full of his own press clippings. More disturbing was a letter to *Life* by Lt. Robert E. Waters of the U.S. Air Force, who as Bob Waters, a Notre Dame undergraduate, had worked for Dooley as a corpsman at Nam Tha in 1957. Waters conceded that "Dooley is a tremendous character doing a decent job against terrifying obstacles. But I object to the way he does this and the way he deals with people. In Dooley's life, there is no room for people as people; only people to be used as tools. I guess this is the worst side of some of our great Americans, and Dooley is one of the great ones." While not a particularly harsh critique, Waters's letter threatened to break the united front of Dooley supporters whose character he most vividly embodied as a Catholic, a Notre Damer, an ex-corpsman, and a current member of the U.S. military.[28]

While *Life* published several letters in Dooley's defense ("Possibly, his job could be done better," wrote a woman from New Mexico, who then offered a rebuttal that set the tone for years to come: "But *he went there* and *he is doing it.* That is the final answer to his critics"), there was little anyone could do to fully restore his public reputation. He tried to blithely dismiss the article, dusting off a favorite "Chinese proverb" he had used in less perilous times: "Man who raises head above bushes gets hit with rotten egg." But he was deeply wounded by the impact the article had on young American Catholics in particular. A high school student from Massachusetts was particularly offended by one of the photographs in the *Life* spread: "We sent you money to help you take care of the poor and sick people in Asia," she wrote, "and not to enable you to take pretty girls riding on the back of your fancy motor scooter."[29]

Sometimes Dooley went too far in reminding people how much "I like my blonds and bars," but his real problem was that since Catholic schoolchildren throughout America—along with their parents—had been encouraged to view his life as a martyrdom in progress, any deviation from that script could prove costly to MEDICO at a time when Dooley hoped to merge his own persona with the organization's public profile. "He could have opened an office here in the U.S.," wrote a fourth grader in an essay contest sponsored by Newark's diocesan newspaper, "and probably he would have become a very wealthy doctor, but no, he gave up his friends and the pleasures of home to help the Asians. To me he is one American who can make Americans proud." Had Catholics not been among *Life*'s readership, had the efforts of "integralists" to create an all-encompassing counterculture which included a "magazine apostolate" (with *Extension* magazine serving as the Catholic *Life*) not foundered, this strictly ascetical vision of Dooley might have prevailed in the conflict of interpretations.[30]

He had never discouraged his most devout followers from viewing him as the special target of "critics . . . in high places." In 1959 a young girl had responded to the critics with her own tribute:

> Dr. Dooley is a man who deserves much respect
> But criticize they must
> Loafer, com. (communist) and derelict
> Way out in Laos jungles
> Where no man dares to tread
> He starves himself
> to help keep the people fed.

But it was he who courted the secular media with his own evangelical fervor. Not only did Tom Dooley know where the forks went, but he knew where the real money came from, as much as he loved the schoolchildren who conducted "Dooley Dollar" days in their parochial schools.[31]

Tom Dooley was an enigma if ever there was one, but as a coconspirator in the making of his own legend, he could not honestly expect his disciples to untangle the contradictions of his character. Secular journalists did no better than their counterparts in the devotional media, but the *Life* exposé raised the specter of an even more damaging revelation that would destroy Dooley and MEDICO as well. His fear that Scot Leavitt would at least imply that he was a homosexual had proven groundless, but now he was deeply afraid that it was only a matter of time before scandal erupted. A report cabled to the CIA noted that

> he was a target for opposing, jealous and/or rpt and/or malicious persons in the US rpt US due to his prominance [sic] and recent, critical Life magazine article. Although he says his naval record has been pulled in Department of Defense, to avoid documentary proof of his undesirable discharge, he feels that if any damaging publicity resulted, it would be detrimental to MEDICO's success in the field and damaging, from the standpoint of character defamation in Southeast Asia area, to US rpt US prestige at this time.[32]

The report indicated that Dooley had approached the navy about having his discharge upgraded and was told that there was a "possibility" it might be done to avoid "embarrassment." "Dooley is sick—scared and apprehensive," the report concluded. "If worse comes, he will pull out of MEDICO, but thereby pull the plug on fund raising. He is not rpt not vindictive nor rpt nor threatening." This passage is followed by the familiar blacked-out handi-work of agency censors, but the effect is chilling enough without requiring further details. The relative sympathy of the CIA for Dooley's plight is revealing, especially in contrast to the attitude of J. Edgar Hoover's FBI. Hoover had been invited in March 1960 to speak that June at a Washington meeting of the Religious Heritage of America, Inc., a nonsectarian body associated with the Heritage Foundation. But not even the presence of Billy Graham, who was slated to introduce him, could overcome Hoover's aver-sion to appearing on a program along with Dr. Tom Dooley, who was to be presented an award by the Religious Heritage that same evening.[33]

Although the FBI had kept a file on Dooley since his ouster from the navy, the bureau's chief public relations operative, Cartha "Deke" DeLoach, reiter-ated in a memo of March 9, 1960, that "Dr. Dooley, according to our files, was discharged from the Navy because of homosexuality." "Certainly the Director would not desire to appear on a program with Dooley," advised DeLoach. Hoover not only concurred, but asserted that he would have nothing to do with the Religious Heritage in the future. Unlike his enemies at the CIA, Hoover had no investment in Dooley and was indifferent to the fundraising concerns of MEDICO.[34]

Dooley responded to his mounting woes by becoming more singlemind-edly devoted to MEDICO than ever before. He took no interest in the Lao elections of April 1960, in which the overwhelming triumph of rightist CDNI candidates "would have surprised even the most adept American big-city machine politician." One U.S. Foreign Service officer "flatly told an observer . . . he had seen CIA agents distribute bagfuls of money to village headmen." Since "no attempt was even made to hide the fraudulent nature of the elections that were staged by Phoumi [Nosavan] in April 1960," the day had long passed when Dooley's politics of compassion were of value even as window-dressing for American military interests and their favorite Lao general who now ran the country. Laos was no longer an issue for Dooley; his only concern was that MEDICO would outlast his own life and provide him a worthy legacy.[35]

In May Dooley returned to New York for tests to determine whether his cancer had been contained or spread to other parts of his body. En route he made a stop in Kenya to visit Dr. Mungai Njorge at MEDICO's Chania Clinic northeast of Nairobi. Although another installation was planned for Riruta, Njorge told Dooley he was receiving no support from MEDICO at his facil-ity. Dooley fired off a memo to Peter Comanduras reporting that "Mungai is very depressed and feels (as does Manny [Voulgaropoulos] and Tom Dooley) that the New York office is not supporting us at all." He then traveled to Rome, "to see all my friends who are storming the Kingdom of Heaven with prayers and perfuming the whole of Heaven with spiritual bouquets." Those friends included Lorraine and Kevin Brennan and the ubiquitous Paul Hellmuth, as well as the Oblates of Mary Immaculate stationed at "my Motherhouse" in Rome, who had arranged an audience for Dooley with Pope John XXIII. Dooley was ambivalent about the prospects of a miraculous cure. The previous December he had "snuck off to Lourdes for a few hours" while visiting Paris en route to Laos. He told publicist Bob Copenhaver: "Personally, I believe that if someone is going to work a miracle for Dooley, it will not be dependent on whether or not Dooley went to Lourdes." He certainly did not resemble a supplicant in Rome, where he stayed at the Hassler, Rome's most expensive hotel, and partook fully of "la dolce vita" in full bloom just down the hill along the Via Veneto and environs.[36]

Immediately on his return to New York, Dooley underwent a series of tests at Memorial Hospital, which reportedly gave no indication that his cancer had spread. He then embarked on yet another grueling fundraising tour: "55 speeches in 41 cities between May 15 and June 24." The high point of the tour, and one of the brightest moments of Dooley's life, occurred at the University of Notre Dame where, on June 5, he received an honorary doctorate that more than compensated for the bachelor of science degree he had failed to earn a dozen years earlier. At the graduation ceremonies, Dooley stole the show from a group of honorees that included President Dwight D. Eisenhower and Giovanni Cardinal Montini, the archbishop of Milan who in 1963 became Pope Paul VI. At a luncheon for the honored guests, "President Eisenhower asked Father Hesburgh, President of Notre Dame: 'Where's Tom Dooley? I want to meet him and have a talk.' Dooley was seated beside the President and spent most of the time during luncheon answering Ike's questions about Medico's field operations, finances, logistics problems, and relations with foreign governments."[37]

Paul Hellmuth had intensively lobbied his alma mater to honor Dooley. During a meeting in December 1959, with Hesburgh's "right-hand man," executive vice-president Reverend Edmund P. Joyce, C.S.C., Hellmuth "spent considerable time telling Father Joyce of the circumstances surrounding my first meeting and how the situation developed thereafter. He feels, as I do, that an active, helpful hand must, of necessity, be turned by me in Tom's direction." The following March Hellmuth wrote to another Notre Dame administrator, Reverend John Wilson, C.S.C., thanking him for his "wonderful kindnesses" during Hellmuth's recent visit to the campus, at which time he had intensified his efforts on behalf of an honorary degree for Tom

Dooley. "If this occurs, as we discussed, I would consider it a great personal privilege if I could personally give Tom the letter from Father Hesburgh announcing the University's intention in this direction."[38]

On April 12 Hellmuth wrote to Hesburgh: "I cannot tell you how good it made me feel to receive your letter of a few days ago telling me that Notre Dame has decided to award Tom Dooley an honorary degree this coming Commencement." Hesburgh had thanked Hellmuth on April 6 "for the great part you have had to play in this decision which I believe is the right one under the circumstances." Hellmuth "felt very proud and happy indeed to be a part of the Notre Dame organization which approached and handled this somewhat difficult problem so resolutely." While it is not clear precisely to which difficulties Hellmuth referred, the critical article in *Life* appeared within days of his letter of April 12. On April 20 he explained to Father Hesburgh that since "Life is espousing the Hope Ship and because this has certain competitive aspects with Medico, we feel that this article might have been intended to give their Hope fund raising program a little bit of an edge over Medico. However, so much of the publicity that has come out on Tom has been so very favorable that you cannot expect to bat 100% all the time."[39]

Hellmuth had his wish fulfilled: in early May, as he walked down the Spanish steps with Dooley in Rome, he presented his friend with a letter from Hesburgh informing Tom that he would be receiving "the long-awaited degree from Notre Dame," an honorary doctor of science. Hellmuth reported that Dooley was "overjoyed to read your letter," which was especially welcome as "he had not been feeling too well during the last couple of weeks. I also thought he looked much more haggard and worn than when I saw him two months before in Laos." Hellmuth planned to bring Dooley to Notre Dame in mid-May, where he would be introduced to the university trustees and present a speech to the student body. Hellmuth made arrangements though a priest at Notre Dame for a double room to be shared by Dooley and himself at the Morris Inn, a campus hotel; a corner room was reserved for Mrs. Dooley.[40]

An honorary degree is a far cry from canonization, but given the special circumstances linking Dooley to Hellmuth and Notre Dame in 1960, the decision to award him this most conspicuous and enduring honor was extraordinary. Under Hesburgh's visionary leadership Notre Dame was on the verge of a major breakthrough into the ranks of America's leading universities: in the year of Dooley's honorary degree, "Notre Dame was rewarded with selection by the Ford Foundation as one of five rapidly improving universities to receive six million dollars in unrestricted funds if it could raise twelve million dollars." Hesburgh was the first Catholic educator to truly become a mainstay of the American establishment. "Beginning with the National Science Foundation," wrote Joel R. Connelly and Howard J. Dooley, "Hesburgh started to get invitations to serve as a member or adviser to the foundations and government—invitations he accepted with alacrity." By 1961 he served on an astonishing variety of national and international advisory boards, on nearly all of which, Hesburgh noted, "I've been the only Catholic."[41]

After 1960 observers often contrasted the "New Notre Dame"—a well-funded, research-oriented modern Catholic university—with the older model founded on devotionalism and the intellectual defensiveness and rigidity of "ghetto Catholicism." Paul Hellmuth clearly believed that as one of the world's leading international humanitarians, Tom Dooley (who "has many years ahead of him") "can be a tremendously constructive force and very helpful to Notre Dame and its aims over a period of time." But, he explained to the Reverend John Wilson, "the first problem is to indoctrinate him and see if we cannot get him to generate the same kind of thinking and enthusiasm for Notre Dame as he has been doing for Medico."[42]

Yet Dooley as usual presented a dilemma: was he more representative of the "old" or the "new" Notre Dame? Having become a primary icon of devotional Catholicism, he appealed to those whose loyalties "were tied to the Old Notre Dame of myth and memory," though many had never actually visited the campus. As one alumnus told *Look* magazine, "The people who are most sentimental about Notre Dame are the people who never attended school there." But Dooley had also built bridges to non-Catholic worlds as diverse as Madison Avenue and Laos. If Hesburgh's "policy was again one of striking a delicate balance between the Old and the New," then Dooley must have been particularly compelling as a symbol of that creative tension on which Notre Dame thrived during a time of dramatic change.[43]

Writing in the 1961 Notre Dame student yearbook, Hesburgh cited Dooley as an example of an alumnus who had complained of the school's rigid discipline, only to wonder, virtually from his deathbed, "Do the students ever appreciate what they have, while they have it?" At the time, few observers could have known that Dooley's sentimental musings were somewhat disingenuous, given that he had routinely ignored the college's regulations—whether to attend a horse show or appear in a chorus line behind Hildegarde at the Palmer House—without apparently suffering the consequences. Neither is it at all clear whether Father Hesburgh was aware in the spring of 1960 that J. Edgar Hoover, for instance, took pains to avoid being seen in public with Tom Dooley. In lauding Hesburgh for so resolutely handling the "somewhat difficult problem" of Dooley's honorary degree, Paul Hellmuth was perhaps acknowledging that Notre Dame's president shared "the remarkable courage and great Christian charity" he attributed to Tom Dooley in bestowing on him such an exalted honor.[44]

There was not much to be gained in prestige for the university, as Dooley was already associated in the minds of many with Notre Dame; if anything, his flamboyance threatened to detract from the presence of President Eisenhower at commencement. Hellmuth's connections to the CIA most likely played a role in his ardent lobbying for the degree: many years later a priest who had served as president of another large Catholic university expressed his long-standing belief that Hesburgh had been pressured into making his decision (in one of the few indications we have that Dooley himself knew that Hellmuth was no ordinary friend of MEDICO, he instructed his brother Malcolm to book an airplane flight from Newark to South Bend for Tom and himself—to be charged to MEDICO's account—as well as a reservation on the same fight for Hellmuth: "And pay for it in cash . . . I repeat pay in cash"). As with so many issues at Notre Dame, as in Tom Dooley's life, indiscernible spiritual considerations undoubtedly played a role as well. In Tom's case, Notre Dame was a focal point in his life both for the Marian piety it represented and for the devout young men on which, he believed, the legacy of his vocation depended. During his visit to Notre Dame in May he spent time with members of the Blue Circle, a student organization centered around devotion to the Blessed Mother. He became close with several of the young men in this group and visited with some of them in their home towns while on a lecture tour later that summer.[45]

One of these young men wrote to Dooley in August, thanking him for a gift of St. Christopher cuff links Dooley had bestowed on him at Notre Dame. Having just graduated from the university, he expressed his admiration for both Dooley and Paul Hellmuth, "who seems willing to cut short his career for charity." He also wrote of his romantic life with young women in a manner blending idealism and despair in a manner not uncommon among individuals of his age and experience. Dooley received the letter in Laos but carried it to New York in October, where he underwent another checkup, then "carried it all the way back to Laos last week, stopping off in Afghanistan and India" before finally responding in early December. In the interval Dooley had seen the young man again, this time in Toronto. "As usual," he wrote, "you were squiring around a beautiful girl. I just hope your philosophical interest in females doesn't upset your philosophical interest in philosophy. Ancient Chinese saying, 'He who flies alone, flies highest.' Of course, it depends upon what you want to do in life. And it also probably depends upon whether you want to fly or not."[46]

This letter is characteristic of the eroticized mysticism Dooley cultivated with increasing fervor in the final year of his life, particularly evident in writings directed to young, male Catholics (he seemed to prefer above all Notre Dame students). "Be careful," he warned his friend, "of that natural biological impulse which can be damn materialistic at times. Otherwise you'll be caught in the snare . . . the snare of love and charm and beauty and softness and sweetness and . . . oops, there I go. Signed . . . Anxious." To another Notre Dame correspondent he had befriended at commencement, Dooley wrote: "I certainly did enjoy hearing from you and remember you very very well. I hope my letter brings back some of the fast moments that we had . . . not so very long ago." He also informed his friend: "I'm working on a new book now; I hope to write with the bright flame that a young man writes with when he believes that many will read his thoughts . . . know his thoughts, and love them . . . and him too."[47]

The book was to be entitled "The Night of the Same Day." Although it was never completed, the manuscript fragments that survive reveal much about Dooley's method of composition as well as his turn toward a more explicit homoerotic mysticism. The fragments consist primarily of inspirational litanies Dooley either wrote or compiled from his reading, ranging from pious bromides to the startling assertion that MEDICO could become the "cornerstone" for "transmigration" programs, through which Dooley evidently envisioned Americans resettling in developing nations such as Laos (the "transmigration concept . . . what America was made great by"). He also foresaw "interplanetary living" becoming an option in the near future.[48]

His musings were dominated by a vision featuring what some might term a "Whitmanesque" quality: "America's greatness is not the splendor of sun-tanned summer vacationists, not the temple of the supermarket . . . not the sweet smell of excess in opulent hotels . . . prestige cars, and gadgets. Our country's beauty is the spirit of YOU . . . young men." He was more explicit in detailing his own role in fostering the national character: "I force a lad into experience, and the more unpleasant it is the more he must face up to his own weakness and overcome it. What I think we should seek is what is often called, 'The Aristocracy of Accomplishment.'" This is the point at which the horizons of Dooley's philosophy and sexuality merge. While he did not necessarily "force a lad" into sexual experience, he was by his own admission intent on rescuing a chosen few from the "snare" of heterosexual conformity and the mediocre quality of the spiritual life he ascribed to that estate.[49]

In his study of gay Americans persecuted by the U.S. military, Randy Shilts contended that "Tom Dooley had done everything he could to overcome the singular defect that in his eyes made him less than human. . . . The Catholic Church had said he could not see the face of God because of his sin, so he struggled to be the best Catholic he could be, performing acts of kindness and obediently following the ideology of the Church." It was ironic but not surprising that Shilts—a journalist committed to gay liberation—would essentially follow the lead of Dooley's most impassioned Catholic disciples in grossly exaggerating the dimensions of his martyrdom, while profoundly underestimating his resourcefulness as a human being. Since Dooley was not the first devout Catholic who also happened to be a homosexual, he presumably had access to the counsel of others who shared his experience.[50]

The same was true for his career in the military where Dooley had come to expect special favors from superior officers he felt were attracted to him. In fact, the Saint Louis University School of Medicine had been the first and only institution to demand that Dooley fulfill the same requirements as everyone else, such as attending class, taking examinations on the scheduled date, and performing the duties of a rotating internship. The fact that Tom was genuinely shocked to learn that he could not charm his way through medical school indicates the extent to which other patrons had covered for his erratic behavior. He need not have been homosexual to receive such special treatment, but since he was, he logically sought the support and protection of those who could relate to his predicament.[51]

Yet Dooley's relationship with the military was always a superficial one compared with his profoundly intimate life as an American Catholic. In the 1950s there was obviously no open discussion of homosexuality within the Church. There is little if any evidence of the manner in which gay Catholics communicated their intimate concerns during that era, though several of Dooley's lovers insisted that he believed God had "made him" that way for a reason and that since so many men found him desirable, he could offer his sexuality as a "gift." At the same time, his sexuality may have oriented him toward a broadly ecumenical outlook: as a member of a "community" crossing the boundaries of race, class, and religion, Dooley could perhaps more readily plead that "we must transcend nationalistic and materialistic aims." He seemed unconcerned, however, that such formulations as his statement that "all men must look with pride on generosity" were more exclusive, given his ideology, than such typically "gendered" utterances of alleged universality.[52]

Dooley's sexuality proved highly "functional" in the context of his vocation. From the exalted if not arrogant perspective of his world humanitarianism, any emotional commitment with individuals could be dismissed as trivial or superfluous to one's calling. As distinct from the many heterosexual Americans who had an affective preference for working in Southeast Asia, there were no interpersonal "rules" for Dooley to break in pursuing sexual adventures, since he never acknowledged homosexual behavior as a morally negotiable issue in the first place. Yet while the concept of "denial" is a tempting one to ascribe to Dooley's sexual identity, it is largely irrelevant in the context of his life and times. We can only speculate as to how his homosexuality "worked" for him as an American Catholic, but it is not implausible to suggest that he found his place in the Church as one among those who were understood to be marked by a sexual "difference" that could be theologized in more ways than one. He bore a burden whose very rarity may have served, in some quarters, to further confirm and exalt his unique spiritual prowess.

On August 7, 1960, Tom Dooley arrived "back in the valley I have learned to love so much." Before returning to Muong Sing he had completed a lecture tour whose frenetic pace was now mere routine to him. In the days following his triumph at Notre Dame he was feted at a luncheon in Washington hosted by Sen. and Mrs. Styles Bridges (Vice-President Nixon was among the guests), served as honored guest speaker before the National Press Club in Washington, and was guest of honor at a tribute dinner, attended by over eight hundred persons, at New York's Commodore Hotel. The principal speaker of the evening, Ambassador Henry Cabot Lodge, proclaimed that "Americans have, from the beginning of our history to the present day, a tradition of pioneer neighborliness, of helping people because we like them. Dr. Dooley symbolizes that tradition. If we lived up to it all around the world, many of our worries would fall away. But he is more than a fighter in our cause. In a deeper sense the quality of courageous compassion which he typifies really is our cause."[53]

"At this gala event," it was reported in MEDICO's newsletter, "Dr. Tom was presented the Medallion of the City of New York. Mr. Spyros Skouras, Vice President of Twentieth Century–Fox, served as Co-Chairman and Master of Ceremonies." Skouras was a Greek immigrant who had worked his way from a restaurant in St. Louis to leadership of the most powerful studio in Hollywood. During a visit by Nikita Khrushchev to Los Angeles in September 1959, "guests at a star-packed luncheon at the 20th Century–Fox Studio gasped" as he and Skouras exchanged barbs in a heated debate over the merits of a free market economy. Skouras informed the agitated Soviet leader that he and his two brothers had "worked as humble bus boys" before becoming highly successful businessmen.[54]

As a fellow cold warrior as well as a St. Louisan, Skouras possessed a greater incentive to bring the Tom Dooley story to the screen than anyone else in Hollywood. In the spring of 1960 Twentieth Century–Fox purchased the rights to all three of Dooley's books for "well over $100,000," Tom told a reporter, "enough money to care for 150,000 kids in Medico hospitals."

Martin Manulis, a successful television producer best known for his work on the acclaimed "Playhouse 90" program, sold Skouras a treatment he had created after meeting with Dooley in May. Just prior to the jungle doctor's departure for Laos in July, Manulis threw a lavish party in Tom's honor at his Brentwood estate. Robert Anderson, the recent recipient of an Academy Award for his screenplay of *The Nun's Story*, was commissioned to write a script for the Dooley story, with production slated to start on location in Thailand or Laos in September 1960.[55]

En route to Laos in July Dooley stopped over as always in Hawaii, where in preparation for reentry into Asian culture he attended the Honolulu Community Theater's premiere performance of the Rodgers and Hammerstein musical *Flower Drum Song*. The event was heralded with ten thousand firecrackers "signaling the start of a traditional lion dance by members of the Chinese Physical Culture Association. . . . This procession wended its way through the auditorium to the stage, where a Chinese traditional ceremonial dance was given to drive out evil spirits." Following the performance members of the audience were served Chinese fortune cookies while they perused watercolors "utilizing Chinese calligraphy hung on the theater picture wall." Dooley had always been comfortable amid Orientalist kitsch; he had been serving up his own versions for years. But the Honolulu setting for the "first non-professional production" of *Flower Drum Song* was particularly appropriate as he entered the final act of his own melodrama. Returning to Laos, he found that the original anticommunist conceit of his mission had exhausted its purpose; he focused instead on a broad dichotomy between Western affluence and the suffering of peoples in "developing" countries in a final effort to leave a permanent mark on the world.[56]

But first he had to acquaint himself with the many new personnel staffing MEDICO's growing network of clinics throughout Southeast Asia and beyond. There were now seventeen hospitals in twelve nations in Asia, Africa, South America, and the Middle East. Dooley told the *St. Louis Globe-Democrat* in July that "in the last six months I have been able to build five more village hospitals in southeast Asia. . . . Two weeks ago I sent out 26 young American doctors and nurses to staff these hospitals. Yes, I got more volunteer doctors and nurses than I know what to do with." In reality Dooley now had little influence in the selection of MEDICO sites and personnel. The conventional wisdom regarding the internal conflict that beset MEDICO—which pitted Dooley's great desire to maintain the program's grassroots, person-to-person character against Secretary General Peter Comanduras's emphasis on medical professionalism—only confirmed the success of a disinformation campaign that deflected attention from the real sources of decision making in Washington.[57]

Comanduras and Dooley were *both* figureheads, though to be sure they represented radically divergent points of view concerning medical humanitarianism. Dr. Donald F. Proctor, a member of MEDICO's medical advisory board, recalled arguing with Dooley "that what was needed was help to needy nations in developing their own talents in medical care. Dooley was equally convinced that any physician who was willing to devote time to the problem should devote his entire energies to the actual treatment of patients. We never reached an agreement." Proctor indicated that he was among a group of physicians with a background in refugee work who were instrumental in founding MEDICO: "It was apparent that many of our concerns were similar to those which had occupied Tom Dooley's interest." In discussing "our mutual interests" Dr. Proctor found Dooley to be "a most dynamic individual who could have sold iceboxes to natives of the Arctic Circle. I don't mean that to be a pejorative statement. He was simply an Irishman endowed with their special talents. He was also absolutely devoted to his ideas."[58]

Yet while the medical professionals advising MEDICO marginalized Dooley, they were even less equipped than he was to make the political judgments necessary to enhance the program's effectiveness. Just as the decision to build a clinic at Quang Ngai was made outside of MEDICO, the recruiting and placement of new personnel had changed dramatically since the days when Dooley selected Dwight Davis and Earl Rhine largely on the basis of intuition. Peter Comanduras was authorized to hire replacement physicians for MEDICO programs, but he could not tell them where they would be assigned. During his visit to New York in May, Dooley had met one of these recruits, Ronald Wintrob, a young Toronto physician who had been frustrated by delays in enlisting in a Canadian program for international medical service. Wintrob recalled that although he himself was on an extremely tight schedule "on the obstetrics service at King's County Hospital" in Brooklyn, Dooley was two-and-one-half hours late for their scheduled interview. He then asked Wintrob to walk with him to the Waldorf. "By one o'clock he had not said more than ten sentences bearing directly on my activities with Medico, except that he would find something for me to do."[59]

Wintrob "bitterly resented" Dooley's arrogance, lack of consideration, ignorance of common courtesy." When Wintrob was assigned in the summer of 1960 to replace an elderly Austrian physician who had been serving at Muong Sing since the departure of Davis and Rhine, Dooley immediately ordered Wintrob to shave his beard, since the Lao associated facial hair with French colonials. Wintrob was perhaps the first MEDICO recruit who, as a liberal Canadian, shared few of Dooley's cold war assumptions. Another MEDICO recruit was Dr. Estelle Hughes, a young African American physician who had worked her way through Howard University Medical School. Assigned initially to a new clinic at Ratanakiri, Cambodia, she was quickly moved to the less "primitive" facility at Ban Houei Sai, where her twelve-year-old son, Everard, was able to attend school for a brief period with Lao children. Dooley treated Everard with the same kindness that he had always shown children, placing him in charge of the paint brushes at the clinic and generally "making Everard feel like he was a big and important person." Like Wintrob and virtually all of MEDICO's recruits from the period following Dooley's cancer surgery, Dr. Hughes never became well acquainted with Tom Dooley, though she was willing to serve in a precarious environment largely due to his earlier example.[60]

"It is only fair," wrote Agnes Dooley in *Promises to Keep,* "that the people who supported Medico so faithfully because of Tom should know the full story of the disappointment which he felt in those final months. He was caught in a tragic dilemma, because just at the moment when he felt that administrative reform was needed, he was fatally ill." Most accounts of this period of MEDICO's history have pitted Dooley's strong desire to maintain the program's person-to-person focus against the wishes of Peter Comanduras and his medical advisory board to export modern medicine on a large scale. Yet this convenient scenario serves to obscure the more significant underlying issues of the painful final months of Dooley's life. Since neither he nor the doctors on MEDICO's board were in complete control of the program, his final "tragedy" actually served as a smokescreen, though the subplot was quite revealing.[61]

By August 1960, Malcolm Dooley "was making a real attempt to run Medico," according to Teresa Gallagher, "but despite Tom's request that Malcolm be given authority, it was limited and restricted." Yet Malcolm had no experience and little aptitude for running an international aid program; it was inevitable that he would be ignored when he was not bearing the brunt of hostility whose real target was much more elusive. Malcolm and Teresa Gallagher were consoling allies, but Paul Hellmuth stood alone among Dooley's Catholic connections as someone who understood what was really happening behind the scenes at MEDICO, yet he was in a precarious position of his own and could do only so much. In the accounts by Teresa Gallagher and others of Dooley's final months, Hellmuth's presence flickers more faintly than in the brave period following Tom's surgery. He backed out of a trip to Laos with Malcolm Dooley and Bob Copenhaver scheduled for the autumn of 1960; by the end he was barely in the picture at all.[62]

Not even such a skilled professional dramatist as Robert Anderson was able to pierce the jungle doctor's riddle. Anderson had met Dooley at a party in Hollywood not long after Tom's surgery; he saw him again in June at the tribute dinner held at Manhattan's Commodore Hotel where, Anderson recalled, Dooley lyrically evoked "my high mountain valley" in a performance that had the audience shedding tears and opening their checkbooks. Martin Manulis commissioned Anderson to draft a Dooley screenplay for Twentieth Century–Fox. Anderson's wife had died of cancer in 1956 and he found Dooley's travail quite compelling. Anderson's 1953 play, *Tea and Sympathy,* had been hailed as a groundbreaking treatment of homosexuality, but as its author often insisted, it was more accurately about the qualities of manliness. Anderson arrived in Bangkok in early August 1960 to gather material for his screenplay. His first impression of Dooley was of "a wiry, tough, Irish hombre" who was "like a nerve" in his taut, hyperactive demeanor. The doctor possessed indefatigable energy as well as the markings of a "classic bully." Anderson witnessed episodes of Dooley's patented taunting of his crew and guests; at the same time, it became clear to the screenwriter that, where Lao officialdom was concerned, his host was the most important white man in Southeast Asia.[63]

Anderson observed Dooley in action at the new clinic at Ban Houei Sai. Tom baldly asserted that he could easily be replaced in a month's time, since he generally treated the symptoms of but three diseases. Yet Anderson concluded that while Dooley did not perform heroic *deeds,* his mere presence in Laos constituted a different sort of heroism that was harder to capture on paper (he watched, for instance, as Dooley sat up all night with a dying patient). When Anderson later submitted the first draft of the screenplay, Spyros Skouras thundered in response: "Where are the serpents?" The screenplay offered a solidly conventional treatment of Dooley's character and motivations: by Anderson's admission, the project was rendered extremely difficult, if not impossible, by the "ambiguity" of Dooley's personal situation. He was curious as to why Dooley seemed to spend so much time on the second floor of Bangkok's Erawan Hotel. According to MEDICO pilot Ted Werner, that floor was one of the central preserves of Dooley's gay life in Southeast Asia, as least as of 1960, but it was strictly off limits as a subject of discussion between screenwriter and subject.[64]

Robert Anderson figured in one of the many bizarre incidents from Dooley's final tour of Laos that resembled absurdist comedy more than straightforward tragedy. In the early morning hours of August 9, 1960, Capt. Kong Le, a twenty-six-year-old commander of a Royal Lao Army paratroop battalion, staged a coup d'état while nearly all of official Vientiane was in the ancient capital of Luang Prabang, participating in the "final arrangements for the ceremonial cremation of the late King Sisavang Vong. He had been lying in state, embalmed on a sandalwood bier, since last October, awaiting a propitious time for his funeral." A young journalist from New Zealand, Peter Arnett, had remained in Vientiane, in part because he planned to interview Dr. Tom Dooley for the *Vientiane World,* a weekly news supplement he edited. After spending an evening with "a comely young lady popular for her impassioned rendering of 'I Left My Heart in Bangkok, Thailand,'" Arnett "pulled aside the curtains and two stories below several Patton tanks were driving by, their Lao crews sprawled over the guns and on the steel turrets, calling out to one another in evident joy and waving opened bottles of beer and swigging on them. I knew that the Lao were not early-morning drinkers; I dressed hurriedly and ran to the streets."[65]

Arnett and everyone else in the capital soon learned that Kong Le—who had been trained and "earned his promotions at the American-run Camp Vincente Lim in the Philippines," and who later had water-skied with Tom Dooley near Vientiane—had decided it was time for "Lao to stop killing Lao" while a corrupt elite pocketed most of the benefits provided by a gargantuan foreign power. Not long after the coup, Kong Le called Arnett to his office "and announced apologetically that the *Vientiane World* was being closed down because it was financed by the CIA. I did not demur. It was not the case, but the Vientiane I had known was gone."[66]

Tom Dooley could have shared Arnett's sentiments. Despite their water-skiing experiences and for all his rhetorical support of Lao self-determination, Dooley failed to express any sympathy or understanding for Kong Le's nationalism. From a peasant family, Kong Le was an outsider to the world of the Lao elites with whom Dooley had grown accustomed to dealing. According to the British scholar Hugh Toye, Kong Le attempted, "almost it would seem for the first time in Laotian history, to appeal to the people themselves over the heads of their leaders new and old." There was no place for Kong Le in the paternalist model of American aid fostered even by such avant-gardists as Dooley and Hank Miller of USIS. When, in May 1960, the "Red Prince" Souphanouvong and other leaders of the Pathet Lao had "escaped" from a Vientiane prison, Hank Miller, according to Arnett, "pulled up in his jeep at the street-side end of the bar of the Constellation Hotel and shouted, 'Have they caught Soupy yet?'"[67]

Souphanouvong and his fellow prisoners had actually driven out of prison in a police truck, accompanied by their jailers, who had been converted by the captives over the course of their six-month confinement. Some even speculated that Lao strongman Phoumi Nosavan was pleased to see the Pathet Lao contingent returned to the jungles of northeastern Laos. In any case, the affair was perceived by Americans as a typically Lao misadventure. There was nothing lighthearted about the aftermath of the August coup. Dooley feared for MEDICO's airplane as well as the fate of supplies waiting to be shipped from Bangkok to various MEDICO outposts. "He was also worried about communications with Medico in New York and with the families of people on the Medico teams in Laos. During this period there was no cable connection between Laos and the outside world except through Vientiane. Everything to and from the rest of Laos stopped right there."[68]

Dooley had recently told his friend Bob Burns, an American intelligence officer attached to USIS who called himself "just a typist in the service of the Lord": "I came to Laos knowing that the Communists would take over the country sooner or later." Kong Le was not even a communist, but he had produced the first genuine crisis in Dooley's experience of Laos. Unlike the earlier "phantom" wars, the coup cast the future of MEDICO in Laos into grave doubt. In the short term there was great anxiety in New York over the communications blackout. In Hollywood Martin Manulis—fearing for the personal safety of the screenwriter he had dispatched to Laos—frantically sought to make contact with Robert Anderson, who was with Dooley in Muong Sing when a runner appeared at the door of the compound, bearing a "cable from 20th Century–Fox asking if Frank Sinatra or Jack Lemmon would be acceptable for the lead in the Tom Dooley film" (in Tom's version, Manulis wanted to know if he thought "Monty Clift would be better than Jack Lemmon, or Sinatra over them both"). As Bob Burns recalled, "This one cable came through to Luang Prabang promptly and in perfect English, which was exceptional also. The rebel censors must have been impressed by the names of the movie stars."[69]

☆ 10 ☆

"And miles to go . . ."

Tom Dooley returned to the "mossless jungle" of New York on October 7, 1960. After undergoing his second series of tests at Memorial Hospital he reported that the results proved negative for the further spread of his cancer, "gratifying news which convinced many of his lay friends that a miracle had occurred and led even some doctors to say hopefully that perhaps Tom Dooley 'had the thing beaten.'" At an October MEDICO board meeting he managed to get himself elected vice-chairman, but while "there was an atmosphere of victory and joy" at a gathering that evening of his supporters, Malcolm Dooley, MEDICO's executive director, "did not feel there was any cause to celebrate." One of Dooley's main adversaries, Dr. Edgar Berman, was made president at the same meeting, ensuring that the impasse which had wracked the organization since early that year would only intensify.[1]

MEDICO was truly in a shambles. Peter Comanduras's relationship with Dooley had steadily deteriorated; in June he tendered his resignation as president of the corporation—in a gesture of disgust—but he remained as secretary general of the organization. In September he had written to Dooley concerning their profound disagreement over MEDICO's future, reiterating his belief that "to continue to send general practitioners to various countries and not to attempt to improve the medical and surgical operations in these areas with visiting specialists is, I think, a poor representation of present day

American medicine." Comanduras was also an advocate of expensive medical surveys "in practically all of the newly emerging countries." He recommended that the surveys be funded by grants from corporate or foundation sources, but therein lay the fundamental flaw of his position: MEDICO had proven itself wholly incapable of raising funds apart from direct appeals by Dooley himself, strictly on behalf of the simple village medicine with which he was so powerfully identified.[2]

The implacable enmity between Dooley and Comanduras was evident at MEDICO's board meeting of October 14, 1960. Dooley prefaced his report as chairman of the Projects Committee by reiterating that "he was interested only in how the Board of Directors will help him care for the sick in his village," though he presumably referred as well to the villages where other MEDICO staffers toiled. He insisted that, according to the agency's philosophy and bylaws, doctors working in the field should remain autonomous and their work must take precedence over specialty programs and medical surveys. In his secretary general's report, Comanduras responded that since "Medico is the representative of American medicine abroad, Medico must be based on what American medicine actually is or else it becomes merely medical propaganda and public relations." He noted that physicians in many developing nations "Know what good medical care is and unless they see the American doctor offering such care they will tell us that Medico is bluffing."[3]

The hostilities between the two men finally exploded at an October 26 meeting of the MEDICO board's executive committee, in which Dooley presided as acting chairman. Dooley announced that he intended "to make this chair the fulcrum of our ideas. . . . If he, who is asked to perform the policies of this committee does not or is technically or administratively incompetent, I intend to ask for and to accept resignations." This was a barely veiled assault on Comanduras and the other members of the medical profession serving on MEDICO's board, who had indeed proven woefully inept in all matters beyond their narrow expertise. Yet Dooley's raving only vindicated their own thinly disguised contempt for him, as both a person and a physician. Dooley informed the board: "No further projects will be considered that will cost us money. Anyone who wishes to bring such a project up will not be given the floor." When Comanduras huffed in reply that Dooley was not empowered to decide unilaterally on new programs ("You have been lecturing to us," he complained), Dooley thundered back: "You are an invited guest [Comanduras had earlier resigned from the board], and you are out of order." A lengthy squabble ensued over Comanduras's right to remain at the meeting.[4]

Dooley's histrionics tempt comparison with all manner of doomed heroes from the world's dramatic literature, as he roared through the meeting in a godly rage, drowning his adversaries in a torrent of self-righteousness. Requests by board members to "please leave the emotional aspects out of it" only fueled his indignant rant: he even indicated that it was about time MEDICO stopped funding the dental program conducted at the hospital of the board's favorite "authentic" jungle physician, Albert Schweitzer. Dooley paused just long enough to enable a Dr. Pollack to scold: "If this organization is going to extend beyond purely an individual one, where one man is so completely responsible as you are, then you have got to have a solid basis and not continue on a crash program. What you are doing is repeating your same pattern of action, if I may say so."[5]

By ignoring the attacks on his person, Dooley raised the ante until, by the meeting's end, there was no doubt that his voice was the only one that counted. "What I believe to be the policy of Medico is not what Dr. Comanduras and not what Dr. Berman believes. . . . I stand in front of my Prime Minister and my King and I say, this is the policy." Shortly afterward he proclaimed: "Gentlemen, I have dinner with the Prime Minister of Malaya and a bunch of people in Washington"; moments later he was out the door, leaving his fellow board members to consider the fate of a visionary program wholly dependent on the persona of their nemesis. Earlier in the meeting Dooley had reminded the board: "If I drop dead tomorrow, there is no one who knows about all the involved intricacies of Southeast Asia. There should be an area commander and we should have some other man to keep up to date on the problems we have in Asia." Yet every time his adversaries proposed a scheme to establish a more "solid basis" for MEDICO than his own charisma, Dooley threw obstacles in their path: it had to be done *his* way, which meant that for all his talk of locating an eminent person to become chairman of MEDICO, he refused to loosen the grip on his own creation.[6]

The many hagiographic accounts of Dooley's final days contrast his spiritual commitment to village medicine with the soulless bureaucrat-physicians who, according to their critics, wished to impose a kind of antiseptic, stainless-steel tyranny of "modern medicine" on the world's poor. Teresa Gallagher most vigorously promoted this view; she was convinced that Dooley hoped to split MEDICO in half: one part "would be involved with setting up village-type hospitals such as Tom was operating, and the other branch would set up interim programs and do research." Gallagher tended to divide the world down the middle between Dooley's largely Catholic allies ("It seemed to me that Tom had some of the nicest friends in the world," she wrote) and the secular if not cynical medical establishment.

Among the former she prominently counted Kevin Brennan, a young insurance executive from Hartford who had joined MEDICO's board, and his wife, Lorraine, who had first met Dooley in 1943 along the "Irish Riviera" at Spring Lake, New Jersey.[7]

Paul Hellmuth remained the most important friend of all. Yet while on October 14 the MEDICO board authorized a letter of appreciation to Hellmuth for his service to the organization, Dooley never proposed him as a possible chairman of the organization. Hellmuth was curiously absent during the tumultuous final months of 1960, though his impact was felt even if it could not be acknowledged. At the October 26 meeting Dooley announced that his brother Malcolm, in his capacity as MEDICO's executive director, would soon depart for a tour of their Asian facilities. He had received a "special grant" from an unnamed "foundation" to fund the trip, on which he was accompanied by Dooley's public relations "volunteer," Bob Copenhaver (Hellmuth was scheduled to make the journey as well but he "dropped out"). Tom Dooley continued to enjoy connections in the political and intelligence communities that seemed beyond the ken of Comanduras and his medical cronies. At the October 26 meeting the secretary general had reminded Dooley that he was not entitled to align MEDICO with any outside agency of his choosing (he cited the Asia Society, a creation of the Rockefeller family, as well as the National Health Council).[8]

Yet MEDICO had been doing precisely that, in Dooley's name, since the agency split from the IRC in September 1959. MEDICO helped support, for example, the 400-bed orphanage of Madame Ngai. Some programs, such as the hospital built at Quang Ngai, were handed over to MEDICO by parties with a strategic investment in their operation; in cases like these Dooley took full credit though he had no more say in their direction than Comanduras or any other officer of MEDICO. Dooley lectured the board at great length about Southeast Asian politics and the likelihood of communist takeovers of Laos and Burma. For someone who was credited with espousing the "little way" of village medicine, it was Dooley and not the haughty physicians on MEDICO's board who played an integral if obscure role in furthering the goals of the only "establishment" that really counted, where the fate of American influence in Southeast Asia was concerned.[9]

The spiritual narrative of Dooley's heroic last stand was therefore skewed by the forces that concealed the intimate relationship between his faith and his funding. In an August 1960 letter to Bob Copenhaver, Teresa Gallagher described a "petit summit" she had held with Malcolm Dooley and Hellmuth in order to locate more allies to place on MEDICO's board. Paul Hellmuth was personally humble in the tradition of the "little way," but he was part of a network that seemed designed to shelter Dooley, as much as possible, in the space where Catholicism and the U.S. intelligence community intersected.[10]

The disinformation campaign that highlighted the misleading contrast between village medicine and sterile bureaucracy served all of Dooley's patrons, from the Church to the CIA to Madison Avenue. In the spring of 1961 Leo Cherne attempted to place the definitive spin on Dooley's break with the IRC: "When he first faced the possibility of death, Tom had readily understood and accepted advice which suggested separating Medico from IRC, because it seemed to him that he was separating something that was direct and personal and still small from something larger, with its complex of fund-raising and office staff. He thought then that Medico would go back to simple beginnings." Cherne reported that a year later, "he really came to see me because he discovered that he hadn't solved that problem at all, that in its turn, largely because of his own efforts and his own genius, Medico had become a large complex apparatus—even larger and more complex than the one he had divorced himself from in the fall of 1959."[11]

In the end there was no solution, nor was there any future for MEDICO without Tom Dooley, not because he was unable to establish a permanent foundation for the agency, but simply because he was as uniquely *compromised* as he was charismatic. If the board of directors was incompetent, which was probably by design, what could Dooley possibly have done about it, living as he did under the constant fear of "exposure"? He had expressed his dilemma with perfect clarity in a February 5, 1960, memorandum to Paul Hellmuth: "I as Tom Dooley do not like MEDICO to be so dependent on me and my personality. If I ever err beyond the straight and narrow MEDICO might collapse. I do not think the foundation should be built on such shifting sands. On the other hand I realize that the mass of Americans must always have a personal identification, and they can do that through me. O.K.? I'll buy it, but I don't particularly like it." As Dooley's last handler, Hellmuth's job may have been to keep his spirit intact so that he might remain useful in his final months, or at least to preclude a public unraveling of the Dooley myth that might bring others down with him.[12]

Hellmuth and Teresa Gallagher bore their burden in an intensely theological spirit: Tom Dooley was human, but his sufferings and humiliations were read as perhaps final tests of his sanctity. Teresa was the most important person in his life: she was uncompromised, a pawn of neither the CIA nor any other interested party. She was a profoundly devoted Catholic who was certain that Tom had been chosen by God to perform a work whose divine inspiration was perhaps not meant to be immediately discerned. En route to Japan from Hawaii in July, Dooley had written to her from aboard an airplane, just as Mount Fujiyama first came into view, "all snow-capped, serene, and majestic. So many thanks to you, Teresa, for the time and effort and sweat and love you have given to me and mine. You give of yourself, and this is something beyond gadgets, money, or time. When I'm home I crave a spiritual sharing of what I am trying to carry on and teach and do. You share this spiritual, tender touching thing with me. Many many thanks. Fuji off the wing tip . . . Asia beneath me once again . . . I'm home!"[13]

In her reply Teresa quoted a prayer composed by John Henry Cardinal Newman that she "kept on my calendar": "God has created me to do Him some definite service; He has committed some work to me which He has not committed to another; I have my mission—I may never know it in this life, but I shall be told it in the next." She added: "There is no explanation for the strong desire I have to help you and the fear when I get tired that I might not be able to . . . you know, you've said it so many times . . . 'the reward for service is the strength to serve.'" In his notes for "The Night of the Same Day" Dooley described "the wonderful nights when I prowl like the beast . . . in the brooding silence of the city's night. Often Teresa comes with me, and we walk through the merciful anodyne of dark. I am not walled by the night. I can reach out to the ends of the earth, only at the night. In my hunger I can eat the very streets my eye can see the hundreds of cities I have seen, my ear can hear the cacophony of languages I hear, my brain can gulp in huge draughts the visions of the millions I have seen suffer and suffer and suffer."[14]

Their relationship was so powerful it could scarcely be acknowledged directly: Tom professed his gratitude only as he returned to Asia, while Teresa confessed that the intensity of their sharing caused her to "often feel it really isn't me, but somebody else standing near me." That feeling was one of Dooley's oldest companions, which perhaps accounts for "something strange" that happened as he bade farewell to Teresa in November 1960, before embarking on his final trip to Asia. "He spoke to me in Lao for several minutes. Very seriously he carried on a conversation directed to me. It never occurred to me to stop him, or insist on knowing what he said. I felt at the time it was his way of saying thank you, so I didn't press for an explanation."[15]

Dooley's final journey to Asia afforded him an opportunity to say numerous good-byes, beginning with Dr. Melvin Casberg, without whose intercession—as the former dean of the Saint Louis University Medical School—Tom would have neither received his degree nor been admitted into the Navy Medical Corps. Casberg was a Protestant missionary serving as dean of the Christian Medical College in Ludhiana, India, when Dooley arrived in late October 1960 to discuss a new program for Tibetan refugees from

Chinese communism. Dooley spoke to the student body of the medical school, where "Tom, in his usual fashion, won their hearts with his earnestness, Irish wit and challenge." Dooley then "spent an evening in the men's dormitory discussing international health problems. Later they joined in song, and Dooley asked the students if they had ever serenaded the ladies' dormitory. The fact that this was unheard of in the Punjab made no difference to Tom. Within a few moments he rounded up the boys and led them in serenading the ladies' dormitory, much to the delight of all the students, and especially the surprised ladies."[16]

In Delhi he spoke before a group of American nuns, nurses "in their starchy white habits" who "spoke and understood Dr. Dooley's language." From there he flew to Bangkok and then up to Muong Sing, where he sat up until 2:00 A.M. the first night, discussing MEDICO's future with Tom Kirby and Dr. Ronald Wintrob, his designated successor at the clinic. Wintrob had not changed his negative opinion of "Tom's character and motivations," but on this occasion and at a final meeting in December, he witnessed Dooley living up to "the highest ideals" he had established for himself, as Tom serenely ran down the needs of the clinic in the months to come. After a stop at Ban Houei Sai, Ted Werner piloted Dooley and a small party of MEDICO personnel into Vientiane, where they were promptly stranded on the battle-decimated landing strip. Capt. Kong Le landed in his Dakota and marched past the MEDICO contingent confined to their Piper Apache. Finally Dooley, in a "desperate gamble," called Souvanna Phouma—who had been brought back into the government yet another time to lead this latest neutralist regime—who then authorized clearance for the MEDICO aircraft to take off for Bangkok. Dooley "grumbled in a frustrated manner, 'Why do they do this to me? They know I am only here to help them.' "[17]

Malcolm Dooley and Bob Copenhaver arrived in Bangkok for their MEDICO inspection tour on November 13. Tom traveled with them to Vietnam before returning to Muong Sing; by the end of the month he was in Hong Kong, where he said good-bye to his brother and Copenhaver (with whom he normally parted with "no goodbyes . . . no shaking of hands"; this time he said, "I'm glad you got to see Laos before anything happened"). Shortly thereafter he called his old friend Travis Fletcher to ask for help in being admitted to a local hospital. Fletcher was a fellow traveler of the Vietnam Lobby who was now field director of the American Emergency Committee for Tibetan Refugees. He arranged a hospital room for Dooley in Hong Kong; on November 30 Tom cabled MEDICO's New York headquarters: "doctors find extreme exhaustion fourteen pound weight loss Anemia Pyelonephritis possible bony hip cancer involvement. Save hip please notify Mother before press finds out. Have never felt so badly. Travis will send bulletins when something worth sending. In good hands however hospital named Saint Teresa."[18]

In early December Dooley was fitted with a brace "to support his disintegrating vertebrae." Days later he flew to Saigon, where he was visited at his hotel by Madame Ngai, whose orphan children had so often buoyed his spirits in the past. Following a tearful reunion he told Madame Ngai: "Keep up your faith. Pray and work, and put all your energy into the great task God has given you. You will never fail." Ted Werner flew Dooley to Quang Ngai the next day, where he gave "an amazing performance," apparently convincing the MEDICO physician stationed there that "he was on the mend." The next morning they flew back to Saigon, where Dooley insisted they walk down Rue de Catinat to visit the sidewalk café of the Continental Palace Hotel, where Tom remembered "how I used to sit there in the old days and watch the Vietnamese girls ride by on their bicycles with their dresses flowing in the breeze." When Dooley was recognized by a former refugee from Haiphong, Werner thought: "This was the best medicine Tom had had in many a month."[19]

Though he undoubtedly would have disobeyed a physician's orders to rest, it was strange, under the circumstances, that Dooley was permitted to burn himself out in manic travel. After a visit to Phnom Penh, he finally collapsed at Bangkok's Erawan Hotel, his longtime personal headquarters. He called a Redemptorist priest, Father John Boucher, to his room, who promptly asked why Tom was not in a hospital. "They can't do anything more for me . . . I just want to be alone, Father. Only a few people know I'm here." Father Boucher replied: "Tom, I don't want to alarm you, but I think it might be wise for me to give you Extreme Unction. You're not really dying yet but I don't have to tell you about your condition." Dooley "seemed entirely relaxed and resigned" throughout the ceremony. "Tom was alone and at peace with God," recalled Father Boucher. He returned two days later, on Christmas morning, to administer Communion to Tom Dooley. "If this is the way God wants it to be," he told the priest, "this is the way I want it, too." Father Boucher "tried to say a few words of assurance, then I gave him Communion. But his words stuck in my mind. Here was a young man in the prime of life, at the peak of his career, saying a thing like that. A couple of thousand years ago a Man of the same age spoke almost the same words in the Garden of Gethsemani: 'Father, if it be Thy Will let this chalice pass from me. Nevertheless not my will but Thine be done.' As I gave him Communion, Tom cried softly. The rosary was still in his hand."[20]

The "agonizing journey home" began on Christmas night in Bangkok and ended two days later, following a stopover in Frankfurt, at New York's Idlewild (now JFK) Airport. Malcolm Dooley, his wife, Gay, and Teresa Gallagher drove out to meet Tom in a taxicab that broke down en route, leaving them temporarily stranded in a snowdrift along the side of the road. When they finally arrived at the airport to begin "the awful period of waiting for the plane to land," Teresa Gallagher became bitterly resentful of "the nonchalance of the ambulance driver and his assistant who were just sitting there talking and smoking as if nothing were wrong." There was always a sense that Dooley had failed by the slightest margin to raise his stature above that of mere celebrity, at least in the eyes of those, like the ambulance driver, not ordinarily inclined to hold vigil for even such a VIP as his prospective passenger. Yet just as Teresa had hoped, Dooley refused the ambulance when he finally arrived and rode instead to Memorial Hospital in a cab with his loved ones.[21]

On December 31 a MEDICO cablegram was brought to his room, informing headquarters that the clinic at Muong Sing had been evacuated in the latest crisis. Dooley was reportedly heartbroken, but the day he had played any meaningful role in U.S. policy toward Laos was long past, if indeed it had ever come. Gen. Phoumi Nosavan, the enforcer for the Lao political figures closest to Dooley, had launched an attack on the latest neutralist (read untenable) regime of Souvanna Phouma. In the battle of Vientiane, rightist forces occupied the capital: while fewer than 40 military casualties were incurred, between 500 and 800 civilians—many of them Chinese and Vietnamese merchants and their families—were killed. The low military casualty rate reflected "the fact that opposing forces usually aimed high, kept well apart wherever possible, and fired off an enormous amount of ammunition."[22]

On January 9, Tom asked Teresa Gallagher, as she sat at his bedside: "Tess, if I die in a month, will you go to work for Malcolm?" On January 17, Tom Dooley's thirty-fourth birthday, Cardinal Spellman paid a visit to the hospital. Malcolm Dooley told Teresa that "Tom had been sleeping and yet, when the Cardinal was announced, he seemed to understand and sat up in bed and clasped his hands in his familiar Asian gesture of prayer and greeting. He listened as Cardinal Spellman spoke. The cardinal later summarized his talk with Tom: "I tried to assure him that in his 34 years he had done what very few have done in the allotted Scriptural lifetime." When Teresa looked at the cardinal, she "saw tears in his eyes."[23]

On January 18 Agnes Dooley, "her own health declining," was sent back to St. Louis. Teresa Gallagher made her daily visit to the hospital on her way home from work later that same day. She "was shocked to find Tom looking so bad. He was propped up in bed, looking very sick. His eyes were closed. One of the many green scapulars that had been sent to him was in my pocket and I took it out and pinned it to the lapel of his pajamas. At the same time I took out a relic of St. Thérèse, the Little Flower, and placed it in his hand. I asked the Little Flower to intercede for Tom, and ask God to take him out of his pain and suffering." Teresa then took out her rosary and "knelt down on the left-hand side of the bed, so that I could look at Tom as I prayed. As I started, I could see his fingers begin to move in the motion of the rosary." She then called in a priest, Father F. X. Finegan, who administered Extreme Unction, the last rites. "I knelt while he proceeded to administer the sacrament, and I listened to his final words as he bent down and whispered into Tom's ear, 'Son, go now and meet thy God.' It was an overwhelming thought."[24]

After the priest departed, Teresa "marvelled how peaceful he suddenly looked. As I picked up his hand and put my other hand to his forehead, I realized he was no longer breathing." Turning to a nurse in the room, she said, "'I think Tom just died.' 'Let me see, let me see. You're right.' 'God is good,' I said as I saw the look of utter peace on Tom's face. It was 9:40 P.M." Teresa immediately reverted to her role as steadfast aide, making the necessary phone calls and ensuring that Mrs. Dooley would have a friend by her side when she heard the news. Only after the hospital room "had been stripped of every sign that he had been there," in the early morning hours, did she finally have "a good cry." "He had come so far and in so much pain to be in New York with the people who loved him and wanted to be with him. And to think that he might have died alone!" Teresa characteristically understated the extent of her unique devotion to Dooley, which stood in stark contrast to his more troubled relationships with virtually everyone else who claimed some intimacy with him.[25]

An autopsy later revealed that "the malignant melanoma had spread to his lungs, brain, liver, spleen, heart—no organ had been spared. The marrow in his bones was supplanted almost completely by tumor." A massive blizzard struck the Northeast on January 19, greatly complicating plans for Dooley's funeral in St. Louis. In the meantime someone was sent to locate Tom's brother Eddie Mike on skid row in New Orleans; he appeared at the wake in a suit purchased for him at a Salvation Army shop. Mrs. Dooley was indisposed in her own way during the proceedings, as she had been through many of the days of her son's ordeal. Much of the Catholic elite of St. Louis was in Rome attending ceremonies marking the election of Archbishop Ritter into the college of cardinals. At the wake, held at the Arthur J. Donnelly Funeral Home on Lindell Boulevard (at one time it was said that the affluent St. Louis Irish could not go to heaven unless they were waked there), Agnes was harassed by an individual who "wanted Mrs. Dooley to make a statement to the effect that Tom might be alive if he had taken a certain cancer cure of herbs and exercise." There was a highly elusive quality to the mourning, as though Dooley's spirit knew no center around which his admirers might gather. There were only a handful of people in the world among the thousands he had met who could truly be described as the friends of Tom Dooley.[26]

Yet Masses and prayers were offered around the globe, from Kenya to India to a Catholic church in Quang Ngai (where, a MEDICO corpsman reported, "there were many more Buddhists than Catholics present, and I think that was a tribute Tom would have enjoyed") to St. Mary's Church in Vientiane, where Father Matt Menger, an Oblate priest, celebrated a requiem Mass. In Rome, Father Paul Reinert, S.J., the president of Saint Louis University, offered a Mass with twenty other priests "at the Tomb of Saint Peter in the grotto below the basilica." In New York, Robert Anderson attended a memorial service at St. Patrick's Cathedral that seemed to him sparsely attended; at St. Louis Cathedral, Khamphan Panya, minister of communications of Laos, bestowed posthumously on Tom Dooley the rank of Grand Officer of the Order of the Million Elephants and White Parasol.[27]

Tom Dooley's diffuse appeal was readily evident in the tributes that poured in. Jim Lucas, a battle-hardened Scripps-Howard reporter who had seen Dooley at his best and worst, wrote an extraordinarily insightful tribute: "In many ways, he was a little boy who never grew up and that—paradoxically—made him the man he was. He demanded much—in the same way a child demands a drink of water from its father in the middle of the night—but always on the assumption that you wanted to give. And he gave unstintingly in return. Tom Dooley's world did not include people who kept things for themselves alone." Sister Madeleva Wolff, the president of Saint Mary's College who had befriended Tom while he was a student at neighboring Notre Dame, wrote to Teresa Gallagher that "the last and best" of Dooley's thirty-four years was "given to go in his suffering members." Teresa treasured equally a letter from another American who was a Methodist and did not "know all the processes of your religion," including presumably the nature of the theology of the Mystical Body of Christ as invoked by Sister Madeleva. "However we all feel that someday Dr. Thomas Dooley will be placed on an equal footing with Bernadette and all the other saints—none with better right! And if that day comes in my lifetime, here is one Protestant who will bow down and pray to be more like him."[28]

In the 1970s a priest of the Oblates of Mary Immaculate—the order with which Dooley was most closely associated—directed an intensive if ill-fated campaign to promote the cause of Dooley's sanctity in the Roman Catholic Church. A physician who had known Dooley but briefly assumed the leadership of the Tom Dooley Foundation. He was rather dubious of the spiritual component of Dooley's vocation, and the resulting fallout, which saw Teresa

Gallagher struggle heroically to sustain a "Tom Dooley Heritage," was as heartbreaking as it was predictable. The Tom Dooley Heritage sponsored refugee camps on the Thai border for Hmong refugees from Dooley's territory—northwestern Laos—who became pawns in the "secret war" launched in the region by the CIA shortly after Tom's death. Dooley's legacy would be debated and sometimes ridiculed, but a Canadian journalist who had found Tom to be a fanatic and an egotist testified to his undeniable achievement:

> His "miracle," and it was virtually that, was *not* that he became obsessed with, or committed to, helping the people in a remote corner of the world, but that by dint of his personality and his relentless, singleminded drive, energy, and force of will, he made his cause a worldwide issue and inspired North America to help the sick and deprived of Northern Laos. If not a saint, he was certainly an exceptional human being who worked courageously and tirelessly and deserved some form of immortality.[29]

Few knew at the time how great were the obstacles in his path, and while Tom Dooley's personal ordeal rendered his canonization highly unlikely, a more worldly event that occurred as his body was being flown to St. Louis confirmed his role as a secular saint. The triumph of John Fitzgerald Kennedy, who was inaugurated the nation's thirty-fifth president on January 20, 1961, affirmed the magnitude of Dooley's spiritual authority. Just as an American Methodist could express a deep spiritual affinity for the Irish Catholic jungle doctor of Laos, so too did a sufficient number of Protestant Americans find themselves casting ballots for John F. Kennedy in 1960, while many others who chose for various reasons not to do so at least accepted the legitimacy of his candidacy, a courtesy far fewer had bestowed on Alfred E. Smith thirty-two years earlier.

Tom Dooley's life had roughly spanned the era between these two events. When he first came to prominence in 1955, it was Joseph P. Kennedy, father of the future president, who warmly embraced him, perhaps as a successor to his friend, the ailing and disgraced Sen. Joseph McCarthy of Wisconsin. By 1959 Dooley enjoyed the adulation of millions of American Catholics, but he was also lauded in the pages of the *Christian Century,* voice of the liberal Protestant establishment and avowed enemy of the sectarian cultural politics it ascribed to Joseph Kennedy, Joe McCarthy, and Francis Cardinal Spellman. In "The Ballad of the Good Tom Dooley," a *Christian Century* editorialist extolled the deceased medical missionary for standing in "the succession of Albert Schweitzer and Gordon Seagrave and the other great Christian physicians of our time." Dooley surely helped make it more likely as well for John F. Kennedy to be viewed by non-Catholics as standing in the succession of Woodrow Wilson and Franklin D. Roosevelt.[30]

Shortly after his election, in proposing the creation of the Peace Corps,

Kennedy cited "the selfless example of Dr. Tom Dooley in Laos," whose work stood in such stark contrast to "the examples of the 'Ugly American.'"[31] Though Dooley's celebrity had originally been designed to serve a distinctly secular vision of American internationalism, in the end he provided the bridge between Joe McCarthy and Jack Kennedy, to the great benefit of the latter. While that accomplishment might have paled, in Tom Dooley's own estimation, before the more universal aims of his vocation, it ushered in a new dispensation in American life, rich in the kind of tragedy and hope this "old romantic" had so ardently cultivated in his own brief lifetime.

NOTES

I have listed below the archival sources cited most often in the text. In the notes, I have used the abbreviations listed in the left-hand column; full citations are given in the right-hand column.

AFV Papers, Lubbock — American Friends of Vietnam Papers, Center for the Study of the Vietnam Conflict, Texas Tech University, Lubbock.

Buttinger Papers, HY — Joseph Buttinger Papers, Harvard-Yenching Library, Cambridge, Massachusetts.

CARE/MEDICO Papers, NYPL — CARE/MEDICO Papers, Manuscripts and Archives Section, New York Public Library.

Cherne Papers, BU — Leo Cherne Papers, Special Collections and Archives, Boston University.

CRS Papers, Baltimore — Catholic Relief Services Papers, Catholic Relief Services, Baltimore.

Dooley Collection, SLU — Thomas A. Dooley Collection, Saint. Louis University Archives.

Dooley Papers, UMSL — Thomas A. Dooley Papers, Western Historical Manuscript Collection, University of Missouri-St. Louis.

Dulles Papers, PU — Allen W. Dulles Papers, Seeley Mudd Library, Princeton University.

Emmet Papers, HIWRP — Christopher Emmet Papers, Hoover Institution on War, Revolution and Peace, Stanford, California.

Fall Papers, JFK Library — Bernard Fall Papers, John F. Kennedy Library, National Archives and Records Administration, Boston.

Fishel Papers, MSU — Wesley Fishel Papers, Michigan State University Archives and Historical Collections, East Lansing.

Halpern Papers, UMASS — Joel Halpern Papers, Archives and Manuscripts Department, University Library, University of Massachusetts, Amherst.

Hesburgh Papers, AUND — Rev. Theodore M. Hesburgh Papers, Archives of the University of Notre Dame, Notre Dame, Indiana.

Lansdale Papers, HIWRP — Edward G. Lansdale Papers, Hoover Institution on War, Revolution and Peace, Stanford, California.

Lederer Papers, UMASS — William J. Lederer Papers, Archives and Manuscripts Department, W.E.B. Du Bois Library, University of Massachusetts, Amherst.

Mission to Laos, RG 469, NA — Records of U.S. Agency for International Development, Mission to Laos, Record Group 469, National Archives and Records Administration, College Park, Maryland.

Operational Archives, NHC   Operational Archives Branch, Naval Historical Center, Washington Navy Yard, Washington, D.C.

Oram Papers, IUPUI   Harold Oram Papers and Records of the Oram Group, Inc., Special Collections and Archives, Indiana University-Purdue University Indianapolis.

Prologue: The Man in the Song

1. *St. Louis Post-Dispatch,* December 1, 1959.

2. Interview with Crawford King, June 12, 1991.

3. James Monahan, ed., *Before I Sleep . . . : The Last Days of Dr. Tom Dooley* (New York: 1961); *St. Louis Post-Dispatch,* December 3, 1959; interview with Reverend Paul Reinert, S.J., May 2, 1995; Dooley's medical school class rank is indicated in an internal memorandum from the CIA's Office of Security dated October 10, 1956. The document bears the heading "Synopsis" and the file number 147058; it was obtained from the CIA under the Freedom of Information Act (FOIA).

4. Crawford King interview; Monahan, *Before I Sleep,* 38–40.

5. Fred Bronson, *The Billboard Book of Number One Hits: The Inside Story behind the Top of the Charts* (New York, 1985), 45; Roger Lax and Frederick Smith, eds., *The Great Song Thesaurus* (New York, 1989), 398; John Foster West, *Lift Up Your Head, Tom Dooley* (Asheboro, N.C., 1993), 9, 12, 43, 49.

6. West, *Lift Up Your Head,* 12–13, 56–57.

7. John A. and Alan Lomax, *Folk Song, U.S.A.* (New York, 1947), 285; Robert Cantwell, *When We Were Good: The Folk Revival* (Cambridge, Mass., 1996), 2–3; West, *Lift Up Your Head,* xvii; see also John Foster West, *The Ballad of Tom Dula: The Documented Story behind the Murder of Laura Foster and the Trials and Execution of Tom Dula* (Durham, N.C., 1977).

8. William J. Bush, "Kingston Trio," in Phil Hood, *Artists of American Folk Music* (New York, 1986), 61–62; Robin Callot and Paul Suratt, "Kingston Trio," liner notes, *The Kingston Trio Collectors Series,* Capitol C4-92710.

9. *The Gallup Poll: Public Opinion, 1935–1971,* vol. 3, *1954–1971* (New York, 1972), 1647; telephone interview with Bob Shane, February 26, 1992.

10. Telephone interview with Gabrielle Dooley, October 12, 1992; "Peggy" [Agnes Dooley] to "Tess" [Teresa Gallagher], February 7, 1963, Box 10, Dooley Papers, UMSL; Monahan, *Before I Sleep,* 40.

11. Bush, "Kingston Trio," 64; *Cash Box,* March 12, 1960.

12. Philip Rieff, *The Triumph of the Therapeutic: Uses of Faith after Freud* (New York, 1966), 2.

13. *St. Louis Post-Dispatch,* July 22, 1979.

14. Bush, "Kingston Trio," 60; Pete Seeger of the Weavers revealed his ambivalence over the success of the Kingston Trio in *The Incompleat Folksinger* (New York, 1972), 24: "The Weavers' . . . example encouraged first the Kingston Trio, and then hundreds of other young strummers, to become professional folk interpreters. Some saw fit to parody and belittle the country people whose lifework they were looting for the sake of a fast buck. At their best, though, some of the groups introduced a commercial public to music which ignored worn-out formulas and said something about real people's lives."

15. Monahan, *Before I Sleep,* 36.

16. George B. Leonard, Jr., quoting Will Holt, in "Pied Pipers to the New Generation," *Look,* January 3, 1961, 60.

17. Lucille Selsor, *Sincerely, Tom Dooley* (New York, 1969), 78; Monahan, *Before I Sleep,* 39.

18. "Tin Pan Alley," *Time,* July 11, 1960, 56; Leonard, "Pied Pipers to the New Generations," 56–60.

19. Ben Blake, "The Kingston Trio," liner notes, *The Kingston Trio: Special Double Play,* Capitol C4-96748; Bush, "Kingston Trio," 61–63.

20. Jim Winters, "Tom Dooley: The Forgotten Hero," *Notre Dame Magazine* (May 1979): 11.

21. *Honolulu Advertiser,* July 15, 1960.

22. In announcing the formation of the Peace Corps, President Kennedy cited Dooley's "selfless example" as one of the inspirations for the program; see Gerald T. Rice, *The Bold Experiment: JFK's Peace Corps* (Notre Dame, Ind., 1985), 5.

23. *The Cash Box,* March 12, 1960; Bush, "Kingston Trio," 66.

24. Bush, "Kingston Trio," 65.

Chapter One: What Tommy Knew

1. Thomas A. Dooley III passport applications, dated January 30, 1948, May 7, 1952, January 28, 1957, October 7, 1958, United States Department of State passport files, FOIA.

2. The legend of Tom Dooley as athletic hero–orchestra soloist appears to have been invented by Dooley himself in an interview with R. J. Allen, "The Amazing Dr. Dooley," *Catholic Digest* (October 1958): 28; versions of the story appear repeatedly in Dooley literature, including in Barbara Jencks, *Tom Dooley, American Saint* (Providence, R.I., 1961), 5; see also Diana Shaw, "The Temptation of Tom Dooley," *Los Angeles Times Magazine,* December 15, 1991, 43–50, 80; Debbie M. Repp, "The Splendid American," *Liguorian* (June 1991): 4–12.

3. The program and menu for the Thomas A. Dooley Sr. testimonial are in Box 1, Dooley Papers, UMSL; *St. Louis Post-Dispatch,* February 17, 1929.

4. T. J. Jackson Lears, *No Place of Grace: Antimodernism and the Transformation of American Culture* (New York, 1981), 4–7; Alexander Scot McConachie, "The 'Big Cinch': A Business Elite in the Life of a City, St. Louis, 1895–1915" (Ph.D. diss., Washington University, 1976), viii.

5. McConachie, "The 'Big Cinch,'" 35–36; Etan Diamond, "Kerry Patch: Irish Immigrant Life in St. Louis," *Gateway Heritage* 10 (fall 1989): 23–30; see also William E. Foley and C. David Rice, *The First Chouteaus: River Barons of Early St. Louis* (Urbana, Ill., 1983); Ernest Kirschten, *Catfish and Crystal* (St. Louis, 1989), 50–56.

6. McConachie, "The 'Big Cinch,'" 31; *St. Louis Post-Dispatch,* February 17, 1929; Benedict Crowell and Robert Forrest Wilson, *How America Went to War: Demobilization* (New Haven, 1921), 156, 179; Thomas A. Dooley to W. K. Bixby, February 12, 1919, Bixby Collection, Missouri Historical Society, St. Louis.

7. Dooley to Bixby, February 12, 1919; William M. Reedy, quoted in Julius K. Hunter, *Westmoreland and Portland Places: The History and Architecture of America's Premier Private Streets, 1888–1988* (Columbia, Mo., 1988), 49.

8. McConachie, "The 'Big Cinch,'" 141–42; Hunter, *Westmoreland and Portland Places,* 56; Dooley to Bixby, February 12, 1919.

9. McConachie, "The 'Big Cinch,'" 288.

10. Agnes W. Dooley, *Promises to Keep: The Life of Dr. Thomas A. Dooley* (New York, 1962), 4–5.

11. Terry Morris, *Doctor America: The Story of Tom Dooley* (Hawthorne, N.Y., 1963), 17.

12. Warren I. Susman, *Culture as History: The Transformation of American Society in the Twentieth Century* (New York, 1984), 271–85; Mrs. Thomas A. Dooley, as told to Terry Morris, "My Son Tom Dooley," *Redbook,* June 1961, 40.

13. Kirschten, *Catfish and Crystal,* 35; Parkview Agents, *Urban Oasis: 75 Years in Parkview, a St. Louis Private Place* (St. Louis, 1980).

14. Interview with Frank Finnegan, June 12, 1992.

15. Morris, *Doctor America,* 19–20.

16. Dooley family home movies, Green Lake, Wisc. 1936–37, on videocassette in the Dooley Collection, SLU; telephone interview with Abbot Edward Volmer, O.S.B., October 12, 1995.

17. *St. Louis Register,* August 15, 1941; Frank Finnegan interview; interviews with Michael Harrington, January 28, 1984, and William Miller, November 17, 1990; telephone interviews

with John McHale Dean, June 12, 1992, Robert Human, June 14, 1992, and Ralph Schumaker, April 15, 1993.

18. For an excellent intellectual history of American Catholicism between 1920 and 1940, see William M. Halsey, *The Survival of American Innocence: American Catholicism in an Era of Disillusionment, 1920–1940* (Notre Dame, Ind., 1980); for the American cultural significance of the Mystical Body see James Terence Fisher, *The Catholic Counterculture in America, 1933–1962* (Chapel Hill, N.C., 1989), 71–99.

19. Kirschten, *Catfish and Crystal,* 30–33.

20. Arnold Sparr, *To Promote, Defend, and Redeem: The Catholic Literary Revival and the Cultural Transformation of American Catholicism, 1920–1960* (New York, 1990), 23, 33–35; Charles Dickens is quoted in Kirschten, *Catfish and Crystal,* 114; William Barnaby Faherty, S.J., *Dream by the River: Two Centuries of St. Louis Catholicism, 1766–1980* (St. Louis, 1981), 169.

21. Interview with Janet McMahon, August 20, 1992; telephone interview with Katherine Albrecht Gunn, June 17, 1992; Agnes W. Dooley, unpublished manuscript, Scrapbook IV, Dooley Collection, SLU.

22. William Miller interview; Daniel Lord, S.J., to Tom Dooley, February 19, 1944, 1943–44 Scrapbook, Dooley Collection, SLU; Dooley's retreat notes are also found in this scrapbook.

23. Michael Harrington, *Fragments of the Century* (New York, 1973), 4–13.

24. Ibid.

25. Miles Davis with Quincy Troupe, *Miles: The Autobiography* (New York, 1990), 7–9, 38; Chuck Berry, *Chuck Berry, The Autobiography* (New York, 1987), 1.

26. Interview with Maryanne Sell Pernoud, June 12, 1992.

27. Ibid.; 1943–44 Scrapbook, Dooley Collection, SLU.

28. Maryanne Sell Diaries, January 13, 1942, February 24, March 21, April 25, 1943, Dooley Papers, UMSL; Maryanne Sell Pernoud interview.

29. Maryanne Sell Pernoud interview; John McHale Dean interview; interview with John Padberg, S.J., September 14, 1995.

30. Janet McMahon interview; interview with Lorraine and Kevin Brennan, January 10, 1991; souvenirs from Dooley's summer 1943 trip to New York are contained in his 1943–44 Scrapbook, Dooley Collection, SLU.

31. P. B. to Tom Dooley, n.d., and E. V. F. to Tom Dooley, December 17, 1943, 1943–44 Scrapbook, Dooley Collection, SLU.

32. Rev. Charles F. McCarthy to Thomas A. Dooley III, November 2, 1943; E. V. F. to Tom Dooley, n.d., 1943–44 Scrapbook, Dooley Collection, SLU.

33. Dale Warren Mark, "The Rhetoric of Thomas A. Dooley, M.D." (Ph.D. diss., University of Oregon, 1971), 19–20.

34. *Notre Dame Scholastic,* July 7, 1944; see also the detailed account of the wartime programs in Philip Gleason, *Contending with Modernity: Catholic Higher Education in the Twentieth Century* (New York, 1995), 211–13; Agnes W. Dooley, *Promises to Keep,* 18–22.

35. Agnes W. Dooley, *Promises to Keep,* 22; Tom Dooley listed his service in the "Pacific Theater of War" in a passport application he filled out in Vientiane, Laos, January 28, 1957, U.S. Department of State passport files, FOIA; telephone interview with E. M., July 27, 1992.

36. Agnes W. Dooley, *Promises to Keep,* 27.

37. Richard Sullivan, *Notre Dame* (New York, 1951), 146–47; telephone interviews with Raymond Fagan, September 5, 1992, Thomas McMahon, December 2, 1992, and Dr. Philip Utz, April 15, 1993.

38. Telephone interview with Hildegarde, January 16, 1993.

39. In his syndicated column of February 16, 1949, Walter Winchell noted that "Hildegarde's opening at the swanky Brook Club brought out the elite. She introduced her accompanist, Salvatore, as one of 'Kinsey's whimseys.'" See the *St. Louis Post-Dispatch,* February 16, 1949. The controversial Kinsey Report on male sexuality (1948) had not of course appeared at

the time Tom Dooley first met Hildegarde; Allan Bérubé, *Coming Out under Fire: The History of Gay Men and Women in World War Two* (New York, 1990), 115.

40. Michael Harrington interview; telephone interview with E.M., July 27, 1992.

41. Agnes W. Dooley, *Promises to Keep,* 22.

42. Mark, "The Rhetoric of Thomas A. Dooley, M.D.," 20; R. J. Allen, "The Amazing Dr. Dooley," *Catholic Digest* (October 1958): 29; *The Dome* 38 (Notre Dame Yearbook, 1947): 312.

43. Agnes W. Dooley, *Promises to Keep,* 26–27.

44. Ibid.

45. Sullivan, *Notre Dame,* 5.

46. Tom Dooley to Mother and Dad, June 16 through 26, 1948, Box 1, Dooley Papers, UMSL.

47. Agnes W. Dooley, *Promises to Keep,* 35.

48. Telephone interview with John P. O'Hare, February 18, 1993; Agnes W. Dooley, *Promises to Keep,* 47; Tom Dooley to Mother and Dad, June 26, 1948, Box 1, Dooley Papers, UMSL.

49. John P. O'Hare interview; telephone interviews with Daniel Yee, October 21, 1991, Dr. Charles Doyle, July 30, 1992, Dr. Ted Dubuque, November 21, 1992, and Dr. C. Rollins Hanlon, March 5, 1993; Mrs. Thomas A. Dooley, Jr., "My Son Tom Dooley," 104.

50. Undated clipping (ca. February 1950), Box 11, Dooley Papers, UMSL.

51. Interviews with Jeanne R. McFall and David Moxley, June 22, 1990.

52. Mrs. Thomas A. Dooley Jr., "My Son Tom Dooley," 104; *St. Louis Post-Dispatch,* November 29, 1948; Thomas A. Dooley Jr. to Tommy, January 17, 1944, 1943–44 Scrapbook, Dooley Collection, SLU.

53. Mrs. Thomas A. Dooley Jr., "My Son Tom Dooley," 104; William Miller and John P. O'Hare interviews; *Omaha World-Herald,* November 10, 1959; *St. Louis Post-Dispatch,* October 29, 1990.

54. Kirschten, *Catfish and Crystal,* 171; for a discussion of Schwitalla's role in Catholic graduate education, see Gleason, *Contending with Modernity,* 174–75, 177–79.

55. Daniel Yee interview; interview with Paul Reinert, S.J., May 2, 1995; Dr. Philip Utz interview.

56. Stephen Birmingham, *America's Secret Aristocracy* (Boston, 1987), 170–71; Peter Hernon and Terry Ganey, *Under the Influence: The Unauthorized Story of the Anheuser-Busch Dynasty* (New York, 1991), 125–26, 171–72.

57. Telephone interview with James Human, June 10, 1992.

Chapter Two: The Storyteller on Ice in Haiphong

1. Agnes W. Dooley, *Promises to Keep: The Life of Dr. Thomas A. Dooley* (New York, 1962), 150–52.

2. In recent years, Dooley has been gradually reemerging as a minor character in historical studies of the cold war era. He is briefly mentioned, for instance, in Richard Gid Powers's comprehensive study, *Not without Honor: The History of American Anticommunism* (New York, 1995), 275. Powers inaccurately claims, however, that Dooley "toured Latin America, and mobilized American support for the right-wing regimes that protected Church interests there against leftist insurgencies."

3. Agnes W. Dooley, *Promises to Keep,* 48; *San Francisco Chronicle,* August 26–27, 1950.

4. Telephone interviews with Dr. Ted Dubuque, November 21, 1992, and Dr. C. Rollins Hanlon, March 5, 1993; Dooley discussed the intervention of Drs. Casberg and McMahon in a letter to Agnes W. Dooley, October 22, 1954, Box 1, Dooley Papers, UMSL. For his orders to the Philippines, see Agnes W. Dooley, *Promises to Keep,* 66.

5. William Conrad Gibbons, *The U.S. Government and the Vietnam War: Executive and Legislative Roles and Relationships, Part I: 1945–1960* (Princeton, 1986), 256.

6. Edwin Bickford Hooper, Dean C. Allard, and Oscar P. Fitzgerald, *The United States Navy and the Vietnam Conflict,* vol. 1, *The Setting of the Stage to 1959* (Washington, D.C., 1976), 272.

7. Tom Dooley to Agnes Dooley, August 8 and 15, 1954, Box 1, Dooley Papers, UMSL. (Letters from Dooley to his mother will hereafter be cited TD to AD.)

8. TD to AD, August 20 and 26, 1954, Box 1, Dooley Papers, UMSL.

9. TD to AD, August 20, 1954, Box 1, Dooley Papers, UMSL.

10. TD to AD, August 20, September 1 and 8, 1954, Box 1, Dooley Papers, UMSL.

11. Capt. Julius M. Amberson, "Operation Passage to Freedom," *Navy Medicine* (January–February/March–April 1989): 28.

12. TD to AD, September 1, 1954, Box 1, Dooley Papers, UMSL.

13. Neal Sheehan, *A Bright Shining Lie: John Paul Vann and America in Vietnam* (New York, 1988), 138; Evan Thomas, *The Very Best Men: Four Who Dared: The Early Years of the CIA* (New York, 1995), 9, 57; David L. Anderson, *Trapped by Success: The Eisenhower Administration and Vietnam, 1953–1961* (New York, 1991), 76; for Operation Exodus/Passage to Freedom, see the Senator Gravel Edition, *The Pentagon Papers: The Defense Department History of United States Decisionmaking on Vietnam* (Boston, 1971), 1:248; Hooper, Allard, and Fitzgerald, *The United States Navy and the Vietnam Conflict,* 294–96; Amberson, "Operation Passage to Freedom," 26–32; Daniel M. Redmond, "Reminiscences of Passage to Freedom," *Navy Medicine* (January–February/March–April 1989): 33–36.

14. Thomas, *Very Best Men,* 57.

15. Howard R. Simpson, *Tiger in the Barbed Wire: An American in Vietnam, 1952–1991* (Washington, D.C., 1992), 127; TD to AD, September 14, 1954, Box 1, Dooley Papers, UMSL; regarding the administration of DDT to the refugees, Julius M. Amberson noted in 1989: "DDT's adverse and long-lasting impact on the environment was unknown in 1954 but, in fairness, it was the most effective insecticide then available." See Amberson, "Operation Passage to Freedom," 30.

16. TD to AD, August 26, 1955, Box 1, Dooley Papers, UMSL.

17. Interview with Pat Lansdale by historian Jonathan Nashel, October 14, 1992, courtesy of Jonathan Nashel.

18. TD to AD, September 15, 21, and 22, 1954, Box 1, Dooley Papers, UMSL.

19. TD to AD, September 21 and 29, 1954, Box 1, Dooley Papers, UMSL.

20. TD to AD, October 11, 1954, Box 1, Dooley Papers, UMSL.

21. Interview with Norton Stevens, April 24, 1992; TD to AD, September 29, 1954, Box 1, Dooley Papers, UMSL.

22. TD to AD, October 13 and 18, 1954, Box 1, Dooley Papers, UMSL; Rear Adm. Lamont Pugh to Tom Dooley, September 20, 1954, Box 1, Dooley Papers, UMSL.

23. TD to AD, October 25 and 27, 1954, Box 1, Dooley Papers, UMSL.

24. TD to AD, October 27, 1954, Box 1, Dooley Papers, UMSL.

25. Dwight D. Eisenhower quoted in Will Herberg, "Religion and Culture in Present-Day America," in Philip Olson, ed., *America as a Mass Society: Changing Community and Identity* (New York, 1963), 380; Townsend Hoopes, *The Devil and John Foster Dulles* (Boston, 1973), 44–45.

26. Eisenhower quoted in *New York Herald-Tribune,* November 11, 1954.

27. David L. Anderson, *Trapped by Success,* 6; Hoopes, *The Devil and John Foster Dulles,* 255–56.

28. Denis Warner, *The Last Confucian* (New York, 1963), 68–69, 72; for additional discussion of Diem and Confucianism, see Ellen J. Hammer, *A Death in November: America in Vietnam, 1963* (New York, 1987), 47–49.

29. Robert Shaplen, *The Lost Revolution: The Story of Twenty Years of Neglected Opportunities in Vietnam and of America's Failure to Foster Democracy There* (New York, 1965), 109–10.

30. Piero Gheddo, *The Cross and the Bo Tree: Catholics and Buddhists in Vietnam* (New York, 1970), 26, 33; Sheehan, *Bright Shining Lie,* 176.

31. Chester L. Cooper, *The Lost Crusade: America in Vietnam* (New York, 1970), 124–25; Stanley Karnow, *Vietnam: A History* (New York, 1983), 217; Diem's stay in the United States has been routinely recounted in historical treatments of the origins of U.S. support for his

regime, though a detailed account of his activities between 1951 and 1953 has yet to appear. See, for example, Anderson, *Trapped by Success,* 47; Hammer, *Death in November,* 45–47; George C. Herring, *America's Longest War: The United States and Vietnam, 1950–1975* (New York, 1979), 14; and Bernard Fall, *The Two Viet-Nams: A Political and Military Analysis* (New York, 1963), 242–43; for more speculative treatments, see Robert Scheer, *How the United States Got Involved in Vietnam* (Santa Barbara, Calif., 1965), 14, and Robert Scheer and Warren Hinckle, "The Vietnam Lobby," *Ramparts* (July 1965): 18–20. In the version of the article in *Ramparts Vietnam Primer* (n.p., 1966), Scheer and Hinckle deleted their original claim that Diem was "in the 17th year of a self-imposed exile" as of 1950. The correction may have been prompted by an unpublished letter to the editor of *Ramparts* by Wesley Fishel, a Michigan State University professor and controversial adviser to Diem beginning in 1950. See Wesley R. Fishel to The Editors, July 6, 1965, Box 11, Emmett Papers, HIWRP. As the origins and nature of the Vietnam Lobby comprise an important element of the present study, see chapter 4 for a fuller discussion.

32. Anderson, *Trapped by Success,* 53–56; Fall, *The Two Viet-Nams,* 244; Sheehan, *Bright Shining Lie,* 175.

33. Cecil B. Currey, *Edward Lansdale: The Unquiet American* (Boston, 1988), 128–29, 140, 142.

34. Memorandum for the Record, January 30, 1954, Gravel Edition, *Pentagon Papers,* 1:443–47; see also Lloyd C. Gardner, *Approaching Vietnam: From World War II through Dien-bienphu* (New York, 1988), 296; Currey, *Edward Lansdale,* 136.

35. Gibbons, *The U.S. Government and the Vietnam War,* 265; Fall, *The Two Viet-Nams,* 153–54.

36. Harry Haas and Nguyen Bao Cong [pseud.], *Vietnam: The Other Conflict* (London, 1971), 15, 20–22; *Advocate* (Newark, N.J., diocesan newspaper), August 9, 1954; Catholic Relief Services, *Annual Report, 1954–55,* 48–49, Catholic Relief Services Archives, Baltimore, Md.

37. Haas and Nguyen Bao Cong, *Vietnam,* 22; U.S. Department of Defense, "Failure of the Geneva Settlement," book 2, in *United States–Vietnam Relations, 1945–1967* (Washington, D.C., 1971), 11; Sheehan, *Bright Shining Lie,* 136.

38. David L. Halberstam, *The Best and the Brightest* (Greenwich, Conn., 1972), 158. In *Vietnam: A History* Stanley Karnow wrote of Lansdale: "One American did influence Diem in those days, though his clout has been exaggerated by both his admirers and his critics" (220); TD to AD, September 29, 1954, Box 1, Dooley Papers, UMSL; telephone interviews with Everet Bumgardner, March 30, 1993, and Rufus Phillips, March 30, 1993.

39. TD to AD, November 30, 1954, Box 1, Dooley Papers, UMSL.

40. TD to AD, October 29 and December 4, 1954, Box 1, Dooley Papers, UMSL.

41. Simpson, *Tiger in the Barbed Wire,* 136; TD to AD, November 11 and 30, 1954, Box 1, Dooley Papers, UMSL.

42. TD to AD, January 9, 1955, Box 1, Dooley Papers, UMSL.

43. Thomas A. Dooley, M.D., *Deliver Us from Evil: The Story of Vietnam's Flight to Freedom* (New York, 1956), 75; TD to AD, January 1, 1955, Box 1, Dooley Papers, UMSL; "Lansdale Team's Report on Covert Saigon Mission in '54 and '55," *Pentagon Papers,* as published in the *New York Times* (New York, 1971), 62.

44. Joseph Alsop, *New York Herald-Tribune,* December 31, 1954; Homer Bigart, *New York Herald-Tribune,* December 22, 1954, and January 1, 1955.

45. Bigart, *New York Herald-Tribune,* January 2, 1955.

46. *New York Times,* December 18, 1954; Memorandum of a Conversation between the Special Representative in Vietnam (Collins) and Bishop Ngo Dinh Thuc, Saigon, March 25, 1955, *Foreign Relations of the United States, 1955–1957,* vol. 1, *Vietnam* (Washington, D.C., 1985), 145–46; John Cooney, *The American Pope: The Life and Times of Francis Cardinal Spellman* (New York, 1984), 243–44.

47. General J. Lawton Collins, *Lightning Joe: An Autobiography* (Baton Rouge, 1979), 388–

89; Gregory Allen Olson, *Mansfield and Vietnam: A Study in Rhetorical Adaptation* (East Lansing, 1995), 52.

48. Cooney, *The American Pope,* 243–44; Sheehan, *Bright Shining Lie,* 143.

49. David Caute, in *The Great Fear: The Anti-Communist Purge under Truman and Eisenhower* (New York, 1978), 108–9, provides a fairly typical interpretation of the sources of American Catholic anticommunism: "Catholic anti-Communism has tended to assume particularly virulent forms in the United States . . . The American Catholic Church remained [in the McCarthy era] . . . under Irish domination; it produced not so much poets, scholars, scientists and artists as security officers, immigration officers, policemen, customs officers and prison wardens."

50. TD to AD, November 28, 1954, Box 1, Dooley Papers, UMSL.

51. Ibid.

52. Ibid.

53. *Advocate,* February 27, 1954.

54. *St. Louis Post-Dispatch,* May 16, 1955; *Saint Louis Globe-Democrat,* December 10, 1955.

55. "Letter of Father Dominique Pham Quang-Phuoc of the Diocese of Haiphong Directed to the Catholics of Haiphong," *Catholic Patriots,* February 24, 1955, Box 1, Dooley Papers, UMSL; Gheddo, *The Cross and the Bo Tree,* 85.

56. Haas and Nguyen Bao Cong, *Vietnam,* 21; Roy Palmer Domenico, "America, the Holy See and the United States, 1939–1945," in Peter C. Kent and John F. Pollard, eds., *Papal Diplomacy in the Modern Age* (Westport, Conn., 1994), 207.

57. TD to AD, February 12, 1955, Box 1, Dooley Papers, UMSL.

58. Tape recording, Tom Dooley at the orphanage of Madame Ngai, n.d., Dooley Collection, SLU; TD to AD, January 18, 1955, Box 1, Dooley Papers, UMSL.

59. Agnes W. Dooley, *Promises to Keep,* 61; TD to AD, November 23, 1954, Box 1, Dooley Papers, UMSL.

60. TD to AD, December 1, 1954, and February 12, 1955, Box 1, Dooley Papers, UMSL.

61. TD to AD, February 11, 1955, Box 1, Dooley Papers, UMSL.

62. TD to AD, January 29, February 8, and February 18, 1955, Box 1, Dooley Papers, UMSL.

63. TD to AD, March 1, 1955, Box 1, Dooley Papers, UMSL.

64. TD to AD, March 24, 1955, Box 1, Dooley Papers, UMSL.

65. TD to AD, March 2, 1955, Box 1, Dooley Papers, UMSL.

66. TD to AD, May 1, 5, 6, and 9, 1959, Box 1, Dooley Papers, UMSL.

67. TD to AD, May 11 and 12, 1955, Box 1, Dooley Papers, UMSL.

68. TD to AD, May 12, 1955, Box 1, Dooley Papers, UMSL.

69. Ibid.; Scheer, *How the United States Got Involved in Vietnam,* 29; interview with Edward G. Lansdale by Will Brownell, courtesy Mr. Brownell.

70. "Report of 'Operation Passage to Freedom,'" January 3, 1955, Post-1946 Command File, Operational Archives, NHC.

71. TD to AD, May 12, 1955, Box 1, Dooley Papers, UMSL; William C. Gibbons and Patricia McAdams, Congressional Research Service interview with Edward G. Lansdale, November 19, 1982, and April 29, 1983.

72. TD to AD, May 12, 1955, Box 1, Dooley Papers, UMSL; Shaplen, *Lost Revolution,* 121.

73. Shaplen, *Lost Revolution,* 122–24; Currey, *Edward Lansdale,* 176–77.

74. Shaplen, *Lost Revolution,* 124; Frances FitzGerald, *Fire in the Lake: The Vietnamese and the Americans in Vietnam* (Boston, 1972), 76.

75. Currey, *Edward Lansdale,* 172–77; Rufus Phillips interview.

76. Gravel Edition, *Pentagon Papers,* 1:237–39.

77. Simpson, *Tiger in the Barbed Wire,* 151; Currey, *Edward Lansdale,* 176.

78. Interviews with Silas Spengler, October 10, 1991, and Joseph Albanese, October 24, 1991; Norton Stevens interview.

79. TD to AD, August 26, 1955, Box 1, Dooley Papers, UMSL.

80. Ibid.

81. Joseph Albanese and Norton Stevens interviews; TD to AD, August 26, 1955 (this letter is distinct from the aforementioned letter of the same date: it begins, "I received a cable from the *Saturday Evening Post*"), Box 1, Dooley Papers, UMSL.

82. *St. Louis Globe-Democrat,* December 10, 1955; newspaper clipping, Box 1049, CARE/ MEDICO Papers, NYPL.

83. Dooley, *Deliver Us from Evil,* 214.

Chapter Three: Deliver Us from Dooley

1. Dale Warren Mark, "The Rhetoric of Thomas A. Dooley, M.D." (Ph.D. diss., University of Oregon, 1971), 23.

2. Thomas A. Dooley III, "Passage to Freedom," unpublished manuscript, n.d., Box 2, Dooley Papers, UMSL.

3. Lt. (jg) Thomas A. Dooley III, "Bui Chu Means Valiant," *U.S. Naval Institute Proceedings* 82 (January 1956): 45–47; T. A. Dooley, "Report from Indochina," unpublished manuscript, n.d., Box 2, Dooley Papers, UMSL.

4. T. A. Dooley III, "Liberty in Saigon," unpublished manuscript, n.d., Box 2, Dooley Papers, UMSL.

5. Ibid.

6. Ibid.

7. Interview with Norton Stevens, April 24, 1992.

8. Ibid.

9. Tom Dooley to Norton Stevens, April 7, 1955, courtesy of Norton Stevens.

10. Interview with William Lederer, March 13, 1991; Dooley referred to Lederer as a commander, but he apparently became a navy captain during 1955.

11. "That Man Lederer," *Saturday Evening Post,* January 14, 1950, 116; Cecil Currey interview with Edward G. Lansdale, February 15, 1984, courtesy of Jonathan Nashel.

12. William Lederer interview; TD to AD, December 7, 1954, Box 1, Dooley Papers, UMSL.

13. William Lederer interview; "That Man Lederer," 116.

14. "That Man Lederer," 116.

15. W. J. Lederer, "They'll Remember the Bayfield," *Reader's Digest,* March 1955, 1–8.

16. Ibid.

17. TD to AD, May 13, June 5, and June 8, 1955, Box 1, Dooley Papers, UMSL.

18. TD to AD, June 10 and 30, 1955, Box 1, Dooley Papers, UMSL.

19. Tom Dooley to William Lederer, n.d., Box 2, Dooley Papers, UMSL.

20. William Lederer, "Hymie O'Toole Is Never Wrong," in Lederer, *All the Ship's at Sea* (New York, 1950), 130–43.

21. Thomas A. Dooley, *Deliver Us from Evil: The Story of Viet Nam's Flight to Freedom* (New York, 1956), 23, 46; Lederer, "Hymie O'Toole," 143.

22. Lederer, "Hymie O'Toole," 131.

23. Dooley, *Deliver Us from Evil,* 46, 212.

24. John Heidenry, *Theirs Was the Kingdom: Lila and DeWitt Wallace and the Story of the Reader's Digest* (New York, 1993), 512.

25. Agnes W. Dooley, *Promises to Keep: The Life of Dr. Thomas A. Dooley* (New York, 1962), 161; W. J. Lederer to Thomas Dooley, July 28, 1955, Box 1, Dooley Papers, UMSL; TD to AD, August 12, 1955, Box 1, Dooley Papers, UMSL.

26. Allen Dulles to Adm. Felix Stump, May 11, 1955, Lederer Papers, UMASS.

27. Cecil Currey interview with Edward G. Lansdale, February 15, 1984; courtesy Jonathan Nashel.

28. TD to AD, June 15, 1955, Box 1, Dooley Papers, UMSL; DeWitt Wallace to William J. Lederer, December 16, 1955, Lederer Papers, UMASS.

29. Heidenry, *Theirs Was the Kingdom,* 321; James Monahan, ed., *Before I Sleep: The Last Days of Dr. Tom Dooley* (New York, 1961), vii.

30. Fred Landis, "The CIA and Reader's Digest," *Covert Action* 29 (winter 1988): 41–47.

31. W. J. Lederer to DeWitt Wallace, May 13, 1958, and W. J. Lederer to Alfred S. Dashiell, April 7, 1959, Lederer Papers, UMASS; Edward G. Lansdale to Noel Bush, April 23, 1963, Box 48, Lansdale Papers, HIWRP.

32. Heidenry, *Theirs Was the Kingdom*, 471–81.

33. John Bainbridge, *Little Wonder: or, The Reader's Digest and How It Grew* (New York, 1946), 59.

34. DeWitt Wallace to Tom Dooley, August 24, 1956, "Letters," Dooley Collection, SLU.

35. Walter J. Ong, S.J., *Frontiers in American Catholicism: Essays on Ideology and Culture* (New York, 1957), 32; W. A. Swanberg, *Luce and His Empire* (New York, 1972), 110–11.

36. Samuel A. Schreiner, Jr., *The Condensed World of the Reader's Digest* (New York, 1977), 46.

37. Heidenry, *Theirs Was the Kingdom*, 323; Memorandum from E. L. to Dr. Dooley, n.d., Box 1, Dooley Papers, UMSL.

38. E. L. Memorandum; William J. Lederer, personal correspondence, March 16, 1986.

39. E. L. Memorandum.

40. Heidenry, *Theirs Was the Kingdom*, 323; Thomas A. Dooley, "Deliver Us from Evil," *Reader's Digest*, April 1956, 43–46, 153–74; cf. Dooley, *Deliver Us from Evil*, chaps. 1, 3.

41. Dooley, "Deliver Us from Evil," 44.

42. Ibid., 174.

43. Memorandum, F. A. Frohbose to A. H. Belmont, December 12, 1959, Federal Bureau of Investigation, Thomas A. Dooley FBI file, FOIA; see also Jim Winters, "Tom Dooley: The Forgotten Hero," *Notre Dame Magazine* (May 1979): 17; David Caute, *The Great Fear: The Anti-Communist Purge under Truman and Eisenhower* (New York, 1978), 321–24.

44. Edwin Bickford Hooper, Dean C. Allard, and Oscar P. Fitzgerald, *The United States Navy and the Vietnam Conflict*, vol. 1, *The Setting of the Stage to 1959* (Washington, D.C., 1976), 294–96.

45. Capt. Julius M. Amberson, "Operation Passage to Freedom," *Navy Medicine* (January–February/March–April 1989): 26–36.

46. Daniel M. Redmond, "Reminiscences of Passage to Freedom," *Navy Medicine* (January–February/March–April 1989): 33–36; Daniel M. Redmond, "Getting Them Out," *Proceedings*, U.S. Naval Institute (August 1990): 44–51.

47. Telephone interview with Daniel M. Redmond, July 27, 1993, and Peter Kessey, May 26, 1993; interviews with Daniel M. Redmond, October 7, 1993.

48. William J. Lederer and Eugene Burdick, *The Ugly American* (New York, 1958), 47, 65; DeWitt Wallace to Tom Dooley, May 3, 1956, "Letters," Dooley Collection, SLU.

49. Agnes W. Dooley, *Promises to Keep*, 164–65.

50. Denver Rotarians' newsletter, *Mile High Keyway*, March 8, 1956, Scrapbook, "Lectures I," Dooley Collection, SLU; Dooley, *Deliver Us from Evil*, 71.

51. Agnes W. Dooley, *Promises to Keep*, 163–64.

52. Press Officer to Public Information Officer, March 16, 1956, Thomas A. Dooley Office of Naval Intelligence (ONI) file, Operational Archives, NHC.

53. Ibid.

54. Chief of Naval Personnel to Director of Naval Intelligence, January 26, 1956, Dooley ONI file, Operational Archives, NHC.

55. Interview with Ted Werner, January 6, 1992.

56. John D'Emilio, *Sexual Politics, Sexual Communities: The Making of a Homosexual Minority in the United States, 1940–1970* (Chicago, 1983), 38; see also Allan Bérubé, *Coming Out under Fire: The History of Gay Men and Women in World War Two* (New York, 1990).

57. Seymour Cholst, M.D., personal correspondence, May 19, 1986. George Chauncey, *Gay New York: Gender, Urban Culture, and the Making of the Gay Male World, 1890–1940* (New York, 1994), 2–6.

58. Interview with R. C., January 7, 1991; O. S., personal correspondence, October 12, 1992.

59. Report of surveillance of Tom Dooley in New York, February 4, 1956, Dooley ONI file, Operational Archives, NHC.

60. Statement of R.D.L.P., District Intelligence Office, Third Naval District, March 18, 1956, Dooley ONI file, Operational Archives, NHC.

61. Report of surveillance for February 17, 1956, and journal entry of January 17 and March 8, 1956, in Dooley ONI file, Operational Archives, NHC.

62. "How *Reader's Digest* Helps Your Sales," *Deliver Us from Evil* scrapbook, Dooley Collection, SLU.

63. Transcript of telephone conversation between Tom Dooley and his brother Malcolm; see also purloined journal entry of February 2, 1956, Dooley ONI file, Operational Archives, NHC.

64. Ibid.

65. Adm. Arleigh Burke, foreword to Dooley, *Deliver Us from Evil,* vii–viii; Report of ONI surveillance of Tom Dooley, January 31, 1956, Dooley ONI file, Operational Archives, NHC.

66. Chief of Naval Personnel to Director of Naval Intelligence, January 26, 1956; Director of Naval Intelligence to District Intelligence Officer, March 16, 1956, Dooley ONI file, Operational Archives, NHC.

67. Report of surveillance of Tom Dooley, March 17, 1956, Dooley ONI file, Operational Archives, NHC.

68. Report of surveillance of Tom Dooley in Miami, Florida, January 31, 1956, and District Intelligence Officer, Third Naval District, to Director of Naval Intelligence, March 8, 1956, Dooley ONI file, Operational Archives, NHC.

69. District Intelligence Officer, Third Naval District, to Director of Naval Intelligence, March 8, 1956, Dooley ONI file, Operational Archives, NHC.

70. Ibid.; interview with Alden Vaughan, April 15, 1988; Agnes W. Dooley, *Promises to Keep,* 166–67.

71. Director of Naval Intelligence to District Intelligence Officer, Third Naval District, March 14, 1956, Dooley ONI file, Operational Archives, NHC.

72. Statement of informant to District Intelligence Office, Third Naval District, March 18, 1956, Dooley ONI file, Operational Archives, NHC.

Chapter Four: The Vietnam Lobby

1. *Des Moines Register,* May 27, 1956; *New Yorker,* May 5, 1956, 167–68.

2. *New York Post,* April 22, 1956.

3. *San Francisco Chronicle,* June 5, 1958; *San Diego Union,* May 6, 1956.

4. Father James A. Murphy, review of *Deliver Us from Evil* in *American Ecclesiastical Review* 157 (September 1957): 214–15; Sister Mary Francille, "The Mystical Body of Christ and the Spiritual Life," *Spiritual Life* 3 (March 1957): 10–15; *The Crusader* (Holy Cross College), April 20, 1956.

5. One of the earliest public declarations that Dooley had left the navy was made on the floor of the United States Senate on April 9, by Mike Mansfield of Montana, a key supporter of Ngo Dinh Diem. The news was so fresh that Mansfield mistakenly reported that Dooley was "preparing to return with a medical team to Vietnam to help the people there." Congressional Record—U.S. Senate, 84th Congress, April 9, 1956, 5915; *South Bend Tribune,* April 14, 1956.

6. Director of Naval Intelligence to District Intelligence Officer, Third Naval District, March 14, 1956, Dooley ONI file, Operational Archives, NHC; James E. Norton, C.S.C., to Rear Adm. B. W. Hogan, April 23, 1956, Dooley Collection, SLU.

7. Thomas A. Dooley, M.D., *The Edge of Tomorrow* (New York, 1958), 5.

8. Joseph Gerard Morgan, "The Vietnam Lobby: The American Friends of Vietnam, 1955–1975" (Ph.D. diss., Georgetown University, 1992).

9. Ibid., 57; *Saturday Evening Post* article quoted in Roberta Ostroff, *Fire in the Wind: The Life of Dickey Chapelle* (New York, 1992), 180–81.

10. Ostroff, *Fire in the Wind,* 184; Joseph E. Persico, *Casey: From the OSS to the CIA* (New York, 1990), 45–46.

11. Ostroff, *Fire in the Wind,* 181; Eric Thomas Chester, *Covert Network: Progressives, the International Rescue Committee, and the CIA* (Armonk, N.Y., 1995), 6–13; see also Aaron Levenstein, *Escape to Freedom: The Story of the International Rescue Committee* (Westport, Conn., 1983), 6–25, 51–52; for Joseph Buttinger see Morgan, *The Vietnam Lobby,* 62–77, and Muriel Gardiner, *Code Name "Mary": Memoirs of an American Woman in the Austrian Underground* (New Haven, 1983), 67–87, 133–35, 165–70; for his writings on Vietnam see Joseph Buttinger, *The Smaller Dragon* (New York, 1958), and *Vietnam: A Dragon Embattled* (New York, 1967), 2 vols.

12. Chester, *Covert Network,* 14–17; Thomas W. Braden, "I'm Glad the CIA is 'Immoral,'" *Saturday Evening Post,* May 20, 1967, 10–12.

13. Chester, *Covert Network,* 105–7.

14. Ibid., 149–52; William Conrad Gibbons, *The U.S. Government and the Vietnam War: Executive and Legislative Roles and Relationships,* pt. 1: *1945–1960* (Princeton, 1986), 301, n.69; Gregory Allen Olsen, *Mansfield and Vietnam: A Study in Rhetorical Adaptation* (East Lansing, 1995), 51.

15. Morgan, *The Vietnam Lobby,* 62–77, 84–93; Duke was killed in a rollerblading accident in 1995; for an obituary see the *New York Times,* April 30, 1995; for Harold Oram see Levenstein, *Escape to Freedom,* 9; interview with Harold Oram, August 12, 1986; Oram's obituary is in the *New York Times,* August 23, 1990; critics of Buttinger who cite his book *In the Twilight of Socialism* (New York, 1953) as evidence of his loss of ideological nerve have overlooked Buttinger's conclusion, that radicals like himself remained "determined to continue the age-old battle, in spite of all defeats, all authorities, all powers of society, and in this determination they feel as close as ever to Marx. The real failure of a Socialist, to them, is not his inability to interpret correctly the brutal facts of social existence, but rather his willingness to reconcile himself to these facts" (549).

16. Morgan, "The Vietnam Lobby," 84–89.

17. *New York Post,* April 22, 1956.

18. Interview with Gilbert Jonas, September 19, 1991.

19. Robert Scheer and Warren Hinckle, "The Vietnam Lobby," *Ramparts* (July 1965): 17, 22.

20. Warren Hinckle, *If You Have a Lemon, Make Lemonade* (New York, 1974), 145.

21. Robert Scheer, "Hang Down Your Head Tom Dooley," *Ramparts* (January–February 1965): 28.

22. Interview with Leo Cherne, December 7, 1990. Marvin Liebman, *Coming Out Conservative* (San Francisco, 1992), 92.

23. Jane Miller interview with Leo Cherne and Richard Salzmann, Box 1, Cherne Papers, BU; *Honolulu Star-Bulletin,* November 22, 1955.

24. Levenstein, *Escape to Freedom,* 6–37; Liebman, *Coming Out Conservative,* 85; Miller interview with Cherne and Salzmann.

25. Claiborne Pell to Leo Cherne, June 29, 1956, Box 23, Cherne Papers, BU; interview with Angier Biddle Duke, March 19, 1991.

26. Angier Biddle Duke interview; for an insightful treatment of the intergenerational issues separating members of the noncommunist Left of the fifties (in particular Joseph Buttinger and Irving Howe) from the New Left, see Maurice Isserman, *If I Had a Hammer: The Death of the Old Left and the Birth of the New Left* (Urbana, Ill., 1993), 105–8; see also Todd Gitlin, *The Sixties: Years of Hope, Days of Rage* (New York, 1987), 171–75.

27. Allen W. Dulles to Leo Cherne, May 9, 1953, Box 56, Dulles Papers, PU; *New York Times,* February 20, 1976; William C. Gibbons, *The U.S. Government and the Vietnam War: Executive and Legislative Roles and Relationships, Part I: 1945–1960* (Princeton, 1986), 301; for a defense of Leo Cherne, see Levenstein, *Escape to Freedom,* 154.

28. Cecil B. Currey, *Edward Lansdale: The Unquiet American* (Boston, 1988), 159–60; Carolyn Campbell, "This Is Oscar Arellano," *Catholic Digest* (April 1957): 79; Dooley, *The Edge of*

Tomorrow, 11; Dooley told his mother the idea for Operation Brotherhood was "plagerized" from the Filipinos: TD to AD, September 5, 1956, Box 2, Dooley Papers, UMSL.

29. William C. Gibbons and Patricia McAdams, Congressional Research Service interview with Edward G. Lansdale, November 19, 1982, and April 29, 1983.

30. Gilbert Jonas interview.

31. Donald F. Crosby, S.J., *God, Church, and Flag: Senator Joseph R. McCarthy and the Catholic Church, 1950–1957* (Chapel Hill, N.C., 1978), 3.

32. "TV Panel Makes More Noise than Sense," *Life*, April 14, 1952.

33. Persico, *Casey*, 40; Liebman, *Coming Out Conservative*, 83; for Cherne's involvement in Liberal Party politics, see his speech on behalf of Rudolph Halley, November 1, 1951, Box 24, Cherne Papers, BU; the FBI was apparently incensed by Cherne's remark about McCarthy's support from communists: see Natalie Robins, "Inside the FBI," *National Review*, May 11, 1992, 44.

34. Liebman, *Coming Out Conservative*, 82.

35. Seymour Martin Lipset, *Political Man: The Social Bases of Politics* (Garden City, N.Y., 1960), 516–17; Godfrey Hodgson, *America in Our Time* (Garden City, N.Y., 1976), 95.

36. Neil Jumonville, *Critical Crossings: The New York Intellectuals in Postwar America* (Berkeley, 1991), 71; Christopher Lasch, "The Cultural Cold War: A Short History of the Congress for Cultural Freedom," in *The Agony of the American Left* (New York, 1969), 61–114; on CIA funding of CCF, see Peter Coleman, *The Liberal Conspiracy: The Congress for Cultural Freedom and the Struggle for the Mind of Postwar Europe* (New York, 1989), 46–50, 219–34.

37. Hilaire du Berrier, *Background to Betrayal: The Tragedy of Vietnam* (Belmont, Mass., 1965); Christopher Shannon, "A World Made Safe for Differences: Ruth Benedict's *The Chrysanthemum and the Sword*," *American Quarterly* 47 (December 1995): 660, 662.

38. For the role of personalism in the Diem regime, see Frances FitzGerald, *Fire in the Lake: The Vietnamese and the Americans in Vietnam* (New York, 1972), 127–28; Bernard Fall, *The Two Viet-Nams: A Political and Military Analysis* (New York, 1963), 2:1095–96, n.2; for Emmanuel Mounier see John Hellman, *Emmanuel Mounier and the New Catholic Left* (Toronto, 1981).

39. Robert Scheer, "The Genesis of U.S. Support for Ngo Dinh Diem," in Marvin E. Gettleman, ed., *Vietnam: History, Documents, and Opinions on a Major World Crisis* (New York, 1965), 246–64.

40. Telephone interview with Peter White, January 28, 1993; Peter White, personal correspondence, February 13, February 23, and March 11, 1993.

41. "American Mother," *Jubilee* (October 1953): 6–15; Peter White, "An American in Vietnam," *Jubilee* (July–August 1956): 2–3.

42. Peter White, personal correspondence, March 11, 1993.

43. Emmanuel Jacques, S.J., "Opportunities in Vietnam," *Worldmission* 4 (spring 1953): 91.

44. Edwin Halsey, "The Third Force," *Integrity* (May 1951): 33–39.

45. James O'Gara, "American Catholics and Isolationism," *Commonweal* 59 (November 15, 1953): 134–39; Angier Biddle Duke to Father Emmanuel Jacques, January 4, 9, and 26, 1956; Angier Biddle Duke to Christopher Emmett, January 9, 1956; Gilbert Jonas to Father Mc-Cluskey, S.J., January 9, 1956; and Rev. Emmanuel Jacques to Angier Biddle Duke, January 11 and 18, 1956, Box 12, AFV Papers, Lubbock.

46. Peter White, personal correspondence, March 6, 1993.

47. Ibid.; Peter White interview.

48. "Catholics and the Evanston Assembly," *America* 91 (August 14, 1954): 00.

49. Patrick Allitt, *Catholic Intellectuals and Conservative Politics in America, 1950–1985* (Ithaca, N.Y., 1993), 28.

50. Will Herberg, *Protestant-Catholic-Jew: An Essay in American Religious Sociology* (Garden City, N.Y., 1955); Winthrop Hudson, "Protestantism in Post-Protestant America," in Thomas T. McAvoy, ed., *Roman Catholicism and the American Way of Life* (Notre Dame, Ind., 1960), 20–27.

51. O'Gara, "American Catholics and Isolationism," 138.

52. Harold Oram interview. Two decades earlier American Catholicism's "most prominent liberal," Msgr. John A. Ryan, had resigned from the American Civil Liberties Union after Norman Thomas and Roger Baldwin—a Harold Oram client—"made excuses for the Mexican regime's persecution of the Church"; Richard Gid Powers, *Not without Honor: The History of American Anticommunism* (New York, 1995), 109–10.

53. Ostroff, *Fire in the Wind,* 187–88; Levenstein, *Escape to Freedom,* 51–54.

54. Harold Oram, draft memorandum, March 27, 1958, Box 30, Oram Papers, IUPUI; Levenstein, *Escape to Freedom,* 55; Christopher Emmet, Memorandum on the Madison Square Garden Rally, November 16, 1956, Box 30, Oram Papers, IUPUI.

55. Emmet Memorandum, November 16, 1956; *New York Times,* November 9, 1956; Elizabeth Nagy to Angier Biddle Duke, November 9, 1956, Box 27, Cherne Papers, BU.

56. Liebman, *Coming Out Conservative,* 91; Emmet Memorandum, November 16, 1956.

57. Emmet Memorandum, November 16, 1956; Leo Cherne to Daly C. Lavergne, October 13, 1954, Box 32, Cherne Papers, BU; Gardiner, *Code Name "Mary,"* 70.

58. Emmet Memorandum, November 16, 1956; "A Hungarian American" to Leo Cherne, November 8, 1956, Box 27, Cherne Papers, BU.

59. Emmet Memorandum, November 16, 1956.

60. Paul Blanshard, *Communism, Democracy, and Catholic Power* (Boston, 1951).

61. Gilbert Jonas interview.

62. *A Symposium on America's Stake in Vietnam* (New York, 1956), 3, 36; "Operation Laos," Box 17, Fall Papers, JFK Library; see also News Release, "International Rescue Committee Announces Formation of Operation Laos," June 6, 1956, "Laos" Scrapbook, Dooley Collection, SLU.

63. "Operation Laos," Box 17, Fall Papers, JFK Library; Leo Cherne's annual prognostications are described in William F. Buckley's column *New York Daily News,* September 6, 1991.

64. Jane Miller interview with Leo Cherne; Persico, *Casey,* 41.

65. Persico, *Casey,* 42.

66. Allen W. Dulles to Leo Cherne, May 9, 1953, Box 56, Dulles Papers, PU.

67. TD to AD, February 14, 1957, Box 2, Dooley Papers, UMSL.

Chapter Five: A Madison Avenue Schweitzer

1. Thomas A. Dooley, M.D., *The Edge of Tomorrow* (New York, 1958), 11; Dooley inaccurately dated his departure for Hawaii as "July," when it is clear he was still in San Francisco as of August 6; see TD to AD, August 6, 1956, Box 2, Dooley Papers, UMSL; see Agnes W. Dooley, *Promises to Keep: The Life of Dr. Thomas A. Dooley* (New York, 1962), 173, for the correct date of departure.

2. Tom Dooley et al., "Dear Friends of Operation Laos," September 30, 1956, Box 2, Dooley Papers, UMSL.

3. Tom Dooley to Adm. Arleigh Burke, June 21, 1956, Box 2, Dooley Papers, UMSL; *Hollywood Citizen,* April 12, 1956; *Worcester Telegram,* May 3, 1956.

4. Cable from John Foster Dulles to American Embassies in Saigon and Vientiane, July 30, 1956, U.S. Department of State central decimal file 032, FOIA.

5. William C. Gibbons and Patricia McAdams, Congressional Research Service interview with Edward G. Lansdale, November 19, 1982, and April 29, 1983.

6. Ibid.; in 1953 the United States Information Service [USIS] was moved from the State Department to become a separate agency, the USIA, though USIS remained the designation for overseas stations of the USIA; interview with Robert Tollaksen, May 28, 1986.

7. Robert Tollaksen interview.

8. Ibid.

9. TD to AD, August 9, 1956, Box 2, Dooley Papers, UMSL; Dooley, *The Edge of Tomorrow,* 24–72.

10. Teresa Gallagher, *Give Joy to My Youth: A Memoir of Dr. Tom Dooley* (New York, 1965), 18.

11. Dooley, *The Edge of Tomorrow*, vi, x–xiv.

12. Ibid., 2.

13. Ibid.; American official quoted in frontispiece to Charles A. Stevenson, *The End of Nowhere: American Policy toward Laos since 1954* (Boston, 1972); according to Arthur J. Dommen, *Lao* has customarily been used "to refer to the lowland Lao" [those, that is, who are "ethnically Lao"] while *Laotian* has been used "to refer to the inhabitants of the state or country of Laos." More recently, Sucheng Chan wrote that "*Laos* is the name of the country that is today called the Lao People's Democratic Republic. *Laotian* refers to all persons who are citizens of Laos, regardless of the ethnic group they belong to (Laos has more than sixty ethnic groups)." For purposes of simplicity, and because "Laotian" still has a French-colonial ring to it (Tom Dooley used the terms interchangeably but clearly favored "Lao"), I have chosen to use the term "Lao" to designate all those living in the nation of Laos. When appropriate, I refer to lowland inhabitants as "ethnically Lao." See Arthur J. Dommen, *Laos: Keystone of Indochina* (Boulder, Colo., 1985), 7 n.2; Sucheng Chan, *Hmong Means Free* (Philadelphia, 1994), xxiv.

14. Martin Stuart-Fox and Mary Kooyman, *Historical Dictionary of Laos* (Metuchen, N.J., 1992), 49.

15. Sisouk Na Champassak, *Storm Over Laos: A Contemporary History* (New York, 1961), 15; Timothy N. Castle, *At War in the Shadow of Vietnam: U.S. Military Aid to the Royal Lao Government* (New York, 1993), 16.

16. Walter S. Robertson to Thomas A. Dooley, November 21, 1956, Box 2, Dooley Papers, UMSL; Carter de Paul to Leo Cherne, February 6, 1955, Cherne Papers, BU.

17. William Prochnau, *Once upon a Distant War* (New York, 1995), 102–3.

18. Dooley, *The Edge of Tomorrow*, 19; J. Graham Parsons to John Foster Dulles, October 2, 1956, Office of the Director, Subject Files (Central Files), 1955–59, Box 17, Mission to Laos, RG 469, NA.

19. CIA memorandum (author and office blacked out), October 8, 1956, Dooley CIA file, FOIA; Milton J. Esman to Carter de Paul, July 13, 1956, Office of the Director, Subject Files (Central Files) 1955–59, Box 17, Mission to Laos, RG 469, NA; Dooley, *The Edge of Tomorrow*, 9, 21.

20. W. W. Blancke to J. Graham Parsons, October 5, 1956, Office of the Director, Subject Files (Central Files), 1955–59, Box 17, Mission to Laos, RG 469, NA; Stevenson, *The End of Nowhere*, 29.

21. Alex Moore Jr., to Carter de Paul, October 16, 1956; Carter de Paul to J. Graham Parsons, October 16, 1956; and J. Graham Parsons to Carter de Paul, October 17, 1956, Office of the Director, Subject Files (Central Files), 1955–59, Box 17, Mission to Laos, RG 469, NA.

22. J. Graham Parsons to Carter de Paul, October 17, 1956.

23. Stevenson, *The End of Nowhere*, 43; Howard R. Simpson, *Tiger in the Barbed Wire: An American in Vietnam, 1952–1991* (Washington, D.C., 1992), 112–13; TD to AD, October 1, 1956, Box 2, Dooley Papers, UMSL.

24. Tom Dooley to Carter de Paul, June 11, 1956, and Carter de Paul to J. Graham Parsons, October 26, 1956, Office of the Director, Subject Files (Central Files), 1955–59, Box 17, Mission to Laos, RG 469, NA.

25. TD to AD, October 20, 1956, Box 2, Dooley Papers, UMSL; Dooley, *The Edge of Tomorrow*, 24.

26. Dooley, *The Edge of Tomorrow*, 26.

27. Ibid., 28.

28. Tom Dooley to Adm. Arleigh Burke, October 19, 1956, Box 2, Dooley Papers, UMSL; Dooley, *The Edge of Tomorrow*, 30–31.

29. Ibid., 34–35.

30. Ibid., 40–41.

31. Ibid., 38, 40, 43–44.

32. Diane Shaw, in "The Temptation of Tom Dooley," *Los Angeles Times Magazine,* December 15, 1991, 43–50, 80, wrote: "Much of Dooley's Vientiane [sic] clinic project was a sham." For an eyewitness account see Joel Halpern, "Field Trip to Vang Vieng and Environs," Halpern Papers, UMASS; interview with Joel Halpern. The medicines were provided to Dooley free of charge by leading American pharmaceutical companies who received ample free publicity in Dooley's books and broadcasts. Though critics later charged that most of the medicines came from expired stock, there is no reason to believe the multitude of pills he administered had lost their potency.

33. Halpern, "Field Trip."

34. Ibid.

35. For background on "That Free Men May Live," see publicity materials in "Laos IV" Scrapbook, Dooley Collection, SLU; for an obituary of Robert Hyland, the visionary general manager of KMOX radio who hired Dooley, see the *New York Times,* March 7, 1992.

36. John W. Henderson to Eric Kocher, February 21, 1957, U.S. Department of State, RM/R Central Files, 851J.49/2-2157, FOIA; Dr. Tom Dooley, "That Free Men May Live," audiotape of KMOX radio broadcast, February 23, 1957, Dooley Collection, SLU; Dooley, "That Free Men May Live," transcript of KMOX broadcast, February 9, 1958, Box 12, Dooley Papers, UMSL.

37. Dooley, "That Free Men May Live," July 23, 1956, audiotape, Dooley Collection, SLU; Dooley, *The Edge of Tomorrow,* 46.

38. Dooley, *The Edge of Tomorrow,* 39.

39. Interview with Gilbert Jonas, September 19, 1991; Dooley, "That Free Men May Live," audiotape of KMOX broadcast, September 14, 1957, Dooley Collection, SLU.

40. Dooley, "That Free Men May Live," audiotape of KMOX broadcast, September 14, 1957, Dooley Collection, SLU.

41. Dooley, *The Edge of Tomorrow,* 12; interview with Dr. Dennis Shepard, January 5, 1992; telephone interview with Peter Kessey, May 26, 1993.

42. Dr. Dennis Shepard and Peter Kessey interviews.

43. Dooley, *The Edge of Tomorrow,* 48; TD to AD, November 6, 1956, and January 20, 1957, Box 2, Dooley Papers, UMSL.

44. William Warren, *The Legendary American: The Remarkable Career and Strange Disappearance of Jim Thompson* (Boston, 1970); for Dooley's friendship with Jim Thompson, see TD to AD, April 29, 1959, Box 3, Dooley Papers, UMSL; interview with S. Z., January 9, 1991; interviews with Ted Werner, January 6, July 15, and August 28, 1992.

45. Ted Werner interview; Dooley, *The Edge of Tomorrow,* 23, 162.

46. Joseph A. Boone, "Vacation Cruises; or, the Homoerotics of Orientalism," *Publications of the Modern Language Association* 110 (January 1995): 89.

47. Ibid., 98; Dooley, *The Edge of Tomorrow,* 23.

48. Dr. Dennis Shepard and Peter Kessey interviews; TD to AD, October 20, 1956, Box 2, Dooley Papers, UMSL. For a fascinating discussion of family ideology as a vehicle of American cultural hegemony in Asia in the postwar era, see Tina Klein, "Family Ties and Political Obligation: Middlebrow Culture and Cold War Commitment to Asia," in Christian Appy, ed., *Cold War Constructions: The Political Culture of United States Imperialism, 1945–1963* (Amherst, Mass., forthcoming).

49. Boone, "Vacation Cruises," 100.

50. Interview with Ngoan van Hoang, June 22, 1990; Jonathan Root, *Halliburton: The Magnificent Myth* (New York, 1965), 105; my thanks to Edward Maisel for alerting me to the Halliburton connection.

51. Excerpt from "That Free Men May Live," *Portrait of a Splendid American: A Documentary Tribute to Dr. Tom Dooley,* Columbia Records, ML-5709.

52. Dooley, *The Edge of Tomorrow,* 44–45; Len E. Ackland, "No Place for Neutralism: The Eisenhower Administration and Laos," in Nina S. Adams and Alfred W. McCoy, eds., *Laos: War and Revolution* (New York, 1970), 149.

53. Cecil B. Currey, *Edward Lansdale: The Unquiet American* (Boston, 1988), 159–60.

54. Carolyn Campbell, "This Is Oscar Arellano," *Catholic Digest* (April 1957): 78–81; Currey, *Edward Lansdale*, 378 n. 15.

55. International Rescue Committee press release, March 10, 1955, Box 31, Cherne Papers, BU; Leo Cherne to Ngo Dinh Diem, March 18, 1955, Box 14, Cherne Papers, BU; International Rescue Committee telegram to donors, May 8, 1955, Box 31, Cherne Papers, BU.

56. Leo Cherne to Gene Gregory, October 24, 1955, Box 31, Cherne Papers, BU; Leo Cherne to Ngo Dinh Diem, January 25, 1956, Box 31, Cherne Papers, BU.

57. TD to AD, April 10, 1957, Box 2, Dooley Papers, UMSL; Dooley, "That Free Men May Live," transcript of KMOX broadcast, June 18, 1957, Box 12, Dooley Papers, UMSL.

58. Stuart-Fox and Kooyman, *Historical Dictionary of Laos*, xlix, 3–4.

59. D. C. Lavergne to the Ambassador, April 9, 1959, Office of the Director, Director's Subject Files, 1955–60, Box 1, Mission to Laos, RG 469, NA; Rufus Phillips to Michael H. B. Adler, April 28, 1958, Office of the Director, Director's Subject Files, 1955–60, Box 2, Mission to Laos, R469, NA.

60. Milton J. Esman to Carter de Paul, July 13, 1956; CIA Memorandum, October 8, 1956, Dooley CIA file.

61. Joseph Burkholder Smith, *Portrait of a Cold Warrior* (New York, 1976), 179.

62. Personal correspondence from Miguel A. Bernad, S.J., January 26, 1993; Miguel A. Bernad, S.J., *Adventure in Viet Nam: The Story of Operation Brotherhood, 1954–57* (Manila, 1974), 423; Edward G. Lansdale, *In the Midst of Wars: An American's Mission to Southeast Asia* (New York, 1972), 214; Smith, *Portrait of a Cold Warrior*, 252.

63. Dooley, *The Edge of Tomorrow*, 60–63; for a brief discussion of Lao religious ritual see Frank E. Reynolds, "Ritual and Social Hierarchy: An Aspect of Traditional Religion in Buddhist Laos," in Bardwell L. Smith, ed., *Religion and the Legitimation of Power in Thailand, Laos, and Burma* (Chambersburg, Pa., 1978), 166–74.

64. For background on the coalition agreement see Marek Thee, "Background Notes on the 1954 Geneva Agreements on Laos and the Vientiane Agreements of 1956–1957," in Adams and McCoy, *Laos: War and Revolution*, 121–38; for the temporary suspension of U.S. aid see Stevenson, *The End of Nowhere*, 42–43.

65. TD to AD, January 10, 1957, Box 2, Dooley Papers, UMSL.

66. Paul J. Rappaport to J. Graham Parsons, December 7, 1956, and Thomas Dooley to Ambassador Parsons, January 10, 1957, Office of the Director, Subject Files (Central Files), 1955–59, Box 17, Mission to Laos, RG 469, NA.

67. J. Graham Parsons to Dr. Thomas A. Dooley, January 12, 1957; J. Graham Parsons to Eric Kocher, January 16, 1957; and N. Carter de Paul Jr. to Dr. Raymond T. Moyer, January 23, 1957, Office of the Director, Subject Files (Central Files), 1955–59, Box 17, Mission to Laos, RG 469, NA; TD to AD, January 25, 1957, Box 2, Dooley Papers, UMSL.

68. Tom Dooley to Norton Stevens, April 9, 1957, courtesy Norton Stevens.

69. Interview with Michael Harrington, January 28, 1984; TD to AD, February 11 and 14, 1957, Box 2, Dooley Papers, UMSL.

70. TD to AD, February 14, 1957.

71. Ibid.

72. Ibid.

73. TD to AD, February 26 and April 10, 1957, Box 2, Dooley Papers, UMSL.

74. TD to AD, May 18, 1957, Box 2, Dooley Papers, UMSL.

75. TD to AD, April 13, 1957, Box 2, Dooley Papers, UMSL.

76. TD to AD, May 11, 1957, Box 2, Dooley Papers, UMSL.

77. TD to AD, May 30, 1957, Box 2, Dooley Papers, UMSL.

78. For ethnicity in Laos see Richard S. D. Hawkins, "Contours, Cultures, and Conflict," Georges Condominas, "The Lao," and Guy Morechand, "The Many Languages and Cultures of Laos," in Adams and McCoy, *Laos: War and Revolution*, 3–34; Dooley, *The Edge of Tomorrow*, 83; Joel Halpern, "Dr. Dooley in Nam Tha," June 17, 1957, Halpern Papers, UMASS; TD to AD, May 15, 1957, Box 2, Dooley Papers, UMSL.

79. TD to AD, May 15, 1957; Tom Dooley to Joel and Barbara Halpern, June 30, 1957, Halpern Papers, UMASS.

80. Dooley, *The Edge of Tomorrow,* 112–13.

81. Ibid., 25.

82. Ibid., 108, 125, 145–46.

83. Ibid., 78–80; 108; TD to AD, July 2, 1957, Box 2, Dooley Papers, UMSL.

84. Dooley, *The Edge of Tomorrow,* 170–71; TD to AD, July 2, 1957, Box 2, Dooley Papers, UMSL.

85. Dooley, *The Edge of Tomorrow,* 150–51.

86. Ibid., 173–90.

87. Jack Kerouac, *On the Road* (New York, 1979), 299; Dooley, *The Edge of Tomorrow,* 180.

88. Dooley, *The Edge of Tomorrow,* 180.

89. Ibid., 187; TD to AD, July 25, 1957, Box 2, Dooley Papers, UMSL.

Chapter Six: Jungle Doctor for a New Age

1. Tom Dooley to Dolf Droge, January 13, 1958, courtesy of Dolf Droge; TD to AD, August 1, 1957, Box 2, Dooley Papers, UMSL.

2. *New York Times,* August 31, 1957.

3. The most richly detailed portrait of Schweitzer is found in James Brabazon, *Albert Schweitzer: A Biography* (New York, 1975); see also George Marshall and David Poling, *Schweitzer* (Garden City, N.Y., 1971), Norman Cousins, *Dr. Schweitzer of Lambaréné* (New York, 1960), and Frederick Franck, *Days with Albert Schweitzer: A Lambaréné Landscape* (London, 1959). Cousins became an enthusiastic supporter of Dooley and served for a time on the board of MEDICO; Dr. Franck was a dentist who established a MEDICO-sponsored clinic in Lambaréné. Dooley on Spinoza is from an interview with Randy Hamilton, January 8, 1987.

4. Marshall and Poling, *Schweitzer,* 37–38; Thomas A. Dooley, M.D., *The Night They Burned the Mountain* (New York, 1960), 37; Randy Hamilton interview.

5. Brabazon, *Albert Schweitzer,* 116.

6. Ibid., 117, 406–8.

7. Thomas A. Dooley, M.D., *The Edge of Tomorrow* (New York, 1958), v–vi; Tom Dooley to Dolf Droge, January 13, 1958, courtesy of Dolf Droge.

8. Ali Silver to Thomas A. Dooley, June 2, 1957, Box 6, Dooley Papers, UMSL; Brabazon, *Albert Schweitzer,* 436–37; Tom Dooley to Agnes Dooley, August 1, 1957, Box 2, Dooley Papers, UMSL; *New York Times,* August 1 and December 22, 1957.

9. Tom Dooley to Father Birch, August 4, 1957, Dooley Collection, SLU; TD to AD, July 10, 1957, Box 2, Dooley Papers, UMSL; Agnes W. Dooley, *Promises to Keep: The Life of Dr. Thomas A. Dooley* (New York, 1962), 192; in 1959, in describing the photojournalist and filmmaker Erica Anderson to his mother, Dooley wrote: "I knew her when I first met Schweitzer (she was in Gunsbach)." This passage supports the most likely scenario, that Dooley briefly met with Schweitzer in Europe, not Africa. See TD to AD, April 20, 1959, Box 3, Dooley Papers, UMSL.

10. Brabazon, *Albert Schweitzer,* 392–93, 415; Albert Schweitzer to Agnes Dooley, February 1961, French original and English translation, Clippings VI, Dooley Collection, SLU.

11. Albert Schweitzer to Agnes Dooley, February 1961.

12. Dooley to Dolf Droge, January 13, 1958.

13. Ibid.

14. Walter S. Robertson to Thomas A. Dooley, November 21, 1956, Box 2, Dooley Papers, UMSL; N. Carter de Paul to Raymond T. Moyer, January 23, 1957, Office of the Director, Subject Files (Central Files), 1955–59, Box 17, Mission to Laos, RG 469, NA.

15. Joel Halpern, "Dr. Dooley in Nam Tha," June 17, 1957, Halpern Papers, UMASS; Howard Kaufman to Alex Moore Jr., December 3, 1956, Office of the Director, Subject Files (Central Files), 1955–59, Box 17, Mission to Laos, RG 469, NA.

16. Dooley, *The Edge of Tomorrow*, 5–6; "Operation Laos," Box 17, Fall Papers, JFK Library; Agnes W. Dooley, *Promises to Keep*, 191–92.

17. TD to AD, April 10, 1957, Box 2, Dooley Papers, UMSL.

18. TD to AD, May 18, 1957, Box 2, Dooley Papers, UMSL.

19. Harold Oram, draft memorandum, March 27, 1958, Box 30, Oram Papers, IUPUI.

20. Ibid.

21. Report of the National Information Bureau on International Rescue Committee, Inc., including MEDICO, July 17, 1958, Box 30, Oram Papers, IUPUI.

22. Address by His Excellency Ngo Dinh Diem, Waldorf-Astoria Hotel, May 13, 1957, UA 1269, Box 5, Fishel Papers, MSU; on Diem's trip to the United States, see David L. Anderson, *Trapped by Success: The Eisenhower Administration and Vietnam, 1953–1961* (New York, 1991), 160–64; Dinner Program, Ambassador Hotel, New York, May 13, 1957, Box 1, Oram Papers, IUPUI.

23. Graham Greene, *The Quiet American* (New York, 1955); Alfred Katz to Harold Oram, February 13, 1956 and May 2, 1956, Box 12, AFV Papers, Lubbock, Texas.

24. Edward G. Lansdale to Joseph L. Mankiewicz, March 17, 1956, Box 35, Lansdale Papers, HIWRP; Jonathan Nashel, "Edward Lansdale and the American Attempt to Remake Southeast Asia, 1945–1965" (Ph.D. diss., Rutgers University, 1994), 282–96; Kenneth L. Geist, *Pictures Will Talk: The Life and Films of Joseph L. Mankiewicz* (New York, 1978), 275–76; Graham Greene's forthright dismissals of the Lansdale-as-Pyle theory have apparently failed to take hold in the historical record, but those unwilling to take the Englishman at his word need only consider the period in which Greene was writing the novel: 1952–1954. For all but the very end of that time, Lansdale was located elsewhere, with the one brief exception of a trip to Vietnam in June 1953, when Greene would have enjoyed precious few opportunities to observe him on the job. *The Quiet American* is based on incidents Greene observed in Vietnam long before Lansdale arrived on the scene.

25. Interview with Gilbert Jonas, September 19, 1991; Nashel, "Edward Lansdale," 291.

26. Nashel, "Edward Lansdale," 290; Edward G. Lansdale to Lt. Gen. John W. O'Daniel, August 5, 1963, Box 39, Lansdale Papers, HIWRP; Thomas A. Dooley, "That Free Men May Live," KMOX radio broadcast, ca. 1959, Dooley Collection, SLU; Gilbert Jonas interview.

27. Tom Dooley to Hank and Anne Miller, November 30, 1957, CIA, FOIA; International Rescue Committee Press Release, February 4, 1958, Box 3, Dooley Papers, UMSL; for the announcement of MEDICO's founding, see the *New York Times*, February 5, 1958; for statements of "MEDICO's Story" and MEDICO's Purpose," see the *New York Times*, March 7, 1958.

28. Gordon S. Seagrave, *Burma Surgeon* (New York, 1943), 151; Barbara W. Tuchman, *Stilwell and the American Experience in China, 1911–45* (New York, 1971), 272.

29. Seagrave, *Burma Surgeon*, 51; Tom Dooley to Hank and Anne Miller, November 30, 1957.

30. Brabazon, *Albert Schweitzer*, 130, 149.

31. Tom Dooley to Hank and Anne Miller, November 30, 1957.

32. Terry Morris, *The Story of MEDICO* (Baltimore, n.d.), 15–17; A. L. Singleton, "Our Healing Ambassador," *Washington Star Magazine*, October 26, 1958; Jane Miller interview with Leo Cherne and Richard Salzmann, Box 1, Cherne Papers, BU; telegram from Albert Schweitzer, Leo Cherne, and Peter Comanduras to Tom Dooley, February 4, 1958, Dooley Collection, SLU.

33. Dr. Peter D. Comanduras, "Medico," Box 15, Fishel Papers, MSU; *New York Times*, March 9, 1958.

34. Jim Winters, "Tom Dooley: The Forgotten Hero," *Notre Dame Magazine* (May 1979): 10–11.

35. TD to AD, January 20, 1957, Box 2, Dooley Papers, UMSL.

36. "Do-It-Yourself Samaritan," *Life*, March 17, 1958.

37. TD to AD, May 30, 1957, Box 2, Dooley Papers, UMSL; Thomas A. Dooley, "Foreign Aid—The Human Touch," *New York Times Magazine*, April 20, 1958, 12, 96.

38. Daniel J. Boorstin, *The Image: A Guide to Pseudo-Events in America* (New York, 1961), 54.

39. Suzi Leslie to Tom Dooley, ca. February 1958, Clippings VI, Dooley Collection, SLU.

40. Letter to Agnes Dooley from Barat Hall School, St. Louis, March 27, 1958, Dooley Collection, SLU.

41. Rod Brownfield to Agnes Dooley, February 25, 1958, Clippings VI, Dooley Collection, SLU.

42. Rev. Harold W. Rigney, S.V.D., *Four Years in a Red Hell: The Story of Father Rigney* (Chicago, 1956); Fulton J. Sheen, foreword to Father George (as told to Gretta Palmer), *God's Underground* (New York, 1949), vii.

43. David Caute, *The Great Fear: The Anti-Communist Purge under Truman and Eisenhower* (New York, 1978), 108; Robert Scheer, "Hang Down Your Head, Tom Dooley," *Ramparts* (January–February 1965): 23–28; Nicholas von Hoffman, "Hang Down Your Head, Tom Dooley," *Critic* (November–December 1969): 16–22.

44. "The Name Is Dooley," *Oblate Digest* (March 1958): 7–11.

45. *Dubuque Telegraph-Herald,* March 18, 1956.

46. Ibid.; Tom Dooley to Hank and Anne Miller, November 30, 1957; "Tall Man's Task in a Hot Spot," *Life* (December 23, 1957), 100.

47. Tom Dooley to Hank and Anne Miller, November 30, 1957; Garry Wills, *Bare Ruined Choirs: Doubt, Prophecy, and Radical Religion* (New York, 1972), 48.

48. *San Francisco Chronicle,* June 5, 1958; *New York Times,* May 27 and September 7, 1958.

49. *Best Sellers,* June 15, 1958; *Ave Maria,* July 26, 1958, 28; Albert H. Miller, review of *The Edge of Tomorrow,* in *Critic* (June–July 1958): 35.

50. Teresa Gallagher, *Give Joy to My Youth: A Memoir of Dr. Tom Dooley* (New York, 1965), 25–27.

51. Ibid., 35–37.

52. Teresa Gallagher to Agnes Dooley, February 7, 1958, Box 2, Dooley Papers, UMSL.

53. Agnes Dooley to Teresa Gallagher, March 9, 1958, Box 2, Dooley Papers, UMSL; Agnes Dooley, quoted in Gallagher, *Give Joy to My Youth,* 44.

54. Gallagher, *Give Joy to My Youth,* 48–49; Teresa Gallagher to Tom Dooley, June 24, 1958, Box 2, Dooley Papers, UMSL.

55. Interview with Ted Werner, January 6, 1992; Gallagher, *Give Joy to My Youth,* 45.

56. Gallagher, *Give Joy to My Youth,* 41; R. J. Allen, "The Amazing Dr. Dooley," *Catholic Digest* (October 1958): 27–31; *Brooklyn Tablet,* May 16, 1959.

57. Gallagher, *Give Joy to My Youth,* 44–45. In a 1968 essay on Eugene J. McCarthy, Wilfrid Sheed wrote: "Humility is hammered perhaps a little too roughly into young Catholic skulls. I have known more promise gone to waste for want of a doting Jewish mother than history will ever hear about. After this boot training in self-abnegation, you may find that no matter how hard you come to believe in the secular world and what needs doing there, you will retain this reflex about yourself: I must not use it for my own glory—even if what it needs is my own glory." From "Eugene McCarthy: The Politician as Professor," in Wilfrid Sheed, *The Morning After: Selected Essays and Reviews* (New York, 1971), 129. This passage is offered not as historical evidence but as a particularly astute observation on the cultural style of 1950s liberal Catholicism, by a veteran participant-observer.

58. Teresa Gallagher to Agnes Dooley, March 13, 1958, Box 2, Dooley Papers, UMSL.

59. Dooley, *The Night They Burned the Mountain,* 26; Gallagher, *Give Joy to My Youth,* 51.

60. Interviews with Earl Rhine, January 9, 1992, and Dwight Davis, August 22, 1992; Dooley, *The Night They Burned the Mountain,* 29–35.

61. Dooley, *The Night They Burned the Mountain,* 31; Tom Dooley to Teresa Gallagher, August 23, 1958, Box 2, Dooley Papers, UMSL.

62. T. S. to Teresa Gallagher, July 29, 1958, Box 2, Dooley Papers, UMSL; Teresa Gallagher to Tom Dooley, September 17, 1958, Box 2, Dooley Papers, UMSL. Gallagher, *Give Joy to My Youth,* 48–49; Agnes W. Dooley, *Promises to Keep,* 199–201; Dooley, *The Night They Burned the Mountain,* 36–40.

63. *Los Angeles Times,* February 23 and July 14, 1958.

64. Dooley, *The Night They Burned the Mountain,* 37; TD to AD, August 15, 1958, Box 2, Dooley Papers, UMSL.

65. TD to AD, August 2 and 31, 1958, Box 2, Dooley Papers, UMSL; Agnes W. Dooley, *Promises to Keep,* 199.

Chapter Seven: The Handsome American

1. Thomas A. Dooley, M.D., *The Night They Burned the Mountain* (New York, 1960), 40–41.

2. TD to AD, September 15, 1958, Box 2, Dooley Papers, UMSL; Dooley, *The Night They Burned the Mountain,* 41.

3. Interview with Dwight Davis, August 22, 1992; TD to AD, October 11, 1958, Box 2, Dooley Papers, UMSL.

4. Interview with William Lederer, March 13, 1991; for an insightful discussion of *The Ugly American* as cold war jeremiad, see John Hellmann, *American Myth and the Legacy of Vietnam* (New York, 1986), 3–38.

5. William Lederer interview; William J. Lederer to John Zinsser Jr., May 23, 1962, Lederer Papers, UMASS.

6. William J. Lederer and Eugene Burdick, *The Ugly American* (New York, 1958), 110–14, 205–13.

7. William J. Lederer to Alfred S. Dashiell, April 7, 1959, Lederer Papers, UMASS.

8. William Lederer interview; Cecil B. Currey, *Edward Lansdale: The Unquiet American* (New York, 1988), 199.

9. William J. Lederer and Eugene Burdick, "Salute to Deeds of Non-Ugly Americans," *Life,* December 7, 1959, 148–63.

10. Lederer and Burdick, *The Ugly American,* 43–65.

11. William Lederer interview; William Lederer, personal correspondence, March 16, 1986.

12. For Father John Cronin, see Garry Wills, *Nixon Agonistes: The Crisis of the Self-Made Man* (New York, 1979), 35–36; Lederer and Burdick, *The Ugly American,* 44; *Richmond* (California) *Independent,* November 6, 1958.

13. Thomas A. Dooley to William J. Lederer, February 29, 1960, Lederer Papers, UMASS.

14. Lederer and Burdick, "Salute to Deeds of Non-Ugly Americans," 148.

15. Hellmann, *American Myth,* 25; William Lederer interview.

16. *Time,* August 31, 1962, 32; DeWitt Wallace to William J. Lederer, September 21, 1962, Lederer Papers, UMASS.

17. Lederer and Burdick, *The Ugly American,* 109; Hellmann, *American Myth,* 26.

18. Perry Stieglitz, *In a Little Kingdom* (Armonk, N.Y., 1990), 12, 33; Oden Meeker, *The Little World of Laos* (New York, 1959), 39; Keyes Beech, quoted in Andrew Tully, *CIA: The Inside Story* (New York, 1962), 214.

19. R. J. Allen, "The Amazing Dr. Dooley," *Catholic Digest* (October 1958): 29.

20. Diana Shaw, "The Temptation of Tom Dooley," *Los Angeles Times Magazine,* December 15, 1991, 43–50, 80.

21. Dooley, *The Night They Burned the Mountain,* 50–51, 71.

22. Dwight Davis interview; interview with Earl Rhine, January 9, 1992.

23. Dwight Davis interview.

24. Interview with Ngoan van Hoang, June 22, 1990; Shaw, "The Temptation of Tom Dooley," 50; Dwight Davis and Earl Rhine interviews.

25. Dwight Davis and Earl Rhine interviews.

26. Dooley, *The Night They Burned the Mountain,* 125; Dwight Davis and Earl Rhine interviews.

27. Dwight Davis and Earl Rhine interviews; Ted Werner interview; Alfred W. McCoy, *The Politics of Heroin: CIA Complicity in the Global Drug Trade* (Brooklyn, 1991), 296.

28. McCoy, *The Politics of Heroin,* 176–78.

29. Ibid., 339–44.

30. Memorandum of a Conversation, Department of State, Washington, January 13, 1958, *Foreign Relations of the United States [FRUS], 1958–1960,* vol. 16, *East Asia-Pacific Region; Cambodia; Laos,* 413.

31. Ibid., 417.

32. Charles A. Stevenson, *The End of Nowhere: American Policy toward Laos since 1954* (Boston, 1972), 43, 62–63.

33. Telegram from the Department of State to the Embassy in Laos, May 15, 1958, *FRUS, 1958–1960,* 16:440; for accounts of the U.S. role in the early history of the CDNI, see Stevenson, *The End of Nowhere,* 64–65; Martin E. Goldstein, *American Policy toward Laos* (Cranbury, N.J., 1973), 143–45; a prominent member of the CDNI, Sisouk na Champassak, later dedicated a book (*Storm over Laos: A Contemporary History,* New York, 1961) to "the memory of my friend Dr. Tom Dooley."

34. Dooley used the French abbreviation for "the young ones," C.D.I.N.; see Dooley, *The Night They Burned the Mountain,* 156–57; Henry L. Miller, Memorandum to Country Team: CDNI Public Opinion Survey, January 7, 1959, Office of the Director, Director's Subject Files, 1955–60, Box 2, Mission to Laos, RG 469, NA.

35. Daly C. Lavergne to Raymond T. Moyer, November 28, 1958, Office of the Director, General Correspondence, 1954–59, Box 1, Mission to Laos, RG 469, NA.

36. Ibid.; Goldstein, *American Policy toward Laos,* 181–90; Haynes Miller, "A Bulwark Built on Sand," *Reporter* (November 13, 1958): 11–16.

37. "Comments by the Department of State and ICA on the Report of the House Committee on Government Operations: 'United States Aid Operations in Laos,' " Executive Office, Subject Files (Central Files), 1956–60, Box 12, Mission to Laos, RG 469, NA.

38. Telephone interview with Sarah Miller Pease, July 31, 1992; Daly C. Lavergne to Raymond T. Moyer, November 28, 1958.

39. Raymond T. Moyer to D. C. Lavergne, January 8, 1959, Office of the Director, General Correspondence, 1954–59, Box 1, Mission to Laos, RG 469, NA.

40. Dooley, *The Night They Burned the Mountain,* 102.

41. Daly C. Lavergne to Raymond T. Moyer, November 28, 1958; Stevenson, *The End of Nowhere,* 61–62; for the conflict between Henry Hecksher of the CIA and Ambassador Horace Smith, see also John Prados, *Presidents' Secret Wars: CIA and Pentagon Covert Operations since World War II* (New York, 1986), 261–63.

42. William C. Gibbons, *The U.S. Government and the Vietnam War: Executive and Legislative Roles and Relationships, Part I: 1945–1960* (Princeton, 1986), 305; on Lansdale's reassignment from Vietnam see Currey, *Edward Lansdale,* 180–85; interestingly, Currey's notes include several objections lodged by Rufus Phillips, who had apparently read the manuscript prior to publication; Phillips objected to Currey's claims that Lansdale had grown "disheartened" over Diem's failure to institute democratic reforms; Rufus Phillips to Edward G. Lansdale, April 28, 1957, Box 40, Lansdale Papers, HIWRP; for Lansdale and the Hmong, see McCoy, *The Politics of Heroin,* 305–306; see also Richard Drinnon's highly polemical account in *Facing West: The Metaphysics of Indian-Hating and Empire Building* (New York, 1980), 412.

43. "An Analysis of the Termination of the Civic Action Program," n.d. (ca. 1958), Office of the Director, Director's Subject Files, 1955–60, Box 2, Mission to Laos, RG 469, NA; this document, apparently written by Rufus Phillips, reveals a *possible* difference between a key member of the Lansdale team and Henry Hecksher, the CIA station chief in Vientiane. As Phillips noted in his report, Civic Action had become strongly identified in Laos with the personality of Col. Oudone Sananikone, one of the leaders of the CDNI. The dissolution of Civic Action (as proposed by USOM) would probably spell the end of Sananikone's political influence, a fact that did not seem to trouble Hecksher, perhaps because Oudone was the nephew of Phoui Sananikone—who put together a weak ruling coalition to succeed Souvanna Phouma in August 1958—and the CIA wished to keep their options open in a volatile political

climate. On July 24, 1958, Hecksher instructed a USOM program officer to freeze a large allocation of Civic Action funds earmarked for Oudone: "Prefer to retain some leverage in case Colonel Sananikone is removed." The "official" CIA in Laos moved inexorably toward support for a rightist military rulership of Laos ("Colonel" Sananikone was minister of public welfare and health as much as he was an active military leader), while the Lansdale team, from Rufus Phillips to Hank Miller of USIS—as well as Dooley—preferred working with "progressive-minded" figures of a civilian orientation; see Henry D. Hecksher to Joseph L. St. Lawrence, July 24, 1958, Assistant Director for Program and Planning Operations, Subject Files, 1954–60, Box 4, Mission to Laos, RG 469, NA; for the origins of Civic Action, see Edward G. Lansdale, *In the Midst of Wars: An American's Mission to Southeast Asia* (New York, 1972), 210–13; see also Rufus Phillips to Michael Adler, Acting Director, USOM Laos, April 28, 1958, Office of the Director, Director's Subject Files, 1955–60, Box 2, Mission to Laos, RG 469, NA.

44. Dooley, *The Night They Burned the Mountain*, 156–58.

45. Memorandum of a Conversation, Department of State, Washington, May 10, 1957, *FRUS, 1955–1957*, 1:816–17; Rufus Phillips to Director, USOM Laos, September 19, 1957, Office of the Director, Director's Subject Files, 1955–60, Box 2, Mission to Laos, RG 469, NA.

46. Telegram from the Commander in Chief, Pacific (Stump) to the Chief of Naval Operations (Burke), February 27, 1958, *FRUS, 1958–1960*, 16:431–32.

47. Currey, *Edward Lansdale*, 200–205, 386–87, n. 69.

48. Henry D. Hecksher to Director, USOM, n.d. (ca. September 1958); J. L. St. Lawrence to D. C. Lavergne, Director, USOM Laos, September 17, 1958; and Henry D. Hecksher to J. L. St. Lawrence, November 26, 1958, Assistant Director for Program and Planning Operations, Subject Files, 1954–60, Box 4, Mission to Laos, RG 469, NA.

49. Currey, *Edward Lansdale*, 165–67; Timothy Castle, *At War in the Shadow of Vietnam* (New York, 1993), 18.

50. *New York Times*, June 24, 1960.

51. Telegram from the Department of State to the Embassy in Laos, *FRUS, 1958–1960*, 16:440; Lansdale, *In the Midst of Wars*, 105–6.

52. Rosemary Rawson, "Eighteen Years after Dr. Tom Dooley's Death, a Priest Insists He Was a Saint, Not a Spook," *People*, July 30, 1979, 24–25; Tom Braden, "Patriotism Needs No Apology," *Fort Lauderdale News*, July 10, 1979.

53. Dooley, *The Night They Burned the Mountain*, 124.

54. William C. Gibbons and Patricia McAdams, Congressional Research Service interview with Edward G. Lansdale, November 19, 1982, and April 29, 1983.

55. TD to AD, October 13, 1958, Box 3, Dooley Papers, UMSL.

56. Dooley, *The Night They Burned the Mountain*, 20–21.

57. Dwight Davis and Earl Rhine interviews.

58. Dooley, *The Night They Burned the Mountain*, 158–59.

59. Ibid., 169–70; TD to AD, August 8, 1959, Box 3, Dooley Papers, UMSL.

60. Dooley, *The Night They Burned the Mountain*, 183–86.

61. Ibid., 183.

Chapter Eight: This Is Your Life

1. "For Immediate Release," MEDICO Press Release, September 1, 1959, Box 3, Dooley Papers, UMSL.

2. Ibid.

3. The editing of Dr. Peter Comanduras is indicated by "Dr. C," written in the margins throughout the draft; the prayer is found on page four of the same document.

4. Thomas A. Dooley, *The Night They Burned the Mountain* (New York, 1960), 20–21; transcript of CBS Reports, "Biography of a Cancer," broadcast over the CBS television network, April 21, 1960, courtesy of CBS.

5. "Biography of a Cancer," 8; Dooley, *The Night They Burned the Mountain,* 143; interview with Dwight Davis, August 22, 1992; Seymour Cholst, M.D., personal correspondence, May 19, 1986.

6. Memorandum, Assistant Deputy Director of Security to Deputy Director of Security, February 1, 1960, CIA, FOIA.

7. Marlys H. Witte, Charles L. Witte, Linda L. Minnich, Paul R. Finley, and William L. Drake Jr., "Aids in 1968," Letter to the Editor, *Journal of the American Medical Association* 251 (May 25, 1984): 2657; Robert F. Garry et al., "Documentation of an AIDS Virus Infection in the United States in 1968," *Journal of the American Medical Association* 260 (October 14, 1988): 2085–87; I am grateful to Edward Maisel for supplying me with copies of these and other articles dealing with suspected cases of AIDS from years prior to 1980. Mr. Maisel in turn obtained his file on this medical literature from Robert Galagan, M.D., a physician living in Hawaii.

8. T. A. Dooley to Dr. Charles Doyle (ca. November 1957), courtesy Dr. Charles Doyle; telephone interview with Dr. Charles Doyle, July 30, 1992.

9. Dr. Charles Doyle interview; *New York Times,* June 19 and July 15, 1990.

10. James Monahan, ed., *Before I Sleep: The Last Days of Dr. Tom Dooley* (New York, 1961), 4–5.

11. "Biography of a Cancer," 1, 3–5.

12. Ibid., 6.

13. Harold Oram to Leo Cherne, November 17, 1958, Box 24, Cherne Papers, BU; Frank Goffio, personal correspondence, April 19, 1996.

14. Jane Miller interview with Leo Cherne and Richard Salzmann, Box 1, Cherne Papers, BU.

15. Minutes of Executive Committee, Medical Advisory Council, MEDICO, March 12, 1959, and Robert MacAlister to Peter Comanduras, March 6, 1959, Box 1041, CARE/MEDICO Papers, NYPL.

16. Irving Howe, introduction to Joseph Buttinger, "Fact and Fiction on Foreign Aid," *Dissent* 6 (summer 1959): 318.

17. Buttinger, "Fact and Fiction on Foreign Aid," 322, 339.

18. C. Alphonso Smith to Joseph Buttinger, July 17, 1959; Loy W. Henderson to Joseph Buttinger, June 29, 1959; and Elbridge Durbrow to Joseph Buttinger, July 1, 1959, Box 9, Buttinger Papers, HY.

19. "Books That Live," W. W. Norton advertising copy for *The Ugly American,* Box 9, Buttinger Papers, HY.

20. Joseph G. Morgan, "The Vietnam Lobby: The American Friends of Vietnam, 1950–1975" (Ph.D. diss., Georgetown University, 1992), 180–81; Esther Pike to Angier Biddle Duke, March 24, 1958; Angier Biddle Duke, draft of letter to Esther Pike, April 23, 1958, Box 12, AFV Papers, Lubbock; minutes of Executive Committee, Advisory Council, MEDICO, May 12, 1959, Box 1041, CARE/MEDICO Papers, NYPL.

21. *New York World-Telegram and Sun,* July 23, 1959; Morgan, "The Vietnam Lobby," 215–16.

22. Morgan, "The Vietnam Lobby," 209, 214, 217.

23. Ibid., 235–36; Edward G. Lansdale to Maj. Gen. John W. O'Daniel (ret.), August 5, 1963, Box 39, Lansdale Papers, HIWRP.

24. Monahan, *Before I Sleep,* 19.

25. Teresa Gallagher, *Give Joy to My Youth: A Memoir of Dr. Tom Dooley* (New York, 1965), 103.

26. Monahan, *Before I Sleep,* 25–26; Memorandum of Teresa Gallagher to Gloria Sassano, December 13, 1959, Box 3, Dooley Papers, UMSL.

27. *New York Times,* July 24, 1974; *Boston Globe,* July 22, 1974, and August 5, 1986.

28. Sol Stern, "A Short Account of International Student Politics and the Cold War with Particular Reference to the NSA, CIA, Etc.," *Ramparts* (March 1967): 31–32; *Boston Globe,*

July 22, 1974; for his extremely influential condemnation of the CIA's funding of the NSA and other liberal groups, see Christopher Lasch, *The Agony of the American Left* (New York, 1969), 63–114.

29. David M. Alpern, "How the CIA Does 'Business,'" *Newsweek,* May 19, 1975, 25–26; Gallagher, *Give Joy to My Youth,* 108–9; interview with Lorraine and Kevin Brennan, January 10, 1991.

30. Paul F. Hellmuth to Reverend Theodore M. Hesburgh, C.S.C., November 11, 1959, Hesburgh Papers, AUND.

31. Gallagher, *Give Joy to My Youth,* 109.

32. *Boston Globe,* August 5, 1986; Paul F. Hellmuth to Reverend Theodore M. Hesburgh, C.S.C., February 4, 1960, Hesburgh Papers, AUND; Robert J. Allen, "The Amazing Dr. Dooley," *Catholic Digest* (October 1958): 27–31; Thomas T. McAvoy, "The Composition of the Catholic Majority Today," *Commonweal* 77 (October 14, 1962): 189–90.

33. Hellmuth to Hesburgh, November 11, 1959; unidentifiable CIA document (ca. May 1960), FOIA.

34. Gallagher, *Give Joy to My Youth,* 114; *St. Louis Post-Dispatch,* January 19, 1961; interview with Crawford King, June 12, 1991; *Los Angeles Examiner,* November 19, 1959.

35. Speech of Dr. Thomas Dooley, November 9, 1959, Mutual of Omaha auditorium, Omaha, Neb., Dooley Papers, UMSL; "The Splendid American," ABC News and Public Affairs Division documentary, produced and directed by Chad Northshield.

36. TD to Teresa Gallagher/Gloria Sassano, December 15, 1959, Box 3, Dooley Papers, UMSL; Monahan, *Before I Sleep,* 15, 74.

37. TD to AD, August 8, 1959, Box 3, Dooley Papers, UMSL.

38. "This Is Your Life," Ralph Edwards Productions, videotape copy courtesy of Dr. Dennis Shepard; Philip Marchand, *Marshall McLuhan: The Medium and the Messenger* (New York, 1989), 50.

39. Randy Shilts, *Conduct Unbecoming: Lesbians and Gays in the U.S. Military: Vietnam to the Persian Gulf* (New York, 1993), 25; "This Is Your Life."

40. "This Is Your Life."

41. Hy Gardner column, June 2, 1960, clipping, Dooley Collection, SLU.

42. Jack Paar, personal correspondence, n.d. (ca. December 1991); *New York Herald-Tribune,* December 22, 1959.

43. M. N. to Dr. Tom Dooley, October 14, 1959, and S. S. to Dr. Tom Dooley, December 8, 1959, Box 5, Dooley Papers, UMSL.

44. Address of Reverend William A. Donaghy, S.J., College of the Holy Cross, November 2, 1959, courtesy Mr. John F. Spain; for a slightly altered version of the speech see Monahan, *Before I Sleep,* 30.

45. Gloria Sassano to Robert Hardy Andrews, May 7, 1956, Box 1049, CARE/MEDICO Papers, NYPL; Dr. Tom Dooley, Immaculate Heart College Speech, Los Angeles, November 16, 1959, from notes made of tape recording, courtesy of Teresa Gallagher.

46. Dooley, Immaculate Heart College Speech; interview with William Miller, November 17, 1990.

47. Jim Winters, "Tom Dooley: The Forgotten Hero," *Notre Dame Magazine* (May 1979): 11.

Chapter Nine: Where Are the Serpents?

1. *The Gallup Poll: Public Opinion, 1935–1971,* vol. 3, *1959–1971* (New York, 1972), 1647; James Monahan, ed., *Before I Sleep: The Last Days of Dr. Tom Dooley* (New York, 1961), 49–50.

2. Monahan, *Before I Sleep,* 49–50; Agnes W. Dooley, *Promises to Keep: The Life of Dr. Thomas A. Dooley* (New York, 1962), 225.

3. Dr. Tom Dooley to Peter Comanduras, December 31, 1959, Box 3, Dooley Papers, UMSL.

4. Ibid.

5. Ibid.; Tom Dooley to Dolf Droge, November 5, 1959, courtesy of Dolf Droge.

6. For a sampling of headlines generated in the U.S. press by the Laos "crisis," see the *Los Angeles Examiner,* September 3, 4, 6, and 13, 1959; William J. Lederer, *A Nation of Sheep* (New York, 1961), 11–31; Hugh Toye, *Laos: Buffer State or Battleground* (New York, 1968), 127–29; Memorandum from the Secretary of State's Special Assistant (Scranton) to the Acting Secretary of State (Robert Murphy), September 4, 1959, *FRUS, 1958–1960,* 16:590–91.

7. Monahan, *Before I Sleep,* 42; TD to AD, August 3, 1959, Box 3, Dooley Papers, UMSL.

8. Kenneth Conboy (with James Morrison), *Shadow War: The CIA's Secret War in Laos* (Boulder, Colo., 1995), 22–23; for political developments within the Pathet Lao, see Charles A. Stevenson, *The End of Nowhere: American Policy toward Laos since 1954* (Boston, 1972), 72.

9. Dr. Voulgaropoulous and his wife, Rose, had been married in a Buddhist ceremony in Kratie, an event described by Dooley in *The Night They Burned the Mountain:* following the "ancient Khmer" rites, a smaller Christian ceremony had been performed. "The whole Kingdom of Cambodia had heard about this American and his bride being married according to the customs of their country, and they loved it." Thomas A. Dooley, M.D., *The Night They Burned the Mountain* (New York, 1960), 137–38; Monahan, *Before I Sleep,* 69–70.

10. Dr. Tom Dooley to MEDICO Office, New York, February 11, 1960, Box 5, Dooley Papers, UMSL; Monahan, *Before I Sleep,* 70.

11. Interview with Alan Rommel, March 29, 1991.

12. TD to AD, February 27, 1960, Box 4, Dooley papers, UMSL; Monahan, *Before I Sleep,* 97–98.

13. Internal memorandum, CIA, n.d. (ca. May 1960), FOIA.

14. Paul Hellmuth to Teresa Gallagher, n.d. (ca. March 1960), Teresa Gallagher file, Dooley Collection, SLU; Monahan, *Before I Sleep,* 139; Jeff Check, quoted in Monahan, *Before I Sleep,* 139.

15. Sister Louise to Dr. Tom Dooley, January 14, 1960, Box 5, Dooley Papers, UMSL.

16. Interview with Janet McMahon, June 20, 1992.

17. "The Sixth Grade" to Dr. Tom Dooley, May 27, 1960, and Dr. Tom Dooley to "All of You," July 5, 1960, Box 5, Dooley Papers, UMSL; Brian Smith to Dr. Tom Dooley, March 21, 1960, Box 6, Dooley Papers, UMSL.

18. F. Z. to Dr. Tom Dooley, May 16 and June (date obscured), 1960, Box 5, Dooley Papers, UMSL; for a highly sensitive treatment of the spiritual meaning of suffering within devotional Catholicism, see Robert A. Orsi, "'Mildred, is it fun to be a cripple?': The Culture of Suffering in Mid-Twentieth Century American Catholicism," *South Atlantic Quarterly* 93 (Summer 1994), 547–590.

19. Dr. Tom Dooley to T. J., February 10, 1960, Box 6, Dooley Papers, UMSL.

20. Interview with Norton Stevens, April 24, 1992; Monahan, *Before I Sleep,* 116.

21. Eddie Albert to Dr. Tom Dooley, March 17, 1960, and Dr. Tom Dooley to Eddie Albert, April 20, 1960, Box 5, Dooley Papers, UMSL.

22. Interview with Arnold Enker, August 22, 1986; *Portrait of a Splendid American: A Documentary Tribute to Dr. Tom Dooley,* Columbia Records, ML-5709.

23. TD to AD, February 11, 1960, Box 4, Dooley Papers, UMSL; Monahan, *Before I Sleep,* 75.

24. Scot Leavitt, "Tom Dooley at Work," *Life,* April 18, 1960, 113–22.

25. Ibid.

26. Agnes Dooley to Teresa Gallagher, April 21, 1960, Box 5, Dooley Papers, UMSL.

27. Bernard B. Fall, Letter to the Editor, *Life,* May 19, 1960, 20.

28. Lt. Robert E. Waters, Letter to the Editor, Life, May 19, 1960, 20.

29. Monahan, *Before I Sleep,* 102.

30. *Advocate* (Newark, N.J., diocesan newspaper), June 23, 1960.

31. L. H. to Dr. Tom Dooley, August 30, 1959, Box 3, Dooley Papers, UMSL.

32. Internal memorandum, CIA, n.d. (ca. May 1960), FOIA.

33. Ibid.; C. D. DeLoach to Mr. Mohr, Federal Bureau of Investigation memorandum, March 9, 1960, Dooley FBI file, FOIA.

34. C. D. DeLoach to Mr. Mohr, March 9, 1960; see also A. H. Belmont to J. Edgar Hoover, December 11, 1959, Dooley FBI file, FOIA.

35. Arthur J. Dommen, *Conflict in Laos: The Politics of Neutralization* (New York, 1971), 133–34; Len Ackland, "No Place for Neutralism: The Eisenhower Administration and Laos," in Nina S. Adams and Alfred W. McCoy, eds., *Laos: War and Revolution* (New York, 1970), 152.

36. Dr. Tom Dooley to Dr. Peter Comanduras, May 1, 1960, Box 4, Dooley Papers, UMSL; Dr. Tom Dooley to the Reverend J. Birch, Oblates of Mary Immaculate, February 15, 1960, Dooley Collection, SLU; Monahan, *Before I Sleep,* 41–42.

37. Monahan, *Before I Sleep,* 120.

38. Paul F. Hellmuth to Reverend Theodore M. Hesburgh, C.S.C., December 18, 1959, Hesburgh Papers, AUND; Paul F. Hellmuth to Reverend John Wilson, C.S.C., March 28, 1960, Hesburgh Papers, AUND.

39. Paul F. Hellmuth to Reverend Theodore M. Hesburgh, April 12 and 20, 1960, Hesburgh Papers, AUND; Reverend Theodore M. Hasburgh to Paul F. Helmuth, April 6, 1960, Hesburgh Papers, AUND.

40. Reverend Theodore M. Hesburgh to Dr. Thomas A. Dooley, April 12, 1960, Hesburgh Papers, AUND; Paul F. Hellmuth to Reverend John Wilson, March 28, 1960.

41. Joel R. Connelly and Howard J. Dooley, *Hesburgh's Notre Dame: Triumph in Transition* (New York, 1972), 20, 31–32.

42. In one important respect Notre Dame had since the 1930s been more "worldly" than most secular universities: as a haven for émigré European academics such as political scientists Waldemar Gurian and F. A. Hermens, the university became a center for a kind of post-totalitarian internationalist thought. In addition to its European political thinkers, Notre Dame frequently hosted continental theologians and philosophers such as Jacques Maritain and Etienne Gilson, key figures in the "Catholic revival" championed by Frank O'Malley of the English department and other members of the faculty. Robert Schmuhl, *The University of Notre Dame: A Contemporary Portrait* (Notre Dame, Ind., 1986), 7; Paul F. Hellmuth to Reverend John Wilson, March 28, 1960.

43. Connelly and Dooley, *Hesburgh's Notre Dame,* 35.

44. Paul F. Hellmuth to Reverend Theodore M. Hesburgh, April 12, 1960; Reverend Theodore M. Hesburgh to Paul F. Hellmuth, April 6, 1960, Hesburgh Papers, AUND.

45. Dr. Tom Dooley to Malcolm Dooley, May 23, 1960, Box 4, Dooley Papers, UMSL; T. S. to Dr. Tom Dooley, August 27, 1960, and Dr. Tom Dooley to T. S., December 5, 1960, Box 5, Dooley Papers, UMSL.

46. T. S. to Dr. Tom Dooley, August 27, 1960; Dr. Tom Dooley to T. S., December 5, 1960.

47. Dr. Tom Dooley to T. S., December 5, 1960; Dr. Tom Dooley to J. K., December 24, 1960, Box 5, Dooley Papers, UMSL.

48. Dr. Tom Dooley, "The Night of the Same Day," manuscript fragments, Box 9, Dooley Papers, UMSL.

49. Ibid.

50. Randy Shilts, *Conduct Unbecoming: Lesbians and Gays in the U.S. Military: Vietnam to the Persian Gulf* (New York, 1993), 26.

51. Interview with Ed Myers.

52. Michael Harrington interview; interview with R. C.; Dooley, "The Night of the Same Day"; at least one individual has come forward in recent years to claim he was Dooley's "spouse," although by the most generous estimate he spent less than two weeks in close proximity to Tom, who made disparaging references to the young man in letters to his mother: either evidence of his "denial" or part of a strategy to disown his intimate relationships with men.

53. Teresa Gallagher, *Give Joy to My Youth: A Memoir of Dr. Tom Dooley* (New York, 1965), 150–55.

54. "Report from MEDICO," September 1960, Dooley Collection, SLU; *Los Angeles Examiner,* September 20, 1959.

55. Manulis was involved in an automobile accident just prior to the affair; he missed his own party, but the guests included Gary Cooper, Ronald Reagan, and Jack Lemmon. Dooley told reporters that Lemmon was a contender for the lead role, along with Montgomery Clift and his personal choice, Frank Sinatra. *St. Louis Globe-Democrat,* July 7, 1960; interview with Martin Manulis, August 25, 1992.

56. *Honolulu Star-Bulletin,* July 15, 1960.

57. *St. Louis Globe-Democrat,* July 7, 1960.

58. Donald F. Proctor, M.D., personal correspondence, May 23, 1986.

59. Monahan, *Before I Sleep,* 117; in a November 30, 1990, interview, Dr. Wintrob expressed a more positive view of Dooley's work.

60. Monahan, *Before I Sleep,* 133–35, 160–61; *St Louis Post-Dispatch,* July 11, 1960; interview with Dr. Everard Hughes, April 2, 1993.

61. Agnes W. Dooley, *Promises to Keep,* 248.

62. Gallagher, *Give Joy to My Youth,* 162.

63. Interview with Robert Anderson, March 12, 1991.

64. Ibid.; interview with Ted Werner, January 6, 1992.

65. Peter Arnett, *Live from the Battlefield: From Vietnam to Baghdad, 35 Years in the World's War Zones* (New York, 1994), 54.

66. Ibid., 60.

67. Toye, *Laos,* 141; Arnett, *Live from the Battlefield,* 48.

68. Monahan, *Before I Sleep,* 154.

69. Ibid., 152; Robert Anderson and Martin Manulis interviews; TD to AD, August 17, 1960, Box 4, Dooley Papers, UMSL.

Chapter Ten: "And Miles to Go . . . "

1. James Monahan, ed., *Before I Sleep: The Last Days of Dr. Tom Dooley* (New York, 1961), 167; Teresa Gallagher, *Give Joy to My Youth: A Memoir of Dr. Tom Dooley* (New York, 1965), 171–72.

2. Dr. Peter Comanduras to Dr. Tom Dooley, September 14, 1960, Box 1049, CARE/MEDICO Papers, NYPL.

3. Minutes of MEDICO Board of Directors meeting, October 14, 1960, Box 1041, CARE/MEDICO Papers, NYPL.

4. Transcript of MEDICO Board of Directors Executive Committee meeting, October 26, 1960, Box 1041, CARE/MEDICO Papers, NYPL.

5. Ibid.

6. Ibid.

7. Gallagher, *Give Joy to My Youth,* 174; interview with Kevin and Lorraine Brennan, January 10, 1991.

8. Transcript of MEDICO Executive Committee meeting, October 26, 1960.

9. Ibid.

10. Teresa Gallagher to Robert Copenhaver, August 16, 1960, Box 8, Dooley Papers, UMSL.

11. Monahan, *Before I Sleep,* 168–70.

12. Dr. Tom Dooley to Paul Hellmuth, February 5, 1960, Box 1049, CARE/MEDICO Papers, NYPL.

13. Gallagher, *Give Joy to My Youth,* 157.

14. Ibid., 158; for a complete version of this prayer, and Teresa Gallagher's commentary, see the unidentified reproduction among the manuscript fragments in Tom Dooley, "The Night of the Same Day," Box 9, Dooley Papers, UMSL.

15. Gallagher, *Give Joy to My Youth,* 176–77.

16. Monahan, *Before I Sleep,* 161, 174–75, 177–78, 193–94.

17. Ibid., 208–9.

18. Cablegram, Dr. Tom Dooley to MEDICO, New York, November 30, 1960, Dooley Collection, SLU.

19. Monahan, *Before I Sleep,* 219–24.

20. Ibid., 230–36; cf. Agnes Dooley's virtually identical account in *Promises to Keep,* which was also published by Farrar, Straus and Cudahy, as were all three of Dooley's books (by the time Teresa Gallagher published *Give Joy to My Youth,* the firm had become Farrar, Straus and Giroux).

21. Gallagher, *Give Joy to My Youth,* 190–91; cf. Monahan, *Before I Sleep,* 242–44.

22. Martin Stuart-Fox and Mary Kooyman, *Historical Dictionary of Laos* (Metuchen, N.J., 1992), 11.

23. Gallagher, *Give Joy to My Youth,* 197.

24. Ibid., 202–6.

25. Ibid.

26. Interview with Bill Salfen, April 2, 1995; Monahan, *Before I Sleep,* 260.

27. Monahan, *Before I Sleep,* 264–71; interview with Robert Anderson, March 12, 1991; Paul C. Reinert, S.J., to Mrs. T. A. Dooley, January 26, 1961, Box 9, Dooley Papers, UMSL.

28. *Evansville Sunday Courier and Press,* January 22, 1961; Gallagher, *Give Joy to My Youth,* 216.

29. Peter Worthington, *Looking for Trouble: A Journalist's Life . . . And Then Some* (Toronto, 1984), 105.

30. "The Ballad of the Good Tom Dooley," *Christian Century* 76 (September 9, 1959): 132.

31. Gallagher, *Give Joy to My Youth,* 179.

INDEX

295